SCANDALIZING
JESUS

Kazantzakis's *The Last Temptation of Christ*
Fifty Years On

Edited by
DARREN J. N. MIDDLETON

Featuring essays by
MARTIN SCORSESE, PETER BIEN,
& PETER T. CHATTAWAY

continuum

NEW YORK • LONDON

Copyright © 2005 by Darren J. N. Middleton

The Continuum International Publishing Group, 15 East 26th Street, New York, NY 10010

The Continuum International Publishing Group Ltd, The Tower Building, 11 York Road, London SE1 7NX

Unless otherwise indicated, Scripture quotations are taken from the New Revised Standard Version of the Bible, copyright 1989 by the Division of Christian Education of the National Council of the Churches of Christ in the USA. Used by permission. All rights reserved.

Text from *The Last Temptation of Christ* by Nikos Kazantzakis used by permission of Dr. Patroclos Stavrou, Kazantzakis Publications, Athens, Greece.

Cover art courtesy of Dr. Patroclos Stavrov
Cover design by Lee Singer

Library of Congress Cataloging-in-Publication Data

Scandalizing Jesus? : Kazantzakis's The last temptation of Christ fifty years on / edited by Darren J. N. Middleton.
    p. cm.
  Includes bibliographical references and index.
  ISBN 0-8264-1607-1 (pbk. : alk. paper) — ISBN 0-8264-1606-3 (casebound with jacket : alk. paper)
    1. Kazantzakis, Nikos, 1883–1957. O teleftaíos peirasmós. 2. Kazantzakis, Nikos, 1883–1957—Characters—Jesus Christ. 3. Jesus Christ—In literature. I. Middleton, Darren J. N., 1966–
  PA5610.K39T4325 2005
  889'.332—dc22

2005006615
Printed in the United States of America

01 02 03 04 05 06 07 08 09 10   10 9 8 7 6 5 4 3 2 1

TO IVA LOU HILL AND ROBERT E. FLOWERS,

who have taught me more about Jesus

than I could say here or anywhere

CONTENTS

Contents

Don Cupitt

In the writings of Darren J. N. Middleton, Lewis Owens, and others, we have in recent years seen signs of a revival of interest in Nikos Kazantzakis (1883–1957). This is very welcome, not only because of Kazantzakis's value as a lay religious thinker but also because—perhaps like Nietzsche, Dostoyevsky, and Unamuno—he is one of those representative figures who has struggled on our behalf to make sense out of the many conflicting strands in modern Western culture.

Nietzsche, whom Kazantzakis admired so much, illustrates the problem very well. Descended from a line of Lutheran pastors, classically educated, and with a period of military service, he was also a product of our modern liberal-democratic, commercial-industrial culture. And he was much affected by Darwinism. Now, how on earth do you make a morally coherent worldview and personal way of life out of those five quite different value scales?

Kazantzakis, being a Greek, is roughly halfway between Germany and Russia in the way he experiences these conflicts. He is highly aware of the contrast between the compassionate religious humanism of the New Testament (itself another Greek book, to him) and the heroic humanism of Homer: Jesus versus Odysseus, as he puts it. And Kazantzakis is just as vividly aware of the conflict between the timeless and basically supernaturalist idea of truth taught by Plato and the Greek Church, and the historically evolving picture of reality that underlies all modern culture since Hegel. Cosmology, geology, biology are *historical* now, and so are all the human sciences. Must we now learn to think of truth as being not eternal but historical?

These two great conflicts are felt particularly acutely by Kazantzakis because he is himself a Greek. But there is also a third conflict that he gets involved in because he is a novelist: Given the way we now think about "human nature," and given the Church's insistence on Jesus' full humanity, how are we to think about Jesus' human subjectivity—*including* his sexuality?

That topic is trouble, big trouble, as everyone knows. Especially, Martin Scorsese knows. But the very fact that the topic causes so much trouble is all the more reason that it deserves a lot of attention, and we can only be grateful that Kazantzakis had not only larger-than-life literary talent but also larger-than-life courage. We should be grateful, too, that Scorsese managed to get his film made and issued. One wonders whether the studio would back such a risky project with the same determination today, in the much-less-liberal times in which we live now.

I have spent my "career" (such as it was) as a priest and an academic, and I have to admit that technically proficient academic priest-theologians tend to look down on lay religious thinkers, mere literary types such as Kazantzakis. But in the long run, experience has suggested to me that the academic priest-theologians are chiefly interested in defending tradition, the power of the Church, and the interests of the clerical profession. All of this means that their work is much less interesting to the general public, and less interesting to *me*, too, than the work of figures like Kazantzakis. Fifty years ago, we tended to refer to such people as "religious existentialists," and at least a dozen of them were well-known to the public. Do you remember, for example, Berdyayev, Marcel, Weil? Today, sadly, there are few such figures. Updike, maybe? Otherwise, religion is nowadays chiefly discussed not as an intellectually and morally vital subject for everyone but as a rather crazed militant quasi-political ideology, much involved in provoking savage conflicts all around the world. Today, religion is almost nowhere a blessing, and almost everywhere a curse.

That is a profoundly discouraging thought. I hope that books like this will prompt many people to take up again the kind of serious lay thinking about religion, morality, and worldview that so consumed Nikos Kazantzakis. Many of the contributors were at a lively conference about him at Canterbury Christ Church University College, which I happened to attend a few years ago. I am glad for the chance to greet them again and to commend this book warmly.

Don Cupitt
Emmanuel College, Cambridge
April 2004

ACKNOWLEDGMENTS

The idea for this celebratory and critical anthology was sparked by a Kazantzakis conference I attended in Canterbury, England, December 2002. Lewis Owens, inaugural president of the UK branch of the International Society of Friends of Nikos Kazantzakis, organized and convened this event. Lewis and Peter Bien initially encouraged this undertaking, which was then refined and enriched by dialogue with other friends in the world of Kazantzakis scholarship, including Daniel Dombrowski, Howard Dossor, Jen Harrison, Vrasidas Karalis, Gareth Owens, Patroclos Stavrou, and Vasiliki Tsakali.

Meg McCarthy of Cappa Productions helped me establish contact with Martin Scorsese. For his part, Mr. Scorsese generously agreed to step aside from his busy filming schedule to offer some reflections on his cinematic adaptation of Kazantzakis's novel. I am delighted to include such thoughts in our volume.

For the use of the Kazantzakis photographs, I thank my dear friend Patroclos Stavrou—the very model of kindness and cooperation.

Special mention must be made of Austin S. Lingerfelt, my former student assistant, who proofread many essays, cataloged various newspaper articles, and compiled the webliography that appears at the end of this anthology. Most of all, though, I value his comment in my Christianity and Literature class, where he first discovered Kazantzakis: "Any person who reads this novel with an open heart will find themselves born again!" And this from the mouth of a Texas Pentecostal preacher's kid! Thank you, Austin, for shattering a stereotype. My current student assistant, Megan A. Johnson, provided much-needed, last-minute help with the "For Further Reading" section, for which I am grateful.

I owe a word of appreciation to my colleagues in the Religion department at Texas Christian University, especially S. Brent Rodriguez-Plate and Daryl D. Schmidt, for their friendship and support across the years. Further, I would be remiss in not crediting my many students; several have challenged me to refine, sometimes even abandon, my various interpretations of Kazantzakis's literary art.

Henry Carrigan, my Continuum editor, has been an ardent supporter of this project. His close reading has greatly improved the book. Any remaining errors are my own. I also thank Ryan Masteller for his industry and verve.

I acknowledge with gratitude the following permissions for quotations: Kazantzakis Publications (Athens) for all Greek texts authored by Nikos Kazantzakis and/or his wife, Eleni Kazantzaki (= Helen Kazantzakis), and Simon & Schuster (USA) for *The Last Temptation of Christ*.

Finally, I recognize Betsy, my wife, with deep and lasting appreciation for our first ten years of married life.

Darren J. N. Middleton
Lent 2005

Each essayist in this volume has made every effort to clarify the referent when writing about Nikos Kazantzakis's novel and/or Martin Scorsese's film. Generally, Kazantzakis's imaginative re-creation of Jesus' life, *O teleftaíos peirasmós* (*The Last Temptation*) was completed in 1951 and published in Greek in 1955. The Greek title does not include "of Christ." Translated into English by Peter Bien in 1960, *O teleft-aíos peirasmós* appeared as *The Last Temptation* in the United Kingdom and *The Last Temptation of Christ* in the United States. Martin Scorsese's 1988 cinematic adaptation of Kazantzakis's text uses the American title of the novel.

Some contributors to this anthology cite the Greek text of Kazantzakis's novel, albeit sparingly, and/or use other specialized Greek words, phrases, or expressions. When they do, each writer uses the (phonetic) transliteration scheme developed by *The Journal of Modern Greek Studies* with slight variations.

Literary Lord, Screen Savior

Darren J. N. Middleton

Of the Devil's Party

Cretans buried their native son Nikos Kazantzakis (1883–1957) on November 5, 1957. Forming a grand funeral procession, thousands accompanied his body as it was taken from Heraklion's St. Minas's Cathedral to the Martinengo rampart on the Venetian walls. Local students held copies of Kazantzakis's books as they walked directly behind the coffin. In sketching the scene for the periodical *Spitha*, the Archdean Augustinos Kantiotis depicted Satan as leading the students. Grinning impishly, Satan clutches his own copy of *O teleftaíos peirasmós* (*The Last Temptation [of Christ]*).[1] This sketch has haunted me for years. Whenever my literature students are tempted to think that fiction is a neutral territory upon which all educated people can stand and debate openly, I show them Kantiotis's cartoon.

As my students soon discover, compelling storytelling is frequently subversive, even threatening, and often likely to incite others. But this is perhaps as it should be. Persuasive fiction habitually protests easy solutions, time-worn moralities, and prevailing orthodoxies. It resists tradition's tyranny, or whatever it is that holds us in thrall to the past, functioning like an ax for the frozen sea within.[2] Poets and writers often find that they must attend the devil's party before conjuring those characters who pose difficult questions about life, reality, meaning, and God.[3] As critic Frederic Koeppel writes:

> We turn to great literature—all great art—for the challenge of complexity, for the shock of recognition, for the bracing bath of humanity in all its weakness and greed and illicit longing, qualities that may not get us into heaven but certainly make for the exquisite and heartbreaking tensions great art requires, not to mention providing a rip-roaring reading. . . . The (author's) wisdom lies in the telling, in the narrative, in

language itself, and it forms a kind of powerful morality of choice that draws us to literature, even to the same books, over and over again.[4]

Behind Kantiotis's sarcastic sketch lies an anxious attitude toward art and literature, one that seems as real today as it did upon Kazantzakis's death in 1957. Published in 1955, Kazantzakis's *The Last Temptation* remains one of the most controversial novels of the twentieth century. Lured by a "powerful morality of choice," the essayists featured here have reread and reappreciated this modern literary classic as it celebrates its fiftieth anniversary. Before I introduce their contibutions, however, some commentary on what I refer to as Kazantzakis's reverence for Jesus seems in order.

Kazantzakis's Reverence for Jesus

Arguments about Kazantzakis's religiosity began in 1930 when, not long after he published *The Saviors of God: Spiritual Exercises*, some contemporaries accused him of atheism. A trial date was then set. Although he was never summoned, opposition to his ideas subsequently intensified. In 1953 several religious leaders censured Kazantzakis for scandalizing the Church's official teaching (both Orthodox and Catholic).[5] Hostilities culminated with the Greek publication of *The Last Temptation* in 1955. While most of Kazantzakis's texts courted controversy, *The Last Temptation* was the only one listed in the Vatican's Index of Forbidden Texts.[6]

Given such ecclesiastical resistance, it is understandable why later Christians have continued to dismiss Kazantzakis. But if we read his writings closely, we discover that Kazantzakis approaches Jesus reverentially. Consider the following notebook entry, composed after hearing the twelve Gospels of Holy Thursday, March 1915:

> Great emotion in church. The Crucified seemed to me more mine, more myself. I felt the "suffering God" deeply within me and said: May the Resurrection come with perseverance, love, and effort. Joy, victory over passion, dematerialization, freedom. Simplicity and serenity, composed of the essence of all the passions, which have been subordinated to the divine Eye. Spirit like light and like the clear water of the fountain.[7]

Kazantzakis holds that our best attributes are to be found in Jesus of Nazareth's life and teaching. In both his love for God and his behavior toward others, Jesus exemplifies our ideal. But since Jesus' message requires our inner evolution, our being born again, so to speak, Jesus also challenges us to follow him, making our ideal real. Kazantzakis confesses:

> I kept gazing at Christ's virile, ascetic figure in the gentle glow of the cressets. [Here Kazantzakis writes about venerating the sacred icons at St. Catherine's Monastery in the Sinai desert.] Perceiving the slender hands which maintained a firm grip on the

world and kept it from falling into chaos, I knew that here on earth, for the full span of our lives, Christ was not the harbor where one casts anchor, but the harbor from which one departs, gains the offing, encounters a wild, tempestuous sea, and then struggles for a lifetime to anchor in God. Christ is not the end, He is the beginning. He is not the "Welcome!" He is the "Bon voyage!" He does not sit back restfully in soft clouds, but is battered by the waves just as we are, His eyes fixed aloft on the North Star, His hands firmly on the helm. That was why I liked Him; that was why I would follow him.

What attracted me and gave me courage above everything else was how—with what striving and derring-do, what frantic hope—the person who found himself in Christ set out to reach God and merge with Him, so that the two might become indissolubly one. There is no way to reach God but this. Following Christ's bloody tracks, we must fight to transubstantiate the man inside us into spirit, so that we may merge with God.[8]

By "bloody tracks," Kazantzakis means Christ's struggle as revealed in his temptations. Like us, Jesus was tempted. But since Jesus did not succumb to the devil's snare, Kazantzakis thinks that we can draw strength from Jesus' example.[9] As the focal instance of the divine-human person, Jesus is the firstborn son of salvation. Victorious in his own ascent to God, Jesus now beckons us to the lofty peak, which is union with the divine: *theōsis*. Whenever we heed Jesus' call, a deepening of God's incarnation occurs, or as Kazantzakis puts it, we show that "a Messiah is always on the march."[10]

There can be little doubt that *The Last Temptation* is a controversial novel. But we need not disbelieve—or, as with Kantiotis, discredit—Kazantzakis's reverence for Jesus, even if we must acknowledge that he did not label himself "Christian." As this brief section shows, he approaches his subject with passionate spiritual feeling:

This book [*The Last Temptation*] is not a biography; it is the confession of every man who struggles. In publishing it I have fulfilled my duty, the duty of a person who struggled much, was much embittered in his life, and had many hopes. I am certain that every free man who reads this book, so filled as it is with love, will more than ever before, better than ever before, love Christ.[11]

Fifty Years Later

Nearly fifty years after *The Last Temptation*'s publication, the essayists of *Scandalizing Jesus?* reassess both the novel and its 1988 cinematic adaptation (*The Last Temptation of Christ*) by Martin Scorsese. The anthology is divided into two parts. In the first, "Literary Lord," contributors focus on Kazantzakis and the novel. The first three essays here consider Kazantzakis's primary sources in writing *The Last Temptation*. Peter Bien indicates that Kazantzakis read Ernest Renan's *Vie de Jésus* (1863) very carefully in October 1950, copying long passages into the special notebook that he was using for his then-new project. Renan's influence was pervasive. Yet Bien insists that we must not overstate it. Perhaps Renan merely reinforced ideas that Kazantzakis had developed on his own. Following Bien, W. Barnes Tatum acknowledges that *The Last Temptation* possesses its own integrity as a literary work. However, he maintains that Kazantzakis's retelling of the Jesus story draws upon the four canonical Gospels alongside issues raised during the continuing two-hundred-year historical quest for Jesus. That Kazantzakis's novel reflects a sensitivity to historical-Jesus issues becomes understandable when one recognizes that he admired Renan's work and shared a personal friendship with Albert Schweitzer—towering figures in what has become known as the quest of the historical Jesus. In his essay, Lewis Owens analyzes Kazantzakis's notebooks, especially his marginalia, and shows that Carl Gustav Jung's influence is to be found not only in Jesus' characterization, which is predominantly Freudian, but also in the portrayal of Pontius Pilate. Like Bien and Tatum before him, Owens's source criticism provides an invaluable insight into the primary literature and philosophy that shaped Kazantzakis's thought during his novel's composition.

The next three, more speculative essays establish connections between Kazantzakis, *The Last Temptation*, and Christianity. Daniel Dombrowski explores orthodoxy and heterodoxy in Kazantzakis's fictional Christology. He argues that it can most profitably be seen as a contemporary version of Monophysitism (from the ancient Greek: *mon-* [one] + *physis* [nature]), holding that Jesus has one nature. Although this view is at odds with what has been traditionally seen as the orthodox, Chalcedonian view (Jesus' having two distinct natures), Dombrowski thinks it is nonetheless a more defensible view of Jesus in light of the recent revolt against dualism. Kazantzakis, then, helps us to see the inadequacies of a two-tiered view of the universe and of Jesus wherein the "supernatural" is arbitrarily inserted into the natural world or invades it. Pamela Francis demonstrates how Kazantzakis's Jesus exemplifies the mysticism of the Orthodox Fathers, especially that of the Cappadocian Gregory of Nyssa. For Francis, Kazantzakis and Gregory's views are parallel in their understandings of God, humanity, and Christ. Her analysis of Gregory's writing in relation to the Greek Orthodox tradition yields a fresh understanding of Kazantzakis's own relationship to that tradition, and in turn its relation to the other strains of thought found in *The Last Temptation*. Vrasidas Karalis examines some of these strains as seen in the christological debates of the early Church. He holds that Kazantzakis's Jesus models the concept of theandric union as framed but not fully articulated by the ecumenical councils.

Roderick Beaton then turns us toward a more non-Christian reading of *The Last Temptation*. First, he questions the conventional assumption that "Jesus" and "Christ" are one and the same person for Kazantzakis. In an even bolder move, he claims that the last temptation was not so much a temptation as a dream or even an alternative reality. Finally, he compares Kazantzakis's novel with Jorge Luis Borges's fictional texts, texts that lead away from Christianity, and thus he attempts to move our own interpretations of *The Last Temptation* in a similar direction.

After Beaton, C. D. Gounelas gives a Platonic reading of *The Last Temptation*, which sees Kazantzakis as exploring the question of how matter and spirit harmonize in a World-Psyche. References to Plato, Angelos Sikelianós, and Édouard Schuré on Jesus provide a context of mystical insight toward which Kazantzakis's novel seems to be reaching, Gounelas says.

Both Charitini Christodoulou and Jen Harrison see *The Last Temptation* through a feminist lens. Christodoulou draws heavily upon Julia Kristeva's work on the struggle between the symbolic and the semiotic to analyze Jesus' relationship with his mother and Mary Magdalene. Taking cues from Rosemary Radford Ruether, Elizabeth Schüssler-Fiorenza, and Marcus Borg, Harrison claims that Kazantzakis's trinity of Marys encapsulates the range of misogynist myths and fears about women, highlighting the humanness of the pre-Easter Jesus and humanity's fundamental need of redemption. Redeemed man, of course, bears no such fear of woman, since in Christ the two are equal.

Mini Chandran closes the first part of *Scandalizing Jesus?* by examining *The Last Temptation*'s impact in Kerala, an area of India with a strong Christian presence. Given its highly combustible religious elements, India has never reacted kindly to scriptural reconfigurations. As she recounts, many Indian religious leaders reacted with outrage over Kazantzakis's novel and its manifestation in a street play. Chandran concludes by pointing to similar reactions to Aubrey Menen's *Rama Retold* and Salman Rushdie's *The Satanic Verses*.

Recognizing that Martin Scorsese's cinematic adaptation of Kazantzakis's novel has been a significant part of *The Last Temptation*'s reception history since the film's release in 1988, the essays in part 2, "Screen Savior," critically reassess this landmark event. Elizabeth H. Flowers and Darren J. N. Middleton explore evangelical reaction to Scorsese's film. Focusing on Texas, they argue that evangelical critique can actually better help us understand the human side of Kazantzakis's/Scorsese's Jesus. Middleton and Flowers indicate that sex, the ultimate temptation of Jesus to engage in sex with Mary Magdalene, forms an important part of Texas evangelical critique of *The Last Temptation of Christ*. In the next essay, however, Peter Chattaway argues that Scorsese emphasized sex as "the last temptation" to a greater degree than Kazantzakis's novel, and that those who protested the film focused on it almost exclusively. Yet for Chattaway, the irony is that both the film and its protestors hold sexuality and spirituality as mutually incompatible.

Following Chattaway, Lloyd Baugh questions this focus on sexuality, which tends to overlook Kazantzakis's/Scorsese's deeply problematic anthropology and Christology. While highlighting their weaknesses, Baugh maintains that the novel and film are nonetheless capable of stimulating believers to think theologically. Melody D. Knowles and Allison Whitney share Baugh's final point. As teachers at Chicago's McCormick Theological Seminary, they chart their students' surprising reactions to their classroom use of Scorsese's film. Overall, they argue for its pedagogical potential in raising issues that are often left unaddressed in the training of clergy.

The next two essays grapple with the relationship between word, sound, and image in Kazantzakis's/Scorsese's artwork. Randolph Jordan shows how cinema's dual sound/image apparatus enhances our understanding of Christ's own duality. According to Jordan, Scorsese's film achieves a truly unified medium where the auditory and the visual are understood as two parts of the same thing, just as God the Father and God the Son are one and the same. Eftychia Papanikolaou explores how Peter Gabriel's sound track to *The Last Temptation of Christ* highlights the ideological bond between Kazantzakis and Scorsese. As she maintains, the music becomes a third voice that acts as a bridge between author and filmmaker. Although vital as an autonomous and abstract work of art, the music is inextricably infused with the same dialectic that penetrates the film's narrative, that between flesh and spirit, the human and the divine.

The last word in *Scandalizing Jesus?* goes to Martin Scorsese. Scorcese looks at the years between his first reading of the novel in 1973 and his film's release in 1988. The result is an honest self-profile. Scorsese contemplates what inspired him to make the film and touches upon the surrounding controversy. In the end, though, he moves beyond himself to offer hope that now, in the early part of the twenty-first century, we are perhaps finally ready to reappreciate *The Last Temptation*.

Conclusion

According to the Nobel Prize–winning South African writer J. M. Coetzee, "The classic defines itself by surviving." After fifty years of heated debate, Kazantzakis's novel is still going strong. It continues to provoke, agitate, and excite persons of faith and those of no faith. While some see it as an example of satanic arrogance, others view it as part of their outlook on God. Either way, people continue to bring to it questions whose answers do not come easily. In one sense, then, there is no real difference between Kantiotis's hostile sketch and our own broadly celebratory volume. As Coetzee says, "The interrogation of the classic, no matter how hostile, is part of the history of the classic, inevitable and even to be welcomed. For as long as the classic needs to be protected from attack, it can never prove itself classic." On such grounds, the critic is "duty-bound to interrogate the classic." The essayists of *Scandalizing Jesus?* have tried to discharge this duty as we approach the fiftieth anniversary of the publication of Nikos Kazantzakis's classic *O teleftaíos peirasmós*.[12]

Notes

1. The sketch is reproduced in George I. Panagiotakis, *The Life and Works of Nikos Kazantzakis*, trans. Ioannis Panagiotis (Heraklion, Crete: Typokreta, 2002), 308.

2. The phrase belongs to Franz Kafka. See Joyce Carol Oates, "The Importance of Childhood," in *The Writing Life: Writers on How They Think and Work*, ed. Marie Arana (New York: PublicAffairs, 2003), 15.

3. Here I am paraphrasing William Blake's famous remark about John Milton's being "of the Devil's party without knowing it."

4. Frederic Koeppel, "It's Fiction; What's Goodness Got to Do with It?" *The Commercial Appeal* (Memphis), Sunday, September 29, 1996, G2.

5. The details are so well documented that it seems unnecessary to rehearse them in this introduction. For more information, see the essays in Darren J. N. Middleton and Peter A. Bien, eds., *God's Struggler: Religion in the Writings of Nikos Kazantzakis* (Macon, GA: Mercer University Press, 1996).

6. See Helen Kazantzakis, *Nikos Kazantzakis: A Biography Based on His Letters*, trans. Amy Mims (New York: Simon & Schuster, 1968), 524.

7. Ibid., 58.

8. Nikos Kazantzakis, *Report to Greco*, trans. Peter Bien (New York: Simon & Schuster, 1965), 289.

9. Nikos Kazantzakis, *The Last Temptation of Christ*, trans. Peter Bien (New York: Simon & Schuster, 1960), 1–4.

10. Helen Kazantzakis, *Biography*, 496. Cf. N. Kazantzakis, *Last Temptation*, 227. Also see 2 Cor 6:16–18 and Heb 2:10–18; 4:15.

11. Nikos Kazantzakis, *Last Temptation*, 2–3. Also see H. Kazantzakis, *Biography*, 505–6.

12. J. M. Coetzee, *Stranger Shores: Literary Essays, 1986–1999* (New York: Viking, 2001), 16.

PART ONE
Literary Lord

CHAPTER 1

Renan's *Vie de Jésus* as a Primary Source for *The Last Temptation*

Peter Bien

Throughout his career Nikos Kazantzakis had been concerned with the Christ-theme.[1] By the time he determined to write a novel on this theme, he already had many possible approaches in mind. Nevertheless, with his accustomed diligence he set himself to school afresh in order to discover the best treatment, and there is some likelihood that this schooling gave him the book's central trick of having happiness emerge as a last temptation at the time of Jesus' death. If so, then the precise source for this treatment is Ernest Renan's *Vie de Jésus* (1863), which Kazantzakis read or reread carefully in October 1950, copying long passages into the special notebook he was using for his new project. My suspicion is that Renan gave him the central idea, or at least activated something earlier that had remained in Kazantzakis's subconscious. This theory is strengthened by the fact that it was not until November 1950—directly after his reading of Renan—that Kazantzakis designated "the last temptation" as the "probable title" of his work in progress.[2] In any case, he was attracted by the following passage in Renan (I quote the authorized English translation; Kazantzakis obviously read the original French):

> All the recitals agree, in attributing to him [Jesus], before his arrest, a moment of hesitation and of trouble, a kind of anticipated death-agony. . . . Human nature awoke for a moment. He began perhaps to doubt of his work. . . . Terror, hesitation seized upon him and threw him into a dejection worse than death. The man who has sacrificed repose and the natural compensations of life to a great idea, experiences a moment of sad reflection, when the image of death presents itself to him for the first time, and seeks to persuade him that all is vanity. Perhaps some one of those touching recollections which even the strongest souls preserve, and which at times pierce them like the sword, came to him at this moment. We know not.

Renan goes on to wonder:

> Did he recall the clear fountains of Galilee . . . ; the young maidens who might per
> haps have consented to love him? Did he curse his bitter destiny, which had forbidden
> to him the joys conceded to all others? Did he regret his too lofty nature, . . . did he
> weep because he had not remained a simple artisan of Nazareth?

We cannot be sure, Renan admits; but one thing is sure: "His divine nature soon
resumed the ascendancy. . . . The love of his work gained the victory."[3]

Renan's speculations include the entire kernel of Kazantzakis's novel. Kazantzakis copied out most of the passage in a mixture of languages, turning the questions
into affirmations and omitting Renan's cautious "perhaps" each time it occurred.
Then, presumably during a subsequent review of all his notes, he underlined the following portion of the above passage:

> Les ordres pour l'arrêter étaient donnés. Tous les récits s'accordent pour lui prêter
> avant son arrestation un moment d'hésitation et de trouble, une agonie. . . . La ter
> reur, l'hésitation s'emparèrent de lui, il se prit à douter de son oeuvre. *Thimíthike tin
> ómorfi Galilaía, . . . Magd., metániouse pou* trop grand *ki ékhase tóses harés.*[4]

But Renan's influence, in the areas of both specific points and overall attitude,
was even more pervasive than what I have already suggested. Before proceeding, I
should add that Kazantzakis's reading notes for *Vie de Jésus* are by far the most
extensive in the notebook devoted to his schooling for *The Last Temptation*, and that
he digested the same author's *Les Apôtres* as well. It is worth remembering that
Renan had affected him ever since the start of his career in Athens, and he was not
alone in his admiration. Renan, whose daughter Naomi had married the influential
demoticist Yannis Psichari, was well-known in the intellectual circles of Athens, and
in particular was an important figure for the generation active around the turn of
the century—for Theotokis and Hatzopoulos, for example—because of his skepticism.[5] Thus it is no surprise to find Kazantzakis citing him as early as 1909 in his
essay "*I epistími ekhreokópise?*" There he calls Renan an "*ipérohos skeptikistís*" (superb
skeptic) and shows evidence of having followed the evolution of the Frenchman's
intellectual position from the "premature and juvenile enthusiasm for science" to the
calm skepticism of the final years.[6] Closer to the years we are considering, we find
Kazantzakis citing Renan again—this time his *L'Avenir de la science* (Paris: Calmann
Lévy, 1890)—in his own plans for "Faust, Part III."[7] It was natural for him to feel
especially attracted to Renan's famous series of religious biographies when he embarked on his systematic research for *The Last Temptation*. He may have discovered
the kernel of his novel there, as we have just seen. Among other specific points that
were either derived in the first instance from Renan or, if Kazantzakis had thought of
them earlier, reinforced by Renan's views, we may list the following ten:

> 1. The physical characteristics of Saint Paul. In Jesus' final hallucination in *The
> Last Temptation*, Paul appears as a squat hunchback with bald head, fat belly,

and crooked legs.[8] These repulsive characteristics seem to derive from Renan's *Les Apôtres*, from which Kazantzakis copied into his notebook: "La mine de Paul était chétive; il était laid, de court taille, épais et voûte. Ses fortes épaules portaient bizarrement une tête petite et chauve" (Paul was puny in appearance; he was ugly, short in stature, heavy-set, stooped. His strong shoulders bizarrely supported a small bald head).[9] Renan's source is the apocryphal *Acts of Paul and Thecla* (1:3): "And he saw Paul coming, a man small in size, bald-headed, bandy-legged, well built, with eyebrows meeting, rather long-nosed."

2. The motif whereby Simeon, the old rabbi, cannot die until he has been assured that the Messiah has come.[10] This derives from Luke 2:25–26 and is emphasized by Renan.[11]

3. The inability of Jesus' family, including Mary, to understand his mission. Renan cites John 7:3–5.[12]

4. The ambition of Zebedee's sons, James and John, as well as the other disciples, to be rewarded in heaven.[13]

5. The psychosomatic basis of Jesus' miracles.[14] Kazantzakis follows this most closely in his treatment of the healing of the centurion's daughter. (Later, we shall see incontrovertible evidence that he considered the daughter's paralysis to be hysterical in nature.) He follows Renan as well when he places the walking on the waves in Peter's dream.[15] Renan declares that a miracle "always implies gullibility or deception."[16] The only miracle that Kazantzakis seems to take at face value is the raising of Lazarus, contrary to Renan's efforts to imagine a moribund but still living Lazarus, wrapped prematurely in his grave-windings and already shut within the family tomb, emerging in this garb when Jesus called him forth.[17] "This appearance," concludes Renan, "would naturally be regarded by everyone as a resurrection." On the subject of miracles, however, we must remember that Kazantzakis desired a certain "madness" or "delirium" to govern his book, and therefore resisted Renan's thoroughgoing skepticism. Indeed, one of the novel's strongest points is its ability to allow fantastic intrusions at the same time that it continues to be convincingly naturalistic.

6. Jesus' momentary doubt on the cross, followed at the end by a reaffirmation of his mission. Renan's formulation glosses Kazantzakis's final chapters perfectly:

> For a moment . . . his heart failed him . . . and he cried out: "My God, my God, why hast thou forsaken me?" But his divine instinct resumed its sway. In proportion as the life of his body was extinguished, his soul became serene and gradually returned to its celestial source. He regained the consciousness of his mission.[18]

7. Nazareth, not Bethlehem, as Jesus' birthplace. Renan shocked the readers of his day by opening his second chapter with the blunt assertion, "Jesus was born at Nazareth, a small town in Galilee."[19] Later, he explains the "grave difficulty" of Jesus' birth in Nazareth and the substitution of Bethlehem so that Jesus' life could conform to the messianic prophecies.[20] Kazantzakis has Matthew worry about the same problem.[21] Jesus grows furious at Matthew when he reads what the publican has been writing about him: "'What is this?' he screamed. 'Lies! . . . I was born in Nazareth, not in Bethlehem; I've never even set foot in Bethlehem.'"[22]

8. Emphasis on the vision of Daniel as the ultimate expression of the messianic idea. Kazantzakis seems to have responded to Renan's claim that Daniel "furnished the staging and the technical terms of the new messianism."[23] Summarizing in his notebook Renan's ideas on Jesus' definitive view of the kingdom of heaven, Kazantzakis copied: "L'accomplissement littéral [des visions apocalyptique] de Daniel et d'Hénoch" (the literal accomplishment of the apocalyptic visions of Daniel and Enoch).[24] Kazantzakis's interest in Daniel was stimulated by his other research as well. In his notes for P.-L. Couchoud's *Jésus, le Dieu fait homme* (Paris, 1937), for example, he copied and underlined: "Quand le Fils de l'homme de Daniel aura assimilé l'Homme de douleurs d'Isaïe, le Christianisme sera né" (When Daniel's Son of man will have assimilated Isaiah's Man of sorrows, Christianity will be born).

9. Treatment of the Zealots. Kazantzakis copied into his notebook and underlined Renan's characterization of the Zealots as "pious assassins who imposed upon themselves the task of killing whoever disobeyed the Law."[25] He also seems to have noticed Renan's detail that these political agitators harassed the authorities by acts such as pulling down the Roman eagles set up by Herod.[26] Compare *The Last Temptation*:

> This Zealot was the last of the long lineage of the Maccabees. . . . One night Herod . . . had smeared forty adolescents with tar and ignited them as torches because they had pulled down the golden eagle he had fastened to the . . . lintel of the Temple. Of the forty-one conspirators, forty were caught, but the leader escaped, . . . and this was this Zealot.[27]

In addition, Kazantzakis copied out Renan's long passage on the insurgent known as Juda[s] the Gaulonite, and later added a line in the margin of his notebook, showing his particular interest in this material. The following appears in his notebook:

> Un mouvement qui eut beaucoup plus d'influence sur Jésus fut celui de Juda le Gaulonite ou le Galiléen. *Ekhtrós tou* cens, *tou* impôt. . . . Dieu est le seul maître que l'homme doive reconnaître, payer la dîme à un souverain profane, c'est en quelque sorte le mettre à la place de Dieu. . . . Juda fut le chef d'une

secte galiléenne, préoccupée de messianisme, et qui aboutit à un mouvement politique. . . . Jésus vit peut-être ce Juda qui conçut la révolution juive d'une façon si différente de la sienne; Jésus rêva un autre royaume et une autre déliverance.[28]

A movement which had much more influence upon Jesus was that of Juda the Gaulonite or the Galilean. Enemy of the census, of taxation. . . . God being the only master whom man should recognize, to pay tithes to a mundane sovereign is in some sort to put him in the place of God. . . . Juda was . . . the chief of a Galilean sect, which was full of Messianism, and which ended in a political movement. . . . Jesus, perhaps, saw this Juda who had so different a conception of the Jewish revolution from his own; Jesus . . . looked to another kingdom and another deliverance.[29]

It is clear that Kazantzakis used this, conflating these insurgents with the Zealots. For example, he makes the Zealot who pulled down Herod's eagle speak words taken almost verbatim from the passage in Renan just cited: "'We have only one master—Adonai,' he used to proclaim. 'Do not pay poll tax to the earthly magistrates.'"[30] This Zealot is executed at the novel's start, but Kazantzakis then conflates Judas Iscariot, in a general way, with Juda the Gaulonite, who, as Renan says, "conceived of the Jewish revolution in a fashion so different from [that of Jesus]."[31]

10. Primacy of Matthew's Gospel. Renan believed (erroneously, as we now know) that of all the evangelists Matthew was the most authentic, and that in his Gospel we have recorded the actual speeches that Jesus made.[32] Accepting this view, Kazantzakis makes Matthew follow Jesus with pad and pen in hand, recording on the spot or soon afterward, like a journalist.

Obviously, some of these ten points are more important than others are. But as we extend the list—and many more could be added—we construct by accumulation a convincing case for Kazantzakis's indebtedness to Renan. This indebtedness extends well beyond the specific borrowings dealt with above to overall attitudes that sit at the heart of Kazantzakis's definitive treatment of the Christ-theme. Let us now list at least five of these:

1. Jesus was truly and fully a man in the sense that he was not perfect. For Renan, this is a central axiom: "He was not sinless; he conquered the same passions which we combat."[33]

2. The "divinity" of Jesus must be understood wholly in natural rather than in supernatural terms, in that Jesus—more than any other person—progressed toward the realization of an ideal conception of all that is most elevated in human nature. "We may call [him] divine," says Renan, "in this sense that Jesus is that individual who has caused his species to make the greatest advance towards the divine. . . . In him is condensed all that is good and lofty in our nature."[34]

3. Jesus' unique contribution to the political realm was his conception of inward rather than outward freedom. Elsewhere, I have tried to show Kazantzakis's own increasing recourse to this view as he matured and was repeatedly frustrated in the outward realm, although not in the inward. In *Alexis Zorbas, Christ Recrucified,* and *The Last Temptation,* we see inward strength replacing outward, individual integrity replacing political liberation. Kazantzakis did not derive this conception from Renan, or even from Jesus. But Renan reinforced his mature view and encouraged him in his increasing certainty that the Christian myth was the most paradigmatic for him in the final stage of his own career. Jesus, says Renan, "revealed to the world the truth that country is not everything, and that the man is anterior and superior to the citizen. . . . The idea of omnipotence through suffering and resignation, of triumphing over force by purity of heart, is indeed an idea peculiar to Jesus."[35] That Kazantzakis responded positively to this kind of assertion is shown by the passage he copied out and then marked with a line for emphasis. He characteristically omitted Renan's cautious "peut-être" (perhaps). "Many times perhaps this supreme question was presented to him, Shall the kingdom of God be realized by force or by gentleness, by revolt or by patience?"[36] Most interestingly, although Renan presents this "doctrine of the liberty of souls" as foreign to the ancient Greek, Kazantzakis—certainly from *Alexis Zorbas* onward—places it at the core of the modern Greeks' ability to survive.[37] Insofar as it is valid to distinguish the ancient Greek and the Christian view of liberty in this way, we may consider Kazantzakis the inheritor of both. He veers toward the ancient conception in *Kapetán Mihális,* to be sure, but attempts in *The Last Temptation* to synthesize the two within the larger context of his Bergsonian worldview. In such an evolutionary process, the union of the Christian with the Hellenic (figured, say, in Judas because of his desire for outward liberation) impels the spirit to a still higher level of freedom. We need to call this eschatological, even though Kazantzakis's worldview admits of no supernatural kingdom in the orthodox sense.

4. Jesus' doctrine of inner freedom brought him inevitably into conflict with the official world of power, making him a champion of the dispossessed. Once again, Kazantzakis copied out a relevant passage from Renan:

> Jésus comprit bien vite . . . que le monde officiel de son temps ne se prêterait nullement à son royaume. Il en print son parti avec une hardiesse extrême. Laissant là tout ce monde au coeur sec . . . , il se tourna vers les simples. . . . Le royaume de Dieu est fait (1) pour les enfants et pour ceux qui leur ressemblent *kai tous ómoioús tous,* (2) pour les rebutés de ce monde . . . , (3) pour les hérétiques . . . , publicains, samaritains, païens. . . .
>
> Le pur *ébionisme,* . . . la doctrine que les pauvres (*ébionim*) seuls seront sauvés, que le règne des pauvres va venir, fut . . . la doctrine de Jésus.[38]

Jesus, indeed, soon comprehended that the official world of his time would give no countenance to his kingdom. He resolved upon his course with extreme boldness. Leaving all this world to its hardness of heart and its narrow prejudices, he turned towards the simple. . . . The kingdom of God is: first, for children and for those who are like them; second, for the outcasts of this world . . . ; third, for heretics . . . , publicans, Samaritans and pagans. . . .

Pure Ebionism, . . . the doctrine that the poor (*ebionim*) only shall be saved, that the reign of the poor is at hand, was . . . the doctrine of Jesus.[39]

5. The ministry and passion of Jesus cannot be understood without their eschatological component. We must not subtract this component simply because we ourselves cannot believe in an afterlife. This point was extremely important for Renan and also for Kazantzakis. Of the various overall attitudes that sit at the heart of *The Last Temptation*, it is the most complicated. In this regard Kazantzakis found Renan helpful, I believe, because of the latter's attempt to confront and master the eschatological complexity instead of banishing it by retreating to a wholly ethical perspective. In other words, Kazantzakis felt such a close affinity to Renan because here was a skeptic whose doubt was not so doctrinaire that it excluded mysticism. Renan clearly expounds both sides of the paradox. On the one hand, Jesus was a moralist keenly interested in improving this world as opposed to ending it in favor of a heavenly kingdom. Jesus, he writes,

undertook to create a new condition of humanity, and not merely to prepare for the end of that which existed. . . . He often declares that the kingdom of God has already commenced, that every man carries it in himself, and may . . . enjoy it; that each creates this kingdom . . . by the true conversion of the heart. The kingdom of God is then only the good, an order of things better than that which exists. . . . Jesus . . . had . . . faith . . . in the reality of the ideal.[40]

The revolution which he desired to bring about was always a moral revolution. . . . A visionary who had no other idea than the proximity of the last judgment would not have had this care for the amelioration of man.[41]

On the other hand, and in apparent contradiction with this moralism, Renan stresses Jesus' conviction that the present state of human existence was about to terminate in a great cataclysm ushering in a supernatural kingdom. Kazantzakis copied Renan's view into his notebook as follows, adding in a parenthesis his own sense that the cataclysm imagined by the ancient apocalyptic writers (Daniel and John) might well be at hand because of the atomic bomb:

Les idées apocalyptique de Jésus:

L'order actuel de l'humanité touche à son terme. Ce terme sera une immense révolution, "une angoisse" semblable aux douleurs de l'enfantement; une *palinyenesía* précédée de sombres calamités et annoncée par d'étranges phénomènes . . . un grand orage déchirant la nue, un trait de feu d'Orient en Occident (bombe atomique). Le Messie apparaîtra dans les nuages, revêtu de gloire au son des trompettes, entouré d'anges. . . . Les morts ressusciteront et le Messie procédera au jugement.[42]

> The apocalyptic ideas of Jesus:
> The end of the present order of humanity is at hand. This end will be an immense revolution, a *palingenesis* preceded by sombre calamities and announced by strange phenomena . . . a great tempest rending the sky, a bolt of fire from the East to the West (atomic bomb). The Messiah will appear in the clouds, clothed in glory, with the sound of trumpets, surrounded by angels. . . . The dead will then arise, and the Messiah will proceed to the judgment.[43]

The paradox appears most blatantly, of course, in the full contradictoriness of Jesus' sayings that (1) the kingdom of God is at hand and (2) the kingdom of God is within us. The first assumes that the world as we know it is about to end; the second, because it implies the need and possibility of moral regeneration, assumes that the world as we know it is going to continue.

Kazantzakis refused to ignore, reject, or explain away Jesus' eschatological mysticism in favor of his moralism. I believe that he was helped in this by Renan, who likewise refused that dodge. Indeed, Renan, after expounding the contradiction so clearly, rejoiced in it and argued for its need. It was precisely this contradiction, he declared, that "assured the success" of Jesus' work:

> The millenarian alone would have possessed no power. The millenarianism gave the impulsion, the morality secured the future. In this way, Christianity united the two conditions of great success in this world, a revolutionary starting-point, and the possibility of life. Everything which is made to succeed must respond to these two needs; for the world demands at the same time to change and to endure. Jesus, while he announced an unparalleled revolution in human affairs, proclaimed the principles upon which society has reposed for the last eighteen hundred years.[44]

Kazantzakis goes well beyond Renan in the complexity of his explanation, because he sees biblical millenarianism in evolutionary terms in ways that Renan could never have imagined, writing as he was only a few years after Darwin published his *On the Origin of Species by Means of Natural Selection, or, the Preservation of Favoured Races in the Struggle for Life* (1859), and decades before Bergson. But Kazantzakis, in his general attitude toward the eschatological problem, as in so many other areas, found support from Renan.

All in all, then, we ought now to be able to recognize and acknowledge Renan's influence on *The Last Temptation* in both individual points and generic attitudes that sit right at the heart of Kazantzakis's definitive treatment of the Christ-theme.

But central as Renan is to Kazantzakis's thinking, we must not overstate his influence or treat *The Last Temptation* as a fictionalization of *Vie de Jésus*. First of all, Renan merely reinforced many ideas and attitudes that Kazantzakis had developed on his own in the course of his obsessive concern with Christ over six decades.

Second, although the reading notes on Renan are more extensive by far than those on any other single author, Kazantzakis's self-schooling for *The Last Temptation* involved dozens of additional sources, many of them quite different from Renan. Third, Kazantzakis was never content with redoing what someone else had already done. He aspired to absorb his many sources in all their diversity, to assimilate them into his own system, and then, synthesizing everything, to create something new and entirely his own that, at the same time, would be recognizably rooted in tradition. His statement to Börje Knös in November 1951, after he had finished the novel, is relevant to everything I have just been saying:

> For a whole year I took out of the library at Cannes all the books—those written about Christ, about the Judaeans of those times; the chronicles, the Talmud, etc.— and thus all the details [in *The Last Temptation*] are historically accurate, although I recognize the poet's right not to follow history slavishly; *poíisis filosofóteron istorías* [poetry is more philosophic than history].[45]

The extent of this reading is prodigious in both amount and variety. As he indicated to Knös, his main objective was to immerse himself in the "facts" of the time, insofar as they are known. Thus, for example, he paid particular attention to geography, recording precise distances between towns, figuring how long it would have taken Jesus and his disciples to walk, say, from Galilee to Jerusalem, and so on. He noted climatic conditions, topography, and the dominant characteristics of the landscape as seen from the towns that Jesus frequented. Much of this came once again from Renan's *Vie de Jésus*, since Renan had written this book while on a visit to the Holy Land and was meticulous in his eyewitness descriptions. But Kazantzakis read as well Adolphe Lods's *Israël: Des origines au milieu du VIIIe siècle* (Paris, 1930), taking notes on rainfall and prevailing winds, and also André Louis Chevrillon's *Terres mortes: Thébaïde-Judée* (Paris, 1897) and Pierre Loti's *Jérusalem* (Paris, 1895). His research on Jewish history included more Renan (volume 5 of his *Histoire du peuple d'Israël* [Paris, 1887–1894]), covering the Pharisees, Sadducees, Essenes, the Roman occupation, and the beginning of Jesus' ministry. He also studied Charles Guignebert's *Des prophètes à Jésus: Le monde juif vers le temps de Jésus* (Paris, 1935) and Adolphe Lods's *Historie de la littérature hébraïque depuis les origines jusqu'à la ruine de l'état juif, 135 après J.-C.* (Paris, 1950). As for Jesus himself, besides Renan's *Vie*, Kazantzakis read Marius Lepin's *Le Problème de Jésus: En reponse à MM. A. Loisy et Ch. Guignebert* (Paris, 1936), Charles Guignebert's *Jésus* (Paris, 1933), and studies by Paul-Louis Couchoud and Alphonse Séché—*Jésus: Le Dieu fait homme* (Paris, 1937) and *Histoire merveilleuse de Jésus* (Paris, 1926), respectively. For the early Church, his source was Henry Daniel-Rops's *L'Eglise des apôtres et des martyrs* (Paris, 1948).

However, Kazantzakis did not confine himself to an investigation of the facts about Jesus, his times, and his land. From this center he branched out in many directions. For example, he read Solomon Reinach's *Orpheus: Histoire générale des religions* (Paris, 1909) on the reliability of the Gospels. He also read in Gnostic literature, recording in his notebook that this heresy claimed that Christ survived eighteen months after the crucifixion and in this time conveyed all of his major teachings to the disciples. In addition, Kazantzakis perused Henri Delacroix's *Etudes d'histoire et de psychologie du mysticisme: Les grands mystiques chrétiens* (Paris, 1908) and dipped into the original writings of Boehme, Meister Eckhart, Gerlach, Saint Teresa, Ruysbroeck, and Maria Magdalena dei Pazzi. From these Western mystics he proceeded to Symeon the New Theologian, Cabasilas, and Maximos the Confessor in the Greek Orthodox tradition. The purpose—or at least one purpose—for this extensive investigation of mystical experience becomes apparent when we read his notes drawn from an article in the *Revue Bleue* of March 15, 1902, on the relation between mystical ecstasy and eroticism: "Une question est posée: l'extase ne serait elle pas comme une équivalent épuré, une sublimation de la vie instinctive la plus profonde?" (A question is posed: Would not rapture [sexual climax] be like a purified equivalent, a sublimation of the profoundest instinctive life?) He learned more about this subject from René Allendy's *La Justice intérieure* (Paris, 1931), copying out statements such as this: "flagellation = symbole de l'amour renversé par autopunition" (flagellation = a symbol of sex turned upside down by self-punishment). Allendy helped him as well on the relation between psychosomatic symptoms and miracles. "Le soulagement de la culpabilité pour la prison" (the relief of guilt for prison), Kazantzakis entered in his notebook, with a line for emphasis in the margin, "est comparable à l'apaisement de l'angoisse pour le symptôme somatique de conversion hystérique: paralysie, cécité, aphasie, etc." (is comparable to the allaying of anguish for the bodily symptom of hysterical conversion: paralysis, blindness, aphasia, etc.), after which he added in a parenthesis, "(= *tháma KHS:kóri* 100arkhos)," in other words Christ's miracle [with the] daughter [of the] centurion (*ekatóntarkhos*), referred to earlier as evidence for Kazantzakis's agreement with Renan that the miracles have a psychosomatic basis.[46] From these concerns about the relation of religious behavior to sexuality and the connection between miracles and abnormal psychological states, Kazantzakis branched out more generally to a review of basic psychoanalysis. He read C. G. Jung's *Die Beziehungen zwischen dem Ich und dem Unbewussten* (Zurich: Rascher, 1945) and Sigmund Freud's *Vorlesungen zur Einführung in die Psychoanalyse* (Leipzig: Heller, 1917), both in French translation. In *L'Homme à la découverte de son âme: Structure et fonctionnement de l'inconscient*, the translation of Jung's book, Kazantzakis concentrated once again on the relation between psychology and religiosity, noting and marking with emphasis ideas such as these:

> Accès s'incons[cient] *ekson apo ta óneira = k' i* activité religieuse de l'esprit. Elle est dans l'homme moderne encore plus profondément enfouie que la sexualité ou l'adaptation sociale. Il y a des personnes pour lesquelles la rencontre intér[ieur] avec la puissance étrangère en elles = Dieu. Dieu et une image que crée l'esprit humain dans son insuffisance pour exprimer l'expér[ience] intime de quelquechose d'impensable et d'indicible.[47]

Access to the subconscious apart from dreams = also the soul's religious activity. It is more deeply buried in modern man than is sexuality or social adaptation. There are people for whom the inner encounter with the external power in themselves = God. God is an image created by the human spirit in its inadequacy in explaining the intimate experience of something unbelievable and ineffable.

The notes on Freud's lectures concentrate (1) on the role of the unconscious, (2) on the suppression of sexual passion, (3) on artistic creativity as a conscious elaboration of unconscious drives, and (4) on myths, legends, and fairy tales as expressing the same persistent desires that are expressed in dreams. After dreams Kazantzakis added, in Greek, "This is the source of religion," and then, in French:

1. Individual unconscious (Freud)
2. Collective unconscious (Jung)
3. Universal unconscious (Christ)[48]

Thus far, we have seen Kazantzakis setting himself to school with a dual purpose. First, he sought to acquire factual knowledge so that he could convincingly root his novel in the known accounts (the Gospels and parallel sources such as Josephus, which he mined indirectly through Renan and the other scholars), as well as in the geography and topography of the Holy Land. Second, he sought to acquire a wider perspective vis-à-vis later Church history, mysticism, and psychology. I should add that he was also interested in how others had done what he hoped to do. Thus he read Giovanni Papini's *Storia di Cristo* (Firenze, 1921) in a French translation, and may have absorbed some (but not too much, thank goodness!) of the gushiness seen in passages like the following, which he copied out in French and which I give (freely) in Dorothy Canfield Fisher's translation:

> Overcome by joy, Martha rushes to meet him, to see what He needs, if He wishes to wash, eat, lie down; she goes to the well, lights a fire, fixes dinner; she borrows some fresh fish, eggs, figs, olives. . . . Mary, motionless, has fallen into an ecstasy. She sees and hears nothing but Jesus.[49]

As if this wasn't enough, he took time out in late February or early March 1951, when he was about halfway through *The Last Temptation*, to read Pär Lagerkvist's *Barabbas* (Stockholm, 1950), his disparagement of which reveals what he felt he was accomplishing better in his own book:

> I've read *Barabbas*. It's well written, the theme is very interesting. But no lofty creative invention. A "tidy" work, as we say in Greek—that is, one produced by a tidy person. The work of a good artisan, full of good sense, devoid of madness.[50]

All this reading—which continued, as we have seen, even after he had begun his own novel—is truly prodigious. I have tried to convey both its extent and its breadth, starting with the various books by Renan, Kazantzakis's major source. What we should marvel at, however, is not so much the industry that this self-schooling manifests as the fact that Kazantzakis, when all was said and done, did not become a slave to his sources. Instead, he assimilated them and produced something that is recognizably his own (*poíisis filosofóteron istorías!*) while at the same time also recognizably "factual." If we want to think of the Christ-story as a myth (which Kazantzakis certainly did), then we can say that, stretching the orthodox material, he deepened and broadened this myth into a new version that still functions as the original. Thereby he proved once more that a myth is really the sum of all its versions and may be renewed by being "supplemented." Let us mention apropos Kazantzakis's statement of intent: "I wanted to renew and supplement the sacred story that underlies the great Christian civilization of the West."[51]

If we marvel at his assiduity, we should do so out of the realization that Kazantzakis had already lived with the Christ-story all his life. He knew the Bible and the Apocrypha intimately, had written repeatedly about Christ in the past, and in addition lived in a culture whose folklore and also sophisticated literature are suffused with Christianity. Thus he could easily have embarked on this new novel with only a minimum of further preparation.

Let me elaborate on this cultural background in an attempt to demonstrate the extent to which Kazantzakis, even without individual effort, was immersed in the Christ-theme simply because he was part of Greek culture. Treatments of Christ in the sophisticated literature of Greece are so legion that we cannot even begin to survey them in a short space. So I will cite just one because of its marked similarity in certain respects to *The Last Temptation*. This is Kostas Varnalis's *To fos pou kaíei* (*The Burning Light*, 1922), a work that Kazantzakis most certainly knew.[52] In it we already find, for example, the attitude toward Mary that orthodox Christians considered so shocking when Kazantzakis's novel appeared three decades later. Varnalis's Mary, like Kazantzakis's, objects to her son's role as a public figure and wishes that he had remained an anonymous carpenter so that he could have been a respectable paterfamilias, returning home each evening to his smiling wife and adorable children! But Varnalis's audacity, like Kazantzakis's, is rooted in a much older tradition. In Romanos's *kontakion* (long poem) "Mary at the Cross," for example, which dates from the sixth century, the Mother of God (Theotokos) is shown acting like an ordinary Greek mother.[53] This perception of Mary is surely at the deepest level a folkloristic one, surfacing here and there in sophisticated texts. If we turn to folklore proper, we find in the demotic ballads a curious detail employed by Kazantzakis: gypsies forge the special nails used in crucifixions. A vagrant smith who forges the crucifixion nails appears as well in the medieval passion play *Christos Paschon*.[54] Many of these folklorist traditions must go back, in turn, to the apocryphal gospels, which we know that Kazantzakis reread in 1942 in connection with his plan to write the "Memoirs of Jesus."[55] Again, to trace just one detail employed by Kazantzakis, that of Joseph's flowering rod, we find in chapter 8 of the *Gospel of Pseudo-Matthew* the tradition of Joseph's being chosen to receive Mary and keep her in his house because a dove flew out of his rod.[56] Then, in chapter 7 of the *Gospel of the Nativity [Birth] of*

Mary, a later adaptation of *Pseudo-Matthew*, this is modified to include the flower. The story goes that the high priest heard the Lord's voice say:

> According to the prophecy of Isaiah, a man should be sought out to whom the virgin ought to be entrusted and espoused. For it is clear that Isaiah says: A rod shall come forth from the root of Jesse, and a flower shall ascend from his root; and the Spirit of the Lord shall rest upon him. . . . According to this prophecy, therefore, [the high priest] predicted . . . that he whose rod . . . should produce a flower, and upon the end of whose rod the Spirit of the Lord should settle in the form of a dove, was the man to whom the virgin ought to be entrusted and espoused.[57]

Kazantzakis could have picked up his detail of Joseph's flowering rod from this source. But it is just as likely that the story was "in the air" because of folkloristic analogues and that he just knew it, as he knew about the gypsy blacksmiths, without effort, simply because he had grown up in the Greek culture.

Thus I return to my point that Kazantzakis could easily have embarked on his new novel in 1950 without the systematic self-schooling that we have observed— something that makes his assiduity all the more remarkable. But perhaps we ought not to separate the prodigious program of reading in 1950–51 from what had gone before. We should consider it simply the final phase of a recurrent preparation. This had begun with his exposure to the *sinaksária* (saints' lives) when he was scarcely more than an infant. It had continued in negative form through the 1908–10 period, when he was absorbing the Nietzschean critique of Christianity. It had turned positive again in 1914–15, with the visit to Mount Athos and the sketching out of the plays *Nikiforos Fokas* and *Christos*. Then it was negative once more in the anti-Christian polemics of 1924–25 and the regretful dismissal of Christ in his *Odyssey* (1938). It turned positive anew in 1942, when the theme returned to tempt him, and in 1948, when he wrote *Christ Recrucified*. Finally, it came to a boil, one might say, when Kazantzakis had completed *Kapetán Mihális* and decided in July 1950 to embark on his new novel, which he described to Prevelakis as the one "*me théma ókhi ellinikó, pio fardhí*"(with a non-Greek theme, broader).[58]

Notes

1. See my chapter "Kazantzakis's Long Apprenticeship to Christian Themes," in *God's Struggler: Religion in the Writings of Nikos Kazantzakis*, ed. Darren J. N. Middleton and Peter Bien (Macon, GA: Mercer University Press, 1996), 113–31.

2. Pandelis Prevelakis, *Tetrakósia grámmata tou Kazantzáki ston Prevelaki* (Athens: Ekdhóseis Eléni N. Kazantzáki, 1965), 630.

3. Ernest Renan, *The Life of Jesus*, trans. Charles Edwin Wilbour (New York: Carleton, 1864), 317–18. The French original is *Vie de Jésus*, 2nd ed. (Paris: Michel Lévy Frères, 1863).

4. Nikos Kazantzakis, Unpublished Notebook VI:22. Compare the translation of the passage in question from Renan: "All the recitals agree, in attributing to him, before his arrest, a

moment of hesitation and of trouble, a kind of anticipated death-agony. . . . He began perhaps to doubt of his work. Terror, hesitation seized upon him. . . . Did he recall the clear fountains of Galilee . . . , the young maidens who might perhaps have consented to love him? . . . Did he regret his too lofty nature, and . . . did he weep because he had not remained a simple artisan of Nazareth?" (Renan, *Life*, 317–18). Helen Kazantzakis (1903–2004), wife of Nikos, kindly made the unpublished notebooks available to me. The numbering of the notebooks is entirely arbitrary—by me, not by Kazantzakis. The notebook and page numbers simply allow me to find things in these resources. In any case, for *The Last Temptation*, my number is VI.

5. Kleon Paraschos, "*To révma tis apaisiodhoksías sti néa ellinikí logotekhnía*," *Kainoúria Epohí* (Spring 1956): 142–45.

6. Nikos Kazantzakis, "I epistími ekhreokópise?" *Néa Estía* 64 (September 15, 1958): 1377.

7. Prevelakis, *Tetrakósia grámmata*, 625.

8. Nikos Kazantzakis, *O teleftaíos peirasmós* (Athens: Difros, 1955), 453, 474. *The Last Temptation of Christ*, trans. Peter Bien (New York: Simon & Schuster, 1960), 453, 473.

9. Ernest Renan, *Les Apôtres* (Paris: Michel Lévy Frères, 1866), 170.

10. Kazantzakis, *O teleftaíos peirasmós*, 317; *Last Temptation*, 317.

11. Renan, *Vie*, 18; *Life*, 63–64.

12. Renan, *Vie*, 134; *Life*, 145.

13. Renan, *Vie*, 159; *Life*, 162. Kazantzakis, *O teleftaíos peirasmós*, 335, 338, 439; *Last Temptation*, 335, 337–38, 439.

14. Renan, *Vie*, 259–60; *Life*, 232–33.

15. Kazantzakis, *O teleftaíos peirasmós*, 342–43; *Last Temptation*, 341–43.

16. Renan, *Vie*, lii; *Life*, 45.

17. Renan, *Vie*, 361–62; *Life*, 305–6.

18. Renan, *Life*, 349–50; *Vie*, 424.

19. Renan, *Life*, 65; *Vie*, 19.

20. Renan, *Life*, 218; *Vie*, 239–40.

21. Kazantzakis, *O teleftaíos peirasmós*, 349; *Last Temptation*, 349–50.

22. Kazantzakis, *O teleftaíos peirasmós*, 391; *Last Temptation*, 392.

23. Renan, *Life*, 61; *Vie*, 15.

24. Renan, *Vie*, 271; *Life*, 240.

25. Renan, *Life*, 92; *Vie*, 59.

26. Renan, *Life*, 92; *Vie*, 58.

27. Kazantzakis, *O teleftaíos peirasmós*, 38; *Last Temptation*, 36.

28. Kazantzakis, Notebook VI:15; Renan, *Vie*, 59–61.

29. Renan, *Life*, 93–94.

30. Kazantzakis, *O teleftaíos peirasmós*, 38; *Last Temptation*, 36.

31. Kazantzakis was encouraged in the conflation of the two Judases and the Zealots by what he read in Charles Guignebert's *Des prophètes à Jésus: Le monde juif vers le temps de Jésus* (Paris, 1935): "Une certain Galiléen, nommé Judas . . . , se met en révolte; il cherche à soulever

le peuple et ne réussit qu' à former quelques bandes. . . . Toutefois le sentiment et la tendance d'où procédait leur initiative auraient persisté après eux et la faction des zélotes en serait issue" (221). (A certain Galilean named Judas began to revolt; he sought to arouse the population and succeeded only in forming some bands. . . . Nevertheless, the feelings and sympathies from which their initiative originated would persist after them, and the faction of the Zealots would be the outcome.) Guignebert's subsequent description, taken from Josephus, of the Zealots' tactic of knifing their opponents seems to have been used by Kazantzakis in the encounter between Judas and Jesus in the desert (chapter 11). In chapter 8 we see Judas trying to gather his rebel band.

32. Renan, *Vie*, xxi, xxxvii; *Life*, 22, 34.

33. Renan, *Life*, 375; *Vie*, 458. In a letter to Tea Anemoyanni written after *The Last Temptation* was published, Kazantzakis recounts how some theologians in Holland were shocked that his Christ had real temptations and comments: "but . . . I definitely knew that great temptations, extremely enchanting and often legitimate ones, came to hinder him on his road to Golgotha. But how could the theologians know all this?" See Eleni N. Kazantzaki (= Helen Kazantzakis), *Níkos Kazantzákis, o asimvívastos* (Athens: Eleni N. Kazantzaki, 1977), 604; Helen Kazantzakis, *Nikos Kazantzakis: A Biography Based on His Letters*, trans. Amy Mims (New York: Simon & Schuster, 1968), 515–16. Those who were so scandalized by this aspect of Kazantzakis's treatment of Jesus and who called the author blasphemous for having dared to make Jesus imperfect seem to have forgotten Heb 5:9, which implies that Christ was made perfect only through the crucifixion. Similarly, Heb 2:18 shows the ancients' assumption that Jesus' temptations were real. And Heb 4:15 is also relevant: "For we do not have a high priest who is unable to sympathize with our weaknesses, but we have one who in every respect has been tempted as we are, yet without sinning." Finally, we should remember John Milton's famous solution to this problem in *Paradise Lost* (5.117–21), where Adam instructs Eve:

Evil into the mind of God or Man
May come and go, so unapproved, and leave
No spot or blame behind; which gives me hope
That what in sleep thou didst abhor to dream
Waking thou never wilt consent to do.

34. Renan, *Vie*, 457–58; *Life*, 375.

35. Renan, *Life*, 137–38, 141; *Vie*, 123, 128.

36. Renan, *Life*, 135; *Vie*, 120.

37. Renan, *Life*, 136; *Vie*, 121. It is true, says Renan, that in Greece "many Stoics had found means of being free under a tyrant. But, in general, the ancient world had imagined liberty as connected with certain political forms."

38. Renan, *Vie*, 178–79.

39. Renan, *Life*, 176–77.

40. Ibid., 249–50; Renan, *Vie*, 283–84.

41. Renan, *Life*, 135; *Vie*, 120–21.

42. Renan, *Vie*, 272–73.

43. Renan, *Life*, 242.

44. Ibid., 140; Renan, *Vie*, 126–27.

45. Helen Kazantzakis, *Biography*, 505; Eleni Kazantzaki, *Asymvívastos*, 591.The phrase in ancient Greek is slightly misquoted from Aristotle's *Poetics*, chapter 9: "Dió kai filosofóteron kai spoudaióteron poíisis istorías estín. I men gar poíisis mállon ta kathólou, i d' istoría ta kath' ékaston légei" (Poetry is something more philosophic and of graver import than history, since its statements are of the nature of universals, whereas those of history are singulars.)

46. Kazantzakis, Notebook VI:31.

47. Ibid., 35.

48. Ibid., 73–74.

49. Ibid., 52; Giovanni Papini, *Life of Christ*, trans. Dorothy Canfield Fisher (New York: Harcourt, Brace, 1923), 221.

50. Letter of March 3, 1951, to Börje Knös, printed in Helen Kazantzakis, *Biography*, 495. This paragraph is curiously omitted from Eleni Kazantzaki, *Asymvívastos*, 578–79; and also from idem, *Le Dissident: Biographie de Nikos Kazantzaki* (Paris: Plon, 1968), 503.

51. Eleni Kazantzaki, *Asymvívastos*, 591; Helen Kazantzakis, *Biography*, 505.

52. He commented on Varnalis's work in general in his 1929 article "La Littérature grecque contemporaine" (*Monde*, March 16, 1929, 5), planned to include him in an anthology he hoped to produce in 1930 (Prevelakis, *Tetrakósia Grámmata*, 172–73), and cited him as one of Greece's best poets in a 1949 letter (Eleni Kazantzaki, *Asymvívastos*, 558; Helen Kazantzakis, *Biography*, 479). In addition, Kazantzakis and Varnalis traveled in the same circles in the early years. In Varnalis's work, see especially the section called "*I mána tou Khristoú*." This was brought to my attention by Theano Michaïlidou's Ph.D. thesis "K. Varnalis' Work" (University of Birmingham, 1980).

53. Margaret Alexiou, "The Lament of the Virgin in Byzantine Literature and Modern Greek Folk-Song," *Byzantine and Modern Greek Studies* 1 (1975): 113–14.

54. Ibid., 134–36.

55. Helen Kazantzakis, *Biography*, 407; not in Eleni Kazantzaki, *Asymvívastos*.

56. Alexander Roberts and James Donaldson, eds., *Ante-Nicene Christian Library*, vol. 16, *Apocryphal Gospels, Acts and Revelations* (Edinburgh: T & T Clark, 1870), 26–27.

57. Ibid., 57–58. Isaiah's prophecy occurs at 11:1–2 in the Vulgate and Septuagint translations. Protestant Bibles have a branch instead of the flower. Other apocryphal writings that seem likely to have provided Kazantzakis with individual details are the *Protevangelium of James* and *The History of Joseph the Carpenter*. The "Index of Principal Matters" at the end of Roberts and Donaldson's *Apocryphal Gospels* is most helpful.

58. Prevelakis, *Tetrakósia Grámmata*, 627.

CHAPTER 2

The Novel, the Four Gospels, and the Continuing Historical Quest

W. Barnes Tatum

I wanted to renew and supplement the sacred Myth that underlies the great Christian civilization of the West. It isn't a simple "Life of Christ." It's a laborious, sacred, creative endeavour to reincarnate the essence of Christ, setting aside the dross—falsehoods and pettinesses which all the churches and all the cassocked representatives of Christianity have heaped upon His figure, thereby distorting it.

—Nikos Kazantzakis, on *The Last Temptation*[1]

Introduction

The Last Temptation of Christ possesses its own integrity as a literary work. The novel gives expression to Kazantzakis's distinctive philosophy of life, which he eloquently articulates in the prologue and dramatically unfolds in the narrative. This philosophy owes much to the evolutionary thought of Henri Bergson, who views God as the élan vital, or life-force, that evolves matter forward and upward.[2] However, *The Last Temptation* is about Christ, the one named Jesus. Thus Kazantzakis's Jesus-story not only serves his own personal viewpoint but also draws upon the canonical Gospels of Matthew, Mark, Luke, and John.

By 1955, the year *The Last Temptation* first appeared in print, these four Gospels had been analyzed for more than a century and a half, not only as theological documents but also as literary sources for recovering what Jesus was like as a historical figure. Albert Schweitzer's 1906 volume, later published in English as *The Quest of the Historical Jesus*, stands as a magisterial reminder of this nineteenth-century quest.[3] Born of the Enlightenment, this "old quest" presupposed a distinction between the Christ of faith and the Jesus of history, between Jesus as portrayed in the Church's Gospels and Jesus as discovered through historical research.

19

Theologians and scholars proceeded with the confidence that they could and ought to discover what Jesus was really like within the setting of first-century Roman Palestine. The result was a succession of historical "lives" that arranged Jesus' life into distinct periods and explored his self-understanding and motivations. Many of these works were motivated by the desire to liberate Jesus as a human figure from the shackles of Christian credal orthodoxy, with its claim that Jesus was one person of the divine Trinity, with two natures, divine and human.

In this volume Peter Bien has demonstrated that Ernest Renan's *Vie de Jésus* (1863) greatly influenced Kazantzakis. Renan's biography of Jesus, perhaps the most widely read in the nineteenth century, reads like a novel.[4] Church authorities considered Renan's historical "life" as subversive, and so also Kazantzakis's novel years later.[5]

When Kazantzakis wrote *The Last Temptation* in the early 1950s, the "old quest" had been largely abandoned. Historians increasingly recognized difficulty in using the four Gospels to discover what Jesus was like, and theologians came to consider such a discovery irrelevant for theology. However, that decade also saw the emergence, initially in Germany, of a "new quest."[6] Although these scholars disavowed the possibility of writing a biography of Jesus, they believed it possible and necessary to establish some continuity between the Church's contemporary confession of Jesus as the Christ and Jesus as the human figure who lived and died in the first century.

In recent decades, the accessibility of other ancient (noncanonical) gospels, the broadened understanding of the social setting of early Judaism, and refined historical methodologies have resulted in a renewed interest in the historical Jesus, not only by scholars but also—through them—by a broader public, especially in the United States. This sometimes-called "third quest" continues today.[7]

Although characterized by great diversity, much of the current debate over the historical figure of Jesus revolves around two historical models for understanding what he was all about as a first-century Jew. Some scholars understand Jesus to have been an apocalyptic preacher who expected God, in some sense, to end the world in his own lifetime.[8] Other scholars consider Jesus to have been a wisdom teacher who spoke about God more indirectly through parables.[9] Representatives of both positions have articulated their views in ways that critique the Church's teaching about Jesus as the Christ.

Twenty-five years have passed since I first read *The Last Temptation*.[10] In this essay, I intend to show how Kazantzakis, in his restatement of "the sacred Myth," has imaginatively used the Church's four Gospels as well as perspectives from the continuing historical quest to subvert the Church's Jesus-story. In what follows, I discuss the novel in relation to the four Gospels, then in relation to the historical quest, and conclude with summary observations.

The Four Gospels

The four Gospels represent confessions of faith in narrative form. They know Jesus by many names. The expression "Christ" itself became the title that has remained attached to the personal name Jesus (already in Mark 1:1; Matt 1:1). In popular usage, the title Christ often replaces altogether the given name Jesus as a way of identifying him, as in the (USA) English title of the novel—*The Last Temptation of Christ.*[11]

Names. Kazantzakis also turned to names for Jesus when he began thinking about ways to develop his own Jesus-story. His notebook for his prospective novel included a fourfold scheme in these words: "Son of the Carpenter, Son of Man, Son of David, and Son of God."[12] These four names, among others, abound throughout the novel on Jesus' lips and others' lips, although seldom together and never in this order.[13] However, Peter Bien and Darren Middleton convincingly use these four names as heuristic markers in their explorations of Jesus' evolving messianic consciousness.[14] Certainly, nothing in the novel appears more subversive to the Church's Jesus-story than the psychological ambivalence and struggle that beset Kazantzakis's Jesus to the very end of his life. Kazantzakis derives these four names from the canonical Gospels themselves, and each name functions as an appropriate identifier for a stage in Jesus' life and messianic career.

"Son of the Carpenter" appears only once in the Gospels (Matt 13:55; cf. Mark 6:3). In the novel, the name identifies Jesus from the outset of his spiritual development, while he still lives with his parents in Nazareth at the level of day-to-day ordinariness. He has a job. He does his job. But more than this, Kazantzakis's identification of Jesus as a woodworker enables Kazantzakis to invent a harrowing view of what Jesus works in wood: crosses for the Romans.

"Son of Man" appears repeatedly and exclusively on Jesus' lips in the Synoptic Gospels (Matthew, Mark, Luke), as though this name were Jesus' chosen self-designation. The title represents the most complicated and variously interpreted of all the names ascribed to Jesus in the Gospels because of its varied origin within Jewish tradition and its different uses in the Gospels.[15] In the novel, Kazantzakis identifies the source of the name as the vision of the end times in the apocalyptic book of Daniel: "Behold, one like a son of man came with the clouds of heaven" (Dan 7:13 WBS).[16] The abbot of the monastery in the desert interprets this passage to be a messianic text. But later in the novel, Kazantzakis's application of this text to Jesus identifies him as the expected Messiah who has arrived, not some messianic figure yet to come upon clouds of heaven. Shortly after Jesus' sojourn in the monastery, he inaugurates the "Son of Man" phase of his messianic career by proclaiming a message of universal love for humankind on a mount in Galilee.

"Son of David" does not appear in the Gospels as a self-designation used by Jesus. However, it occupies a position of honor, particularly in the Gospel of Matthew, where the Gospel writer has a special interest in Jesus' descent from King David and thus his fulfillment of the Jewish expectation of a royal messiah (Matt 1:1–17).

In the novel, after Jesus' baptism by John and his testing in the wilderness, he inaugurates the "Son of David" phase of his messianic career outside the synagogue in Nazareth. He complements his message of love with a call for justice—symbolized by the ax of John and the sword of David.

Of the four names selected by Kazantzakis to identify phases of Jesus' life and messianic career, "Son of God" represents the title most prominent in the Gospel of John and in the subsequent christological debates of the emerging Church. But the name already appears in the Synoptic Gospels. Both Matthew and Mark associate the ascription, and thus Jesus' divine sonship, specifically with his obedient death on the cross (Matt 27:54; Mark 15:39). In the novel, Kazantzakis also presents Jesus' obedient death on the cross as the realization of his divine sonship. Although not without premonition, Jesus finally confronts the possibility that his messianic calling requires him to die when he discovers the decaying body of the scapegoat in the wilderness. He eventually embraces his messianic destiny when he has a vision of the prophet Isaiah holding up a goatskin containing words from the Suffering Servant passage in Isa 53: "Despised and rejected by all, he went forward without resisting, like a lamb that is led to the slaughter."[17]

In spite of the frequent dismissive responses to Kazantzakis's overall characterization of Jesus, his presentation of Jesus' death as a self-conscious fulfillment of Isa 53 corresponds to a view common not only in the Church's theology but also in some quarters of historical Jesus scholarship.[18] Nonetheless, Kazantzakis immediately subverts this traditional interpretation of Jesus' death by ending the novel with Jesus on the cross and without vindication by his subsequent resurrection from the dead.

Kazantzakis undergirds his account of Jesus' spiritual journey by creating for him two geographical journeys, which take him from Galilee to Judea and Jerusalem (chaps. 15, 24), each of which occurs respectively during the "Son of Man" and the "Son of David" phases of his public ministry. Thus Kazantzakis follows neither the Synoptic outline of one journey from Galilee to Judea nor the Fourth Gospel's presentation of multiple journeys.

Scope. The four Gospels have been described collectively as "passion narratives with extended introductions."[19] The passion of Jesus traditionally refers to the sufferings endured by Jesus during his last hours. More inclusively, the passion narratives represent the accounts of Jesus' final week in Jerusalem from his entry to his crucifixion (Mark 11–15; Matt 21–27; Luke 19–23; John 12–19).

Accordingly, the Gospel of Mark introduces Jesus' passion by reporting Jesus' sayings and stories from the time of his association with John the Baptizer in the wilderness (Mark 1–10). Matthew and Luke also connect Jesus' public activity with the ministry of John (Matt 3–20; Luke 3–19), but begin their accounts with events related to Jesus' birth (Matt 1–2; Luke 1–2). The Gospel of John similarly connects the beginning of Jesus' public activity with John the Baptizer, but opens with words that recall the opening phrase of Genesis, "In the beginning" (John 1:1).

By contrast, Kazantzakis has framed his Jesus-story between a dream Jesus experiences as a "young man" who makes crosses for the Romans (chap. 1) and a fantasy Jesus experiences on a Roman cross that he himself has borne (chaps. 30–33). The novel narrates how Jesus the cross-maker becomes a cross-taker, how Jesus actualizes his call to become the Son of God. Details about Jesus' conception and birth, and events from his earliest years, are subordinated to the broader narrative by being reported through remembrances and dreams.[20]

Sayings (Words). The four Gospels contain two sharply conflicting characterizations of Jesus and his message. According to the Synoptic Gospels, Jesus speaks about the "kingdom of God" (although Matthew prefers the "kingdom of heaven") most distinctively through parables. According to the Gospel of John, Jesus speaks about himself through a series of "I am" sayings that are reminiscent of the way God talks in Jewish Scripture. These "I am" sayings appear within the context of longer discourses that interpret actions performed by Jesus—such as his climactic raising of Lazarus from the dead.

In the novel, Jesus' speech contains and juxtaposes statements that reflect the varied intellectual and literary traditions that have shaped Kazantzakis's own view of life. These statements include sayings from the four Gospels with the characteristic turns of phrase "kingdom of heaven" and "I am." Also, more than fifty individual sayings by Jesus from the canonical Gospels can be identified, including six parables.[21] The Gospel of Matthew represents the greatest contributor of individual sayings, many from the Sermon on the Mount (Matt 5–7). In addition to incorporating Jesus' sayings from the Gospels into larger discourses of diverse background, Kazantzakis uses the words subversively in several ways.

First, the phrase "kingdom of heaven" frequently suggests a realized rather than a futuristic eschatology, often with echoes of Luke 17:21 that the kingdom is "within you" (KJV) or "in the midst of you" (RSV). To Judas, Jesus says, "The kingdom of heaven is not in the air, but it is within us, in our hearts."[22] Later, he says to Peter, "The kingdom of heaven is within us."[23] Still later, when Jesus approaches, a shout goes forth: "The kingdom of heaven is here."[24] The kingdom of heaven, not earth, manifests itself where and when there is a reconciliation of opposites, whether Israelites and Romans, Judeans and Samaritans, rich and poor, Matthew and Peter.[25] The apocalyptic-sounding phrase "end of the world" appears throughout the novel.[26] But it becomes clear that these words do not signify an approaching cosmic upheaval any more than the expression "kingdom of heaven." As the last line of the novel suggests, the end of the world comes with Jesus' death, which paradoxically becomes the beginning.

Second, the emphasis on the realized kingdom receives reinforcement through the use of the "I am" formula. Kazantzakis places only one of the seven metaphorical "I am" sayings from John onto Jesus' lips: "I am the road" (cf. John 14:6).[27] The novel significantly omits Jesus' dramatic declaration that precedes his raising of Lazarus from the dead: "I am the resurrection and the life" (John 11:25). Nonetheless, the "I am" formula does appear in several other statements, including two consistent with

Jesus' self-sacrifice: "I am the goat" and "I am the lamb" (the latter based on John 1:29, 36).[28] However, in the novel Jesus explains his daring use of the first-person pronoun in ways that go beyond any explicit statement in the Gospels: "When I say 'I,' . . . I do not speak of this body—which is dust; I do not speak of the son of Mary—he too is dust, with just a tiny, tiny spark of fire. 'I' from my mouth means God." This daring claim of his being not just the Son of God, but God himself, prompts Jesus to affirm laughingly: "I am Saint Blasphemer, and don't forget it."[29]

Third, two parables included in the novel provide Kazantzakis himself with an opportunity to comment on the kingdom by changing their endings: the parable of the rich man and Lazarus (Luke 16:19–31) and the parable of the ten virgins (Matt 25:1–13).[30] The former parable, as in the Gospel of Luke, contains futuristic eschatological subject matter. The latter parable, in the Gospel of Matthew, appears within a literary setting that gives it futuristic eschatological meaning as well. In the novel, Jesus originally concludes both parables with Gospel-based endings: the rich man is consigned to eternal torment; the five foolish virgins are excluded from the wedding. But in response to protests by his hearers, Jesus provides different conclusions. The rich man is taken up to paradise. The five foolish virgins have the doors opened to them. In the same letter that provided this essay with its epigraph, Kazantzakis explained his modifications this way: "Parables which Christ could not possibly have left as the Gospels relate them I have supplemented, and I have given them the noble and compassionate ending befitting Christ's heart."[31]

Fourth, no doubt "compassion" was included in what Kazantzakis considered to be "the essence of Christ." Jesus as "Son of Man" opens the love phase of his public ministry with the parable of the sower (Matt 13:3–9).[32] He interprets the parable allegorically by identifying himself as the sower, the stone and thorns and field as his hearers, and the seed as the command to "love one another" (John 13:34) He places on Jesus' lips the words, "God is love" (1 John 4:8, 16).[33] Later, disciples remind Jesus that he commanded them, "You must love your enemy" (cf. Matt 5:44).[34] Although the "Son of David" phase with the accent on justice succeeds the "Son of Man" phase in Jesus' messianic career, this does not require Jesus' turning away from love but rather his incorporating justice into love as one of its expressions. After baptizing Jesus, John asks Jesus, "Was it all for nothing then that I carried the ax and placed it at the root of the tree? Or can love also wield an ax?" Jesus later recalls John's words and says, "Who knows, perhaps love carries an ax."[35] Subsequently, after the inauguration of this stage of Jesus' public ministry, "love" continues alongside "justice" in Jesus' discourse as Jesus reaffirms his theme that the kingdom of heaven involves inclusiveness and a radical egalitarianism.[36]

Stories (Deeds). The four Gospels diverge in specific stories they tell about Jesus during his public ministry. Although the Synoptics and John include the account about Jesus' action in the temple, the Synoptics locate the episode during his final days, whereas John places the episode at the outset of his activity. In John, the raising of Lazarus serves as the climactic event that precipitates his arrest and eventual execution.

In the novel, there are stories about Jesus that have no basis in the Gospels. But Kazantzakis does incorporate stories from the four Gospels in several ways.

Sometimes he uses stories to support themes that run through his overall narrative, such as the brief vignette involving Simeon that underscores the imminence of the Messiah's coming and Jesus' fulfillment of that expectation (Luke).[37] In other instances, stories are more expansively narrated, often in ways and with details that challenge traditional understandings of the reported events. Among these are the stories of Jesus' baptism and his threefold testing in the wilderness (Synoptics).[38]

Then there are those stories about women of dubious reputation and behavior, unnamed in the Gospels themselves, but identified in the novel as Mary Magdalene: the woman taken in adultery who is forgiven by Jesus (John), the sinful woman who washes his feet and wipes them with her hair (Luke), and the woman who anoints him for burial (John).[39] The identification of these women as Mary Magdalene reinforces rather than subverts Church tradition. Nevertheless, Kazantzakis's use of these stories in conjunction with more imaginative aspects of Mary Magdalene elsewhere in the novel challenges more traditional views on Jesus' sexuality or asexuality.

Kazantzakis's subversive use of stories about Jesus can be clearly seen in his treatment of Jesus' miracle-working and specific miracle stories. Seemingly, Kazantzakis allows for the possibility of healings and exorcisms but explains away nature miracles and raisings of the dead. Like the Synoptic writers, he includes periodic summary statements about Jesus' reputation as a healer of various physical ailments such as leprosy, epilepsy, lameness, and blindness.

Kazantzakis has the man from whom demons are cast report how they entered pigs, sending them hurling to their deaths into the sea (Synoptics).[40] He also creates a composite story about the healing of a Roman centurion's daughter, based on miracle stories from the four Gospels: the centurion's slave (Matt and Luke); the official's son (John), and Jairus's daughter (Synoptics, especially Mark). Jesus revived the young paralyzed woman with a touch of his hand, a look into her eyes, and a simple word: "Rise, my daughter!"[41]

This healing occurs at Cana; but earlier when Kazantzakis narrates Jesus' attendance at a wedding feast in Cana, he omits any reference to Jesus' turning water into wine.[42] Literarily, the wine miracle has been erased by the healing miracle. Elsewhere in the novel, the story of Jesus' walking on the water (Synoptics and John) has been reduced to Jesus' ironic wish that he could walk from one side of the lake to the other in order to avoid Capernaum.[43] Later, the novel explains this story as having originated in a dream by Peter. Likewise, the story of the transfiguration (Synoptics) originated as a recurring dream of Simeon.[44]

However, the most telling treatment of a miracle story from the four Gospels involves the resuscitation of Lazarus, which serves as important a function in the novel as it does in the Gospel of John.[45] In the Gospel, Jesus interprets the meaning of his dramatic act with the equally dramatic words, "I am the resurrection and the life" (John 11:25). Thus Jesus brings eternal life to anyone who believes in him. In the novel, Jesus' raising of Lazarus from the dead is reported to a crowd in Jerusalem by a character named Melchizedek. The narrator explains Jesus' response to this occurrence: "This was the sign [Jesus] had been waiting for. The hopelessly rotted world was a Lazarus. The time had come for [Jesus] to cry out, 'World arise.'"[46] However, after being brought back to life—sort of—Lazarus is eventually murdered by Barabbas.[47] The point is clear: No one gets out of here alive.

Kazantzakis's presentation of the Lazarus story anticipates his ending his Jesus-story with crucifixion, not resurrection. In comparison with traditional Church teaching, Carnegie Samuel Calian accurately states, "In his search for God, Kazantzakis became a prophet of non-hope."[48]

Passion. The four Gospels agree most closely in their respective accounts of Jesus' final week in Jerusalem. There are only slight, although not necessarily unimportant, differences of detail among the four Gospels. The Gospels share a common core of eight events: Jesus' entry into Jerusalem on a donkey at Passover time, a conspiracy by the Jewish authorities, his betrayal by Judas, his Last Supper with his disciples, his arrest by the Jewish authorities, his nighttime appearance before the Jewish authorities, his morning appearance before the Roman governor, and his crucifixion on a Roman cross.

Kazantzakis's account of Jesus' final days in Jerusalem narrates the same seven events.[49] He harmonizes the four Gospel narratives. However, he sometimes borrows details from one Gospel and sometimes another, often with imaginative touches of his own. Throughout, he selectively incorporates into the dialogue words recalling specific sayings of Jesus from the Gospels. There are strikingly subversive moments even in Kazantzakis's retelling of these core events.

First, the betrayal by Judas takes on quite different meaning in the novel, given the role played by Judas. Judas has his own personal journey, from the role of Zealot antagonist with opposing views of the kingdom to that of a confidant who ensures Jesus' faithfulness to his calling. Jesus says to Judas: "God will give you the strength, as much as you lack, because it is necessary—it is necessary for me to be killed and for you to betray me. We two must save the world. Help me."[50]

Second, in the novel, the accounts of the Last Supper and the Jewish proceedings against Jesus contain features that shift emphasis away from a futuristic eschatology and toward a realized eschatology.[51]

As in the Synoptics, the Last Supper is a Passover meal, on which occasion Jesus anticipates his own death by pronouncing words over the bread and the wine. Kazantzakis underscores Jesus' approaching death by having him explicitly identify himself as the Passover lamb to be slaughtered in fulfillment of Isa 53. Correspondingly, Kazantzakis omits Jesus' vow that he will not drink wine again until he drinks in the coming kingdom (Synoptics). As in John, Jesus washes the disciples' feet and talks about the imminent coming of "the Comforter, or Spirit of truth." The promise of the Comforter, a name in John for the Holy Spirit, appears quite appropriate in the setting of the Last Supper in the novel. Like John, the novel does not hold forth the expectation of Jesus' coming on the clouds of heaven as the exalted "Son of Man" (cf. Dan 7:13).

Similarly, in the account of the Jewish proceedings against Jesus, Kazantzakis has Jesus openly acknowledge his identity before Caiaphas by declaring, "I am the Christ, the Son of God" (based on Mark 14:61–62). Kazantzakis omits the remainder of Jesus' confession wherein Jesus suddenly talks apocalyptically about coming on the clouds of heaven as the exalted "Son of Man" (cf. Dan 7:13).[52]

Third, on the cross, Jesus declares only two of the so-called seven last words spoken by him in the four Gospels. These sayings frame his illusionary "last temptation": "Eli, Eli, . . ." (Matt 27:46; cf. Mark 15:34) and "It is accomplished" (cf. John 19:30).[53] Then come the closing words of the novel: "And it was as though he had said: Everything has begun."[54] Carnegie Samuel Calian described Kazantzakis as a prophet of no hope. However, from Kazantzakis's distinctive view of Jesus and life, these closing words are full of hope, since the basic temptation that confronts all humans had been resisted, and Jesus thus provides a model to be followed.

The Historical Quest

In *The Last Temptation*, Kazantzakis uses not only the Church's four Gospels but also perspectives from the historical quest to subvert the Church's Jesus-story. Toward the conclusion of the novel, Jesus himself assumes and articulates these perspectives in his interactions with Matthew and with Paul. Jesus thereby calls into question the accuracy of the apostolic text and the truthfulness of the apostolic message.

Apostolic Text. Kazantzakis introduces Matthew into his story in Nazareth, as Jesus leaves town after inaugurating the "Son of David" phase of his ministry by preaching outside the local synagogue. As in the Gospels, so here, Matthew is a tax collector, specifically a customs official, whom Jesus summons to follow him. Thereafter, Matthew appears in the story on at least nineteen occasions, the last three during Jesus' fantasy on the cross.[55]

Kazantzakis imaginatively portrays Matthew as a scrupulous observer and chronicler of everything Jesus says and does. Matthew interrogates others to learn details about happenings that occurred prior to his becoming a follower, such as John's baptism of Jesus and John's execution. Indeed, Matthew begins writing his Gospel during Jesus' lifetime, with quill and ink, in a blank ledger carried as a notebook. In describing the process of Matthew's writing, Kazantzakis also borrows from the iconographic tradition, which depicts an angel dictating into Matthew's ear what to write. Although Kazantzakis presents Matthew as a contemporary and eyewitness of happenings in the life of Jesus, he also shows how the involvement of this angelic figure in the writing process makes the emerging Gospel text less than historically accurate.

On one occasion, Kazantzakis describes how Matthew's zealousness for fulfilling his role as chronicler results not only in his reporting but also in his creating an event for the written record.[56] Peter dreams about Jesus' walking on the water and his own failed attempt, which results in a near-drowning experience. But Peter's dream becomes transformed into an event that happened. Upon awakening, Peter's conversation with the vigilant Matthew leads to Peter's suggestion, "Perhaps it wasn't a dream. . . . What do you think, Matthew?" Matthew replies: "It most certainly wasn't a dream. This miracle definitely took place."[57] So the dream finds its way into the written Gospel as a miracle story, now recorded in Matt 14:22–33.

On another occasion, Kazantzakis points out how Matthew's knowledge of the Scriptures leads him to match up "the prophecies and Jesus' life."[58] This results in what John Dominic Crossan has called "prophecy historicized" in contradistinction to "history remembered."[59] That is, the Gospel writers, and prior transmitters of the Gospel tradition, have created details in the Gospel stories about Jesus in order to bring those stories into line with specific scriptural texts. When Matthew begins writing about the events related to Jesus' birth, he suddenly finds himself tussling with the angel over what to write. When Matthew starts to write that Jesus was "the son of Joseph," the angel insists that Matthew call Mary "a virgin" in accordance with the text in Isa 7:14. When Matthew begins to write that Nazareth was the place of Jesus' birth, the angel again wins out and forces him to identify Bethlehem as the site in accordance with the text in Mic 5:2. Matthew angrily protests, "It's not true. I don't want to write, and I won't." Nonetheless, he continues, and these details find their way into his written account (Matt 1:18–2:6).[60]

On a later occasion, Matthew proudly presents his notebook to Jesus to read. After skimming the contents, Jesus throws the emerging Gospel to the ground and shouts, "Lies! Lies! Lies! The Messiah doesn't need miracles. He is the miracle—no other is necessary."[61] After denying the accuracy of particular details on record and listening to Matthew's defense that an angel made him do it, Jesus relents and tells him to write what the angel dictates.

Still later, even after the preceding conversation, Jesus again complains to Matthew: "I say one thing, you write another, and those who read you understand still something else! I say: cross, death, kingdom of heaven, God, . . . and what do you understand? Each of you attaches his own suffering, interests and desires to each of these sacred words, and my words disappear. . . . I can't stand it any longer!"[62]

Thus, in the novel, Jesus himself questions the accuracy of the apostolic text and recognizes the tendency of persons to use his words to support their own interests. The problem of the historical Jesus begins during Jesus' own lifetime.

Apostolic Message. The canonical Gospels nowhere mention Paul as having any contact with Jesus during his lifetime. However, Kazantzakis introduces Paul into his story in Jerusalem, shortly after Jesus' entry into the city on the donkey and his subsequent disruption in the temple. Paul—still Saul—suddenly steps forth from the crowd and throws a lemon rind that strikes Peter in the face. Jesus and his followers simply continue their return to Bethany. This brief appearance represents Paul's only appearance in the narrative of Jesus' public activity. The two other appearances, more substantive, occur during Jesus' imaginings on the cross.[63]

Paul—still Saul—first appears during Jesus' marriage to Mary Magdalene. While Jesus sleeps, Paul confronts Jesus' wife: "Mary Magdalene, whore! I am Saul."[64] Now

Saul throws not a lemon rind but the first stone, and those with him continue stoning her unto death. During Mary's final moments, she says to Saul: "I was just thinking, Saul—and sighing—just thinking what miracles you would perform if God suddenly flashed within you and you saw the truth! To conquer the world, my beloved needs disciples like you."[65]

Saul—now Paul—next appears after Jesus has become the head of Lazarus's household and taken Mary and Martha as wives. Paul announces to Jesus, whom he takes to be Lazarus, that he has been transformed on the road to Damascus and become a preacher of "Good News" throughout the world:

> Jesus of Nazareth . . . was not the son of Joseph and Mary; he was the Son of God. He came down to earth and took on human flesh in order to save mankind. The wicked priests and Pharisees seized him, brought him to Pilate and crucified him. But on the third day he rose from the dead and ascended to heaven. Death was conquered, . . . sins were forgiven, the Gates of Heaven opened up![66]

In the heated exchange that follows between Jesus and Paul, Jesus makes it clear that he rejects most of Paul's claims about him. He repeatedly exclaims: "Liar! . . . Liar! . . . Liar! Liar! . . . Liar! Liar!"[67] Paul likewise makes it clear that he has gone his own way. Paul declares, "I create the truth." Later, he continues: "I shall become your apostle whether you like it or not. I shall construct you and your life and your teachings and your crucifixion and resurrection just as I wish. Joseph the Carpenter of Nazareth did not beget you; I begot you—I, Paul, the scribe from Tarsus in Cilicia." Paul concludes: "It's been delightful meeting you. I've freed myself, and that's just what I wanted: to get rid of you. Well, I did get rid of you and now I'm free; I'm my own boss. Farewell."[68]

This conversation between Paul and Jesus reflects the dialectic that runs throughout the historical quest for Jesus: the dialectic between the Christ of faith and the Jesus of history. But throughout its history this quest was concerned not to liberate Paul from Jesus but to free Jesus as a historical figure from the Church's claims about Jesus as the Christ.

Conclusion

Fifty years ago, Nikos Kazantzakis's restatement of "the sacred Myth" underlying Western civilization appeared in print under the title *The Last Temptation*. In this retelling of the Jesus-story, Kazantzakis necessarily used the four Gospels. His use of the canonical Gospels was by no means an innocent borrowing. He imaginatively used the Church's Gospels as well as perspectives from the historical quest to subvert the Church's Jesus-story.

Retrospectively, *The Last Temptation* itself reflects many characteristics of "old quest" biographies. Kazantzakis assumes a distinction between the Christ of faith and the historical Jesus. He chronologizes by laying out the events of Jesus' life and career in a sequential order. He also psychologizes by entering the mind of Jesus as the latter struggles to discover his messianic identity and his messianic mission.

Fifty years after the publication of *The Last Temptation*, Jesus as a historical figure has once again become the center of much attention, among theologians, scholars, and even the general public. In comparison with the two alternative models for understanding Jesus historically, Kazantzakis's Jesus appears to have less in common with Jesus the apocalyptic preacher than with Jesus the wisdom teacher.

However, in spite of his familiarity with the historical quest, Kazantzakis thus concluded the letter that provided this essay with its epigraph: "And so all the details are historically correct, even though I recognize the right of the poet not to follow history in a slavish way. . . . 'Poetry is more philosophical than history.'"[69] Therefore, Kazantzakis's lifelong personal quest was not a search for the historical Jesus nor a search for the Christ of faith. Instead, in his own terms, he sought the essential Christ.

Notes

1. These words, and others cited later in this essay, appear in a letter, dated November 13, 1951, addressed by Nikos Kazantzakis to his friend Börje Knös shortly after he had completed the manuscript of *The Last Temptation*. See Helen Kazantzakis, *Nikos Kazantzakis: A Biography Based on His Letters*, trans. Amy Mims (New York: Simon & Schuster, 1968), 505–6.

2. Nikos Kazantzakis's philosophy, with its indebtedness to Henri Bergson, has much in common with process philosophy and process theology and their emphases on the becoming, not the being, of God. For additional information, see Daniel A. Dombrowski, *Kazantzakis and God* (Albany, NY: SUNY Press, 1997); Darren J. N. Middleton, "Vagabond or Companion? Kazantzakis and Whitehead on God," in *God's Struggler: Religion in the Writings of Nikos Kazantzakis*, ed. Darren J. N. Middleton and Peter Bien (Macon, GA: Mercer University Press, 1996), 189–211.

3. Albert Schweitzer, *The Quest of the Historical Jesus: A Critical Study of Its Progress from Reimarus to Wrede*, foreword by Delbert R. Hillers, preface by F. C. Burkitt (Baltimore: Johns Hopkins University Press, 1998). Kazantzakis and Schweitzer became friends in their later years. Kazantzakis even dedicated his novel *Saint Francis* to the missionary doctor as "the Saint Francis of our era." Schweitzer visited Kazantzakis on his deathbed, in Freiburg, in the fall of 1957. But there is no confirmation that Kazantzakis had read Schweitzer's work on Jesus.

4. Ernest Renan, *The Life of Jesus*, trans. Charles Edwin Wilbour (New York: Carleton, 1864). The French original is *Vie de Jésus*, 2nd ed. (Paris: Michel Lévy fréres, 1863).

5. For additional information on the controversies surrounding Kazantzakis's novel, see Michael Antonakes's essay in *God's Struggler*, ed. Middleton and Bien, 23–35.

6. The most widely read "new quest" work on Jesus remains Günther Bornkamm's *Jesus of Nazareth*, trans. Irene McLuskey and Fraser McLuskey, with James M. Robinson (New York: Harper & Brothers, 1960).

7. The discussion herein of the four Gospels and the historical quest presupposes the survey of these matters in my *In Quest of Jesus: Revised and Enlarged* (Nashville: Abingdon, 1999).

8. These include E. P. Sanders, *The Historical Figure of Jesus* (London: Allan Lane, Penguin, 1993); Dale C. Allison, *Jesus of Nazareth: Millenarian Prophet* (Minneapolis: Fortress, 1998); Bart D. Ehrman, *Jesus: The Apocalyptic Prophet of the New Millennium* (London: Oxford University Press, 1999); Paula Fredriksen, *Jesus of Nazareth, King of the Jews* (New York: Random House, 1999).

9. This understanding represents the collective view and emerges out of the cooperative scholarship of the Jesus Seminar. The Jesus Seminar was founded in 1985 with Robert W. Funk and John Dominic Crossan as cochairs. Because of my long-standing interest in Gospel scholarship and Jesus research, I became a Fellow of the Jesus Seminar in 1988. The Seminar has produced two volumes presenting the results of its deliberations in response to two basic historical questions: (1) What did Jesus really say? See Robert W. Funk, Roy W. Hoover, and the Jesus Seminar, *The Five Gospels: The Search for the Authentic Words of Jesus* (New York: Macmillan, 1993). (2) And what did Jesus really do? See Robert W. Funk and the Jesus Seminar, *The Acts of Jesus: The Search for the Authentic Deeds of Jesus* (New York: HarperCollins, 1998). A recent publication contains fourteen essays by individual Fellows of the Seminar and is appropriately titled *Profiles of Jesus*, ed. Roy W. Hoover (Santa Rosa, CA: Polebridge, 2002). Over the years, many Fellows have also published monographs historically reconstructing Jesus' life or some aspect thereof.

10. I first read *The Last Temptation of Christ* in the late 1970s in response to an invitation by a colleague, Edward O. Coleman of the English faculty, to review a book of my choosing for a literary forum sponsored by the James Addison Jones Library at Greensboro College. My first published words about Kazantzakis's literary portrayal appeared shortly thereafter in the 1982 edition of my *In Quest of Jesus*. In the introduction, I briefly discuss Kazantzakis's literary treatment under the rubric "Jesus the Monk." More recently, I have included an analysis of Martin Scorsese's film adaptation of the novel in my survey of Jesus-films, *Jesus at the Movies: A Guide to the First Hundred Years,* rev. and exp. ed. (Santa Rosa, CA: Polebridge, 2004). Therein I use the rubric "Jesus the Reluctant Messiah."

11. The Greek title in 1955 was *O teleftaíos peirasmós* (Athens: Difros), to be translated into English as *The Last Temptation* (with the added phrase *of Christ*). For this essay, where needed, the original Greek edition of the novel has been consulted.

12. Peter A. Bien, *Tempted by Happiness: Kazantzakis' Post-Christian Christ* (Wallingford, PA: Pendle Hill, 1984), 4–5.

13. Nikos Kazantzakis, *The Last Temptation of Christ,* trans. Peter Bien (New York: Simon & Schuster, 1960), 147, 356. These are the only two passages where I have identified the four names together, but not in the notebook order.

14. Darren J. N. Middleton, *Novel Theology: Nikos Kazantzakis's Encounter with Whiteheadian Process Theism* (Macon, GA: Mercer University Press, 2000), 53–106.

15. Tatum, *In Quest*, 162–68.

16. Nikos Kazantzakis, *Last Temptation*, 101.

17. Ibid., 387; also 425–26.

18. This view was common among British scholars of an earlier generation: Archibald M. Hunter, *The Work and Words of Jesus* (Philadelphia: Westminster, 1950); Vincent Taylor, *The Life and Ministry of Jesus* (Nashville: Abingdon, 1955); and C. H. Dodd, *The Founder of Christianity* (New York: Macmillan, 1970).

19. Martin Kähler, *The So-Called Historical Jesus and the Historic, Biblical Christ*, trans. Carl E. Braaten (Philadelphia: Fortress, 1964), 80n11.

20. Nikos Kazantzakis, *Last Temptation*, 13, 22, 25–26, 31–33, 38, 42, 60, 70, 93–94, 134, 145, 169, et al.

21. Whereas most scholars today assume the priority of the Gospel of Mark, Kazantzakis continued to accept the traditional view, well established after Augustine in the fifth century, that Matthew was the earliest Gospel. Where there is a saying of Jesus preserved in the Gospel of Matthew, I adopt the convention of giving the chapter and verse from Matthew, although it may have a parallel in Mark and/or Luke. The page numbers in parentheses indicate the location of the Jesus-saying in the novel: Matt 3:15 (239); 4:19 (209); 5:3 (186–87); 5:4 (186); 5:5 (186–87); 5:6 (186); 5:10–11 (186–87); 5:17 (356, 346); 5:21f. (345f.); 5:27 (346); 5:37 (157, 177–78); 5:44 (188, 201); 6:10 (139, 193); 6:26f. (196); 6:28f. (196); 6:31f. (196); 7:13–14 (331–32); 7:26–27 (411); 8:30 (192); 9:13 (315); 9:15 (196); 9:17 (380); 10:14 (313); 10:16 (361); 10:29 (348); 10:37 (346); 12:22–24 (140, 312); 12:48–50 (181, 188–89, 309, 312); 13:3–9 (parable of the sower, 183); 13:45 (parable of the pearl of great price, 272); 15:4f. (346); 16:16–19 (378); 16:21 (420); 18:22 (201); 20:20–21 (336, 406, 408); 22:15–22 (315, 384–85); 23:24 (385); 24:2 (366); 25:1–13 (parable of the ten virgins, 216–17); 26:11 (416); 26:26, 28 (424); 26:39a (431f.); 26:39b (432); 27:46 (443, 495). Luke 4:18–19 (307); 12:13–21 (parable of the rich fool, 338); 14:16–24 (parable of the great banquet, 314); 16:19–31 (parable of the rich man and Lazarus, 200–201); 17:21 (196, 299, 328); 22:35–36 (425). John 2:4 (192 et al.); 1:29, 35 (402, 426); 2:19 (326); 3:16 (226); 4:13–14 (221); 4:23–24 (222); 8:7 (176); 8:11 (213–14); 11:43 (369); 13:34 (186–87); 14:6 (414); 14:16–17 (427); 18:36 (382); 19:5 (437); 19:30 (496).

22. Nikos Kazantzakis, *Last Temptation*, 196.

23. Ibid., 299.

24. Ibid., 328.

25. Ibid., 367.

26. Ibid., 109, 165, 334, 345, 368, 396, et al.

27. Ibid., 414.

28. Ibid., 255, 402, 426.

29. Ibid., 365–66.

30. Ibid., 200–201, 216–17.

31. Helen Kazantzakis, *Biography*, 505.

32. Nikos Kazantzakis, *Last Temptation*, 183–86.

33. Ibid., 186.

34. Ibid., 201.

35. Ibid., 252–54.

36. Ibid., 308, 315, 325, 352, 367, 368.

37. Ibid., 55–56 et al.

38. Ibid., 237–40, 247–64.

39. Ibid., 171–78, 214, 416–17.

40. Ibid., 213.

41. Ibid., 319–424, 334.

42. Ibid., 195–96.

43. Ibid., 128.

44. Ibid., 357, 360, 417.

45. Ibid., 368–72.

46. Ibid., 372.

47. Ibid., 413–14.

48. Carnegie Samuel Calian, *Theology without Boundaries* (Louisville: Westminster/John Knox, 1992), 89.

49. Nikos Kazantzakis, *Last Temptation*, 406–43.

50. Ibid., 421.

51. Ibid., 420–28.

52. Ibid., 435.

53. Ibid., 443, 495–96.

54. Ibid., 496.

55. Ibid., 315–16, 326–28, 341–43, 348–50, 352, 359, 377–78, 389–92, 405, 410, 415, 419, 425, 439–40, 487, 493–94.

56. Ibid., 341–43.

57. Ibid., 343.

58. Ibid., 348.

59. John Dominic Crossan, *Who Killed Jesus? Exposing the Roots of Anti-Semitism in the Gospel Story of the Death of Jesus* (San Francisco: HarperSanFrancisco, 1995), 1–13.

60. Nikos Kazantzakis, *Last Temptation*, 349.

61. Ibid., 391.

62. Ibid., 415.

63. Ibid., 410, 451–55, 473–80.

64. Ibid., 452.

65. Ibid., 453.

66. Ibid., 475.

67. Ibid., 475–76.

68. Ibid., 477–78.

69. Helen Kazantzakis, *Biography*, 505–6. I am indebted to friends and colleagues Walter H. Beale and Rhonda Burnette-Bletsch for reading an early version of this essay and offering helpful suggestions.

CHAPTER 3

Pontius Pilate
Modern Man in Search of a Soul

Lewis Owens

> Great poetry draws its strength from the life of mankind, and we completely miss its meaning if we try to derive it from personal factors. Whenever the collective unconscious becomes a living experience and is brought to bear upon the conscious outlook of an age, the event is a creative act which is of importance to everyone living in that age. A work of art is produced that contains what may truthfully be called a message to generations of men.
>
> —C. G. Jung, *Modern Man in Search of a Soul*

Introduction

Since its publication in Greece in 1955, *The Last Temptation* has continually been placed under a hermeneutical spotlight. Is the book blasphemous? Is it heretical? Is it a refreshingly honest and sympathetic portrayal of the humanity of Jesus? In this chapter I do not wish to use speculation as a main hermeneutical tool; rather, I draw on Nikos Kazantzakis's own marginalia and annotations in order to reveal unknown sources and subsequent influences that may be uncovered beneath the rich text of the narrative itself. This necessary textual analysis of Kazantzakis's marginalia and notes provides an invaluable and hitherto unexplored insight into the literature and philosophy that shaped Kazantzakis's thought while he composed the novel.

During the time Kazantzakis was drafting the novel in the late 1940s and early 1950s, he was deeply troubled by the current world situation. In particular, he was deeply concerned by the Korean War, the Cold War, and above all the potentially catastrophic developments surrounding the A-bomb. The world was in a profoundly dangerous predicament, politically and spiritually. *The Last Temptation* was essentially written in order to try to lift humanity out of its contemporary dark night and into a new spiritual future by using the most powerful myth of Western civilization to express contemporary concerns. When drafting the novel, Kazantzakis was reading and making notes on Carl Gustav Jung, who in the early 1930s was also deeply troubled by the world situation, particularly the rise of scientific rationalism, technology, and "Americanization." Kazantzakis's notes on Jung center primarily upon the notion of the archetypes, the importance of dreams and the unconscious, and the possibility and subsequent means of leading humanity to a higher level of conscious awareness of the contemporary situation. In short, for Kazantzakis, as for Jung, humanity needed to rediscover its soul. In *The Last Temptation*, therefore, Jesus symbolizes the personification of a creative, spiritual force that has the power to lead humanity out of its current perilous existential existence. Yet the character of Pontius Pilate signifies everything that is essentially nihilistic and materialistic, and hence hinders the creative urge of what Kazantzakis called "God." In short, Pilate is a symbol of the decaying contemporary epoch.

Kazantzakis and Jung

Many commentators have obviously focused on Jesus as the most fruitful character from which to distill the essence of Kazantzakis's religious philosophy and assess his supposed heterodox views on Christianity. They also evaluate the Bergsonian dynamism or the Nietzschean will-to-power that clearly pervades this main character as he overcomes all obstacles en route to his crucifixion and filial relationship with God. Likewise, they have repeatedly examined the character of Judas in an attempt to explain and justify the obvious close relationship that existed between Jesus and his traditionally so-called "betrayer."[1] The most interesting trend uses the work of Jung to unpack the layers and reveal the bare bones of the relationship.[2] John S. Bak, for example, is convinced that "Kazantzakis's theory of the unconscious incorporates the work of Carl Gustav Jung just as much as it does the work of Freud."[3] For Bak, Kazantzakis's Christ in *The Last Temptation* seeks "wholeness" or psychic totality by assimilating opposite forces, such as light and darkness, male and female, into a coincidence of opposites; only then can he assume the role of God. This psychological interpretation of the Christ figure is justified. We know that the working title of the novel was *Jesus Has Been Cured*, implying a strong psychological element to the character of Christ. Following Peter Bien, Darren J. N. Middleton observes: "Throughout *The Last Temptation of Christ*, Jesus adventures toward an integration of his own soul, harmonizing psychic contrasts, but this can only be reached as Jesus wrestles with his darker side (Judas), transmuting evil into the service of good. What this aspect of Jesus' characterization indicates is that Kazantzakis believes a healthy, balanced life is found wherever and whenever someone has learned to countenance opposites in his or her character."[4]

These uses of Jung as a means of interpreting the character of Jesus and his relationship with Judas, his apparent "shadow side," are extremely fruitful and entirely justified. Moreover, Kazantzakis would certainly have found elements in Jung's analytical psychology conducive to his own richly Bergsonian philosophy. For example, Jung echoes Bergson's belief that any attempt to understand the human self by using static, abstract concepts will fail to reveal the dynamic and changing character of the self. Moreover, Bergson postulates there to be a life-force (élan vital), which shows itself in all living things and desires life to free itself from the constrictions of inert matter in order to attain self-consciousness. The élan vital consists of a dialectical intertwining of spirit and matter, creation and destruction. Jung also stresses the dynamic, creative principle within evolutionary life that pushes humanity to transcend nature and merely instinctual behaviors and to create culture: "It is the growth of consciousness which we must thank for the existence of problems; they are the dubious gift of civilization. It is just man's turning away from instinct—his opposing himself to instinct—that creates consciousness. Instinct is nature and seeks to perpetuate nature; while culture can only seek culture or its denial."[5] Bergson, Jung, and Kazantzakis all term this life-force that seeks to push humanity to ever-widening cycles of consciousness and culture "élan vital" or "God."[6] Kazantzakis's Bergsonian worldview is particularly captured in the account of Jesus' death in *The Last Temptation*. Middleton comments on the ending of the novel, in which the narrator asserts that after Jesus' declaration "IT IS ACCOMPLISHED," it was as though he had said, "Everything has begun." He correctly stresses the underlying Bergsonian philosophy to transubstantiate not only matter into spirit but also spirit into matter. "With *The Last Temptation*'s final statement—'Everything has begun'—it is clear that the élan vital does not 'die' with Jesus' death; rather, Jesus' crucifixion signals the liberty of the élan to begin the creative process anew."[7] Hence, the end of Jesus' material existence signifies the beginning of a reentry into matter for the élan vital.

However, a close reading of Kazantzakis's notebooks reveals that rather than using Jung to highlight a family resemblance existing between Jung, Bergson, and Kazantzakis, we can pinpoint the exact source of the influence, something that has yet to be assessed in Kazantzakis scholarship. In a notebook entry from around October 1950, when he was drafting *The Last Temptation*, Kazantzakis was engaged in reading a French translation of Jung's *Modern Man in Search of a Soul*. He made sufficient notes, particularly on the articles "The Postulates of Analytical Psychology" and "The Spiritual Problem of Modern Man," to demand attention. We must begin here, therefore, in analyzing the supposed Jungian influence on Kazantzakis, and on the novel in particular.

Modern Man in Search of a Soul

Jung's work, translated as *Modern Man in Search of a Soul,* is a selection of essays, drawn mostly from lectures, that provide a comprehensive overview of Jung's analytical psychology. In it, Jung deals with various issues, including the differences between his approach and Freud's, the relationship between psychology and literature, mythology, and the nature of archaic man, all of which would have immediately appealed to Kazantzakis's own psychology. As evident from Kazantzakis's notes, in which he often quotes verbatim from Jung, he was clearly taken by this work, particularly Jung's views on the "collective unconscious" and the notion of archetypes.[8]

Jung declares the existence of symbols within the subconscious, symbols that are older than historical humanity and outlast all generations. These symbols or archetypes constitute the foundation of the human psyche and are the source of all our conscious thoughts. Jung declares, "It is only possible to live the fullest life when we are in harmony with these symbols; wisdom is a return to them."[9] Moreover, Jung offers the image of the setting sun and the "nocturnal sea of unconsciousness" as symbols of these archetypes, which resonate clearly with symbolism that Kazantzakis uses elsewhere.[10] Consciousness is a late offspring of the subconscious soul, which is symbolized by Kazantzakis in his notebooks as "a sea on which the consciousness of the self would navigate, like a boat. The original subconscious is attacking the individual from every angle."[11] Jung argues that the nocturnal sea symbolizes the darkness of the unconscious that is to be navigated safely. This "journey" can also be symbolized as a spiritual rebirth from the mother's womb. Likewise, death may also be represented as symbolizing a reentry into the mother for rebirth. The mother symbol is an archetype referring to a place of origin, "to nature, to that which passively creates, hence to substance and matter, to material nature, the lower body (womb) and the vegetative function."[12]

Kazantzakis begins his notes on Jung's *Modern Man in Search of a Soul* under the subhead "The Unconscious" and compares the contents of consciousness to those of the subconscious. Quoting Jung, Kazantzakis writes:

> While consciousness is intensive and concentrated, it is transient and is directed upon the immediate present and the immediate field of attention; moreover, it has access only to material that represents one individual's experience stretching over a few decades. A wider range of "memory" is artificially acquired and consists mostly of printed paper.[13]

The characteristics of the unconscious, on the other hand, are entirely different: "It is not concentrated and intensive, but shades off into obscurity; it is highly extensive and can juxtapose the most heterogeneous elements in the most paradoxical way."[14] Moreover, the unconscious is home to the various archetypes transcending merely individual existence and acting as the foundation for a "collective unconscious" that underpins all human psychic activity. Kazantzakis writes of the unconscious containing, "besides an indeterminable number of subliminal perceptions, an immense fund of accumulated inheritance factors left by one generation of men after another, whose mere existence marks a step in the differentiation of the species."[15] If this "immense fund of accumulated inheritance factors" were personified, it would constitute a being representing all of collective humanity. Such a being would represent a *coincidentia oppositorum* combining both male and female characteristics, transcending youth and age and all temporal vicissitudes. And due to its access to the collective knowledge of humanity, it would in a sense be "immortal." "If such a being existed," Kazantzakis continues, still quoting Jung,

> he would be exalted above all temporal change; the present would mean neither more nor less to him than any year in the one hundredth century before Christ; he would be a dreamer of old-age dreams and, owing to his immeasurable experience, he would be an incomparable prognosticator. He would have lived countless times over the life of the individual, of the family, tribe and people, and he would possess the living sense of the rhythm of growth, flowering and decay.[16]

In his following notes, Kazantzakis shows a particular interest in the idea of archetypes and their religious significance. The archetype is the "original image existing in the subconscious. It is the centre charged with energy."[17] Access to these subconscious archetypes, primarily through dreams, constitutes the religious activity of the mind. Dreams contain mythological themes, which have a collective meaning that transcends the individual. The encounter with these "foreign" powers within the soul is an encounter with God, which cannot be captured linguistically: "God is the image which the human mind is creating in his inability to express the intimate experience of something unthinkable and unspeakable."[18]

Thus far, we have observed certain similarities between Kazantzakis and Jung, highlighted by Kazantzakis himself in his unpublished notebooks. But a question immediately surfaces in response to the title of this chapter: What role does Pontius Pilate play in the Christian myth for Kazantzakis? The answer again comes directly from Kazantzakis himself. His notebooks on *The Last Temptation* make it clear that Kazantzakis had a quite specific portrayal of Pilate in mind within the novel. At the top of his second page of notes on Jung, he writes "psych. de Pilate" and reveals his source to be Philo of Alexandria. This "psychology of Pilate" is very much in keeping with his intimate dialectical link between destruction and creation, and the sterility of contemporary modern humanity. It first is necessary to examine the historical portrayals of Pilate contained in the Gospels in order to see how and why Kazantzakis diverges from them.

Pontius Pilate in the Gospels

The Gospel portrayals of Pilate are, on the whole, relatively sympathetic, unlike the thoroughly negative treatment offered by Kazantzakis in the novel. Moreover, Kazantzakis changes the narrative order of the Gospel accounts and is clearly skeptical of the historical accuracy of these accounts.[19] Indeed, he claims in a letter that although he had thoroughly researched all books about Christ, Judea, Jewish history, and the Talmud, he retained the right of the poet to have creative license, claiming that "poetry is more philosophical than history."[20] In the same letter he offers further evidence that his portrayal of Christ is not intended to be historically accurate but is rather imbued with a contemporary and symbolically religious significance. Thus he writes:

> I wanted to renew and supplement the sacred Myth that underlies the great Christian civilization of the West. It isn't a simple "Life of Christ." It's a laborious, sacred, creative endeavour to reincarnate the essence of Christ, setting aside the dross— falsehoods and pettinesses which all the churches and all the cassocked representatives of Christianity have heaped upon His figure, thereby distorting it. . . . Parables which Christ could not possibly have left as the Gospels relate them I have supplemented, and I have given them the noble and compassionate ending befitting Christ's heart. Words which we do not know that He said I have put into his mouth, because He would have said them if His Disciples had had His spiritual force and purity. And everywhere poetry, love of animals and plant life and men, confidence in the soul, certainty that the light will prevail.[21]

The Gospel of Mark, traditionally accepted to be the oldest of the Gospels, portrays Pilate's direct involvement with Jesus in two connected scenes.[22] In the first, the chief priests, elders, teachers of the law, and whole Sanhedrin hand Jesus over to Pilate and accuse him, we infer, of claiming to be "King of the Jews." Pilate interrogates him along that line. The accusers make other charges, and Pilate is astonished that Jesus makes no reply. In the second scene, Pilate apparently does not find the charges proved and offers to release Jesus based on the Passover custom for the release of a prisoner. Deciding to satisfy the crowd, Pilate is impelled to release Barabbas and hands Jesus over for execution.

The account in Matthew's Gospel is similar to that in Mark's, although he adds Pilate's wife's dream, which warns the procurator, "Have nothing to do with that innocent man." As with the Gospel of Mark, Matthew describes Pilate, somewhat hesitantly, as symbolically washing his hands of the affair and handing Jesus over to be crucified.[23] Luke's Gospel predictably follows a similar line, with subtle additions: Pilate, agreeing with the prior exoneration of Jesus given by Herod Antipas, wishes to release Jesus but succumbs to the demands of the people and the chief priests to have him crucified. Barabbas is therefore released and Jesus sent to his death.[24]

Thus far we have the synoptic accounts of the Gospels that, as we know, are intimately linked in time, form, and content. All three Synoptics hint that Pilate thought Jesus was innocent (or at least not deserving of death) but that he ultimately failed in strength of will and succumbed to the demands of the people. John's Gospel, however, does not belong to the synoptic tradition. It not only is the longest Gospel but also bears the strongest relation to the account in *The Last Temptation*.[25] For example, only in John (19:5 Vulgate) does Pilate introduce Jesus with the words (later used by Nietzsche) "Ecce homo" when presenting him to be crucified. *The Last Temptation* also repeats Pilate's question, "What is truth?" found only in John (18:38). The dream of Pilate's wife also plays a central role in the novel. We thus recognize Kazantzakis's interest in Jung's dream-theory and the fact that the novel is sandwiched between two dreams. We also observe Kazantzakis's obvious skepticism toward the historical accuracy of the Gospel narrative and his own admission that he wished to "renew and supplement the sacred Myth that underlies the great Christian civilization of the West." Therefore, it seems reasonable to assume that Kazantzakis was more attracted to the "symbolic" nature of John's Gospel.[26] Furthermore, Kazantzakis would have been attracted to John's portrayal of Judas. John's Gospel is the most sympathetic toward Judas and says nothing about his death, unlike Matthew's Gospel (27:5), which claims that Judas, realizing the error of his ways, hangs himself.

The quest for the historical Pilate is therefore as daunting a task as for any significant figure in early Christian history. Aside from the Synoptics and John's Gospel, the historical sources are relatively sparse. There are apocryphal accounts as well as information given by the Roman historian Tacitus, who refers to the execution of Jesus, and the Jewish writers Josephus and Philo, who relate several incidents during Pilate's tenure in office. Unlike the Gospel writers who had quite specific theological apologetics in mind, the accounts of Josephus and Philo, in particular, are stark and negative, no doubt biased upon their Jewish prejudice. Indeed, it is from Philo, rather than the Gospels, including John's, that Kazantzakis extracts most of his traits for the character Pilate. In his notebooks, Kazantzakis mentions the aforementioned "psych. de Pilate" before referring to Philo and to Pilate's "unbending nature" and arrogance (*"tin physin akampis" kai meta tou authadous ameiliktos*). This characterization is entirely in keeping with Philo's stance in *Legatio ad Gaium*, to which we now turn.

Pontius Pilate in Philo and Kazantzakis

Philo—whose account of the crucifixion of Jesus was, of all existing accounts, written closest to its occurrence—was in the best position to gather firsthand facts. Philo's pro-Jewish agenda must be borne in mind when we read his presentation of Pilate as "spiteful, angry, lacking in courage, inflexible, stubborn and cruel" and given to savagery.[27] In *Legatio ad Gaium* Philo suggests that the Jews suffered mercilessly at the hands of Pilate's procuratorship (or prefecture); in particular, many were massacred for their opposition to an aqueduct that was desired by Pilate. Philo begins by referring to Pilate's setting up of gilded shields in Herod's palace in Jerusalem with the specific intention of "annoying the Jews rather than honouring Tiberius."[28] In response, the Jews called on Pilate to respect their native customs; being a man of "inflexible, stubborn and cruel disposition," his response was, according to Philo, a refusal to respect Jewish custom, which subsequently led the

Jews to suggest a forthcoming revolt. After an appeal from the Jews to the emperor Tiberius, Pilate grew weary of being impeached, probably due to earlier acts of mis-government. In sum, Pilate is characterized by Philo as oppressive, greedy, stubborn, and cruel and is ridiculed according to "his venality, his violence, his thefts, his assaults, his abusive behaviour, his frequent executions of untried prisoners, and his endless savage ferocity."[29]

Kazantzakis's description of Pilate in *The Last Temptation* is equally as negative as Philo's. It represents a personification of passive nihilism, one who blocks the ascent of the spirit, or élan vital ("God"), epitomized by Jesus.[30] Kazantzakis describes Pilate:

> Towering before them, at once fortress and palace, was the tower which guarded with-in the haughty Roman Governor, Pontius Pilate. He detested the Jewish race and held a perfumed handkerchief in front of his nostrils whenever he walked in the lanes of Jerusalem or was compelled to speak with the Hebrews. *He believed neither in gods nor in men—nor in Pontius Pilate, nor in anything.* Consequently suspended around his neck on a fine golden chain was a sharpened razor which he kept in order to open his veins when he became weary of eating, drinking and governing or when the emperor exiled him. He often heard the Jews shout themselves hoarse calling the Messiah to come and liberate them—and he laughed.[31]

Moreover, Pilate ridicules and scoffs at the prominence the Jews give to dreams. As discussed above, Kazantzakis copies from Jung a stress on dreams as providing access to the subconscious archetypes and constituting the religious activity of the mind: "Whatever you Jews yearn for while you're awake, you see in your sleep. You live and die with visions."[32] Kazantzakis therefore uses Pilate to signify an oppressive materiality and nihilism that prevent the creative life-force, epitomized in Jesus, from continuing its perpetual cycle to higher levels of consciousness. This is why Kazantzakis veers away from the traditional Gospel accounts of Pilate, which are rel-atively sympathetic, to an account that is harsh, cruel, and thoroughly negative. As we know from his unpublished notebooks, Kazantzakis almost certainly draws on Philo of Alexandria for this stark portrayal.

Conclusion

Like Jung, who claimed in *Modern Man in Search of a Soul* that humanity was faced with the necessity of rediscovering the life of the spirit, Kazantzakis was greatly aware that modern humanity was deeply in search of a soul. Hence, he used the character of Pontius Pilate to highlight all that represents spiritual emptiness. Moreover, *The Last Temptation* was written with a "collective" aim in mind: Jesus is essentially the subconscious personified. We know from his unpublished note-books that Kazantzakis was particularly interested in the views of Jung, who claimed that any true work of art rises above artistic individuality and speaks instead to the voice of contemporary humanity.[33] Kazantzakis therefore was unlike Pilate, who "believed neither in gods nor in men—nor in Pontius Pilate, nor in anything," and lived by his nihilistic motto "Eat, drink, and be merry, for tomorrow you die." Through his art Kazantzakis sought with the character of Jesus to create a riverbed into which a new creative culture could flow. Naturally, he drew on various political, philosophical, and religious texts, as well as relevant Greek history, in formulating the novel. Nevertheless, we must recognize the importance Kazantzakis placed on Jung, not simply in terms of dreams and the collective unconscious but also as formulating in his art a voice for contemporary and future humanity, which Kazantzakis believed needed to rediscover its soul. *The Last Temptation* was Kazantzakis's finest gift to that search. He believed that contemporary culture remained in an age of "night," although he intuited that this period of "night" may be necessary to exhaust the corrupt elements of the present materialistic age before a new spiritual and cultural dawn might be ushered in. As Jesus claims in the novel, with a phrase that captures the essence of Kazantzakis's creative philosophy, "Love comes only after the flames. First this world will be reduced to ashes and then God will plant his new vineyard. There is no better fertilizer than ashes."[34]

In response to the news that *The Last Temptation* had been listed in the Index of Forbidden Books in 1954, Kazantzakis remarked to Börje Knös: "I've always been amazed at the narrow-mindedness and narrow-heartedness of human beings. Here is a book that I wrote in a state of deep religious exaltation, with fervent love for Christ; and now the representative of Christ, the Pope, has no understanding of it at all, he cannot sense the Christian love with which it was written, and he condemns it! *And yet it is in keeping with the wretchedness and slavery of the contemporary world that I should be condemned.*"[35] Nevertheless, he saw in the archetypal figure of Jesus a symbol for the re-creation of this contemporary world. And he, Kazantzakis, saw himself as an artist charged with a responsibility to shape the unconscious, psychic life of humanity. Moreover, the image of a savior or wise man needs awakening from its unconscious slumber. "The archetypal image of the wise man, the saviour or the redeemer, lies buried and dormant in man's unconscious since the dawn of culture; it is awakened whenever the times are out of joint and a human society is committed to a single error." The "collective" nature of Jesus' personality has clear parallels to the contemporary epoch:

> An epoch is like an individual; it has its own limitations of conscious outlook, and therefore requires a compensatory adjustment. This is effected by the collective unconscious in that a poet, a seer, or a leader allows himself to be guided by the unexpressed desire of his times and shows the way, by word or deed, to the attainment of which everyone blindly craves or expects—whether this attainment results in good or evil, the healing of an epoch or its destruction.[36]

Like Jung, Kazantzakis saw the dreams of individuals and the vision of artists as necessary to restore the psychic equilibrium of the epoch.

Both Jung in the 1930s and Kazantzakis while he was writing *The Last Temptation* were losing faith in the dominant scientific rationality of the world. They were deeply troubled by the inevitable catastrophes that would result if such an imbalance was not redressed. It was necessary for humanity to learn to be humble once more. Jung writes, "But spiritually the Western world is in a precarious situation—and the danger is greater the more we blind ourselves to the merciless truth with illusions about our beauty of soul."[37] It was toward the more spiritual strength of the East that one should look for psychic renewal and to escape this age of Americanization.[38] Therefore, although deeply troubled, both Jung and Kazantzakis were essentially optimistic for the future, providing that a far-reaching spiritual change in Western humanity occurred. As Jung writes, "We are only at the threshold of a new spiritual epoch." And he sees this threshold, like Kazantzakis, as a period of "night" that will nevertheless usher in a new "dawn."[39] For Kazantzakis, destruction and despair are the prerequisites for creativity and optimism, and he sees this intimate dialectical link in the following quote of Jung, which he copied into his notebook: "Any disease which dissociates a world constitutes at the same time a healing process. Decomposition, apparently meaningless and distressing, able to inspire disgust and despair, holds in its lap the germ of a moral light."[40]

By dressing these contemporary concerns and this essential optimism in Jewish attire to represent the most "sacred Myth that underlies the great Christian civilization of the West," Kazantzakis is essentially speaking to contemporary humanity. On the one hand Jesus signifies the hope, optimism, and spiritual creativity. On the other hand Pilate represents the modern nihilistic and material person desperately in search of a soul. When asked by Pilate, "Hey, Messiah, what is this fearful news I hear you bring to the world?" Jesus thus answers, "Fire . . . fire to cleanse the earth. . . . And then on the scorched purified earth, the new Jerusalem shall be built."[41]

Notes

1. As Kazantzakis himself claims in a letter to his Jewish friend Rahel, "And how I've raised and sanctified Judas Iscariot right alongside Jesus in this book I'm writing now." See Helen Kazantzakis, *Nikos Kazantzakis: A Biography Based on His Letters*, trans. Amy Mims (New York: Simon & Schuster, 1968), 477.

2. Elsewhere I have looked at the relationship between Kazantzakis and Jung. See Lewis Owens, *Creative Destruction: Nikos Kazantzakis and the Literature of Responsibility* (Macon, GA: Mercer University Press, 2002), 146–47.

3. John S. Bak, "Christ's Jungian Shadow in *The Last Temptation*," in *God's Struggler: Religion in the Writings of Nikos Kazantzakis*, ed. Darren J. N. Middleton and Peter Bien (Macon: GA: Mercer University Press, 1996), 153–68.

4. Darren J. N. Middleton, *Novel Theology: Nikos Kazantzakis's Encounter with Whiteheadian Process Theism* (Macon, GA: Mercer University Press, 2000), 82. Morton Levitt also draws on Jung in his belief that St. Francis represents Kazantzakis's "shadow side" in the novel *Saint Francis*. See Levitt, *The Cretan Glance: The World and Art of Nikos Kazantzakis* (Columbus:

Ohio State University Press, 1980), 52–53, 55. Also see Adèle Bloch, "Kazantzakis and the Image of Christ," *Literature and Psychology* 15 (1965): 2–11. Finally, see Peter A. Bien, *Tempted by Happiness: Kazantzakis' Post-Christian Christ* (Wallingford, PA: Pendle Hill, 1984), 5–8.

5. Carl Gustav Jung, *Modern Man in Search of a Soul*, trans. W. S. Dell and Cary F. Barnes (London: Kegan Paul, Trench, Trubner, 1933), 110.

6. Elsewhere, Jung claims that similar conceptions to "libido" may be found in Bergson's notion of élan vital and Schopenhauer's "will." See Carl Gustav Jung, *On the Nature of the Psyche*, trans. R. F. C. Hull (London: Ark Paperbacks, 1988), 30. See also James Heisig, *Imago Dei: A Study of C. G. Jung's Psychology of Religion* (Lewisburg, PA: Bucknell University Press, 1979). For Jung, especially in his early thought, the libido, or more generally psychic energy, is characterized by opposing and conflicting desires that strive for consciousness. Libido, or "God," as he later referred to it, is portrayed as both creative and destructive. See Heisig, *Imago Dei*, 153n71.

7. Middleton, *Novel Theology*, 88.

8. Kazantzakis was reading a French translation of Jung's work and making notes in French, unlike the English translation I am using for the purpose of this work. I am extremely grateful to Peter Bien for access to Kazantzakis's unpublished notebooks.

9. Jung, *Modern Man*, 130.

10. Ibid., 122. This symbolism is clearly evident in Kazantzakis's *Odyssey* (1938), where the entire poem takes place between the rising and setting sun. See Owens, *Creative Destruction*, 146–47.

11. Nikos Kazantzakis, Notebook VI:21, with my translation from the original French.

12. Jung, *Modern Man*, 28. Jung, 141, argues that Freud shipwrecks on the question of Nicodemus reported in the New Testament: "Can a man enter his mother's womb a second time and be born again?" Very generally, in *The Last Temptation* Jesus refers to the sterile, maternal, and hence physical temptations as "the Curse." When citing this novel, I use Nikos Kazantzakis, *The Last Temptation of Christ*, trans. Peter Bien (New York: Simon & Schuster, 1960).

13. Jung, *Modern Man*, 215; cited by Kazantzakis in Notebook VI:21.

14. Jung, *Modern Man*, 215.

15. Ibid.

16. Ibid.

17. Kazantzakis, Notebook VI:23, my translation.

18. Ibid., 22, my translation.

19. For example, Barabbas is imprisoned for murdering the resurrected Lazarus, and contrary to the Gospel accounts, Jesus' first visit to Pilate occurs before the Last Supper and Gethsemane.

20. Letter dated November 13, 1951. See Helen Kazantzakis, *Biography*, 505–6. See also Jung's chapter "Psychology and Literature" in *Modern Man*, where he distinguishes between "psychological" and "visionary" art. In the latter category he includes Dante, Goethe, and Nietzsche. Using the criteria set out by Jung, it is also fair to place Kazantzakis in this visionary category.

21. See Helen Kazantzakis, *Biography*, 505.

22. Mark 15:1–15.

23. Matt 27:15–26.

24. Luke 23:13–25.

25. John 18:33–19:16, 19–22.

26. Moreover, we have a suggestion of Kazantzakis's skepticism concerning the Gospel accounts of Jesus' life, especially Matthew's, when Kazantzakis's Jesus chides Matthew for writing lies, although he acknowledges the creative and "spiritual" process of writing. See Kazantzakis, *Last Temptation*, 391–92.

27. Philonis Alexandrini, *Legatio ad Gaium*, trans. E. Mary Smallwood (Leiden: Brill, 1970), §§ 299–306.

28. Ibid., § 299.

29. Ibid., § 302.

30. Pilate's psychology is captured in the engraving on his skull-carved ring: "Eat, drink and be merry, for tomorrow you die." In Martin Scorsese's film Pilate is played by David Bowie, one of only two English characters within the film (the other is the little girl representing the Tempter, who replaces the Negro boy in the book). As Peter Bien suggests, this may have to do with Scorsese's views of the English and is not an interpretation of Kazantzakis. See Peter A. Bien, "Nikos Kazantzakis's Novels on Film," *The Journal of Modern Greek Studies* 18, no. 1 (2000): 161–69.

31. Kazantzakis, *Last Temptation*, 380, with added emphasis. We recall Philo's comment that Pilate feared impeachment by the emperor Tiberius (Phionis Alexandrini, *Legatio ad Gaium*, 302).

32. Kazantzakis, *Last Temptation*, 382.

33. See Jung, "Psychology and Literature," in *Modern Man*.

34. Kazantzakis, *Last Temptation*, 354.

35. Helen Kazantzakis, *Biography*, 523, with added emphasis.

36. Jung, *Modern Man*, 191–92.

37. Ibid., 245–46.

38. Kazantzakis in Notebook VI:23, once more quoting Jung, makes reference to "the old specialist in Chinese matters," Richard Wilhelm.

39. Jung, *Modern Man*, 252. See also Lewis Owens, "Metacommunism: Kazantzakis, Berdyaev and the 'New Middle Age,'" *Slavic and East European Journal* 45, no. 3 (2001): 29–48.

40. Kazantzakis, Notebook VI: 22, my translation.

41. Kazantzakis, *Last Temptation*, 383.

CHAPTER 4

Kazantzakis, Chalcedonian Orthodoxy, and Monophysitism

Daniel A. Dombrowski

Conceptual Background

Nikos Kazantzakis's novel *The Last Temptation of Christ* has created a combustible mixture that has tended to generate more heat than light among its readers.[1] But the light is there for the patient reader to appreciate. In this chapter I explore what is orthodox and what is heterodox in Kazantzakis's Christology. I argue that his Christology can most profitably be seen as a contemporary version of Monophysitism (from the ancient Greek: *mon-* [one] + *physis* [nature]). Although this view is somewhat at odds with what has been traditionally seen as the orthodox, Chalcedonian view (Jesus' having two distinct natures), it is nonetheless a more defensible view of Jesus in light of the contemporary revolt against dualism.[2] Kazantzakis helps us to see the inadequacies of a two-tiered view of the universe and of Jesus wherein the "supernatural" is arbitrarily inserted into the natural world or invades it.

In Kazantzakis's prologue to the novel, he does refer to the dual substance (*ipostasis*) of Jesus in terms of both spirit (*pnevma*) and flesh (*sarks*); indeed, he speaks of the battle between these two. But *this* distinction is quite different from the one found in the Chalcedonian formula to the effect that Jesus is fully God (supernatural) and fully human (natural) and that these are two distinct natures. Thus Kazantzakis is quite clear that divinity is found on *both* sides of the distinction between spirit and flesh: "Every man partakes of the divine nature in both his spirit and his flesh. That is why the mystery of Christ is not simply a mystery for a particular creed: it is universal."[3] In Kazantzakis there is no rigid split between divinity and flesh; likewise, there is no rigid split between divinity and spirit.

In Kazantzakis's view, the mystery of Jesus is universal, presumably because the struggle between spirit and flesh breaks out in every person. In fact, the stronger the spirit and the flesh, the more fruitful the struggle. It is a commonplace in Kazantzakis's writings that God does not favor weak spirits nor flabby flesh. Spiritual struggles with or through formidable fleshly resistance are the loci for the most successful religious lives, he thinks. The telos of these struggles is nothing other than union with God, with "God" conceived in terms of the summit (*koroufi*) of flesh that is transubstantiated into spirit.[4]

Kazantzakis's unique contribution to Christology (discussed below) should not prevent us from also appreciating his continuity with religious tradition. For example, various spiritual masters in the Orthodox Christian tradition from the fourth to the fifteenth centuries, as anthologized in *The Philokalia*, make a point that helps us better to understand Kazantzakis's view: the ancient Greek word *sarx* (flesh) has various senses. It can refer to the human in contrast to the divine, as in Chalcedonian Christology. But it can also refer to the whole spirit-body complex as found in Jesus or in any other human being. In this latter sense of the term, "flesh" refers to the *whole* spirit-body complex insofar as it is fallen, whereas "spirit" refers to the *whole* spirit-body complex insofar as it is redeemed. To be precise, the spirit as well as the body can become fleshly, just as the body as well as the spirit can become divinized. In both *The Philokalia* and *The Last Temptation of Christ*, there is hope for some sort of rapprochement between human embodiment and the process of *theōsis* (deification).[5]

Before moving to some passages from the novel itself, a careful consideration of the logical possibilities, along with the historical evidence cited in the previous paragraph, offers support for Kazantzakis's view. When seeking to explain both spiritual (or mental) experiences in human beings as well as the bodily experiences they have, there are three (not two!) general possibilities to consider. (1) Dualism is the view that such experiences are due to the fact that spirit (or mind) and body are two separate natures that are not reducible to each other. This stance seems to underlie the Chalcedonian view of Jesus. (2) Materialism, by way of contrast, is the view that spirit (or mind) can be reduced to body, such that the sort of love exhibited by Jesus or other human beings can be explained in terms of hormonal secretions or neurons firing in the brain.

Most modern discussion in Christology would center on these two options, with dualists holding aloft the only flickering torches of hope against the rising tide of materialists. Yet we recognize that there is another option: (3) It may be the case that body can be reduced to spirit (or mind or psyche or at least some sort of proto-sentient activity). This last option can come in at least two different forms: (3a) Panpsychism or panexperientialism is the view that ultimate reality exhibits some sort of self-motion or activity. Plato realized this (e.g., *Sophist* 247E) when he said that anything existing exhibits some sort of dynamic power (*dynamis*) to affect, or to be affected by, something else, in however slight a way. (3b) The hylomorphist view of Aristotle holds that anything existing exhibits both a mental or formal pole or structure (*morphē*) as well as a physical pole (*hylē*). In this view it would be best to refer to Jesus and to other human beings as "soulbodies" or "spiritbodies." Doing so would indicate that there is an integral connection between spirit (or mind) and body, and that there is no inert, lifeless stuff that constitutes those who are either divine or made in the image of the divine. Hence, in both views of the last option (3a and 3b), matter literally is internally formed; it is animated with something "far more deeply interfused" (to use William Wordsworth's phrase) than is allowed in either the dualist or materialist hypothesis.[6]

The issue as to whether Kazantzakis is more of a panpsychist or dynamic hylomorphist is not as important as the realization that his Christology (and his anthropology) is decidedly neither dualist nor materialist. To be precise, there *is* an opposition in Kazantzakis between spirit and matter (or flesh), as mentioned above, and this opposition leads some to think of Kazantzakis in dualist terms. But this "dualist" opposition is to be understood within a metaphysical monism. We have seen that in the prologue to *The Last Temptation of Christ*, Kazantzakis states quite clearly that *the* divine nature is found in both the human spirit and the flesh. This ubiquity makes the mystery of Jesus something other than a parochial concern for Christians alone.

Panpsychism/Dynamic Hylomorphism

No doubt certain critics will suggest that the passages in *The Last Temptation of Christ* indicating a commitment to panpsychism leave Kazantzakis open to the charge that he has committed some pathetic fallacy, as when he has trees laughing.[7] But it is entirely plausible that Kazantzakis, like Wordsworth, is noticing not that whole trees are sentient, but rather that parts of trees (such as *living* cells) are at least proto-sentient. As Wordsworth puts the Kazantzakian point: "The budding twigs spread out their fan, / To catch the breezy air; / And I must think, do all I can, / That there was pleasure there."[8] I take it that these "twigs" provide a metaphorical way to refer to the animated, dynamic parts of the tree. In any event, it is by no means clear that this pathetic fallacy, if Kazantzakis commits it, is worse than the apathetic fallacy whereby dualists and materialists (respectively) treat most or all of the world as inert, lifeless stuff, presumably to be manipulated at will.

God's presence is ubiquitous in *The Last Temptation of Christ*: in woods, birds (including their songs), and human beings. All of creation is seen as the Romantic poets saw it: fresh from the hands of the Creator. Even the scorching wind and the lightning bolt, along with the beneficent orchard in bloom, are charged with the grandeur of God, to use Gerard Manley Hopkins's well-known phrase.[9] It is true that the psyche or self-motion of the minutest parts of nature is sometimes hidden from us, but with effort we can appreciate the "face of God" even in the black eye of an ant. Kazantzakis presumably speaks in these panpsychist passages (or better, pan-experientialist passages, in that "psyche" elicits in some readers a conscious mind rather than a more generalized ability to feel or to experience) both from personal experience and from the perspective of Bergsonian philosophy of science, wherein nature is animated with a Zorba-like élan vital. Because of this pervasive animism, God loves the whole world.[10]

Kazantzakis interprets Jesus' cleansing of the temple in a way that illuminates his panpsychism. We should not be too much concerned with a temple building as a locus for spiritual activity if each of our bodies is itself a temple; there is something within ourselves with which we worship and with which we are filled with joy. Elsewhere, Kazantzakis tries to convince us that God is an explosive power who breaks out in each cell, indeed, in the smallest particle of matter.[11]

This is a clue that perhaps enables us to understand the faith healings that are mentioned several times in *The Last Temptation of Christ*, including the healing of the centurion's daughter. "Without speaking, he [Jesus] pinned his eyes on to the two green eyes and felt his soul flow impetuously from the tips of his fingers into the girl's body."[12] Jesus' psyche, as it were, had an influence on the proto-psyche of the girl's microscopic parts that were causing the girl's disease. Thus both faith healings and psychosomatic illnesses are unintelligible as long as it is assumed that a psychic or supernatural reality is arbitrarily inserted into a natural body or invades it. But these phenomena can perhaps make some sense to us if they are explained in terms of natural bodies that contain within themselves animating or psyche-like power to affect others.[13] Further, Jesus' hope in *The Last Temptation of Christ* also seems to be Kazantzakis's own: "Ah, if I could only blow on every soul, he thought, and cry to it, Awake! Then, if it did awake, the body would become soul and be cured."[14]

One of the problems with a dualist metaphysics, such as the one lying behind the Chalcedonian formula, is that it gives the impression that Jesus' divinity is a "ghost in a machine." Thereby it is too easy for the materialist opponent to dualism to exorcize the ghost and then declare that Jesus' divinity is a hoax. These dualist/materialist approaches are too facile, as Kazantzakis sees things in his terror-filled effort to understand Jesus' bloody journey to Golgotha, because they fail to adequately link the "fully human" aspect of Jesus (admitted even in Chalcedonian Christology) to divinity.[15] Dualism fails to do this by not even trying to explain how the two natures interact, whereas materialism fails to do this by, in effect, denying the very existence of divinity. As Kazantzakis sees things, it is in Jesus' very struggle to transubstantiate flesh into spirit that divinity is to be found, rather than in the Chalcedonian deus ex machina.

As mentioned, my primary aim here is to locate Kazantzakis's Christology in opposition to dualist or materialist Christologies. Further, there is a family resemblance between panpsychism and dynamic hylomorphism in that they are both alternatives to dualism and materialism. I have not, however, tried to advance a view regarding whether Kazantzakis was more of a panpsychist or a dynamic hylomorphist. Clearly, Kazantzakis himself was not interested in fine-tuning his view so as to choose between these two. Nevertheless, locating his stance as some combination of panpsychism and dynamic hylomorphism does help us considerably in the effort to understand his Christology.

The textual evidence cited above regarding his panpsychism can be supplemented by the evidence regarding his flirtation with dynamic hylomorphism. In an instructive scene early in the novel, Jesus experiences hunger for food, a hunger not unrelated to the spiritual hunger that pervades the book. Kazantzakis describes the event in the following remarkable terms:

> The son of Mary felt calmed. He sat down on the root of the ancient olive tree and began to eat. How tasty this bread was, how refreshing the water, how sweet the two olives which the old lady gave him to accompany his bread. They had slender pits and were as fat and fleshy as apples! He chewed tranquilly and ate, feeling that his body and soul had joined and become one now, that they were receiving the bread, olives, and water with one mouth, rejoicing, the both of them, and being nourished.[16]

We need not look further than the domestic event of relieving hunger in order to understand the divinizing event of flesh being transubstantiated into spirit: "Wherever children and petty cares and cooking and arguments and reconciliations [are], that's where God is."[17]

In at least one respect, Kazantzakis is a more consistent hylomorphist than Aristotle. The latter abandoned his hylomorphism at a cosmological level when he claimed that the gods were pure actualities and formalities and that they were not characterized by concrete embodiment.[18] Kazantzakis, by way of partial contrast, has a view that is consistent with hylomorphism both at a personal level and at a cosmological level. For example, the natural world is not externally related to God but is rather the concrete receptacle for the divine struggle itself: "The whole earth was a cross on which he [Jesus] was being crucified."[19]

One of the main tensions in *The Last Temptation of Christ* is that between Judas and Jesus. Judas wants to liberate the body from Roman domination and then later worry about the soul. Jesus thinks either that body and soul must be liberated together or that the soul must be liberated first, with the body necessarily following along in tow. "The foundation is the soul," he tells Judas, who tends toward materialism and is anachronistically depicted as a proto-Marxist.[20] In order to avoid Judas's Zealotism, however, one need not try to sequester spiritual concerns away from the material world altogether. In an incarnational religion like Christianity, it would be odd if God did not truly mix with humanity:

> Without man, God would have no mind on this Earth to reflect upon his creatures intelligibly. . . . He would have on this Earth no heart to pity the concerns of others. . . . But man, without God, born as he is unarmed, would have been obliterated by hunger, fear and cold. . . . That God and man could become one.[21]

There indeed are several passages in *The Last Temptation of Christ* that could be seen to offer support for a dualist interpretation of Kazantzakis's Christology. But these passages are also perfectly compatible with Kazantzakis's claim in the prologue (recognized above) to the effect that the divine nature is alive in *both* Jesus' spirit and his flesh. The tension between spirit and flesh is located within a larger whole that is in the process of transubstantiation. For example, at times we hear that when Jesus entered the monastery, he planned to *kill* the flesh.[22] This sort of language could easily lead one to conclude that spirit and flesh are completely different natures, utterly opposed to each other. A more judicious interpretation, I think, can be found by way of appeal to *The Philokalia* (as mentioned above). By killing the flesh, Kazantzakis seems to mean an opposition to the entropic, fallen character of the whole spirit-body complex. Once again, to be redeemed is to allow the whole spirit-body complex to dynamically rise to new levels of freedom and understanding.

It is the abbot in the monastery, not Jesus, who suggests that the body of a human being is accursed and refuses to allow spiritual progress.[23] Kazantzakis associates Jesus with the more defensible view that flesh is not necessarily dirty and opposed to the process of transubstantiation; indeed, flesh plays an essential role in that process. The point is subtle, however, when we realize that even on a dualist basis there is *some* role for the body. Thus it is seen as the camel on which the soul mounts in order to traverse the desert of one's burden in life, or as a mere tent for the soul.[24] But in the Kazantzakian view, the flesh is not a mere passive, supine element in the spiritual life. This is the whole point to the hylomorphist claim that matter is in-formed and has its own Platonic *dynamis*. As I read *The Last Temptation of Christ*, I see occasional flirtations with dualist language. Yet Kazantzakis's Jesus struggles *with* matter rather than *against* it. The spiritual journey from *this* somewhat beautiful world to *that* truly beautiful one is neither a journey for the feet nor an escape from the body altogether.[25] Instead, it is a journey that involves a change in attitude toward *this* world.

Divine Ascent/Ascent to the Divine

In a previous work I referred to Kazantzakis's theism as dipolar.[26] I still think that this is an appropriate designation in that Kazantzakis at times sees the transubstantiation of flesh into spirit itself as divine (divine ascent), and at other times he sees God as the goal or the telos of the transubstantiating struggle (ascent to the divine).

Examples of the former tendency are not hard to find in *The Last Temptation of Christ*. At several points Kazantzakis uses one of his favorite metaphors, examples of which are scattered throughout his writings: a caterpillar struggling to unfold its wings and become a butterfly.[27] This metaphor (perhaps derived from Saint Teresa of Avila) is meant to work against the Chalcedonian assumption that God always *descends upon* humanity, as is implied in metaphors like a thunderbolt striking human beings or a clawing vulture using its talons to catch human beings.[28] Rather, the ascent toward God is itself divine, whether we unfold wings like a caterpillar/butterfly, or advance little by little toward spiritual flight like a simple partridge.[29] A childlike desire to "become God" (*na yinis Theos*) takes us close to Kazantzakis's view of divinity here.[30]

This first tendency in Kazantzakis's theism obviously takes time seriously; divinization is a process that occurs over time, as in the transubstantiation of mud into spirit that happened over the immense ages of evolutionary history.[31] At each moment human beings are on the frontier of this transubstantiation process.[32] A harmonious human life, to the extent that such is possible amid the tragedies that attend such a life, is one in which flesh and spirit work together in this transubstantiating process.[33] No matter how high the spirit soars, however, like an arrow in flight it must come back down to earth.[34] It is presumably for this reason that Peter Bien, in his concluding note at the end of his translation of *The Last Temptation of Christ*, suggests that for Kazantzakis liberation is not a reward for the transubstantiating struggle, but is rather the very process of the struggle itself.[35] It is thus understandable that Jesus is constantly tempted, especially at the end of the novel when he is almost lured into what is, in effect, bourgeois complacency in the domestic life with the sisters Martha and Mary.

Like Plato's divinity in the *Timaeus*, Kazantzakis's struggling God must cajole and negotiate the way through chaos (*khaos*); the divine road involves crosses, to use the Christian metaphor.[36] Or, to use a different device, Kazantzakis's "Jerusalem" is in motion, and at the time of Jesus, this Jerusalem was in motion at a fast pace.[37]

Although less prominent than the first tendency, evidence for the second tendency in Kazantzakis's theism can also be found in *The Last Temptation of Christ*. God thus is not always seen as the transubstantiating struggle between spirit and flesh, but is sometimes seen as the goal of such a struggle when pure spirit is the result.[38] At one point in the novel, the implication is that human beings cannot sprout wings like a butterfly or a partridge until they reach the brink of the abyss. And this abyss clearly is God.[39] We will see that it is not only God's knowledge that is a terrifying abyss or precipice, but also God's love.[40] The two tendencies in Kazantzakis's theism are brought together by spirit, the crucial factor at work in both divine tendencies: a human spirit is a spark of God, but the divine nature itself is a spiritualized or besouled conflagration (*pirkhayia*)![41]

Divine Love as Sublime

There is a superficial resemblance between the apostle Paul's famous battle between the flesh and the spirit and Kazantzakis's battle. The Chalcedonian formula takes Pauline dualism and reifies the two forces at odds with each other as distinct natures, only one of which is associated with Deity. Because of the oppositional language Kazantzakis uses to describe the relationship between flesh and spirit, it might be assumed that there is more similarity between Kazantzakis and the Chalcedonian formula than I have admitted in this chapter.

This assumption, I maintain, should be called into question for at least two reasons: (1) As Kazantzakis makes abundantly clear, divinity is found on both sides of the tension between flesh and spirit, hence showing the appropriateness of calling his position Monophysite: there is one soul-body complex. One consequence of this view, recognized at the Council of Chalcedon itself, is that on the basis of Monophysitism, the divine nature of Jesus was capable of suffering. Kazantzakis does not view this consequence as a reduction of his position to absurdity, as the defenders of the Chalcedonian formula would allege. In fact, he readily admits that his God stumbles and struggles in the process of spiritual liberation. And (2) the driving force that carries along spirit *and* flesh is the sublime love *embodied* in Jesus, a love that bears no trace of sentimentality or syrupy affectation.

At a crucial point in the novel, Jesus tells Ananias a parable so as to help the latter eliminate his nightmares. As its primary effect the extended parable has the affirmation of divine omnibenevolence: God is not only powerful and just but also good.[42] Yet as Kazantzakis's Jesus often speaks in terms of clearing away the rotted wood found in the social and religious beliefs of his contemporaries, this insistent love often appears to be something that is not good.[43] But as an outsider in the novel, the Roman centurion whose daughter was cured by Jesus is quick to notice the difference between a God of justice and vengeance and the God of love described by Jesus and indeed embodied in him. In this light, love is the way, the truth, and the life.[44]

To say that Jesus' love in *The Last Temptation of Christ* is sublime rather than pretty or cute is not to suggest that it is completely beyond the ken of transubstantiating (divinizing) human beings. It is rather to say that it challenges them in ways that are extraordinary. Echoing the famous biblical trope (Matt 10:28–31), we are told that God cares even for the fall of a sparrow. Hence, even if we are of more value than many sparrows, we are called on to have a love for others that is both cosmic in scope and profoundly deep.[45] Even in the story regarding the cleansing of the temple, which many people have interpreted in terms of an abrogation of Jesus' love for others when he violently whips those who had defiled the temple, such love remains in full force. Kazantzakis is a more careful reader of Scripture than many readers and even his admirers realize. He has Jesus carry an oxgoad (*vukhentra*), not a whip, just as the biblical text has Jesus carry a lash made out of rushes (*phragellion ek schoiniōn*, John 2:15) so as to prod the animals out of the temple. In sum, no whip or goad is mentioned at all in the Synoptic Gospels (Matt 21:12–13; Mark 11:15–17; Luke 19:45–46). And the goad mentioned in both John (2:13–17, "whip") and *The Last Temptation of Christ* does not seem to have been the sort of thing that signals violent treatment of other human beings, despite Jesus' momentary rage.[46]

Likewise, in the scene in the garden when Jesus was arrested, Jesus tells Peter, "If we meet the knife with the knife, when will the world ever be free of stabbings?"[47] Although it must be admitted that "love" is not necessarily a simple, tranquil word, Jesus' message *is* a simple one that involves love (*aghapi*) and nothing else, in Kazantzakis's reading.[48] The Monophysite interpretation of Jesus that I offer in this chapter requires that whatever is meant by "love" must engage the body. Hence, we should not be surprised that the love discussed in *The Last Temptation of Christ* seems to involve at least two different ancient concepts, both the spiritual love that does not require love in return (*agapē*) and sexual passion (*eros*). Regarding the latter, Kazantzakis attributes to Jesus early in life a similar psychosomatic illness elicited by (supposedly) illicit sexual passion for Mary Magdalene, which Kazantzakis himself exhibited in 1922 in Vienna.[49] More typical is the allusion to Aristophanes's speech in Plato's *Symposium*, where love signals a desire to acquire what one lacks; hence, it is our bodily or spiritual poverty that requires us to love.[50]

Two Objections

In the prologue to *The Last Temptation of Christ*, Kazantzakis indicates that the relationship between divinity and humanity in Jesus is not something that should be of interest only to Christians. He thinks there is something universal in Jesus' struggles. But this universality is not articulated well in the Chalcedonian Christology, where Jesus' concrete embodiment in the world is outside the divine process. In the Chalcedonian account, divinity is outside of time and history, making unintelligible the divine relationship with the human Jesus, who was clearly in time and who clearly had a history. The euphemism used by defenders of the Chalcedonian account is that this relationship is "mysterious."

We have also seen that Kazantzakis at times admittedly flirts with Chalcedonian dualism when he gives the impression that Jesus' divinity is related to spirit *simpliciter* and that Jesus' humanity is without remainder to be identified with his body.[51] However, I have argued that the issue is complicated in that in Kazantzakis's Christology, divinity is struggling through/with matter, and in his anthropology, a transubstantiating spirit is very much at work. Indeed, the universal appeal of Jesus' struggles and the anthropological import of his message seem to be the causes of Bien's claim that Kazantzakis is not so much interested in Christology but rather in lifting Jesus out of the Church altogether.[52]

Kazantzakis himself puts the point in the following way:

> Christ's every moment is a conflict and a victory. He conquered the invincible enchantment of simple human pleasures; He conquered every temptation, continually transubstantiated flesh into spirit, and ascended. Every obstacle in His journey became an occasion for further triumph, and then a landmark of that triumph. We have a model in front of us now, a model who opens the way for us and gives us strength.[53]

Perhaps we should say that there is no clear boundary between Kazantzakis's Christology and his anthropology. In his view, this interpenetration should make Jesus a figure of universal interest.

No doubt many criticisms could be offered regarding the thesis I defend in this chapter. In that I claim no dogmatic certainty regarding my view, I welcome these criticisms in the common effort to understand and appreciate what Kazantzakis is trying to do in *The Last Temptation of Christ*. As I see things, however, by claiming that Kazantzakis exhibits a contemporary version of Monophysitism, we take a step closer toward both understanding his view and understanding how to respond to those of his critics who do not take his (admittedly, somewhat hetcrodox) Christology seriously.

Before closing, I briefly respond to two criticisms that *are* serious. The first comes from the British philosopher Stephen R. L. Clark, who defends Chalcedonian orthodoxy. At times Clark also defends the dualism on which Chalcedonian orthodoxy depends, although he is a thinker who tolerates a great deal of dissonance in his views, so that he does not pretend to be entirely consistent in his defense of dualism. Clark claims that the Monophysite position is "simple-minded" because he assumes that it, along with other "single-subject theories," is necessarily reductionistic and materialistic. Rather than the three general theoretical options outlined above (dualism, materialism, and panpsychism or dynamic hylomorphism), Clark acknowledges only two. And with these two options, only dualism is acceptable to a theist; if one rejects the dualism that underlies Chalcedonian orthodoxy, then one is left with a purely materialistic Jesus who is divine in no way, he seems to be suggesting.[54]

It is odd that Clark takes this stance, given his own admiration for Aristotle.[55] Kazantzakis, along with Aristotle, is opposed to the idea that matter is lifeless, inert stuff. In Aristotle's language, it is always in-formed. And for Kazantzakis, matter—even single cells, mud, and so on—is the locus for the process of transubstantiation. This divine struggle "breaks out," as it were, throughout the universe, including in human flesh. As I see things, one of the advantages of Kazantzakis's view is that it—rather than Chalcedonian orthodoxy—helps us to understand the traditional divine attribute of omnipresence in addition to helping us understand Jesus' humanity-divinity. There is much that is lost when the third theoretical option provided by panpsychism or dynamic hylomorphism is erased.

The second objection might be that in the Monophysite interpretation I have offered, Jesus' uniqueness is lost; and without such uniqueness the whole point of Christology is also lost. *Some* notion of Jesus' uniqueness is nonnegotiable in Christology. In response to this objection, at the start I emphasize that Jesus' uniqueness might be understood in several ways, with the Chalcedonian view exhibiting only one of the options. Kazantzakis's process view is another, more defensible stance. It must have seemed imposssible from an ancient Hebrew point of view to try to reconcile the divinity and the humanity of Jesus, because the ancient Hebrews recognized God as *totaliter aliter*, totally other. But because Kazantzakis relies as well on the ancient Greeks, the task is not impossible, because the heroes from Greek mythology were half-divine, half-human.

In *The Last Temptation of Christ*, God acts as a (confusing and enigmatic) lure, both for Jesus and for the other characters in the novel. Jesus' uniqueness primarily consists in the acute way in which he experientially "prehends" (Whitehead's term: contrasting with the idea that Jesus intellectually apprehends) the divine lure.[56] Robert Mellert explains the Kazantzakian point:

> Jesus, responding to the promptings of these initial [divine] aims, freely chose to realize that divinity by directing the synthesis of each and every occasion of his life toward the fulfillment of that divine initiative. Every moment of his life was an accep-

tance and a reaffirmation of God's special initiative on his behalf. In religious language, every moment was a moment of grace.[57]

Jesus' uniqueness thus consists not so much in the fact that he alone was arbitrarily lured into a religious life by God (we all receive divine influence), but rather in the intense and cumulatively reinforcing way in which he responded, moment by moment, to such a divine lure.

Jesus' uniqueness, understood in terms of the extraordinary strength of his response to God and his loving relationship with God, differentiates him from most human beings. However, this does not necessarily mean that he is unique when compared with other religious mystics. His moment-by-moment integration of the human and the divine also characterizes several other figures treated favorably in Kazantzakis's writings: Saint Teresa of Avila in *Spain*, Saint Francis of Assisi in the novel devoted to him. Hence, Jesus is indeed unique, but this uniqueness need not require his absolute distinction from all other human beings, as is the case in the Chalcedonian version of Jesus' uniqueness. As Mellert once again ably puts the point:

> Jesus is in fact unique because in his humanity he is a more perfect model of ideal humanity than has ever existed, or, we may believe, will ever exist in the future. . . . He is divine not because of an absolute difference from other men [sic], but because of the realization of divinity within him.[58]

There is no reason to think that talent in any significant activity is distributed among human beings in a strictly egalitarian way: some people jump higher than others, solve math problems better than others, and so on. It is thus also with respect to appropriating divine influence and responding appropriately to the divine lure. But among those who have "talent" in this regard are to be found not only Jesus but also Moses, Mohammad, Dorothy Day, Martin Luther King Jr., Thomas Merton, Saint Gregory of Nyssa.[59]

If there is something really unique about Jesus in the company of these other unique individuals, it seems to lie in the instructive way in which Jesus makes us aware of the fact ("redeems" us, as it were) that divine power lies in an absence of force. It lies in loving persuasion. A recent example is the "power" Mother Teresa exerted over others when she entered a room, a power felt by almost all who met her, and a power that she attributed to "Christ." In light of this sort of power, we might not only call him by the name Jesus but also by the title Christ: the anointed or smeared one, the one marked for slaughter like a lamb. When Jesus speaks with authority in *The Last Temptation of Christ*, as he often does, it is an "authority" based on the eminent sort of response he has made to the persuasive lure of God's loving agency; it is not based on coercive power. Once again, the Roman centurion in the novel grasps this better than the apostles; as a military officer he would certainly recognize coercive power when he saw it, but he did not see it in Jesus.

Unfortunately, throughout the history of the Abrahamic religions, there has been a tendency to think that God (Yahweh, God the Father, Allah) is ultimately something other than, or beyond, responsive love. Kazantzakis's Jesus pulls us back to *this* world, where divinity is to be found not primarily in a hidden divine will that is beyond the world in which we live. Instead, it is found in loving, transubstantiating struggle itself.[60]

Notes

1. Nikos Kazantzakis, *The Last Temptation of Christ*, trans. Peter Bien (New York: Simon & Schuster, 1960). Also see the Greek version, *O teleftaíos pierasmós* (Athens: Difros, 1955). I will use standard Library of Congress transliteration for the ancient Greek; regarding modern Greek, I will use the (phonetic) transliteration scheme developed by *The Journal of Modern Greek Studies*.

2. For the Chalcedonian Definition of the Christian Faith (451 CE), see Alister E. McGrath, ed., *The Christian Theology Reader*, 2nd ed. (Malden, MA: Blackwell, 2001), 269–71.

3. Kazantzakis, *Last Temptation*, 1.

4. Ibid., 2–3.

5. See G. E. H. Palmer et al., trans., *The Philokalia* (London: Faber & Faber, 1979), 1:361. The authors anthologized in *The Philokalia* often defended *both* this rapprochement between human embodiment and the process of *theōsis*, and Chalcedonian orthodoxy regarding Jesus, wherein Jesus' body is externally related to divinity. By way of partial contrast, Kazantzakis sees such rapprochement between embodiment and the process of *theōsis* as a model for both human beings and how we should interpret Jesus.

6. See William Wordsworth, "Lines Composed a Few Miles above Tintern Abbey," lines 92–96, in *Poetical Works* (Oxford: Oxford University Press, 1981).

7. Kazantzakis, *Last Temptation*, 16.

8. See William Wordsworth, "Lines Written in Early Spring," lines 17–20, in *Poetical Works*.

9. See Gerard Manley Hopkins, "God's Grandeur," line 1, in *The Norton Anthology of English Literature*, ed. M. H. Abrams, vol. 2 (New York: W. W. Norton, 1968).

10. Kazantzakis, *Last Temptation*, 57, 59, 118, 142, 150, 157, 224, 226, 432.

11. See Nikos Kazantzakis, *Journeying*, trans. Themi Vasils and Theodora Vasils (San Francisco: Creative Arts, 1984), 92.

12. Kazantzakis, *Last Temptation*, 323.

13. Ibid., 233, 304, 323–24. Also see Marcus Ford, ed., *A Process Theory of Medicine* (Lewiston, NY: E. Mellen, 1987).

14. Kazantzakis, *Last Temptation*, 333.

15. Ibid., 2.

16. Ibid., 71–72. Also see 223, 338, 425.

17. Ibid., 72. Also see 95.

18. Aristotle, *Metaphysics* 12.7–9.

19. Kazantzakis, *Last Temptation*, 80.

20. Ibid., 204.

21. Ibid., 281.

22. Ibid., 82.

23. Ibid., 103, 106.

24. Ibid., 336, 400.

25. Ibid., 430.

26. See Daniel A. Dombrowski, *Kazantzakis and God* (Albany, NY: SUNY Press, 1997).

27. Kazantzakis, *Last Temptation*, 69, 126, 493.

28. See Dombrowski, *Kazantzakis and God*, 55–56. Also see Nikos Kazantzakis, *Spain*, trans. Amy Mims (New York: Simon & Schuster, 1963).

29. Kazantzakis, *Last Temptation*, 259.

30. Ibid., 263.

31. Ibid., 246, 296.

32. Ibid., 346.

33. Ibid., 447.

34. Ibid., 493.

35. See Peter A. Bien, "A Note on the Author and His Use of Language," in Kazantzakis, *Last Temptation*, 504.

36. Kazantzakis, *Last Temptation*, 6, 191.

37. Ibid., 227.

38. Ibid., 222.

39. Ibid., 43, 49.

40. Ibid., 254.

41. Ibid., 347, 380.

42. Ibid., 200–202.

43. Ibid., 298–99.

44. Ibid., 322, 325, 394.

45. Ibid., 348.

46. Ibid., 406, 408.

47. Ibid., 433.

48. Ibid., 478.

49. Ibid., 26. Also see Peter A. Bien, *Kazantzakis: Politics of the Spirit* (Princeton: Princeton University Press, 1989), xix. Finally, see Helen Kazantzakis, *Nikos Kazantzakis: A Biography Based on His Letters*, trans. Amy Mims (New York: Simon & Schuster, 1968), 81–83.

50. Kazantzakis, *Last Temptation*, 42.

51. See Nikos Kazantzakis, *Report to Greco*, trans. Peter Bien (New York: Simon & Schuster, 1965), 290–92.

52. See Bien, "A Note on the Author," 505.

53. Kazantzakis, *Report to Greco*, 291.

54. See Stephen R. L. Clark, *A Parliament of Souls* (Oxford: Clarendon, 1990), 136–54. Clark works at a high level of discourse. For a more basic summary of the Chalcedonian position, see informative articles on the Council of Chalcedon in *The Catholic Encyclopedia* and *The New Catholic Encyclopedia*.

55. See Stephen R. L. Clark, *Aristotle's Man* (Oxford: Clarendon, 1975).

56. See "prehension" in the index of David Ray Griffin, *Reenchantment without Supernaturalism: A Process Philosophy of Religion* (Ithaca, NY: Cornell University Press, 2001).

57. Robert Mellert, *What Is Process Theology?* (New York: Paulist Press, 1975), 81.

58. Ibid., 87–88.

59. See Charles Hartshorne, *Omnipotence and Other Theological Mistakes* (Albany, NY: SUNY Press, 1984), 113–19.

60. See John Cobb and David Ray Griffin, *Process Theology: An Introductory Exposition* (Philadelphia: Westminster, 1976), 95–110.

CHAPTER 5

Reading Kazantzakis through Gregory of Nyssa
Some Common Anthropological Themes
Pamela J. Francis

Introduction

It would have been difficult for Nikos Kazantzakis to have escaped or ignored the Eastern Orthodox aspects of his environment. even as late as 1980, anthropologists observed that in Greece, particularly on the islands, "every stage of the life cycle— birth, marriage, death—was marked by Christian ritual; indeed, the life cycle *was* a Christian cycle."[1] But more exciting to Kazantzakis than the rituals of religion, which tended to be the provenance of women anyway, were the mythic tales of the Bible. In *Report to Greco* he recounts his favorite class in elementary school, Sacred History. He remembers the subject matter as "a strange, intricate and somber fairy tale with serpents who talked, floods and rainbows, thefts and murders."[2] His teacher told his young pupils, "These are God's doings. . . . We're not supposed to understand."[3] Yet he continued to read the legends of the saints, and from them he developed an over-whelming desire for sanctity, second only to his desire for freedom. In *Report to Greco* he observes, "Hero together with saint: such is mankind's supreme model."[4] Indeed, this is the model for all of his protagonists, including the Jesus of *The Last Temptation of Christ*.

The piety of Kazantzakis's fellow Cretans should not be mistaken for theological acumen, however, and one current anthropological study observes of a Greek island community: "It was their *identity* as Christians . . . which was the real object of *pisteuō*—'I believe that I believe.' The rest . . . could safely be left to priests, bishops and theologians: experts whose business it was to be learned in such things."[5] It was fortuitous, then, that Kazantzakis was a high school student in Heraklion under Christos Androutsos. Androutsos was an important Eastern Orthodox theologian, who after his time in Heraklion had advanced to a professorship in systematic theology at the University of Athens and published *Dogmatics of the Eastern Orthodox Church*.

Andreas Poulakidas mentions that Kazantzakis had read this work, and it is most likely that this is where Kazantzakis made his acquaintance with the early Greek theologians known collectively as the Cappadocians.[6] Of these theologians, Gregory of Nyssa (331/40–c. 395) most closely parallels the thought of Kazantzakis, particularly in three ways. The first way is their mutual understanding of the human being as the nexus of spirit and matter. The second parallel is their concept of an upward struggling of humanity and its resultant transubstantiation of matter into spirit. Finally, both thinkers emphasize the essential role that freedom plays in an evolutionary humanity. In both Gregory and Kazantzakis, the historical figure of Jesus, played out in a New Adam typology, is the culmination of this evolutionary process.

In this chapter, I take an anthropological approach to the figure of Jesus rather than a christological approach to the risen Christ. The historical figure of Jesus serves as a symbol of sacred humanity in both Kazantzakis's and Gregory's thought. Several times Kazantzakis wrote on the figure of Jesus. For him, Jesus was not divine in the way that traditional Chalcedonian Christology defines him. Instead, Kazantzakis viewed Jesus as a human who had developed to his highest spiritual capacity, in the same way as several of his characters, particularly Odysseus and Buddha. Similarly, Gregory's work, reflecting a common theme in Eastern Orthodoxy, stressed a spirituality focused more on finding God than Christ. As Anthony Meredith observes, "The sacred humanity, even in authors who defended the divinity of the Saviour, was treated more as a gateway to God than as an end in himself."[7] The Christ figure for Gregory was not an end in itself; rather, Jesus' life served as an example of the virtuous life, an important theme for Gregory. This same idea of Jesus as sacred humanity is evident in Kazantzakis's *The Last Temptation of Christ*; here Jesus serves as an example of one who has fully transubstantiated matter into spirit.

Kazantzakis's life parallels Gregory's in ways that suggest a common interaction between the men and their environments. For instance, each man was political yet somewhat ineffectual in that arena. Gregory of Nyssa was removed from his bishopric at one time and also seems to have been "far from universally popular."[8] Despite Kazantzakis's nomination for the Nobel by non-Greek writers who supported his cause, and holding a position in the Greek government after World War I, he was generally viewed with suspicion at home. A Greek newspaper headline summed up much of the attitude of fellow Greeks: "A Long Discussion of the Anti-Christian Works of the Leftist Writer Kazantzakis."[9]

Likewise, Gregory and Kazantzakis both struggled with the flesh. Unlike his fellow Cappadocians and many other churchmen of his time, Gregory seems never to have been a monastic. He is believed to have been married. Kazantzakis, married twice, often lived apart from his wives and spent a great deal of time alone and in an ascetic existence.

Finally, both men were strongly influenced by the pagan humanistic tradition. Gregory sought to incorporate the pagan philosophical tradition within Christian theology. Kazantzakis sought to remind the modern world of the validity of such humanism within a world in which even religion, once the successor of pagan philosophy, had been superseded by science. In sum, it can be said of them both, as Gerhart Ladner remarks of the Cappadocian Fathers, "Philosophy to them is only a way of approach toward union with God, though in an indispensable and exalted way."[10]

This interest in union with God informs the anthropological conceptions common to both thinkers. These three areas are (1) the nature of humanity, particularly as it pertains to the merging of spirit and matter in a person; (2) the idea of humanity moving toward God, an idea that can be explained through the concept of *epektasis* (extension) in Gregory and "the saving of God" in Kazantzakis; and (3) the absolute necessity of human freedom, incalculably important for both thinkers. These ideas are realized in the person of Jesus, one of Kazantzakis's heroes who has fully transubstantiated his flesh into spirit.

Spirit, Matter, and Humanity

In both Gregory and Kazantzakis, the human being is constituted of matter and spirit. Matter, in its mutability, is downward pushing, while spirit pushes upward toward God. Specifically, Gregory refers to the part of the human that is immaterial as the image of God in humanity. The image of God in humanity, as described in *On the Creation of Man*, is humanity in its fullness, with the divine character in the soul. Gregory describes this condition as *makariotes*, beatitude.[11] It is humanity as created in what Jean Daniélou calls "God's concrete plan."[12]

But the *idea* of humanity in its fullness is far from who we are. The difference is what Gregory, via Genesis, calls the "garment of skin."[13] This garment of skin refers not only to the flesh, the corporeal body, but also to the actions we have in common with the animals, such as sexual procreation. Kazantzakis likewise emphasizes the "dual substance" of humanity in general and Jesus in particular.[14] "The struggle between God and man breaks out in everyone," he writes, "together with the longing for reconciliation." Flesh resists transubstantiation into spirit or, as he puts it in the prologue to *The Last Temptation of Christ*, "union with God." Indeed, the stronger the flesh, "the more fruitful the struggle and the richer the final harmony."[15] *The Last Temptation of Christ* provides us with several figures in various stages of the transubstantiation of matter into spirit. But it is the figure of Jesus, through his painful struggle with God, who has fully transformed his material nature into that of spirit.

We must be careful, however, to avoid a Manichaean understanding of matter. In both Gregory and Kazantzakis, matter is absolutely necessary to the evolutionary process of transubstantiation. For instance, in Gregory, the garment of skin is not only a consequence of sin but also a sort of "medicine" for sin. As Daniélou explains, the fall was humanity's turning away from the spiritual life to a life of carnality; however, if God forces humanity toward the good, human beings have lost their freedom. Therefore, the garment of skin allows humanity to experience disgust with carnality and move instead toward "his former blessedness."[16] Furthermore, as the garment of skin is also our mortality, its dissolution destroys that evil that may not be inherent in the flesh but is so often bound up in the flesh.

We see the same wary but positive understanding of flesh in Kazantzakis as well. Thus Darren Middleton and Peter Bien remind us that "Kazantzakis's system urges us to use the flesh in order to refine it."[17] In *The Last Temptation of Christ*, women most frequently symbolize this downward pushing materiality, and in most cases they do not attempt to struggle against it. For instance, Jesus' mother complains to her rabbi brother-in-law that she doesn't want a prophet for a son: she wants a son like other women's sons, a son who will marry and have children.[18] And when Jesus leaves his mother's home for the monastery, an old woman gives him bread and olives to sustain his body but berates him when she learns where he is heading, exclaiming that God is not found in monasteries but in family life. She scolds him, "Wherever you find husband and wife, that's where you find God. . . . The domestic one, not the monastic: that's the true God."[19] Finally, in the opening of the temptation scene, Jesus and Mary Magdalene make love; afterward, Jesus tells her that he now knows that the flesh is holy as well as the soul and is a sister of the soul. He tells her that he never knew that the joys of the body were not sinful.[20] Domesticity, procreation—the giving in to downward pushing materiality—is not essentially evil here, but it does mark a failure to heed the evolutionary nature of the divine Cry, which impels the transubstantiation of matter into spirit.

Theōsis

Kazantzakis's thought most closely parallels Gregory's in the nature and method of this transubstantiation from flesh into spirit. For both, the object is *theōsis*, deification. In Gregory's anthropology, *theōsis* is the realization of the image of God within us. In Kazantzakis's Bergsonian understanding of the transubstantiation of matter into spirit, we "save" God. This emphasis on deification, evident in both writers, is in keeping with the Eastern monastic tradition, as recognized by Daniel Dombrowski, in which deification "does not suppress humanity but makes it more authentically human."[21] Kazantzakis and Gregory are both thoroughly Orthodox in their understanding of *theōsis*.

Gregory's understanding of *theōsis* is best explained by his doctrine of perpetual progress, or *epektasis*. Translated as "stretching forth," the term is taken from its New Testament usage in Phil 3:13–14: "Straining forward to what lies ahead, I press on toward the goal for the prize of the heavenly call of God in Christ Jesus." *Epektasis* is humanity's move toward the goodness or virtues of God. But in this sense virtue is not an end in itself but a *dynamis*, or movement toward the good, in which we manifest the image of God that we bear within us. As Orthodox scholar Vladimir Lossky points out, "There is for the Christian no such thing as an autonomous good: a work is good in so far as it furthers our union with God."[22] Furthermore, in the soul's ascent toward God, in its participation (*metousia*) with the divine energies, it is continually propelled upward, as God is continually beyond reach. Thus Gregory writes of Abraham, "As he disposed all these things in his heart, he kept constantly transcending what he had grasped by his own power, for this was far inferior to what he sought."[23] Abraham will continue to stretch forth, thereby continuing the process of deification, in essence transubstantiating his own flesh into spirit.

In this move toward perfection, in which participation in God and assimilation to God are one process, the human soul serves as the vital link, the *syndesmos*, between matter and spirit. It is through this conduit that the spirit is propelled forward, increasing in virtue as it advances. In one of Gregory's most well-known passages, he describes this movement as not a mark of deficiency, as the Neoplatonists had viewed humanity's mutability, but rather as a benefit:

> Let us change in such a way that we may constantly evolve toward what is better, being transformed from glory to glory, and thus always improving and ever becoming more perfect by daily growth, and never arriving at any limit of perfection.[24]

However, understanding the "capacity to create oneself" as the divine image within humanity, as Gregory scholar Paulos Gregorios puts it, has often been misunderstood as an undue emphasis on humanism rather than theism. Furthermore, Gregorios states, "Christian theology has been generally reluctant to accept this idea of Gregory's—that Man is not simply a creature pure and simple, but a co-creator of himself and the world."[25] It only remains to observe that certain representatives of institutional Christianity have made the same accusations against Kazantzakis.

In Kazantzakis, *theōsis* takes the form of a struggle, in which substance is transformed into spirit; and indeed, *metousiōsis*, transubstantiation, is our "highest obligation."[26] *The Last Temptation of Christ* demonstrates *metousia* through Christian imagery, specifically the imagery of Eucharistic communion. Transubstantiation is literal in some instances, most notably in the Last Supper scene:

> Each of the disciples ate his mouthful of bread and drank his sip of wine. Their minds reeled. The wine seemed to them thick and salty, like blood; the portion of bread descended like a burning coal into their very bowels. Suddenly, terrified, they all felt Jesus take root within them and begin to devour their entrails.[27]

Later, when Jesus breaks bread with the followers, we read that Andrew's portion was immediately transubstantiated into love and laughter.[28] And in yet another scene, we hear Jesus tell Nathanael that Nathanael need only eat a mouthful of bread and drink a cup of wine to become truly his.[29] Consuming the bread and wine, Nathanael felt it sending strength to his bones and soul, all becoming one in an act of transubstantiation.

In the figure of Jesus himself, the transubstantiation imagery is taken to its evolutionary zenith. He tells the old rabbi Simeon that as a child he shouted to himself, "God, make me God! God, make me God! God, make me God!" words that are later repeated to him and promised fulfillment by the archangel Lucifer.[30] *Metousiōsis*, the transubstantiation from matter to spirit, is not an action upon a subject; it necessarily requires participation by the subject. This *metousia*, participation, in Kazantzakis's works, is the struggle with God, which in turn is both God's essence and humanity's purpose.

Kazantzakis's Jesus thus becomes one of several "mythic depictions of heroes who cooperate with the cosmological process of evolution that, via a materiality that is unmade, progresses toward motion, freedom, and spirit."[31] The structure of *The Last Temptation of Christ* is built around the struggle within Jesus, but the motif is applied to all within the novel. For instance, in the opening pages of the novel, we read of a collective wail from the highest point in the village. Yet it is not a human scream but rather "the whole village dreaming and shouting together, the whole soil of Israel with the bones of its dead and the roots of its trees, the soil of Israel in labor, unable to give birth, and screaming."[32] The struggle comes full circle when, at the end of the last temptation scene, Jesus cries, "IT IS ACCOMPLISHED!" But with the next line, "Everything has begun," we see that Jesus has transformed his garment of skin into pure spirit: he has become God. The struggle, that of all humanity, here represented by the sleeping village, has served as the crucible in which Jesus' flesh has become spirit.

So in both Gregory and Kazantzakis, we see that one must "stretch forward," to use Gregory's terminology, or struggle, as Kazantzakis would have it, for by these methods humans participate in God. The final outcome of both exercises differs significantly, and it is here that Kazantzakis's humanism overtakes the Christian Orthodox notion of becoming. In Gregory, humanity must keep stretching forward, never reaching God's perfection, since that is what separates humanity from God. In Kazantzakis, however, transubstantiation *makes* God, a clear gloss on his insistence against the omnipotence of God.

In both writers, the struggle is evolutionary in that transubstantiation is made in increments and not as a result of one moment of grace. In Gregory's view, the human being contains within itself all previous evolutionary stages of life. In *De hominis opificio*, Gregory relates the three stages of living creatures: vegetative, providing the faculty of growth; animal, providing sense perception; and finally, human, providing the intellectual aspect of humanity. The fully developed human, then, contains all of the previous evolutionary stages.[33] Kazantzakis likewise found an evolutionary view of humanity's progress to be a necessary component of *metousia*, not as a matter of ontology, but in consideration of contemporary science. After telling us in *The Last Temptation of Christ*, "Great things happen when man mixes with God," his narrator further explains how God and humanity are dependent on each other for mutual fulfillment and how deeply he believes that man and God could thus become one.[34]

In sum, in both Gregory and Kazantzakis, we see the impetus to move forward by way of struggle. In this participation or *metousia* between matter and spirit, we see humanity become ever more godlike. In its turn, the God/spirit that increases within also evolves. In the scene in which Kazantzakis's Jesus relates the parable of the rich man and Lazarus, God evolves from only just to just and *good*. Upon the poor man

Lazarus's request, the rich man is brought up from the fires of hell to participate in God's refreshing waters. Kazantzakis's Jesus changes the ending of the parable in order to reflect his belief in the simultaneous coevolution of God and humanity.[35]

The Necessity of Freedom

In Gregory and Kazantzakis, as we have seen, the human is composed of matter and spirit. I have demonstrated the similarity in the two men's understanding of *epektasis*, or stretching forth toward the spirit. Hence, it is inevitable to wonder what exactly propels—or impels—the soul forward. Here both writers are paradoxically at their most humanist, as well as their most Orthodox. In the anthropologies of Gregory and Kazantzakis, the freedom of choice provides the impetus for transubstantiation.

In Gregory, free will is both the image of God within humanity as well as what moves us forward to participate in the good.[36] But contrary to the more Western views of Clement and Augustine, which leave the onus of "becoming" up to God's grace, Gregory insists on human initiative through the action of *synergeia*, "the cooperation of two unequal, but equally necessary forces: divine grace and human will."[37] It is important that we not underestimate the emphasis Gregory placed on human freedom: in Gregory's view, humanity's mutability and freedom are synonymous, and this same mutability provides us the opportunity to change for the better.[38] This decision, this turning of the will, is described by Gregory as *aretē*, virtue in the sense of a striving toward the good. Conversely, when the part of us that is animal gives in to *philēdonia*, love of pleasure, we take on a "likeness to the irrational brutes."[39] This "irrational animal" nature is exacerbated by human reason, so that all passions, such as anger, are even more malevolent.

Similarly, in Kazantzakis, moral goodness is the end result of our "making" of God, which in turn is absolutely dependent on freedom of the will. James Lea observes: "In Kazantzakis' system this prerequisite act [freedom of choice], from which all else follows, is cast as the freely chosen commitment to save God. Zorba chooses to dance and affirm life. . . . El Greco chose to paint penetrating and beautiful portraits of the spirit."[40] Ultimately, in *The Last Temptation of Christ*, Jesus also chooses to save God, doing so by choosing his death on the cross over the life of the flesh, as offered by the tempter, his "guardian angel." The choice comes at the moment in the temptation scene when Judas shames Jesus with his own words by recalling an earlier lesson: "Life on earth means: to eat bread and transform the bread into wings, to drink water and to transform the water into wings. Life on earth means: the sprouting of wings. That's what you told us—you traitor."[41] But here, living with Martha and Mary, Jesus has instead succumbed to his garment of skin; now he asserts that life instead means the shedding of one's wings.[42] He begs forgiveness of those he has betrayed and awakes from his dream to find he has been crucified after all. Kazantzakis closes the text with the parallel statements, "IT IS ACCOMPLISHED!"

and "Everything has begun."[43] Jesus has now become one of Kazantzakis's saviors of God because he has freely chosen to struggle, to consciously transubstantiate matter into spirit.

Although students of Kazantzakis will recognize Jesus as only one of several of the author's heroes—those who have transubstantiated matter into spirit—they must also recognize that for Kazantzakis, the figure of Jesus represents the quintessential anthropological model. Morton Levitt states, "Jesus is most like man in his duality, in the tensions which develop between his body and soul."[44] And in *Report to Greco*, Kazantzakis echoes the prologue to *The Last Temptation of Christ* when he declares, "Every man is half God, half man. . . . That is why the mystery of Christ is not simply a mystery for a particular creed; it is universal."[45] By emphasizing the universality of Jesus, Kazantzakis necessarily omits reference to any preexistent state of divinity. Accordingly, Levitt emphasizes: "In this milieu Jesus of Nazareth is unmistakably a man and only potentially a god; his divinity, in fact, may be no greater than all men are capable of attaining."[46] Although I have traced strains of Kazantzakis's anthropology in the thought of Gregory of Nyssa, Kazantzakis's Christology clearly parts ways with Eastern Orthodoxy.

Yet both Gregory and Kazantzakis emphasize the essential humanity of Jesus by their use of the New Adam typology. Particularly, Gregory believed that humanity is "God's presence consciously immanent, in creation."[47] In the first Adam, this presence—what Gregory referred to as the image of God—was imperfect, a weakened link. Jesus, as the New Adam, retains a more perfect image, which "is so inseparably united to [the] body, mind and soul of humanity that there emerges a new humanity."[48] In Gregory's anthropology, this renewal is God's plan for humanity all along.

In Kazantzakis's mythopoesis, there are a number of these Adams, because with each of his heroes or saviors of God, humanity has transubstantiated matter into spirit. In *The Last Temptation of Christ*, Jesus as a new Adam takes on additional significance. He is both a reworking of the Christian myth and a paean to creative humanism. While dreaming one night, Jesus finds himself as Adam, newly created. In a parade of birds, emphasizing again that life means "the sprouting of wings," a long-nosed blackbird warns Adam that the doors of heaven and hell are alike, and both are attractive, so he must take care in his choosing.[49] Here Jesus is Adam, continually presented with a choice. The first Adam chose his garment of skin, succumbing to matter's downward pull. In Kazantzakis's Jesus, humanity has another chance to choose, and by choosing, to transubstantiate material into spirit.

Conclusion

This investigation into the similar anthropologies of Gregory of Nyssa and Nikos Kazantzakis is introductory. Many of the areas touched upon in this chapter deserve closer scrutiny. In particular, Gregory's notion of *epektasis* and the related function of *metousia* are relevant to Kazantzakis's work, especially in light of recent work on the connections between Kazantzakis and process theology. If, as Lewis Richards claims, the three influences on Kazantzakis's thinking were Nietzsche, Bergson, and his Orthodox upbringing, we must acknowledge that the imprint of his religion has been given far less attention than the role that modern philosophers have played in Kazantzakis's thought.[50] If we ignore or slight the importance of Kazantzakis's discourse with Orthodox religious tradition, we overlook his deeply felt connection to Greece's past and his sense of being an inheritor to something holy. While Nietzsche and Bergson provided modern and humanist understandings of this sense of upward-pushing spirit, the Eastern Orthodox tradition provided a sense of mystery to the élan vital, which transubstantiates all matter—including the human being—into spirit.

Notes

1. Roger Just, "Anti-Clericism and National Identity: Attitudes toward the Orthodox Church in Greece," in *Vernacular Christianity: Essays in the Social Anthropology of Religion Presented to Godfrey Lienhardt*, ed. Wendy James and Douglas H. Johnson (New York: Lilia Barber, 1988), 17.

2. Nikos Kazantzakis, *Report to Greco*, trans. Peter Bien (New York: Simon & Schuster, 1965), 55.

3. Ibid., 55.

4. Ibid., 71.

5. Roger Just, "Anti-Clericism and National Identity," 19.

6. Andreas K. Poulakidas, "Kazantzakis and Bergson: Metaphysic Aestheticians," *Journal of Modern Literature* 2 (1971): 276.

7. Anthony Meredith, S.J., *Gregory of Nyssa*, ed. Carol Harrison, Early Church Fathers (London: Routledge, 1999; reprint, 2002), 26.

8. Hans von Campenhausen, *The Fathers of the Greek Church*, trans. Stanley Godman (New York: Pantheon Books, 1955), 111.

9. Quoted in Michael Antonakes, "Christ, Kazantzakis, and Controversy in Greece," in *God's Struggler: Religion in the Writings of Nikos Kazantzakis*, ed. Darren J. N. Middleton and Peter Bien (Macon, GA: Mercer University Press, 1996), 29.

10. Gerhart B. Ladner, "The Philosophical Anthropology of Saint Gregory of Nyssa," *Dumbarton Oaks Papers* 12 (1958): 62.

11. Jean Daniélou, *From Glory to Glory: Texts from Gregory of Nyssa's Mystical Writings*, trans. Herbert Musurillo (Crestwood, NY: St. Vladimir's Seminary Press, 2001), 11.

12. Ibid.

13. Ibid.

14. Nikos Kazantzakis, *The Last Temptation of Christ*, trans. Peter Bien (New York: Simon & Schuster, 1960), 1–4.

15. Ibid., 2.

16. Jean Daniélou, *From Glory to Glory*, 13.

17. Darren J. N. Middleton and Peter Bien, "Spiritual Levendiá: Kazantazakis's Theology of Struggle," in *God's Struggler*, ed. Middleton and Bien, 9.

18. Kazantzakis, *Last Temptation*, 64.

19. Ibid., 72.

20. Ibid., 450.

21. Daniel A. Dombrowski, *Kazantzakis and God* (Albany, NY: SUNY Press, 1997), 92.

22. Vladimir Lossky, *The Mystical Theology of the Eastern Church* (Crestwood, NY: St. Vladimir's Seminary Press, 1998), 197.

23. Quoted in Daniélou, *From Glory to Glory*, 77.

24. Ibid., 52.

25. Paulos Mar Gregorios, *Cosmic Man: The Divine Presence: The Theology of St. Gregory of Nyssa (ca. 330– 395 A.D.)* (New York: Paragon House, 1988), 154.

26. Dombrowski, *Kazantzakis and God*, 28.

27. Kazantzakis, *Last Temptation*, 424.

28. Ibid., 197.

29. Ibid., 338.

30. Ibid., 145, 263.

31. Middleton and Bien, "Spiritual Levendiá," 11.

32. Kazantzakis, *Last Temptation*, 6.

33. See Ladner, "Philosophical Anthropology," 70.

34. Kazantzakis, *Last Temptation*, 281.

35. Ibid., 202.

36. John Behr, "The Rational Animal: A Rereading of Gregory of Nyssa's *De hominis opificio*," *Journal of Early Christian Studies* 7 (1999): 236.

37. Timothy Ware, *The Orthodox Church* (London: Penguin Books, 1997), 222.

38. Everett Ferguson, "God's Infinity and Man's Mutability: Perpetual Progress according to Gregory of Nyssa," *Greek Orthodox Theological Review* 18 (1973): 69.

39. See Gregorios, *Cosmic Man*, 153.

40. James Lea, *Kazantzakis: The Politics of Salvation* (Tuscaloosa, AL: University of Alabama Press, 1979), 126.

41. Kazantzakis, *Last Temptation*, 493.

42. Ibid., 493.

43. Ibid., 496.

44. Morton Levitt, "The Modernist Kazantzakis and *The Last Temptation of Christ*," *Mosaic: A Journal for the Comparative Study of Literature* 6, no. 2 (1973): 117.

45. Kazantzakis, *Last Temptation*, 290.

46. Levitt, "Modernist Kazantzakis," 105.

47. Gregorios, *Cosmic Man*, 149.

48. Kazantzakis, *Last Temptation*, 232.

49. Ibid., 280.

50. Lewis Richards, "Christianity in the Novels of Kazantzakis," *The Western Humanities Review* 21 (1967): 49–55.

CHAPTER 6

The Unreality of Repressed Desires in *The Last Temptation*

Vrasidas Karalis

Introduction

Nikos Kazantzakis's novel *The Last Temptation* is a paradoxical book that has remained, since first publication, in the gray area between religion and literature without really determining whether it belongs to either of them. Further, it seems to provoke unilateral criticism from the religious side, while the literary merits or demerits of the book pass unnoticed. According to Gore Vidal, it is a "marvellously dead landscape of a book in which not even a weed could grow."[1] Yet to Anthony Bridges the novel is "alive with dialectical power; every page shouts with argument and mental struggle. . . . It glows with the author's personality."[2]

The thesis of this chapter is that we cannot understand Kazantzakis's book in its religious significance if we don't see it first as a narrativized elaboration of a major christological statement—a hybrid form of an anthropological investigation in Christology employing both imagination and history. With Kazantzakis's novel, modern literature seems to be readdressing the foundational question of the Christian world in a manner not known before and in a style that consciously emulates the narrative practices of the canonical Gospels, especially Matthew.

Kazantzakis's Jesus is a daring translation of the originary *mythos* of the Christian mentality from the verbal, conceptual, abstract mode of thinking to the pictorial, visual, iconic mode of representation. Such translation has never been made before as successfully as in this case; and this despite the fact that after the Enlightenment there were similar attempts to textualize Jesus' life through the devices dominant in various eras, starting with David Friedrich Strauss (1835) and Ernest Renan (1863). Kazantzakis's book is the most effective and the densest depiction of the mystery of Jesus' self-perception, in a manner that has to be appreciated as both innovative in form and groundbreaking in its implications.

Whereas previous narrativizations debunked, sentimentalized, or idealized Jesus, throughout its story line Kazantzakis's book maintains a strong aura of *numinosity*, of a transfiguring unknowability around its central character. It does this by depicting his development as a gradual advancement in self-exploration, the unfolding of a realm of subjective potentialities, as unknown to the character as to the readers of the book. The Jesus character learns who he is simultaneously with the reader; his numinosity lies in the sense of unknowability remaining elusive within him, giving at the same time a mysterious presentiment for the emergence of a dimension of being not framed in the narrative itself. Jesus' messianic mission remains a mystery to his humanity. As he is struggling with such mystery within, he becomes aware of his divinity as the ultimate outcome of his wrestling with his human condition.

Herein abides the controversy around the book, and later about the movie by Martin Scorsese (1988): Kazantzakis's Jesus deals with some crucial questions of Western tradition in a way that gave them new life and revived their cultural validation. Kazantzakis reinvented the mythopoeic relevance of the evangelical figure and made it again pertinent to the sociocultural dilemmas of the Western world after the tragic experience of World War II, the Holocaust, and the semantic nihilism that emerged when cultural relativism became a dominant condition of postwar self-definition.

Jesus' Liminality

The central argument of the novel may be found in the condition of interstitiality in which Kazantzakis suspends his character. His Jesus is in a perpetual state of redefinition, of an inner unfolding of his psychic potential; this is reminiscent of Kazantzakis's other hero, Odysseus. Kazantzakis rejects the idea of a core self and its existential coherence. On the contrary, Jesus' self gradually emerges out of his lived time with others, and it is about this sense of shared temporality that his disciples reclaim him from himself during the depiction of his "last temptation." Kazantzakis's Jesus is seen without the Christology accumulated by successive generations of community worship in the historical tradition of Christianity. This Jesus is the individual character in the making, in his attempt to understand himself and transform his name into the symbolic epitome of his community. Jesus' searching for his Christic transformation is the anthropological and psychological ground on which the novel is founded.

Such liminal character(ization) can be constructed only as long as the writer himself maintains its main formal depiction in a position of indeterminacy; the depicted self readjusts itself constantly as it gains awareness of its new positionality. Kazantzakis suspends the book between religion and literature and thus creates a kind of lack of allegiance to any generic conformity. Is his Jesus simply a literary invention, the product of individual creative mythology, the symbolic representation of a preconceived philosophy, or the elaboration of Christianity's main symbol in a somehow pre-evangelical manner?

For the author, Jesus is the focal point of a "strong" dramatic narrative, which arranges and configures patterns of symbolic identification and empathic union for its readers. This explains the controversy about the book and the rather emotional interpretation made by both its detractors and supporters. The book itself posits the extremely difficult question of how we formulate christological statements today: Is Christology feasible after two centuries of searching for the historical Jesus or, indeed, after nineteen centuries of implied Monophysitic and docetic spiritualization of Christ? Kazantzakis deals with the confused and confusing question of the incarnation in a provocative way that puzzles not simply the official representatives of Christianity but also the ordinary person's understanding of Jesus' human personality. Within the mystery of incarnation, Kazantzakis struggles with the issue of Jesus' self-consciousness in a rather challenging and somehow anti-Chalcedonian manner. Similar theological questions were articulated already for Roman Catholicism since Fr. Paul Galtier's 1939 book *The Unity of Christ*, followed after the war by Mgr. Pietro Parente's *L'Io di Christo* (1951) and Fr. Bartholomew M. Xiberta's *El Yo de Jesucristo* (1954).[3] These books, from within the official hierarchy of the Church, might account for the pope's inclusion of Kazantzakis's book in the Index.

However, Kazantzakis was Eastern Orthodox, and within his tradition Jesus' figure has retained a kind of existential fluidity, with the elusive quality of his humanity blurred by the Constantinian triumphalism that still dominates its artistic and theological expression. There are no important christological statements from the East after the Chalcedonian Creed was finalized (unless they were deemed heretical) except in the attempt to depict Jesus as Christ Pantokrator in the Byzantine churches. However, Christ's melancholic depiction in *Hagia Sophia* in Constantinople or in the Andrei Rubliev icons manifests an element of humanity in utter contrition, of a humanity transformed through the experience of suffering, death, and resurrection. Kazantzakis's depiction of Jesus is the most effective contemporary supplement to the actual narrative textualization of Christ's life as found in the Gospels. It is also relevant to the anthropology of today's society—unlike the almost sadomasochistic representation of Jesus' dead body by Western painting after the Renaissance, culminating in the rather anti-Christian depiction of the Christ in Mel Gibson's Monophysitic film *The Passion of the Christ* (2004).

Kazantzakis, the Gospels, and Christian Theology

Kazantzakis's study of the Gospels, or theories about the Gospels, was rather thorough, if we judge from the evidence incorporated in the novel. The manner of compiling all these narratives into the master script of a highly selective biographical synthesis is probably another element that brings Kazantzakis's novelistic strategies close to those of the earliest Gospels. It is particularly like Matthew, in which the combination of earlier sources with Midrash elaborations and Jewish traditions creates a collective imaginative space for the *ekklēsia*. However, we must not make the critical error of trying to reconcile Kazantzakis's Jesus with the image constructed through centuries of creative conceptualization by diverse Christian communities of the accepted narrative Gospels.

Kazantzakis's Jesus is preeminently non-Christianized—indeed, pre-Christian. And he is a Jewish hero. Writing to one of his friends during *The Last Temptation*'s composition, Kazantzakis claims, "For a year now I've been taking out of the library of Cannes all the books written about Christ and Judea, the Chronicles of that time, the Talmud, etc. And so all the details are historically correct, even though I recognize the right of the poet not to follow history in a slavish way."[4] It is obvious that Kazantzakis's sources are more Jewish than Christian since he utilizes references to Jesus found in the Jewish tradition. He may also have used Jewish scholar Joseph Klausner's popular book *Jesus of Nazareth: His Life, Times and Teaching* (1925), which effectively depicts the differentiation of Jesus from his cultural background.

Kazantzakis is close to the various attempts of liberal and postliberal theology to free Jesus from metaphysics and mythology, from the Johannine preexisting Logos, the Pauline Cosmic Christ, and redeeming Savior of early Christian communities. Kazantzakis struggles to reconstruct the reality of a specific individual in all its particularity and psychological specificity. In essence, he is trying to depict not the Jesus of a worshiping community but the I-perception of Jesus as a self-constituting subject. Thus he brings Jesus closer to the Suffering Servant of God of the Hebrew Bible and its continuation in certain Essene beliefs.[5] Through suffering, through the intense experiencing of his humanity, divinity overtakes the individual; and in accordance with the logic of successive ecumenical synods, his divinity overtakes his humanity after his death, resurrection, and assumption. In Kazantzakis's book the historical Jesus remains a riddle and a cipher since his divinity cannot be understood or expressed by his humanity: it remains preconscious and therefore preverbal. Such existential inconsumerability of the character adds the element of numinosity that underpins Kazantzakis's anthropology.

This does not mean that Kazantzakis simply tries to psychologize a religious symbol and thus create a Christianized version of Hamlet. Kazantzakis's Jesus is an epic figure, closer to an Achilles of the post-Enlightenment period. Corroboration for this claim can be found in Albert Schweitzer's *The Mystery of the Kingdom of God* (1914). At the end of his exploration, Schweitzer states that the aim of his book is "to depict the figure of Jesus in its overwhelming *heroic greatness* and to impress it upon the modern age and upon modern theology." Schweitzer claims that through sentimentalization by Renan or modernization by contemporary philosophers, "the heroic element in Jesus was lost and if we want to revive the heroic in our Christianity and in our *Weltanschauung*, then we have to go back to the actual historical individual and know how he created a moral world which bears his name."[6]

This does not mean that Kazantzakis wants to depict Christ as a "folk hero" of the Jewish people, a kind of narrative monomyth encapsulating family dynamics and social conditioning within a rural economy and a primitive economization of the libido.[7] His Jesus is not the male in crisis, as was seen in the 1960s and is evident in Robert Elwood's interpretation: "Fired by its author's rich and profoundly Greek imagination, unorthodox yet enigmatically reverent, *The Last Temptation* portrays Jesus' self-doubts, his hellish apparitions and his erotic dreams of Mary Magdalene, his sightings of angels 'with red and blue wings,' and the agony on the cross by which he finally set it all to rest."[8] Nor can we identify this Jesus completely with the author, as Charlotte Allen has suggested.[9]

Flesh and Spirit

We must notice, though, the presentation of self-doubts that punctuates the dramatic economy and the theological argument of the book. What actually shocks is the extreme uncertainty within the character, the kind of existential vacuum, which makes Jesus vulnerable, fragile, almost an insecure adolescent who cannot find his way in life, and therefore creates an ideal persona, a second self, moving erratically within the realm of an unintegrated selfhood. The shadow of an absent father is also crucial for the understanding of such confusion in the character. And finally, the presence of a remote and even hostile mother is clearly indicative of a crisis in Jesus, of a constant conflict with his own origins. Kazantzakis's Jesus chooses the path of self-invention and personal mythmaking, constructing a dramaturgical narrative of his own that gives him a sense of belonging and orientation. The book portrays the fulfillment of his own narrative mythos: once completed, it becomes a collective network for self-invention and identification.

These elements are interconnected in Kazantzakis's character. The ellipsis within the character emphasizes the two-layered structure that we see throughout the work. The character is progressively defining himself as the plot defines its own making. At the end they both converge in the posthumous life of the individual outside the confines of his own biography. Jesus becomes Christ; and so the new double identity of being both at the same time emerges, although within the time of his life, those were in opposition and beyond each other's horizon of meaning. Such double structure is an important aspect of Kazantzakis's metaphysics.

In the novel's prologue we read about the dual substance of Christ, which is expressed as both an attempt to return to God and yet at the same time "the struggle between God and man."[10] There is some implied confusion here, observed in most of Kazantzakis's presumed dualistic, almost Manichaean, mythological universes. William E. Phipps has condemned the book in the strongest of terms. "Kazantzakis ably articulates the most gnawing heresy in the Christian tradition," he says, "the Platonic-Docetic-Gnostic-Manichaean syndrome that the sensual is evil and that decontamination is effected by pommeling the pleasure drive to death."[11]

However, the metaphor employed by Kazantzakis of a reconciliation between God and man is not commensurate with the idea of a battle between flesh and spirit. In the latter there is a rather rationalistic perception of a conflict of faculties, but in reality there was always a complementarity between them. What Kazantzakis stresses is the indivisible unity of both flesh and spirit in an attempt to disavow the highly spiritualized and disembodied image of Jesus projected by established churches, without at the same time discarding the material dimension of representing his corporeality. W. B. Yeats quotes a strange theosophical poem by the poet and editor Edwin Ellis, who "imagined himself in a fine poem as meeting at Golgotha the phantom of 'Christ the Less,' the Christ who might have lived a prosperous life without the knowledge of sin, and who now wanders 'companionless, a weary spectre day and night.'" Further:

> I saw him go and cried to him,
> "Eli, thou hast forsaken me,"
> The nails were burning through each limb,
> he fled to find felicity.[12]

Undoubtedly, the mystical element of a "double Christ," expressed theologically in the work of the fourteenth-century Byzantine mystic Nicolas Kavasilas, can be seen as the foundational subtext in the synthesis of the character and the structure of the novel. The Gnostic undertones about a historical and a cosmic Christ, also found in the Epistles of Paul, give to Kazantzakis's novel an extremely interesting background for the convergence of both into the integrated self-conscious and multidimensional personality of the specific individual.

In this respect Kazantzakis's Jesus is in the same line of philosophical heroes described by Hegel in his belief about self-consciousness being the central event of the incarnation:

> This incarnation of the Divine Being, or the fact that it essentially and directly has the shape of self-consciousness, is the simple content of the absolute religion. In this religion the divine Being is known as Spirit, or this religion is the consciousness of the Divine Being that is its Spirit. For Spirit is the knowledge of oneself in the externalisation of oneself; the being that is the movement of retaining its self-identity in its otherness.[13]

Kazantzakis's hero gains self-consciousness, thus completing his mission, after he experiences otherness within his own self-identity. So what seemed a dualistic dichotomy now becomes existential unity and integration. "The incessant merciless battle between the spirit and the flesh" is harmonized and therefore annulled after the self-conscious individual gains awareness of an inexplicable self within himself.[14] Essentially, the unifying principle of the novel comes at the end, when Jesus passes over to the new reality of his existence, transformed into the level of symbolic immortality. Kazantzakis depicts a hero who discovers who he is and together with his readers becomes self-reflective; now his biography establishes its own meaning. This coevolution of reader and character—I think the character knows only as much about himself as the reader—is obviously one of the most appealing strategies employed by Kazantzakis in order to frame the experience of self-actualization and self-realization that emerges with the final words on the cross.

The theological significance of the last sentence is extremely important, since it resembles Dante's celebrated expression "Incipit vita nuova" (Here begins a new life) as the beginning of the scriptural transformation of memory. Historically similar words were uttered by Dietrich Bonhoeffer before his execution by Nazis: "This is the end—for me the beginning of life."[15] Kazantzakis offers famous words: "He uttered a triumphant cry: IT IS ACCOMPLISHED! And it was as though he had said: Everything has begun."[16]

The sense of an ultimate self-awareness gained in front of death is another important existential testimony described by Kazantzakis and probably owes much to Tolstoy's immensely influential story *The Death of Ivan Ilyich*: "He searched for his former habitual fear of death and did not find it. 'Where is it? What death?' There was no fear because there was no death either. In place of death there was light. 'So that's what it is!' he suddenly exclaimed aloud. 'What joy!'"[17] Death becomes the ultimate liberation from illusion (*avidya* in Buddhist terms) and false consciousness, from the fallen state of a mind without historical awareness of its position. Essentially, death is the only encounter with freedom.[18] Martin Heidegger built his monumental (and unfinished) *Being and Time* around such experience of Being-toward-Death, when the anticipation of dying causes anxiety for the authentic self, yet releases the individual from "the illusions of the 'they.'"[19]

A Different Christology

Kazantzakis's version of Christ essentially gives a complete, coherent, and unified story line to the narrative translation of Jesus' life, reinventing the mythic structure of his personal approach to dying. This powerful enculturation of the Jesus myth makes the story again relevant to modern dilemmas in an age of global relativization of values and perceptions. Essentially, Kazantzakis's Jesus is the epitome of a transcultural revaluation of the Christian tradition, European as well as Asian. In this Kazantzakis represents his Jesus as the symbol of the post-Nietzschean collapse of identity and subjectivity, with the gradual emergence of a composite self-perception, of a fused definition of how myths function and how individuals mythopoeically express their needs and desires within a polymythic mode of communication.

The most important point of Kazantzakis's christological exploration is the final depiction of what he calls "the last temptation." Within his narrative this special elaboration (or midrash) on the existing Gospel stories of temptation superimposes the ultimate concern of contemporary humanity onto the story of Jesus. The Gospel narratives about Jesus and his encounter with the devil in the desert are of particular interest because Kazantzakis reassembles them in order to prepare the completion of his message. With their tripartite structure (the temptations of pleasure, power, and spiritual authority), the Gospel stories reveal the mystical and esoteric perception of *psychanodia*, a dominant motif in ancient Hellenic metaphysics. One of the most common ideas of ancient Stoic and Neoplatonic moral philosophy is the gradual elevation of the soul beyond any thought of material reward and the denouncement of every fulfilled desire for elevation to the realm of spiritual fulfillment.

For centuries Church theologians have struggled to reconcile the somehow contradictory messages we receive from these stories and the references to test in the Lord's Prayer or the elaborations of the tempted Messiah in the Epistle to the Hebrews. In Luke we read: "When the devil had finished every test, he departed from him until an opportune time" (4:13). A more precise translation would be: "And after having exposed him to all kinds of temptation, the devil departed until the right moment." In the passage both the "*panta peirasmon*" and the temporal indication "*achri kairou*" justify Kazantzakis's elaboration of the story in a completely new way, since these are themselves elaborations of the early Markan tradition.[20] Similar stories from Christian-Gnostic gospels can be detected as sources in the construction of his narrative; however, Kazantzakis's handling of temptation as the ultimate confrontation with mortality, corporeality, and finitude is a novel approach toward a different Christology.

Dietrich Bonhoeffer also talks about "the last temptation" or "the complete temptation," projecting the temptations of Jesus onto every believer:

> The practical tasks of the Christian must, therefore, be to understand all the temptations which come upon him as temptations of Jesus Christ in him, and thus he will be aided. But how does it happen? Before we can speak of the concrete temptations of Christians and their overcoming, the question of the author of the temptation of Christians must be put. Only when the Christian knows with whom he has to do in temptation, can he act rightly in the actual event.[21]

Kazantzakis's vision of temptation is much more radical than Bonhoeffer's, despite striking similarities in their ultimate message.

Kazantzakis stresses the unreality of the last temptation. Whereas all previous temptations happened outside the individual, the last temptation happened in him, within his mental structure. It is a clash between his actual life and his mental world, the confrontation between his reality and his ideality. Kazantzakis does not simply present it as a hallucination. Instead, within the temptation the actual lived experience is stripped of its meaning, its temporal consciousness, and its material gravity. Kazantzakis's hero denounces matter in order to reaffirm its importance after he experiences the enchantment and the illusory bewitchment of its opposite idealistic negation. The world of his dreams is the ultimate nightmare. In this temptation Jesus confronts his unconscious repressed self in the Freudian sense: his unfulfilled desires, when actualized, create a life without orientation and diffuse his internal tension. His temptation is similar to what Norman O. Brown has described: "The essence of repression lies in the refusal of the human being to recognize the realities of his human nature."[22] In the framework of the last temptation, Jesus wrestles with the acedia of his social self to actualize and materialize his life-projects and thus remain in the gray limbo of unfulfilled potentialities.

E. R. Dodds observes that Gregory of Nyssa's "entire work is penetrated by a deep feeling of the unreality of the sensible world, which he calls *goēteia*, a magical illusion echoing a phrase of Porphyry."[23] The concept of the world as illusion can also be found in Kazantzakis's Buddhist-inspired works. But in *The Last Temptation*, Kazantzakis goes beyond the false dilemma of negating or accepting life and places the whole question within the human psyche itself. Jesus has to confront the deepest feelings and the most secret desires of his heart. These are not the temptations of the flesh but the most enticing temptations of the spirit, as Bonhoeffer indicated; in short, *securitas* and *desperatio*.[24] In Kazantzakis's novel, *securitas* is expressed with the self-sufficient and self-consuming structures of the family, the clan, or the tribe. Jesus earns the respect of every decent family man in his temptation, the approval of his mother, the acceptance of his village. He forgets his message and enjoys his moments.[25]

Kazantzakis also explores how Jesus slips into meaninglessness in all levels of his life as long as he evolves into a self without regenerative projects in front of him. His words are still the words of his youth. But he does not really mean anything he says. He employs words as strategies to win acceptance, respect, and authority, but the actual words mean nothing beyond their vague association with his past.

For Kazantzakis, the end of meaning is the outcome of the internal quest for the consolidation of the self; after such consolidation is achieved, the self's corrosion and the emptying of its significance begin. As long as the self remains in the making, meaning is generated; but after this process ends, meaning becomes an ossified fetish, an empty shell of insignificance. Jesus loses his own self under his socially situated subjectivity; he is what others expect him to be.[26]

This temptation to happiness leaves out something extremely important, how time can be meaningfully experienced (the *achri kairou*), and whether happiness is at the same time completeness and plenitude. The more Jesus experiences the allurements of happiness, the more he becomes dependent on them; he then loses his internal tension and wastes the dynamic of his mental anxiety. His last temptation is beyond the pleasures and charms of the flesh. Like Al-Ghazali's Muslim Jesus, Kazantzakis's Jesus knows that "the great temptation for the soul is not simply vice but diversion."[27]

Conclusion

The whole of Jesus' temptation has one purpose: to show the unreality of repressed desires and the need for accepting lived moments in their actuality, tension, and anxiety. Kazantzakis imaginatively expresses the struggle in Jesus' mind in order to accept his historicity. As a symbol of our era, the decentered subject of modern society loses its sense of orientation and falls into the bewitchment of self-consuming interiority. And whereas interiority is the locus where identity is primarily established, it is not the place where it develops its sense of historical responsibility and sense of communitarian selfhood. After defeating the ultimate temptation, which is to remain a prisoner in his own personal adventure, Kazantzakis's Jesus delivers himself to the collective imagining of his community. Therefore, he becomes their binding myth, the dramaturgical narrative through which all communities of the faithful acquire self-recognition and the sense of togetherness. When in the imaginative re-creation of his community Jesus becomes Jesus the Christ, he "redeems" his humanity and "resurrects" his temporal existence.

The Last Temptation brings Jesus Christ back to history in order to become the salvific *imitatio* for another individual, as a symbolic ritual of fusion with tradition. Kazantzakis's depiction of Paul acts as a catalyst so that Jesus' story is transformed into the connecting story of a community. Paul says: "I create the truth, create it out of obstinacy and longing and faith. I don't struggle to find it—I build it. I build it taller than man and thus I make man grow."[28] Thus "Jesus" is transformed into a public drama, a symbolic rite of passage for everyone who develops one's selfhood and wants to participate in rituals of belonging. Jesus Christ is the creative invention of a community as a testimony (*martyria*) to their faith, and *martyria* means the genesis of Scripture.

It is the collectivity encapsulated within Jesus' personality that makes his drama so effective. In Kazantzakis's novel, Paul says, "Joseph the carpenter of Nazareth did not beget you; I begot you—I, Paul, the scribe from Tarsus in Cilicia." Thereby he stresses the early Christian belief in the kingdom of God not within but among people, as is the correct translation of the Jesus saying.[29] The Parousia of the Christ becomes the polyphonic word of the many, not simply within the Church but also in the final quest for the Jesus of history. *The Last Temptation* reaffirms the fascinating numinosity in Jesus' life as a ritual of communal recognition. The triumphant cry of the end can be interpreted as the ultimate cry of despair of a dying human being; and who can ever resist such a call for help? And the act of saving Jesus is the act of becoming part of the *koinonia* he inaugurated.

Notes

1. Gore Vidal, *Palimpsest: A Memoir* (London: Abacus, 1995), 386.

2. Anthony Burgess, *The Novel Now: A Student's Guide to Contemporary Fiction* (London: Faber & Faber, 1971), 180.

3. See Ralph J. Tapia, *The Theology of Christ: Commentary: Readings in Christology* (New York: Bruce, 1971), 447–56.

4. Helen Kazantzakis, *Nikos Kazantzakis: A Biography Based on His Letters*, trans. Amy Mims (New York: Simon & Schuster, 1968), 505–6.

5. See Israel Knohl, *The Messiah before Jesus: The Suffering Servant of the Dead Sea Scrolls*, trans. David Maisel (Berkeley: University of California Press, 2000).

6. Albert Schweitzer, *The Mystery of The Kingdom of God: The Secret of Jesus' Messiahship and Passion*, trans. Walter Lowrie (New York: Prometheus Books, 1985), 174.

7. See Otto Rank et al., *In Quest of the Hero* (Princeton, NJ: Princeton University Press, 1990), 215–16.

8. Robert S. Ellwood, *The Sixties Spiritual Awakening: American Religion Moving from Modern to Postmodern*, (New Brunswick, NJ: Rutgers University Press, 1994), 91.

9. Charlotte Allen, *The Human Christ: The Search for the Historical Jesus* (New York: Free Press, 1998), 225.

10. Nikos Kazantzakis, *The Last Temptation of Christ*, trans. Peter Bien (New York: Simon & Schuster, 1960), 1.

11. William E. Phipps, *The Sexuality of Jesus: Theological and Literary Perspectives* (New York: Harper & Row, 1973), 131.

12. W. B. Yeats, *Mythologies* (London: Papermac, 1979), 338.

13. G. W. F. Hegel, *Phenomenology of the Spirit*, trans. A. V. Miller (Oxford: Oxford University Press, 1979), 459.

14. Kazantzakis, *Last Temptation*, 1.

15. Eberhard Bethge, *Dietrich Bonhoeffer: A Biography: Theologian, Christian, Man for His Times*, rev. and ed. Victoria J. Barnett, trans. Eric Mosbacher et al., rev. ed. (Minneapolis: Fortress Press, 2000), 927.

16. Kazantzakis, *Last Temptation*, 496.

17. Leo Tolstoy, *The Death of Ivan Ilyich and Other Stories*, trans. Rosemary Edmonds (Harmondsworth, UK: Penguin Books, 1960), 60–61.

18. The only modern theologian who has dared to deal with Jesus' self-understanding and how it "was affected by a growing awareness that he could not avoid his approaching death" is Edward Schillebeeckx, *Jesus: An Experiment in Christology*, trans. Hubert Hoskins (London: Collins, 1979), 318.

19. Martin Heidegger, *Being and Time*, trans. John Macquarrie and Edward Robinson (London: Blackwell, 1962), 311.

20. See Ernest Best, *The Temptation and the Passion: The Markan Soteriology* (Cambridge: Cambridge University Press, 1965).

21. Dietrich Bonhoeffer, *Creation and Fall: A Theological Interpretation of Genesis 1–3* (New York: Macmillan, 1959), 108.

22. Norman O. Brown, *Life against Death: The Psychoanalytic Meaning of History* (New York: Random House, 1959), 4.

23. E. R. Dodds, *Pagan and Christian in an Age of Anxiety: Some Aspects of Religious Experience from Marcus Aurelius to Constantine* (New York: Norton Library, 1965), 11.

24. Bonhoeffer, *Creation and Fall*, 123–26.

25. Kazantzakis, *Last Temptation*, 476.

26. Ibid., 471.

27. Tarif Khalidi, ed., *The Muslim Jesus: Sayings and Stories in Islamic Literature* (Cambridge, MA: Harvard University Press, 2001), 43.

28. Kazantzakis, *Last Temptation*, 477.

29. Ibid., 487.

CHAPTER 7

The Temptation That Never Was
Kazantzakis and Borges
Roderick Beaton

Chuang Tzu, some twenty-four centuries ago, dreamt he was a butterfly and did not know, when he awoke, if he was a man who had dreamt he was a butterfly or a butterfly who now dreamt he was a man.

—Jorge Luis Borges (1947)[1]

Introduction

What exactly happens during the last four chapters of *The Last Temptation*?[2] Much of the condemnation of the book, and of the film based on it, has concentrated on the portrayal there of Jesus' sexual relationships, first with Mary Magdalene, then in his bigamous union with Mary and Martha, the sisters of Lazarus. For many Christians, this is blasphemy. Apologists for the book, as also for the film, take their cue from Kazantzakis's own prologue and point out that none of these things "really" happened: they are all part of a dream in which Jesus is tempted by earthly happiness. This is the "last temptation" of the title, a happiness that he finally and gloriously refuses. It therefore follows that even if Kazantzakis was not exactly a Christian, his fictional portrayal of the Son of God is ultimately respectful of the transcendental truth revealed in Scripture.[3]

As the title and epigraph of this chapter already hint, there is another way of reading this key episode in the novel. In a paper published some years ago, I hazarded the possibility, tentatively and within parentheses, that "a robust reading of the novel might suggest that Jesus is not so much tempted as allowed to have his cake and eat it."[4] In this chapter, I figuratively remove the brackets from that suggestion and try to justify it, through a close reading of Kazantzakis's text and also through juxtaposing it with fictional texts by Borges that lead away from the

Christian religious tradition. Hence, I finally propose a radically different and non-Christian reading of Kazantzakis's fictional biography of Jesus.

The place to begin is Kazantzakis's prologue. This starts out with the author meditating on the "substance," the "nature," and the "mystery" of Christ.[5] He describes how in writing the book, he followed "Christ's bloody journey to Golgotha." He lays stress on "that part of Christ's nature which was profoundly human," without which "he would not be able to become a model for our lives." According to this prologue, Christ progressively throughout his life overcame the weaknesses and limitations of his humanity. Even at the supreme moment, dying on the cross,

> his struggle did not end. Temptation—the Last Temptation—was waiting for him upon the Cross. Before the fainted eyes of the Crucified the spirit of the Evil One, in an instantaneous flash, unfolded the deceptive vision of a calm and happy life.

There follows a relatively anodyne summary of the content of the final chapters, after which the prologue continues:

> This was the *Last Temptation* which came in the space of a lightning flash to trouble the Saviour's final moments.
>
> But all at once Christ shook his head violently, opened his eyes, and saw. No, he was not a traitor, glory be to God! . . . He had accomplished the mission which the Lord had entrusted to him. . . . Temptation fought until the very last moment to lead him astray, and Temptation was defeated.[6]

This prologue was presumably written after the novel itself and, like most prologues, with the aim of disposing the reader in a particular way toward the text that follows. The Christian reader is reassured by the devotional, at times even sentimental, tone; it is implied that the story to come is about Christ, the Son of God, and further, that it presents him in a way at once deeply personal to the author and ultimately edifying for the reader. According to this prologue, Christ is exemplary in the supreme act of will that defeats the ultimate temptation.

But this prologue does not form part of the narrative of *The Last Temptation*; the prologue is not only extraneous to the narratives, but also cleanly shorn from it by two deep and unmistakable fissures. First, the object of the author's meditation in the prologue is called, always and only, "Christ." Historically, as is also made clear in the main text, "Christ" was not a name but a title: the "Anointed One," corresponding to the Hebrew title "Messiah," not a name. Within the main narrative, on the other hand, the subject of the fictionalized biography is *never* called "Christ." He is always and only known as "Jesus," the given name of the historical Jesus of Nazareth. As I have argued more fully elsewhere, much of this biographical fiction consists of the quest, by Jesus and others, to discover a true identity for its subject, beyond that given name. First Judas, and then Jesus himself, wonders: Can this be the Messiah? It is only after his baptism by John the Baptist that Jesus in the narrative determines that he *is* the Messiah and sets out to fulfill the role that has been laid down for him in the Jewish Scriptures.[7] Throughout the main text, the designation "Christ" is applied to Jesus *only* in the words of the evangelist Matthew and the apostle Paul, in contexts that explicitly reveal these writers of Scripture embellishing the "real" story of Jesus for posterity.[8] Thus nothing that the prologue says about "Christ" can properly be transferred to the "Jesus" who is the biographical subject of the main text. For this reason, throughout this chapter I insist on the translated title of the novel in the United Kingdom edition, which accurately renders Kazantzakis's title in Greek: *The Last Temptation*. The addition of the words *of Christ* in the United States edition is gratuitous and can be justified only with reference to the prologue, not to the main narrative, which is precisely not about Christ the Son of God but about a man named Jesus.[9]

The other fissure concerns the nature of the last temptation itself. According to the summary given in the prologue, at the end of the deceptive vision, "Christ shook his head violently, opened his eyes, and saw." It may seem like a small point, but in the main text you look in vain for that crucial act of will by which temptation was defeated:

> Jesus rotated his eyes with anguish, and looked. He was alone. . . . He tried with all his might to discover where he was, who he was and why he felt pain.

Even the discovery, which follows almost at once, that what he has experienced has been a temptation, and that he has not succumbed to it, no longer carries the assurance of authorial omniscience. Here, as in much of the rest of the book, the narrative is mediated through the consciousness of Jesus himself. True, while he is adjusting back to the new/old reality of the cross, he seems to have a last glimpse of the "guardian angel" who had accompanied him through the unreal time of his temptation, and who now takes leave with a "cool mocking laugh."[10] But at the end of these four illusionist chapters, who is to say what is real and what is fantasy? Flimsy grounds, perhaps, on which to experience "a wild, indomitable joy" and to conclude, as Jesus now does:

> No, no, he was not a coward, a deserter, a traitor. . . . He had stood his ground honourably to the very end; he had kept his word. The moment he cried ELI ELI and fainted, temptation had captured him for a split-second and led him astray. . . . All—all were illusions sent by the Devil. . . . Everything had turned out as it should, glory be to God![11]

So Jesus' waking on the cross to his moment of final triumph, as told in the novel itself, turns out to be every bit as subjective as the more complex—and interesting—feelings he experiences throughout the illusory time of his temptation. It is time to look in more detail at the content of these four final chapters.

Alternative Realities

Chapter 29 ends with the crucifixion. Halfway through uttering the canonical last words from the cross, the fictional Jesus faints.[12] The next chapter begins with him waking: "His eyelids fluttered with joy and surprise." He discovers himself leaning against a flowering tree in springtime, on which he is delighted to count thirty-three singing birds: "As many as my own years," he muses; as many, too, as the chapters of the book will be by the time the interlude that now begins is over. A smiling angel reassures him, "You lived your entire Passion in a dream."[13] Overwhelmed with joy and relief, Jesus sets out with this new guardian angel, who promises "all the pleasures you ever secretly longed for."[14] For the first time, the tormented ascetic of the preceding chapters discovers the beauty and wonder of earthly life. Consummating his long-denied desire for Mary Magdalene, he confesses to her:

> I went astray because I sought a route outside of the flesh; I wanted to go by way of the clouds, great thoughts, and death. Woman, precious fellow-worker of God: forgive me. I bow and worship you, Mother of God.[15]

Soon afterward, Mary Magdalene is brutally and gratuitously murdered at the instigation of no less a person than the zealot Saul, later to reappear as the apostle Paul. Not least bizarre about this strange episode is the shift of the narrative perspective away from Jesus to Magdalene herself, who incidentally becomes the only person in the whole story to engage directly in dialogue with God.[16] Seemingly, the last moments and death of Magdalene have been only a dream within a dream: "What had he just dreamt? He could not remember. Nothing remained in his mind but stones, a woman, and blood. Could the woman have been Magdalene?"[17] It is unusual, surely, to dream in the third person, to dream of the experiences of someone else. Was the erotic consummation that precedes this also, perhaps, part of the same dream? We are on the border here between dream and the representation of an alternative reality, one that has room for other subjectivities besides that of the dreamer and one in which, as we will see, real events, people, and the flow of real historical time all have a place.

After the death of Mary Magdalene, Jesus' guardian angel brings him to the house of Lazarus's two sisters, Mary and Martha. Now transformed into a little black boy, the angel brings about a change in Jesus' physical appearance. This change enables Jesus without too much difficulty to assume the identity of "Master Lazarus," return to his old vocation as a carpenter, and take up residence as husband simultaneously of both sisters of the original Lazarus, who has in the meantime died a second time.[18] Surrounded by these loving women and the children they bear to him over the years, Jesus learns to experience the earthly happiness that consists in "profound correspondence between body and soul, between earth and man."[19] More time passes; flaws begin to appear in the fabric of bliss. Not even the guardian angel can satisfy Jesus' craving for the happy state to last "for all eternity." With a surely acute insight into the fictional character of Jesus as conceived throughout the novel, the angel for once rebuffs him: "Moments aren't enough for you? If so, you must learn that eternity will not be either."[20] Mary has a horrible dream that all this is nothing but a dream, and that in reality Jesus was crucified.[21] There are now two realities in play: in the one, Jesus died on the cross, having saved humankind; in the other, he lives a fulfilled life, saving his own self. Each reality obtrudes at moments into the other, but only to be dismissed as a dream. How is the reader, let alone the fictional Jesus, to be sure which is the "true" one?

By now, the stage is darkening. Figures from the past begin to arrive at the house of "Master Lazarus." The most unpleasant of these is Paul, the former "bloodthirsty Saul," who contemptuously assures Jesus that Christianity will be founded on the story of the crucifixion and the resurrection even if neither event ever happened in reality.[22] The emotional fulcrum of these final chapters comes at the beginning of chapter 33. Jesus, Mary, and Martha have all grown gnarled and white-haired. A few pages later we learn that Jerusalem has just been burned by the Romans,[23] so we know that historical time has flowed on to the year 70 CE. Although it is not spelled out, this means that Jesus has now reached the age of "three-score years and ten," a person's allotted span according to the Old Testament—an age, too, that Kazantzakis himself was fast approaching when he completed the novel at sixty-eight years of age. The sense of fear at the prospect of old age and death, of time running out, is vividly and movingly conveyed:

> Frightened, he shut his eyes and felt Time run like water from its high source—his mind—down through his neck, breast, loins and thighs, and flow out finally through the soles of his feet.[24]

The little black boy, the disguised guardian angel, now seems a sinister figure, because "he did not grow, he did not age." He is the one who announces explicitly what the elegiac tone of the writing has already signaled for the reader: "The end is near." At first Jesus is even glad of this. "If your purpose was to smother me in honey like a bee," he declares, "your pains have gone to waste. I've eaten all the honey I wanted, all I could, but I did not dip in my wings."[25] As a fulfilled life approaches its natural end, the fictional Jesus prepares to find a conventional consolation in the purity of his soul; but it will not be so easy.

Hard on the heels of news of the destruction of Jerusalem comes "a cluster of tiny old men," the former disciples.[26] These decrepit shreds of humanity have not forgotten; as best they could, they have kept faith and remained true to the teachings of the Jesus they knew. Recollection turns into bitterness: when the testing time came, it was Jesus who betrayed these hopes and that faith through his failure to be crucified. Finally, Judas appears; of the two, Jesus and Judas, Judas has always been the stronger, the man of courage and action, while Jesus has been portrayed throughout the story as passive, vacillating, and physically weak. Now Judas "is the only one who still holds himself erect, . . . full of vigour, and unyielding."[27] Judas's first word to Jesus is "Traitor!"[28] Judas goes on to accuse Jesus as a coward and a deserter: "I don't believe in anything any more, I don't believe in anyone. You broke my heart!" The refrain gathers force, as they all attack Jesus: "Coward! Deserter! Traitor!"[29] The biblical roles of Jesus and Judas have been exactly reversed. And from this crushing annihilation of all that he has been for just over half his life, the seventy-year-old Jesus awakens, *involuntarily*, to the relief of discovering that none of it happened. He is still on the cross, still age thirty-three; he is in time to complete his last words, "IT IS ACCOMPLISHED!" and die. "And," the novel ends, "it was as though he had said: Everything has begun."[30]

So what has happened? Something rather different from the "*vision* of a calm and happy life" promised by Kazantzakis in the prologue.[31] Almost forty years of apparently real time have elapsed, longer than the life of the historical Jesus. In that time, reneging on his mission, Jesus has found fulfillment instead in the satisfactions of an earthly life. Only mortality and the approach of death have prompted him to claim that his soul has been untouched by what he has enjoyed. And that claim was thrown dramatically back in his face by the appearance of Judas and the disciples. Left with nowhere to turn, all his life behind him, the renegade Jesus is forced to face an all-too-human reality, that of having failed to live up to the hopes and ideals of his youth. In despair he cries out to the disciples, "Oh, if I could only relive my life from the beginning!"[32]

It is in answer to that prayer that Jesus "wakes." The polarity between dream and reality, which had seemed miraculously to "save" him from an agonizing death, is now reversed again, just in time to save him from an end more agonizing still. Instead of dying an old man, a renegade, and in despair, Jesus suddenly finds himself back at the moment when his life had split into alternative, irreconcilable paths. *But the moment is not presented as one of choice.* It is by no discernible act of will that Jesus returns to his destiny on the cross. In experiencing joy and triumph at finding himself there, he exercises no choice. The miracle has been accomplished—but how? Of the competing realities, which was the "real" one, which the dream? Within the space of the text, *both* exist, and each at different times has laid claims to the imaginative connivance of the reader. The fictional Jesus has every reason to feel relief at being finally returned to the "reality" of the cross, and at interpreting what has happened to him as a temptation finally overcome. But the reader is just as likely to feel that this Jesus, by the end of his life, has had it both ways.

Time Refuted

If this is an unprecedented and, for some readers, an unacceptable way for Kazantzakis to retell the central story of the New Testament, it is not without parallel in the secular writing of his generation. The Argentinian writer Jorge Luis Borges was sixteen years Kazantzakis's junior; like Kazantzakis, Borges devoted his early years to poetry. Then in Buenos Aires in 1944, he published the first edition of the short fictions that would establish his worldwide reputation.[33] It is conceivable that Kazantzakis, an omnivorous reader who had written a travel book about Spain and published translations of Spanish poetry, knew Borges's work by the time he came to write *The Last Temptation* in 1950–51. Equally, he could have encountered Borges's work in France. Or perhaps the parallels I am about to draw are explicable in terms of the common debt of both writers to the philosophy of Henri Bergson. Whatever the explanation, it is in three thematically linked stories by Borges, published close together in the *Ficciones* of 1944, that we find the most illuminating parallels I know for the last four chapters, and indeed for aspects of the whole conception of *The Last Temptation*.

In "Theme of the Traitor and the Hero," a revolutionary leader turns out to have been the hidden traitor to his own cause. After being exposed, Fergus Kilpatrick willingly participates in a bizarre charade to ensure that his actual execution will go down in history as the martyrdom of a hero whose reputation remains untarnished.[34] "The Secret Miracle" tells of a Czech-Jewish scholar and patriot executed by the Nazis on the annexation of the Sudetenland. In response to his prayer on the eve of his death, Jaromir Hladik experiences a full year of life in the split second between the firing of the fatal shots and the bullets' striking his body. During that time, he completes in his head the unfinished play that was to have salvaged his tarnished intellectual reputation. Typically of Borges's labyrinthine world of mirror images, the subtitle of the fictional Hladik's play is *The Vindication of Eternity*. Its vestigial plot, as given in the story, turns on the discovery that its central character, Baron Roemerstadt, is not the hero himself but his deranged enemy, a former rival in love who now believes himself to be the baron. And so, "the drama has never taken place; it [the whole action of the play] is the circular delirium that Kubin [the deranged rival] lives and relives endlessly."[35]

Finally, "Three Versions of Judas" tells of a Swedish theologian in the early twentieth century and his successive interpretations of the biblical story. The theologian Runeberg first decides that Judas's betrayal "was a preordained fact which has its mysterious place in the economy of redemption," a willing sacrifice of everything Judas holds most dear by "one man [Judas], in representation of all men." According to this version, "Judas in some way reflects Jesus." Later, the hapless Runeberg goes further, concluding that it was Judas, not Jesus, who was the incarnation of God, and finally that in revealing this secret to the world, it is he himself who has become the ultimate betrayer. In this way the third "version" of Judas turns out to be none other than Runeberg himself. According to the first two of Runeberg's "versions," Judas changes place with Jesus; in the third, Judas changes place with the hero of the story.[36]

In all three of these stories, we encounter the paradoxical double, or switched, identity of "the traitor and the hero," which also characterizes the relationship of Jesus and Judas in *The Last Temptation*. In Borges's story, the first "version" of Judas presents Judas's act of betrayal as necessary to his master's design; Judas's character and actions "reflect" those of Jesus. Exactly this relationship underpins the whole psychological interplay between the two men in Kazantzakis's fiction. This relationship reaches its climax shortly before the crucifixion, when Jesus reveals to Judas: "It is necessary for me to be killed and for you to betray me. We two must save the world." Judas, horrified, protests, "If you had to betray your master, would you do it?" to which Jesus concedes, "God pitied me and gave me the easier task: to be crucified."[37] Then in the final chapter, in the context of the temptation-dream, the roles of the previously complementary characters, Jesus and Judas, are completely reversed. There it is *Judas*, the traitor according to tradition, who calls his former master a traitor, in a reversal corresponding to Runeberg's second "version" of Judas.

Even more striking is the similarity between the miraculous and subjective prolongation of the lives, respectively, of Jesus in *The Last Temptation* and of Hladik in "The Secret Miracle." In both narratives, time is mysteriously dilated. A precedent for this can be found in Bergson's theoretical attempt to separate time from space. Bergson conceived time as a product of consciousness and therefore ultimately subjective, while space, being measurable, has an objective existence. In the fictions of first Borges, then Kazantzakis, this philosophical position is tested through a kind of imaginative reductio ad absurdum.[38] Both stories also involve the logical paradox that the content of the subjectively experienced time must be everywhere and forever unknowable, since in both cases the subject dies a split second after it ends. Characteristically, Borges points this up with dry humor: "He [Hladik] was not working for posterity or even for God, whose literary tastes were unknown to him."[39] Hence comes the title of the story "The *Secret* Miracle." But self-evidently, and for the same reason, everything narrated in *The Last Temptation* after the end of chapter 29 must also remain secret, by its very nature incapable of objective corroboration.

Kazantzakis may have been responding directly to these paradoxes as set out by Borges, or, like Borges himself, he may have been elaborating on concepts derived from his study of Bergson. Either way, if we read the end of *The Last Temptation* alongside Borges's fictions, we at the same time distance it from the Christian, religious framework against which it has usually been read. At the heart of *The Last Temptation* lies not the christological anxiety expressed in its prologue but the existential anxiety of the human subject confronted with the finitude imposed by mortality. Kazantzakis had memorably, if bleakly, summed up this anxiety almost thirty years earlier, in his philosophical work *The Saviors of God*: "We come from a dark abyss; we end up in a dark abyss; the bright interval between we call Life."[40]

Read in this way, *The Last Temptation* is not about the mystery of God incarnated as man but about the struggle of a man to transcend the bounds of mortality and become God. This perhaps is not very surprising, since it is also the central theme of *The Saviors of God* and of much that Kazantzakis had been writing ever since. Indeed, understood in this way, the struggle of Jesus in *The Last Temptation* becomes another version of the struggle not only of the Christlike Manolios in *Christ Recrucified* but also of the most *un*-Christlike Kapetan Michalis in *Freedom and Death*. The latter's final enemy turns out to be not the hated Turkish overlords of Crete but mortality itself.[41]

As much as anything, it is the furor created by the accusations of blasphemy against *The Last Temptation* that has diverted attention away from the fundamentally *secular* nature of this book. Its defenders no less than its attackers have been misled—by its prologue and still more by its title in the American edition—into reading Kazantzakis's novel against the background of the Christian tradition. But despite its use of so much Christian material and its radically daring reinterpretation of some of it, there is much to be said for reading *The Last Temptation* instead as a Bergsonian, and indeed a Borgesian, meditation on the time-bound, finite nature of human life.

Notes

1. Jorge Luis Borges, "A New Refutation of Time," in his *Labyrinths: Selected Stories and Other Writings*, ed. Donald A. Yates and James E. Irby (New York: New Directions, 1964; Harmondsworth, UK: Penguin Books, 1970), 266; on the original publication of this text in Spanish, see 252–53.

2. For reasons set out in this chapter, I retain the title of the UK edition, and all quotations and page references are to its paperback: Nikos Kazantzakis, *The Last Temptation*, trans. Peter Bien (London: Faber & Faber, 1962).

3. Darren J. N. Middleton and Peter Bien, "Spiritual Levendiá: Kazantzakis's Theology of Struggle," in *God's Struggler: Religion in the Writings of Nikos Kazantzakis*, ed. Darren J. N. Middleton and Peter Bien (Macon, GA: Mercer University Press, 1996), 7: "We probably should not think of him [Kazantzakis] as Christian—certainly not in a narrow sense. Yet . . . he was a profoundly religious person, and indeed one whose religiosity . . . may speak meaningfully to Christians today." See also Peter Bien, *Nikos Kazantzakis: Novelist* (Bristol: Bristol Classical Press, 1989), 66–78 (esp. 73–76); cf. James F. Lea, *Kazantzakis: The Politics of Salvation* (Tuscaloosa, AL: University of Alabama Press, 1979), 141; and Theodore Ziolkowski, *Fictional Transfigurations of Jesus* (Princeton, NJ: Princeton University Press, 1972), 16–17, 125–26 (both Lea and Ziolkowski are heavily dependent on the book's prologue, on which see below). John S. Bak, "Christ's Jungian Shadow in *The Last Temptation*," in *God's Struggler*, ed. Middleton and Bien, 153–68), brings a new, and secular, perspective to bear but not does not differ significantly on the nature of "Christ's [*sic*] dream on the cross, the 'last temptation'" (160).

4. Roderick Beaton, "Writing, Identity and Truth in Kazantzakis's Novel *The Last Temptation*," *Kampos: Cambridge Papers in Modern Greek* 5 (1997): 1–21 (esp. 17).

5. Kazantzakis, *Last Temptation*, 7.

6. Ibid., 9.

7. Beaton, "Writing," 12–19.

8. Kazantzakis, *Last Temptation*, 334, quoting the opening of Matthew's Gospel in the original New Testament Greek; 485–90, where "Christ" appears only in the direct speech of Paul, at one point explicitly contrasted to Jesus' assumed identity as "Master Lazarus": "Choose! On one side, Christ, the son of God, the salvation of the world; on the other, Master Lazarus!" (490). But Jesus does not choose.

9. The earliest publication of the book was in the Swedish translation by Börje Knös. Like all the translations that appeared during Kazantzakis's lifetime, it retains the unelaborated Greek title: Nikos Kazantzakis, *Den Sita Frestelsen* (Stockholm: Hugo Gebers, 1952).

10. Kazantzakis, *Last Temptation*, 507.

11. Ibid., 506–7.

12. Ibid., 453.

13. Ibid., 455.

14. Ibid., 456.

15. Ibid., 460.

16. Ibid., 461–62.

17. Ibid., 464.

18. Ibid., 471. For the disturbing portrayal of Lazarus's half-life after being resurrected, and the gruesome details of his second death, see Kazantzakis, *Last Temptation*, 376–82, 397–98, 422–24. It is generally supposed that the raising of Lazarus in John 11:17–44 is a prefiguration of the later resurrection of Christ himself. If so, the transposition of these details by Kazantzakis into the genre of the horror story, with specific allusions to the famous Greek folk ballad "The Dead Brother," provides one of the most suggestive indications in Kazantzakis's text that literal resurrection in the flesh is not to be expected of *this* Jesus.

19. Kazantzakis, *Last Temptation*, 478; cf. 475.

20. Ibid., 476.

21. Ibid., 478–79.

22. Ibid., 484–92.

23. Ibid., 493–95.

24. Ibid., 493.

25. Ibid., 494.

26. Ibid., 495–96.

27. Ibid., 499.

28. Ibid., 501.

29. Ibid., 505–6.

30. Ibid., 507.

31. Ibid., 9, emphasis added.

32. Ibid., 505.

33. Borges, *Labyrinths*. For the contents of the 1944 edition of *Ficciones* and for the Spanish texts, see J. L. Borges, *Obras completas*, vol. 1, *1923–1949* (Barcelona: Emecé, 1989).

34. Borges, *Labyrinths*, 102–5.

35. Ibid., 118–24, esp. 121.

36. Ibid., 125–30, esp. 126–27.

37. Kazantzakis, *Last Temptation*, 431. Cristina Mayorga Ruano also cites this dialogue and links it to Borges's "Three Versions," but she does not explore the implications for *The Last Temptation*. See her "Ho Kazantzakis kai to Provlima tou Kakou stin Historia," in *Nikos Kazantzakis: Saranta Chronia apo to Thanato tou* (Chania, Crete: Municipal Cultural Enterprise, 1997): 83–94.

38. Henri Bergson, *Time and Free Will*, trans. F. L. Pogson (London: Allen & Unwin, 1910), 104–12. See esp. 108: "Within myself a process of organization or interpenetration of con-

scious states is going on, which constitutes true duration. It is because I *endure* in this way that I picture to myself what I call the past oscillations of the pendulum at the same time as I perceive the present oscillation" (original emphasis). The locus classicus in Borges's work for a similar, part-parodic philosophical reductio ad absurdum (an elaboration of Bergson's ideas projected back into the philosophical discourse of the mid-eighteenth century) is the essay of 1947 from which the epigraph to this chapter is taken (see note 1).

39. Borges, *Labyrinths*, 124.

40. Nikos Kazantzakis, *Askitiki: Salvatores Dei* (Athens: Ekdoseis E. Kazantzaki, 1971), 9 (my translation).

41. Roderick Beaton, "Of Crete and Other Demons: A Reading of Kazantzakis's Freedom and Death," *Journal of Modern Greek Studies* 16, no. 2 (1998): 195–229 (esp. 205–9). Nikos Kazantzakis, *Christ Recrucified*, trans. Jonathan Griffin (Oxford: Cassirer, 1954); published in the USA as *The Greek Passion*, trans. Jonathan Griffin (New York: Simon & Schuster, 1954).

CHAPTER 8

"This Clay Bird Is the Soul of Man"
A Platonic Reading of Kazantzakis's *The Last Temptation*
C. D. Gounelas

Introduction

Nikos Kazantzakis's *The Last Temptation* follows the final three years of Jesus' life: the predicament over becoming the Messiah, the visit to Magdalene, the formation of the group of disciples, the baptism, the preaching, and the crucifixion. One of Kazantzakis's last two novels (the other being *Saint Francis*), this book represents his final attempt at a story that had preoccupied him since almost the beginning of his writing career. The tragedy *Christ*, begun nearly thirty-five years earlier and published in 1928, presents an apparition experienced by a few faithful at the Holy Communion and recapitulates the tragic events between the crucifixion and the resurrection. Unlike this early verse drama, which focuses on the reaction of the disciples, as well as Mary and Magdalene, to Jesus' death, *The Last Temptation* reads like a historical novel, placing the events in conventional order and allowing rational explanation for each act. Both in chronological sequence and geographic setting, the novel is fairly accurate, containing what is known generally in the Christian tradition and the Bible.[1] Jesus, along with every other character, is depicted as convincingly human, with the usual frailties and weaknesses.

This historical approach is mirrored in the novel in the role of Matthew, who sets himself the task of acting as an eyewitness to Jesus' life and giving an accurate written account of Jesus' activities so that nothing will be lost. In his self-appointed task as scribe, however, he is fated always to miss the truth in Jesus' words, as the latter points out in an exchange that echoes postmodern observations about the unrepresentability of truth:

Thanks to Ruth Parkin-Gounelas for her comments on the text of this chapter and her patience in sharpening my English.

"Your words are obscure, Rabbi," Matthew complained. "How do you expect me to record them in my book?" All this time, he had been holding his pen in the air, unable to understand anything or to write.

"I don't speak in order for you to write, Matthew," Jesus answered bitterly. "You clerks are rightly called cocks: you think the sun won't come up unless you crow. . . . I say one thing, you write another, and those who read you understand still something else!"[2]

Matthew acts as a double of the narrator of the novel itself, since both attempt, with differing degrees of awareness of their failure, to write like a national historian, giving an objective and rational account of the major events.

Kazantzakis presents this realistic and somewhat conventional life story in such a way as to demand an answer to the radical question of whether there is anything to Jesus' life beyond the human dimension. Even the miracles are performed as if by an uninvolved intermediary between God and humanity. Is Jesus deliberately stripped of his divine status, we wonder? This chapter aims to address this question and to explore the relation between Jesus' normal, bodily life and the spiritual implications that so tentatively emerge from his activities. For all the narrator's repeated insistence that the spirit will and does triumph over the flesh, it is the body that remains. It is around this paradox that the novel circles.

Much of the novel is dedicated to the narrator's insistence that reason will prevail. In Peter's role we are given to understand that rationality is of paramount importance. The saying repeatedly used by Peter as well as by Zebedee in arguments with others, "Two and two make four," confirms that certain things have to be faced in square and rational terms. In addition, the narrator insists on the importance of food and drink, reinforcing the impression that what constitutes a human being is the body and its needs. In the role of the disciples (with the exception perhaps of John and Andrew), we are presented with stoic realists with little interest in abstract ideas.

However, the recognition of the importance of rationality runs counter to the urge felt by all, main characters and the mob alike, to await the arrival of the Messiah, the dominant and motivating force in the novel. This impatience for the arrival of the Messiah, it could perhaps be argued, is depicted as the inevitable outcome of a popular demand at a difficult historical moment, when the Romans occupied Israel. The Judaic context of the novel, however, makes clear that the arrival of the Messiah as predicted by the prophets is part of a centuries-long tradition of inner, mystical need. That this Messiah will come to seek his own death in no way undermines the power of this force. Death, he will prove, is both an insight into life and a redemption from it.

Throughout, the novel gives priority to sense experience, reliable spatiotemporal data, what can be verified from outside in objective terms. In spite of this, however, no reader can be oblivious to another dimension that emerges as a certain cosmic and metaphysical insight, something of which we are not fully conscious. To describe this in face of the impossibility of its representation, Kazantzakis uses spatial terms such as *kenó* (the void), *ávissos* (the abyss), or even an ellipsis (. . .), or else as *kravyí* (a cry). All these words indicate a reaching not so much at "spirit" (as an abstract entity, the *opposite* of the body), but rather at matter peeled away or hollowed out to reveal something *within it* that escapes signification. The novel works to show that the world is made up of these two elements, material forms and voidlike formlessness, that must be taken together in order to comprehend its vastness.

The world could thus be said to be constructed upon different sets of opposing phenomena or principles, presented not so much as a battle in which one will triumph, as some critics have argued, but rather as a conflict of complementaries in "harmony." Flesh and spirit, pain and pleasure, love and hatred, altruism and selfishness—these are shown to be inevitable contraries in which each term becomes meaningful only in relation to its opposite. Jesus and Judas are symbols of these primary opposites, depicted in an intricate union that the one demands of the other. The same applies to Jesus and John the Baptist: one proclaims love and the other the ax, their "togetherness" being identified as the cornerstone of Christianity. It is significant that each of these opposing characters is depicted at a strategic moment as kissing Jesus on the mouth, in an act of ritualistic union. Indeed, all the different phenomena in the world are yoked together ("enveloped") by a divine power that determines our universe and our lives:

> The son of Mary sighed. Ants are God's creatures too, he reflected, and so are men, and lizards, and the grasshoppers I hear in the olive grove and the jackals who howl during the night, and floods, and hunger. . . . He felt completely enveloped in God's breath.[3]

This metaphysical insight into the void or the abyss emerges either in signs or as psychic obsessions of individual characters' fear or desire. Our human lives are surrounded with indicators that we have to interpret in order to cope with ourselves and with the divine order of the world. A bird, a fly, a lizard, the scent of a leaf, thunder—Kazantzakis seems to say that all have a purpose and are signs for interpretation. Here are some of the ways in which the narrator tries to describe this mystical intuition: "God and man: all were transposed." "The air was a fire which licked the stones." The individual is "flying in the air just as one flies in one's dreams."[4] Time loses its conventionality, "a split-second" being felt as equal to "a thousand years."[5] It is the half-uttered or even the unuttered word we hear within us, often as a silence or a wild cry.

I call it a formlessness because as evoked by Kazantzakis, it is not unregistered but rather something that does not fit into words or into conventional shapes. No matter how it manifests itself, Kazantzakis gives it a special status, often rendering it similar to what his fellow traveler in the early years, Angelos Sikelianós, had called Cosmic Sexus, Lyricism, or a Cosmic Creative Rythmos.[6] In the years 1914–15 Kazantzakis and Sikelianós had exchanged ideas over the cosmic and the essence of the religious instinct, just before Kazantzakis started writing his tragedy *Christ* in 1915.[7] An important text for Sikelianós had been Édouard Schuré's *Great Initiates: A*

Study of the Secret History of Religions (1889), a book that treats Rama, Krishna, Hermes, Moses, Orpheus, Pythagoras, Plato, and Jesus.[8] This book, translated from French into Greek in 1904, had made an impact at the time, and it is highly likely, both through his association with Sikelianós and through his strong interest in theological and metaphysical questions, that Kazantzakis had read it as well.[9] Schuré's chapter on Jesus links him to an ancient tradition of mysticism, which focuses on the importance of inner revelation. Schuré rejects the Jesus of Strauss, Renan, and Keim, arguing that this tradition of biblical criticism deprives the story of its "light," leaving out "the intuitive sensation and inner knowledge."[10]

This metaphysical state I am referring to here stands for the epicenter of all centers, which unites and harmonizes the world and everything in it, something of which we are both aware and unaware at the same time. Considering the meaning of the world, the old rabbi (Jesus' uncle) reflects:

> Everything is of God, . . . everything has two meanings, one manifest, one hidden. The common people comprehend only what is manifest. They say, "This is a snake," and their minds go no further; but the mind which dwells in God sees what lies behind the visible, sees the hidden meaning. . . . But what is that meaning?[11]

And then he addresses Jesus, using an image that reverberates throughout the novel:

> No one told me; but still, it's possible. I've seen signs. Once when you were a boy you took some clay and fashioned a bird. While you caressed it and talked to it, it seemed to me that this bird of clay grew wings and flew out of your grasp. It's possible that this clay bird is the soul of man, Jesus, my child—the soul of man in your hands.[12]

In this novel about death, life and death are presented as inevitably interimplicated and interwoven, as if the one contains the other. The struggle of the human being to ascend from flesh to spirit has been interpreted by several critics in developmental terms, as progress or "creative evolution" from defeat (of the flesh) to victory (of the spirit). This developmental view, however, does not allow for the predetermined interimplication of opposites at every stage. The world is a result of opposites in unison, a unison that can only be understood as a harmony, the principle of the world's existence, and as a sound of music, leaving a soothing effect on us. Jesus and the disciples sing in ecstasy when they see Jerusalem from a distance, as if they know that this is where they are fated to be tested.

To say that Jesus "creatively evolves," as I elaborate later, is to suggest either that there is an unpredictable change occurring at random in the process, as in the Darwinian schema, or that there is a willed impulse toward improvement. In Kazantzakian terms the world is neither unpredictable, if we read the signs, nor developing, if we consider that the abyss has no time, space, or direction. If we are correct to assume that "harmony," or a unified epicenter as a World-Psyche, as Plato calls it in the *Timaeus,* is closer to what Kazantzakis is suggesting, then the world we live, act, dream, and create in is comparable to a performance. The existentialist Platonist Iris Murdoch writes: "Man is a creature who makes pictures of himself, and then comes to resemble the picture."[13] This same sentiment is expressed in the novel in Jesus' dream when he sees the "redbeard" (Judas) ambitiously aspiring to eternal development as a rebel and scorning the visionary prophet. In the dream Judas rages at the prophet:

> And you, malicious fanatical headstrong ascetic: you look at your own face and manufacture a God who is malicious, fanatical and headstrong. Then you prostrate yourself and worship him because he resembles you.[14]

The implication is that Judas is shortsighted in thinking that he can impose his will on the future and shape it. Prophets recognize the signs and accept the predetermined nature of the world. The Platonic circle of resemblances suggests always the vanity of human will.

It was in relation to concepts like what I have called formlessness that T. S. Eliot expressed his famous struggle for words to define what may be the impulse behind artistic expression. His essay "Tradition and the Individual Talent," he announced, "proposes to halt at the frontier of metaphysics or mysticism."[15] This rather awkward awareness lies behind the powerfully eloquent lines in his *Four Quartets*: "Words, after speech, reach / Into the silence. Only by the form, the pattern, / Can words or music reach / The stillness, as a Chinese jar still / Moves perpetually in its stillness."[16] In similar manner, Kazantzakis depicts the way words or forms ("the form, the pattern") are the manifest signs of a hidden meaning, access to which is available only through an emotional or intuitive leap.

As I read it, neither the world nor human beings can be said to be evolving in Kazantzakis's work in the sense of there being a power that can alter life and its course. Everything returns to death, or to the abyss, as he argued in *Askitiki* (1927), a point that is emphatically reiterated in *The Last Temptation*. "God is an abyss," says the rabbi when the Zealot is crucified, meaning that the destiny of the world is incomprehensible and indeterminable.[17] "Life? Death? What was this silence?" the narrator asks us when Magdalene raises her head to listen for an answer.[18] But this metaphysical dimension also means that the world in its essence is not made up of a singular power. It is more like a deeper sensation of a balance or a harmony, as I will argue. This is almost certainly the implication of Jesus' crucial phrase "Love one another!"[19] In other words, the apparent opposites must unite and constitute a harmony.

Rather than a Bergsonian élan vital, I argue, Kazantzakis's emphasis on transubstantiation (*metusíosis*), the materialization of an innate spirit, is more meaningfully understood in relation to the Platonic idea of World-Psyche, a formless substance that contains everything, or the multifaceted essence of our being.[20]

Monism or Dualism?

Peter Bien's predominantly Bergsonian reading of Kazantzakis interprets the Greek writer as viewing the world "monistically." Thus,

> *god is the entire evolutionary process*: the primordial essence that first wills its own congealment into life and then wills the unmaking of that creative action. . . . The essential thing is the invisible progress on which each visible organism rides during its short interval on earth, . . . [allowing] life's continuity of genetic energy to pass like a current from germ to germ in its ascent towards consciousness or supraconsciousness, . . . [helping reality to] become "productive of effects in which it expands and transcends its own being" (Bergson).[21]

In focusing on this divine energy that moves the world, this interpretation underestimates the significance of the gap between what man wills and what inexplicable nature imposes. The monist view interprets these two forces as one and the same, as both cause and object of activity.

This view takes human freedom ("in the rare moments when this 'thick crust that covers our personal sentiments . . . bursts'") as a given.[22] But, one might argue, if humans are continually subject to the inner power of élan vital, they are compelled to activity, limited by its singular predisposition. The struggle between spirit and flesh, which Kazantzakis depicts in *The Last Temptation* as a constant human battle, suggests that there are two or even more unidentified powers. Jesus expresses ignorance as to his antagonist:

> "I am wrestling," he answered!
> "With whom?"
> "I don't know. . . . I'm wrestling."[23]

If we adopt a monist position and assume that the propelling power is one, then the struggle cannot be but illusory—an illusion, surely, few readers of this powerful novel would want to accept. And again, to what extent can we assume that this propelling force that works for itself and by itself leads to something higher?

When Kazantzakis writes in his prologue to *The Last Temptation* about the "incessant, merciless battle between the spirit and the flesh," we must be careful to avoid interpreting this in value-laden terms.[24] In speaking of Jesus' "ascent,"[25] he means not a triumph of spirit or soul over flesh but rather a victory of union in an incessant and unresolvable struggle: "The stronger the soul and the flesh, the more fruitful the struggle and the richer the final harmony."[26] In his own reading of Bergson forty years earlier, Kazantzakis seems to reject the view of creative evolution as a single power. The philosopher's "flowing, evolving thought," he writes, requires "joining intuitional capabilities to your intellectual ones."[27]

The emphasis on transubstantiation inevitably leads in rational terms to the idea of ascent. A similar reading of Kazantzakis can be found in the study by

Darren J. N. Middleton, who tends to depict Kazantzakian wrestling as a form of ascent, as for example in the following observation:

> This notion of divine-human tussle seems to form the connective tissue holding *The Last Temptation of Christ* and *Saint Francis* together as fictional narratives capable of provoking process theological reflection. Jesus and Saint Francis are major models of spiritual becoming; indeed, Kazantzakis views them as sanctified heroes energized by the desire to redeem God through the incremental conversion of flesh into spirit. In *The Last Temptation of Christ*, Jesus' spirituality ripens through acts of creative *metousiosis*. In Bergsonian terms, Kazantzakis's Jesus helps to "unmake" the élan vital by practicing "spiritual exercises," which enable him to transcend the wonders of the material world.[28]

The main theme of the novel, he writes elsewhere, is "the transubstantiation of Jesus' flesh into spirit, . . . the freeing of élan vital from the confines of matter."[29] There is no doubt that this often seems to have been said by Kazantzakis himself, as for example in *Saint Francis*, where he attributes to his hero the "highest obligation," "the obligation to transubstantiate the matter which God entrusted to us, and turn it into spirit."[30] There is another way of reading this, however, according to which transformation into spirit does not mean the elimination of the flesh. The wonders of the material world are not transcended but rather "enveloped in God's breath," to use the phase from the novel quoted earlier.

In Platonic thought, which I think corresponds quite closely to Kazantzakis's particular version of Christianity, duality (as inherited from the Pythagorean tradition) provides a background against which to read materiality and the metaphysical void as in imperative balance and harmony. Only through this harmony can the human potential attain freedom and simultaneously subjugate itself to the divine will. *The Last Temptation* ends with the enigmatic but climactic phrase: "Everything has begun."[31] Through this we are led to understand that "nothing that happens in the world is without its meaning," a phrase expressed by the greedy old Zebedee, which nonetheless rings true.[32] He is here referring to the sight of a flying fish winging over his head and diving back into the lake. The materiality of the world's signs, through which God takes presence, are there to be read by all. In appearing to the disciples after the crucifixion in fleshly form, Christ manifests his own materiality as if he has never left them.

Kazantzakis's Dual Perception

I began this chapter by saying that Matthew acts to some extent as a double of the narrator, setting things down in historical order. The difference between the two, however, begins to emerge in relation to Matthew's failure to understand inner intention and motivation, and above all the tragedy of Jesus' predicament. The difference between Matthew and the narrator is that one gives an external narrative, while the other explores an individual psyche as well. Dreams occur frequently in the novel as indications of a psychic shift. The novel opens with a long description of a dream of Jesus sleeping in his workshed, a dream that occupies the whole of the first chapter, and finishes with a prolonged dream-vision that Jesus has on the cross. In both of these cases, conveyed through an elaborate narrative in which the unconscious is represented in images, we are given to understand how the World-Psyche manifests itself in the human mind, either in fear or in desire.

The narration of this first dream involves several shifts in point of view, providing a variety of narratives. At times the perspective is of a distant, third-person narrator, a person outside the text who shares our contemporary point of view. At other times the third-person narrative lapses into the second person, as if Jesus is addressing himself, or the narrator is speaking to Jesus directly: "Little by little your eyes became accustomed to the darkness."[33] On other occasions, free indirect speech takes us into the mind of Jesus or gives us the voice of a local person. There is also a dialogue in Jesus' dream between Judas, as a leader of the rebels, and the mob.

This constant shifting of narrative perspective functions to represent the flickering or vacillation between bodily and spiritual experience that the dream seeks to capture. The formlessness of Psyche can only appear evanescently in the material images of dreams. In the dream with which the novel opens, Kazantzakis uses the word "rarefied" (aréose) to suggest the way the entry into or out of the dream state involves the taking on or putting off of material form:

> The dream took fright, began to flee. The mountain rarefied and its insides appeared. It was not made of rock, but of sleep and dizziness. The group of huge wild men who were stamping furiously up it with giant strides—all mustaches, beards, eyebrows and great long hands—they rarefied also, lengthened, widened, were completely transformed and then plucked into tiny threads like clouds scattered by a strong wind. A little more and they would have disappeared from the sleeper's mind.[34]

Here the verbs, beginning with "rarefied," move the passage toward the taking off of form: began to flee, rarefied, lengthened, widened, transformed, plucked, scattered, disappeared. The starkly concrete nouns and adjectives, however, work to retain the material forms (mountains, insides, rock, huge wild men, mustaches, beards, eyebrows, great long hands, threads). They keep the experience grounded in the sensual, reinforcing the way, in Platonic terms, that through form we recollect its essence in Psyche. The passage is characteristic of what could be called a tussle (between verbs and nouns) at the textual level itself. Only in dreams, in this irresolution between form and its essence, can Jesus' innermost impulses (fear, desire, guilt) be represented. Dimly conscious of his predestination, he wonders, still dreaming: "Was this sleep? Or death, immortality, God?"[35]

The rendering of such material immateriality into English presents a particular challenge for the translator of this novel. One example occurs in a second-person passage in this first dream, where Jesus is described as follows: "*Psihanemízusun, osmízusun, ómos den évlepes típote*," which is rendered by Peter Bien as "You sniffed, you sensed, you divined—but saw nothing."[36] *Psihanemízusun* is a characteristic Kazantzakian word formed from *psihí* (psyche) and *ánemos* (breeze), which when compounded in Greek takes on the metaphorical meaning of "to suspect" or "to perceive."[37] Peter Bien's choice of the term "to divine" here conveys powerfully Kazantzakis's connotation of uncanny insight that is part of Jesus' response. He is compelled, however, to use two verbs instead of one ("you sensed, you divined"), thus disjoining what for Kazantzakis is a unified experience, bodily (sensing) and spiritual (divining). In the novel this divination is an important part of the constant expectation that God's voice will be heard, an expectation that is never fulfilled. What predominates is silence or Jesus' one-sided dialogue with God.[38] God's voice can only be registered by the psyche of, for example, Jesus in the desert, or John the Baptist, or the rabbi, or the abbot on his deathbed—as an inner imagining, a cry, an abyss, a nothingness.[39]

Platonic idealism posits the duality of any manifestation that bears a form. For Plato, form is the mental registration of what cannot otherwise be revealed. In order for something to be revealed, it has to take on exteriority, as a harmony or as the "sameness" of the inner with the outer.[40] Elsewhere, Kazantzakis makes use of a Nietzschean reading of the Dionysian and the Apollonian to illustrate the way Apollonian light acts as an outer revelation of inner (Dionysian) impulses.[41]

It is striking how deeply Platonic Kazantzakis is in his definition of soul or psyche as the spring or source of self-motivation. "The foundation is the soul," Jesus says.[42] "When I bend far down into my soul, . . . I don't know how and why the truth always issues from within me."[43] Kazantzakis's depiction of this enveloping soul/psyche in his prologue makes clear that it is the locus where body and spirit (*sárka* and *pnévma*) play out this insoluble antagonism: "My soul is the arena where these two armies have clashed and met."[44] In Greek Orthodoxy, spirit and soul are often conflated; similarly in Kazantzakis's text, "spirit" often functions as that which mediates between the soul and the world. Thus when Andrew is described as rejoicing "with his whole body [*síngorma*], his whole soul [*símpsiha*]—deeply, with the very roots of his being," what is being conveyed is the way body and soul/spirit unite to form psychic harmony.[45] There is yet another term often added to this harmony in Kazantzakis's text, the term *nus* (mind or intellect), which in the late Platonic dialogues suggests both the highest activity of the soul and the divine and the transcendent principle of cosmic order. This sense is intended in the following phrase at the end of *The Last Temptation*, when Christ on the cross is described as "hurling downward [into his *nus*] and perishing"[46] (*gremízuntan mésa sto nu tu ke hánuntan*).[47]

As any user of the Greek language is aware, *pnévma* and *psihí* represent both contraries and a resulting harmony in the Platonic tradition, in particular as it entered early Christianity. In the *Phaedo*, the dialogue glorifying death, Plato elaborates on the concept of psyche in relation to the Pythagorean principle of harmony, suggesting that "every man partakes of the divine nature in both his spirit and his flesh."[48] This Platonic context is most strikingly conveyed by Kazantzakis in his confessional prologue to *The Last Temptation*:

The anguish has been intense. I loved my body and did not want it to perish; I loved my soul and did not want it to decay. I have fought to reconcile these two primordial forces which are so contrary to one another, to make them realize that they are not enemies but rather fellow-workers, so that they might rejoice in their harmony—and so that I might rejoice with them.[49]

Conclusion: Kazantzakis's Theogeny

Schuré's *Great Initiates*, mentioned earlier, gives the following summary of the Pythagorean view of the world:

> The material and spiritual development of the world are two contrary motions which are nonetheless parallel and in harmony [concordants] on the whole scale of being. The one can only be understood through the other, and seen together, they explain the world.[50]

This panoramic vision is very close to that of Kazantzakis, whose decision to deal with Christ the Theanthropos inevitably led him to broad questions touching upon the relation of matter to spirit—in other words, to cosmogony and mysticism. (The view first expressed by Elli Alexiou, that her ex-brother-in-law had one foot on earth and the other in heaven, is a commonplace in Greek assessments of the writer.) These concerns invariably took precedence over matters of social interaction or analysis in all of Kazantzakis's writings, in which the emphasis is on the human being in its confrontation with universal, cosmic demands. Unlike most novelists of his time, he was undaunted by such large, abstract questions: How can Christ be both divine and human? How is death related to life? Or how can we communicate with the World-Psyche, and what form does it take?

In the *Phaedrus*, Plato used the famous tripartite image of the soul as a charioteer controlling and balancing two horses, one noble energy, the other degenerate appetite.[51] In the *Timaeus*, which deserves particular attention as the only surviving dialogue in the early centuries of Christianity and thus influential (along with the Neoplatonists Plotinus, Proclus, and Porphysius) in shaping its development, World-Psyche is described in the broadest possible terms as the cosmological principle that contains everything:

> He [God] made her [psyche] out of the following elements and on this wise. From the being which is indivisible and unchangeable, and from that kind of being which is distributed among bodies, he compounded a third and intermediate kind of being. He did likewise with the same and the different, blending together the indivisible kind of each with that which is portioned out in bodies. Then, taking the three new elements, he mingled them all into one form, compressing by force the reluctant and unsociable nature of the different into the same.[52]

As "third and intermediate kind of being," therefore, psyche contains and combines both body and spirit, same and different, in such a way as to render discussions of them as separate entities ultimately redundant. For Plato (particularly in the *Philebus*), our material bodies are composed of the same substance that composes the universe. In Kazantzakis's text, similarly, Jesus' human form is more emphatically present than are the allegorical implications of his divine being.[53]

The material signs experienced in life need to be deciphered for us to register the realm of universal harmony. Nowhere, I have said, do we have direct access to God's voice in the novel, although we have been led to anticipate it continually. To be in a state of knowing requires solitude, as we are given to understand through Mary's role. Mary, who has experienced God's presence (the moment of conception), when Joseph is struck down by a thunderbolt, says, "God descended in a savage form on top of the mountain and spoke to me in a savage way." She goes on to ask, "What did he say to me?" and after much effort thinks she cannot remember. Again, all of a sudden, she thinks she remembers that God has said, "Hail, Mary," nothing more.[54] By this I believe Kazantzakis wants to suggest that God is neither an abstract presence nor a blind spirit or force pushing the individual upward, but rather a manifestation within things, helping us to distinguish the multiple contrasts within the eternal harmony. Salvation is achieved only when we reach wisdom by recognizing the totality, our being in it. The *content* of God's message, "the actual words," is inaccessible.[55] All that remains is the addressing voice ("Hail, Mary") in all its physical presence. That voice emerges as a combination of the sound of the thunder rolling down "like a creaking ox-cart"[56] and the touch of the dove, its "tiny warm body and beating heart,"[57] which Mary caresses on her knees in her effort to remember. Through a reverberation of images, this dove will be picked up later, as we have seen, when Jesus is described by the old rabbi as having created the soul of man from a clay bird, which grew wings and flew off when caressed by the young Messiah. It is these sense-experiences of the world in our present embodied life that enable us, according to Plato, to return in recollection to the eternal realities.

Notes

1. Peter Bien states that Ernest Renan influenced Kazantzakis. Besides his essay in the present volume, see Bien, *Tempted by Happiness: Kazantzakis' Post-Christian Christ* (Wallingford, PA: Pendle Hill, 1984), 20. Also see Darren J. N. Middleton, *Novel Theology: Nikos Kazantzakis's Encounter with Whiteheadian Process Theism* (Macon, Georgia: Mercer University Press, 2000), 70.

2. Nikos Kazantzakis, *The Last Temptation*, trans. Peter Bien (New York: Simon & Schuster, 1960), 415.

3. Ibid., 127.

4. Ibid., 44.

5. Ibid., 56.

6. Angelos Sikelianós, "*Prólogos*," in *Lirikós Víos* (Athens: Ikaros, 1975), 1:9–81.

7. In his diary of November 29, 1914, written during his visit to Mount Athos with Sike-lianós, Kazantzakis wrote: "Tonight in our beds we continue talking about the essence of our innermost desire—to create religion. Everything is ripe. Ah! How can we externalize what is most sacred and deep in us[?]" See Pandelis Prevalakis, *Tetrakósia Grámmata tu Kazantzáki ston Preveláki* (Athens: Ekdósis Eleni N. Kazantzaki, 1965), 7. Also see Kazantzakis's letter to Prevelakis when Sikelianós died in 1951 (636–37).

8. See Pandelis Prevelakis, *Ángelos Sikelianós: Tría Kefálea Viografías k' Énas Prólogos* (Athens: Morfotikó Ídrima Ethnikís Trapézis, 1984), 55.

9. It is known that in these early years Kazantzakis was reading authors such as Tolstoy, Dante, Homer, and Buddha and translating William James, Nietzsche, J. P. Eckermann, Charles Darwin, C. A. Laisant, Bergson, and several Platonic dialogues. See Prevelakis, *Tetrakósia Grámmata*, 6. See also G. K. Katsimbalis, *Vivliografía N. Kazantzákis A, 1906–1948* (Athens: 1958); and Helen Kazantzakis, *Nikos Kazantzakis: A Biography Based on His Letters*, trans. Amy Mims (New York: Simon & Schuster, 1968).

10. This is how Schuré puts it: "Strauss's life of Jesus is a solar system without the sun. . . . Renan's life of Jesus is a solar system lit by a pale sun, without life-giving magnetism or creative warmth . . . Theodore Keim's life of Jesus is the most remarkable to have been writ-ten since that of Renan, drawing the maximum light from the texts and from history as interpreted *externally*. But the problem is not one that can be solved without intuition, without the esoteric tradition. It is with this esoteric light, the inner flame of all religions, central truth of every fertile philosophy, that I have tried to reconstruct the life of Jesus in its broad sweep" (translation mine). "La vie de Jésus de Strauss est un système planétaire sans soleil. . . . La vie de Jésus de M. Renan est un système planétaire éclairé par un pâle soleil, sans magnétisme vivifant et sans chaleur créatrice. . . . [La] vie de Jésus [de M. Théodore Keim] est la plus remarquable qu'on ait écrite depuis celle de M. Renan. Elle éclaire la question de tout le jour qu'on peut tirer des textes et de l'historoire interprétés *exotériquement*. Mais le problème n'est pas de ceux qu'on puisse résoudre sans l'intuition et sans la tradition *ésotérique*. C'est avec cette lumière ésotérique, flambeau intérieur de toutes les religions, vérité central de toute philosophie féconde, que j'ai tenté de reconstruire la vie de Jésus dans ses grandes lignes." Édouard Schuré, *Les grands initiés: Esquisse de l' histoire secrète des religions: Rama, Krishna, Hermès, Moïse, Orphée, Pythagore, Platon, Jésus* (Paris: Perrin, 1919), 444–45.

11. Kazantzakis, *Last Temptation*, 150.

12. Ibid., 153.

13. Iris Murdoch, *Existentialists and Mystics: Writings on Philosophy and Literature* (London: Chatto & Windus, 1997), 75.

14. Kazantzakis, *Last Temptation*, 10.

15. T. S. Eliot, "Tradition and the Individual Talent," in *Selected Essays* (London: Faber & Faber, 1975), 21.

16. See T. S. Eliot, "Burnt Norton," in *The Complete Poems and Plays of T. S. Eliot* (London: Faber & Faber, 1970), 175.

17. Kazantzakis, *Last Temptation*, 49.

18. Ibid., 175.

19. Ibid., 185.

20. See Peter A. Bien, *Kazantzakis: Politics of the Spirit* (Princeton, NJ: Princeton University Press, 1989), 23–53.

21. Ibid., 38, 41.

22. Ibid., 44.

23. Kazantzakis, *Last Temptation*, 21.

24. Ibid., 1.

25. Ibid., 2.

26. Ibid.

27. Quoted in Bien, *Kazantzakis*, 52.

28. Middleton, *Novel Theology*, 108.

29. Ibid., 83.

30. Quoted in ibid., 108.

31. Kazantzakis, *Last Temptation*, 496.

32. Ibid., 113.

33. Ibid., 5.

34. Ibid., 6.

35. Ibid., 11.

36. Ibid., 5.

37. See Emmánuel Kriarás, *Néo Ellinikó Lexikó tis Sínhronis Dimotikís Glóssas: Graptís ke Proforikís* (Athens: Ekdotiki Athinon, 1995), 1522. This has an entry for the noun *psihanémisma* with an example from Kazantzakis: "to akathóristo psihanémisma gínete mésa mu veveótita."

38. Kazantzakis, *Last Temptation*, 175.

39. Ibid., 56.

40. For a more recent commentary on Plato's view on forms, see Robert William Jordan, *Plato's Arguments for Forms* (Cambridge: Cambridge Philological Society, 1983).

41. See Friedrich Nietzsche, *I Génnisis tis Tragodías*, trans. Nikos Kazantzakis (Athens: Fexis, 1912). For a comparative study of Nietzsche and Kazantzakis in relation to the Dionysian and Apollonian convergence, see C. D. Gounelas, "The Concept of Resemblance in Kazantzakis's Tragedies *Christ* and *Buddha*," *Journal of Modern Greek Studies* 16, no. 2 (1998): 313–30.

42. Kazantzakis, *Last Temptation*, 204.

43. Ibid., 313–14.

44. Ibid., 1.

45. Ibid., 191.

46. Ibid., 495.

47. Nikos Kazantzakis, *O teleftaíos pirasmós* (Athens: Difros, 1955), 514.

48. Kazantzakis, *Last Temptation*, 1.

49. Ibid., 1.

50. Schuré, *Les grands initiés*, 188, with my translation.

51. In the *Phaedrus*, Socrates says: "We ought now to say something about the soul's nature. To state exactly what the soul is would be a job for a god, and a lengthy one at that; for a human being a brief similitude will suffice. Let us talk about it in that way. Let us compare the soul to the combined forces of a team of winged horses and their charioteer. The horses and the charioteers of the gods are entirely good and of good stock, those of other beings vary. In our case, well, in the first place the charioteer drives a pair of horses, and in the second place one of these horses is noble and good and of a stock to match, while the other is of quite opposite character and breeding. Our charioteer's job is of necessity both difficult and troublesome." From *Phaedrus*, 246a–b, quoted in David Melling, *Understanding Plato* (Oxford: Oxford University Press, 1987), 73.

52. Plato, *Timaeus*, 34c–35a.

53. This view is endorsed by the fathers of the Orthodox Church, as explained by Lambros Kamperidis, who describes Christ as "perfect matter and perfect spirit, a perfect man and a perfect God who . . . descends Himself and commingles His immortal spirit with corruptible material out of which humanity is created." See Lambros Kamperidis, "The Orthodox Sources of *The Saviors of God*," in *God's Struggler: Religion in the Writings of Nikos Kazantzakis*, ed. Darren J. N. Middleton and Peter Bien (Macon, GA: Mercer University Press, 1996), 55. It is worth observing that in *Askitiki* (*The Saviors of God: Spiritual Exercises*), *Anayénnisi* (July–August 1927): 599–631, Kazantzakis stresses the need "to make the Spirit visible, to give it a face, to envelop it in words, in allegories, in reflections and exorcisms, so that it will not abandon us." Quoted in Kamperidis, "Orthodox Sources," 56.

54. Kazantzakis, *Last Temptation*, 60–61.

55. Ibid., 61.

56. Ibid.

57. Ibid.

In the Name-of-the-Father
The Semiotic Threat over the Symbolic Logos
Charitini Christodoulou

Introduction

Nikos Kazantzakis brings into his literature the female presence as a mediator. In this chapter I show that between humanity and nature, nature and culture, instinct and intellect, hu/man and divine, the female presence transfers—*metaphorein*—him/her from one to the other, regulating the process of subjectivity's formation. To this end, I draw on Julia Kristeva's work, relating her theory of the semiotic to woman, demonstrating woman's ability to threaten the stability of the Logos of the Father, of the patriarchal law and society, to shake, that is, the authority of the Name.

Kazantzakis, considering his duty to fight boundaries—"I cannot accept boundaries; I choke," he once remarked—gives female characters a presence and a voice that disrupts the corresponding Christian tradition. He invites a threatening dialogue between the semiotic modality of language and the symbolic, the semiotic representing what is not included in the Name-of-the-Father, meaning the dogma of religion and the law.

In the Name-of-the-Father, the Son, and . . . (the) Woman?

In the Name-of-the-Father is an extensively debated phrase that Jacques Lacan originally used to describe the castrating father of the Oedipus complex, who personifies the taboo on incest.[1] Being either a religious allusion, "*In nomine Patris*" (Matt 28:19 Vulgate), or a play on the French words *non* and *nom*, the Name-of-the-Father (*nom-du-pere*) expresses the father's prohibition, "no" (*non-du-pere*), of the child's incestuous desire for his mother. In Lacan's 1955–56 seminar on psychosis, the Name-of-the-Father is the fundamental signifier that confers identity on humans by situating them in the symbolic order. And Lacan claims that the expulsion of the Name-of-the-Father from the symbolic universe of the subject triggers psychosis.

In the context of Christianity, the Name-of-the-Father is related to the Word/Logos of God, implying a center of reference that entails the Truth. It is also related to Logocentrism, which derives from the Greek word *logos*, designating a structure that provides phenomena with an origin and an explanation of their nature.[2] The opening verse of the Fourth Gospel provides the most sublime example of Logocentrism: "In the beginning was the Word, and the Word was with God, and the Word was God" (John 1:1). In Christian theology, the Logos is the Word of God made flesh through Christ. The Word retained its symbolic properties, even after turning into flesh. Kristeva is thus right to point out that filial bonds in the Christian tradition are established not through the flesh but through the name of the Father.[3] Here, Kristeva castigates the privileging of Logocentrism in the subject's accession to society over the not-phallic elements, the semiotic. In the Bible, a family is constituted through the Word that assumes flesh. Even though Jesus' mother is the career of the Word's transubstantiation into flesh, she is not included in the invocation of the Holy Trinity—"In the name of the Father, and of the Son, and of the Holy Ghost"—that represents the Truth and its origin (Matt 28:19 KJV).

While it seems that Kristeva discusses Logocentrism in terms of Phallogocentrism, being consistent with her tendency of subverting what is established, she disturbs the above correlation by arguing that the woman is the phallus. Lacan first claimed that the phallus is not to be perceived as merely an organ, a penis.[4] Following Lacan, Kristeva claims: "As the addressee of every demand, the mother occupies the place of alternity. Her replete body, the receptacle and guarantor of demands, takes the place of all narcissistic, hence imaginary, effects and gratifications. . . . She is, in other words, the Phallus."[5] Kristeva addresses the question of the mother's role in subjectivity's formation. As a biological function and a social presence, the mother fills in the gaps that the symbolic order is unable to complement, justify, or address adequately. She does not really exist as a symbolic subject with due respect to her semiotic aspect, but she exists in the shadow of the symbolic role she is assigned to in Christian tradition. And she is called to *be-come*—a word implying a transformation and a metaphor—what she is not, in this way gratifying the needs of a phallic order. Thus she becomes the metaphor of a phallus.

In "About Chinese Women" Kristeva comments on the book of Genesis:

> When Yahweh says to the serpent, "I will put enmity between thee and woman, and between thy seed and her seed; it shall bruise thy head, and thou shalt bruise its heel" [Gen 3:15 KJV], he established the divergence—of race or "seed"—between God and man on the one hand and woman on the other. Furthermore, in the second part of the sentence, woman disappears completely into seed: generation. This is to say that woman stands to man and God as an other.[6]

Woman and the mother exist to confirm the identity of the One, who in Christianity refers to the Name of the Father. Her presence is sacrificed and exists in exile—she is the other. The question(s) is whether she is set aside so that the Logos is rendered as the ultimate truth, and whether she is doomed to silence and is sacrificed in the Name-of-the-Father. Jacques Derrida says, "Man speaks, . . . but it is because the symbol has made him man [a speaking subject]."[7] For Lacan, the emergence of symbolic structures is essential for the human transition from nature to culture. However, who is the intermediary who is sacrificed, is excluded, and at what point does this *trans*-ition (Kristeva's notion of *metaphorein*) from nature to culture take place?

Kristeva was among the first theoreticians to address these and other related questions. In *Revolution in Poetic Language*, she argues that sacrifice and art represent two aspects of the institution of the symbolic: "Sacrifice reminds us that the semiotic emerges out of material continuity and the violence of death." It thus reproduces both "the foundation of the social code and what it represses."[8] In another text, she continues:

> All religions . . . celebrate the sacred as a sacrifice: that of a plant, an animal, or a man. Judaism, and then Christianity, admit that this sacrifice is the one that inscribes language in the body, meaning in life. And it does so through a prohibition that does not need to kill to cut, but confines itself to setting out a moral system. A *sacre* moral system, laden with revolts and passions.[9]

Jesus was crucified in his Father's Name, which constituted a revolution based on a morality of love, with due respect to equality, and yet woman's existence in Christianity has been marginalized. However, the "porousness of Being" (Edmund Husserl)— what is not represented in language and the sacrifice that establishes society, the point where the flesh intervenes with the spirit and rationalism with feelings—is an aspect of human existence that, according to Kristeva, leans toward the feminine.

In Christianity, the Virgin, the ultimate female presence, is a silent contributor and supporter of the ultimate sacrifice. Kristeva asserts:

> A mistress or a mother, a woman remains a foreigner to sacrifice: she participates in it, she assumes it but she also disturbs it; she can threaten it. We understand, thus, that this vital depth comprises a social danger as well: eventually, what kind of morality can exist if the sacred needs to be confronted with the attack of those women who scream due to their inherent animism?[10]

This is where Kristeva meets Kazantzakis, in whose novel Jesus' mother attacks the sacred with her voice expressing anger and suffering; her "inherent animism" is revealed. Unable to find a rational explanation, she questions the symbolic order. Woman is therefore brought back to the scene of representation and claims a presence. Jesus' mother does not claim a placement, which implies fixity, but a permission to *become in existence*, without the settling adjective in front of the name—Virgin.

In Kazantzakis's *The Last Temptation*, woman becomes a speaking subject, through a struggle between the semiotic and symbolic modalities. In *Revolution in Poetic Language*, Kristeva writes:

> If there exists a "discourse" which is . . . the essential element of a practice involving the sum of unconscious, subjective, and social relations in gestures of confrontation and appropriation, destruction and construction—productive violence in short—it is "literature," or, more specifically, the text.[11]

Identity in literature, therefore, is the outcome of an eternal destruction and reconstruction expressed through the process of writing. I regard *The Last Temptation* as a novel falling within this category of writing that can be discussed in terms of Kristeva's definition of "literature" or "text."

From the Start, Language Is a Translation

The phrase "from the start" between "language" and "translation" is important. I relate it to the Gospel expression "In the beginning" (John 1:1), used repeatedly by Kristeva. From the beginning language is a translation, according to her. Substituting "language" with "Word," we come up with "The Word is, from the start, a translation." Since "in the beginning was the Word," then the Word is a translation. In the Word's transubstantiation into flesh, Jesus became a translation and a metaphor. Moreover, due to his metaphorical existence, humans gain eternity.

I relate this frame of thought to Kristeva's statement: "If I'm no longer capable of translating or metaphorizing, I become silent and die."[12] In Kristeva's theory, a translation and a metaphor are at stake. Both signify a process deriving from her concept of *metaphorein*, operating on the level of "trans" and presupposing an excess, an "indefinite jamming of . . . one into the other."[13] This excerpt conveys Kristeva's struggle against "monolingualism," the monolithic and motionless establishment of a single meaning. She perceives the feminine as the source of the inexpressible, while her main concerns are with the politics of marginality. Her work expresses the desire to produce a discourse that confronts and—in endless process—is the impasse of language, thinking language against itself.

Her notion of "poetic language/text" disrupts the idea of a single, fixed meaning and opens the way to "polyphony." Expanding on Mikhail Bakhtin's legacy, Kristeva perceives the text as a "productivity": texts and language include an "otherness" that destabilizes meaning and erases oneness.

Perceiving language as nonstatic refers to the notion that language is not reducible to dimensions apprehended by consciousness. Concern for the unconscious leads Kristeva to her concept of the subject in process. This subject can never be captured in one form, since its essence involves its unspeakable, repressed form, whose being is realized through its effects.

By acknowledging this otherness of meaning and of subjectivity, Kristeva tries to express what has been repressed or excluded. In effect, she is concerned for the symbolic (cultural, theological) appropriation of the un-analyzable. To address these issues, she escapes into language.[14] As she says in *Desire in Language*, "Meaning's closure can never be challenged by another space, but only by a different way of speaking: another enunciation, another literature."[15] Through discourses opposing the language of the one, Kristeva seeks to find woman. In *The Feminine and the Sacred,* she, in collaboration with Catherine Clement, asks: "Does a specifically feminine sacred exist? What place is there for women in that history dating from the birth of Jesus, what chance for them two thousand years after him?"[16] Studying Christianity in relation to psychoanalysis, she realizes that woman has indeed been sacrificed, existing in the margins of the manifestations of the Name of the Father. Giving birth or participating in death, she is always the necessary other who is not fairly represented. In Kristeva's terms, the semiotic is sacrificed for the sake of the symbolic's dominance.

The Symbolic versus (?) the Semiotic

The dialogue between the semiotic and the symbolic modality of signification is the necessary precondition for the production of meaning articulated by "the speaking subject." This subject is split by definition, is always in a process of becoming, and manifests itself in "poetic language," literature being one of its expressions. As is suggested in *Revolution in Poetic Language,* "it was in literature . . . that the dialectical condition of the subject was made explicit."[17]

The symbolic provides the linguistic structures necessary to communicate, and the semiotic motivates signification while threatening the symbolic. Although the semiotic prompts transgressions and the symbolic demands conformity, both are interdependent, a fact that guarantees a relationship between body (*sōma*) and soul (*psychē*). Language is like a driving force transferred into life, and signification is like a transfusion of the living body into meaningfulness.

The symbolic comprises the entire social order, religion included, into which all human beings are initiated to become speaking subjects. The symbolic refers to the authoritative meaning of the Logos of the Father, imposing censorship on anything that attempts to transgress its boundaries. The semiotic, alluding to manifestations of otherness, is suppressed in favor of the imposition of the symbolic, which denies the existence of one and the other at the same time and thus does not challenge any sense of identity and subjectivity.

The subject's relation to the symbolic is at the heart of psychoanalysis, as the subject's participation in the symbolic is a process that imposes structures on sexuality and allows the subject to emerge. Pre-Oedipal sexuality is likened to a state of nature and unbridled sexuality. The role of the Name-of-the-Father is to disrupt the dual relationship in which the child tries to fuse with the mother in order to establish a legitimate line of descent. For identity to take place, "the subject must separate from and through his image, from and through his objects," which alludes to symbolic castration.[18]

Concern for the subject's formation led Kristeva to the semiotic. It is the language of the senses and the materiality expressed through language, the body and its functions, smells, drives, impulses, dreams being included. Defined as the "kinetic functional stage" preceding "the establishment of the sign," the semiotic precedes and transcends the symbolic.[19] Though its elements turn toward language, they are irreducible to its structures; the semiotic is always "translinguistic" or "non-linguistic."[20]

On the cultural level, the semiotic preserves and expresses the multifarious libidinal desire challenging the Name-of-the-Father and retaining contact with the female element. Having in mind the properties of the semiotic, in *Report to Greco* Kazantzakis says, "I collect my tools: sight, smell, touch, taste, hearing, intellect."[21] And *The Last Temptation* portrays Jesus thus:

> Seeing a fig tree, he started to slow down in order to pick a leaf and smell it. He liked the smell of fig leaves very much: they reminded him of human armpits. When he was little he used to close his eyes and smell the leaves, and he imagined he was snuggled again at his mother's breasts, sucking. . . . But the moment he stopped and put out his hand to pick the leaf, cold sweat poured over his body.[22]

Also, the novel refers to Jesus and Magdalene thus:

> "No, I don't want to go, I don't want to go [to Magdalene's house]!" he murmured in terror. He tried to reverse his course, but his body refused. It stood its ground like a greyhound and smelled the air.[23]

If the semiotic is conceived sensually, Kazantzakis is an author leaning toward the semiotic.

Both Kazantzakis and Kristeva deal with the sacred and its manifestations. Through Jesus, Mary, and Magdalene, the struggle between Kristeva's two modalities is expressed. The reader deals with split personalities that make up a polyphonic narrative. As Kristeva says, "The speaking subject is a divided subject. . . . The linguistic split (signifier/signified) and the split subject (unconscious/conscious, societal constraints/libido) are part of a biological system that itself is based on a system of division."[24] Similarly, Kazantzakis confesses:

> Within me are the dark immemorial forces of the Evil One, human and pre-human; within me too are the luminous forces, human and pre-human, of God—and my soul is the arena where these two armies have clashed and met.[25]

Anticipating postmodernism's general spirit, Kazantzakis speaks of a process that humans go through to find meaning, a process captured in the conclusion that there is no meaning.

Jesus: A Melancholic Subject Caught between the Semiotic and the Symbolic

> As speaking beings, always potentially on the verge of speech, we have always been divided, separated from nature. This split has left within us traces of the pre- or

translinguistic semiotic processes that . . . diachronically constitute a presubject (the infans). Synchronically they display the catastrophic anguish ("passion") of depressive psychosis. . . . We are subjects in process, ceaselessly losing our identity, destabilized by fluctuations in our relations to the other.[26]

Here Kristeva suggests that there is a division in the speaking subject defining identity's formation, which keeps the subject in contact with his/her presymbolic existence. If the processes related to the presymbolic insist synchronically with the entrance into the symbolic, a crisis is triggered, because the subject is reminded of the loss of the mother, upon whom identity is based.

In *Black Sun*, Julia Kristeva claims: "For man and for woman the loss of the mother is a biological and psychic necessity, the first step on the way to becoming autonomous. Matricide is our vital necessity."[27] Subjectivity thus is contingent on loss. An inability to deal with this loss results in a dangerous form of self-exile, as the mother and the child used to be initially one, although two—the one within the other. This exile, exposing the subject to the memory of a forceful separation at its very core, might cause melancholia or psychosis.

The Last Temptation's Jesus can be discussed in terms of the above theory. While reading the novel, I initially viewed Kazantzakis's Jesus as either a madman or someone suffering from melancholia. He is definitely a divided person, hearing voices whose source is invisible and unidentified and wanting to make them go away, not to mention that he bursts into laughter inexplicably. According to some psychologists, both reactions are signs of madness:

But then, suddenly, someone above was speaking to him. He cocked his ear and heard—heard, and shook his head violently, continually, as though saying: No! No! No! . . .

He remained still again and listened:

"What do you say? I can't hear!"

. . . He listened, holding his breath, and the more he heard, the more his face glowed mischievously, contentedly. His thick fresh lips tingled with numbness, and suddenly he burst out laughing.[28]

Kazantzakis's Jesus also feels invisible presences attacking him:

He raised his eyes and looked: no one. But he smelled the bitter stench of a wild beast in the air. He has come again, he thought with terror; he is all around me and beneath my feet and above my head.[29]

Given these extracts, two of many like them, I think Jesus' speech resembles Kristeva's depressed patient's speech in *Black Sun*:

They utter sentences that are interrupted, exhausted, come to a standstill. Even phrases they cannot formulate. . . . On account of the pressure of silence, the melancholy person appears to stop cognising as well as uttering, sinking into the blankness of asymbolia or the excess of an unorderable cognitive chaos.[30]

Jesus cannnot identify with the world of symbols. And he feels responsibility for others' misery. Not surprisingly, his feelings of despair conquer his soul. He is a melancholic subject living in the death of speech, trying to situate himself in the order of language and speak in the Name-of-His-Father. Even Jesus' route to cruci-fixion touches the borders of schizophrenia or madness: "Someone came. Surely it was God, God, . . . or was it the devil? Who can tell them apart?"[31] Kristeva claims that the story "of the torment of the flesh on Golgotha . . . mirrors in glory the essential melancholy of the man who aspires to rejoin the body and name of a father from whom he has been irrevocably severed."[32] Until Kazantzakis's Jesus accepts the otherness within him, he resembles a psychotic subject.

Kazantzakis's Jesus' disgust with the invisible, and his intention to make crosses to crucify all the messiahs sent by God, leads me to another of Kristeva's observations:

> Christ's passion brings into play even more primitive layers of the psyche; it thus reveals a fundamental depression (a narcissistic wound or reversed hatred) that conditions access to human language. . . . The child must abandon its mother and be abandoned by her in order to be accepted by the father and begin talking. If it is true that language begins in mourning inherent in the evolution of subjectivity, the abandonment by the father—the symbolic "other"—triggers a melancholy anguish that can grow to suicidal proportions. "I detest him, but I am he, therefore I must die."[33]

Jesus needs to depart from the dependency of his mother's semiotic enclosure to fulfill his Father's demand. However, the presence of not only Mary, his mother, but also Magdalene shapes Jesus' fate. The things he needs to reject—dependence, pity, desire, lust, fear—resurface, due to the female presences. For instance, he experiences difficulty forgetting the taste of the maternal paradise.[34] And the semiotic, always present in the subject, keeps alive the desire to return to the protective yet suffocating enclosure of the w(t?)omb. Desire arises by a "lack of being," signaling the division of the subject. Jesus is divided and thus lacks the stability that identity provides. He exists between his human and divine nature. Jesus' first urge is to harm himself, then to harm others, and finally to lead himself to death. For Kristeva, the continuous pursuit of death is related to suppressed sexuality. "Even the death instinct is a manifestation of sexuality when it subtends aggressive desires, desires to inflict pain on another person or on oneself (even to the point of death)."[35] Jesus' sexuality within Kazantzakis's novel has two referees and receivers: Mary, his mother, and Mary Magdalene.

Jesus' Mother: A Career of the Semiotic Threat

Jesus' mother, Mary, and Magdalene are agents of the narrative's desire to move forward toward death and life. They are agents of the death drive, leading narrative to closure, only for the genesis of meaning to be set in motion once again, through destruction, death of the ultimate signified and signifier, the sacrifice itself.

Kazantzakis emphasizes Jesus' mother's human aspect, depriving her of the symbolic property of being a virgin with no desires of the flesh. In *The Last Temptation*, the reader confronts a representation of Mary that completely contradicts the traditional figuration of the Virgin.[36] After all, the Bible does not provide an extensive reference to the Virgin's life. And Catherine Clement, addressing Kristeva, wonders about the Virgin's presence in the Bible:

> When does Mary step in? When she is fourteen at the time of the Annunciation; then, during her pregnancy and Jesus' early childhood. When Jesus is twelve, Mary makes herself scarce. Once the presentation of Jesus at the temple is over, exit Mary, until the crucifixion. What an absence. What becomes of Mary for twenty-two years? It's a mystery. Her body has almost no story, or rather, it has only two: gestation without impregnation by the male and the final Dormition. I am undoubtedly too much of a pagan to accept a body that is incarnated but at the same time escapes sex and death.[37]

Kazantzakis addresses the historicity and the "body" of Jesus' mother. His Mary attacks the Christian tradition. She not only speaks against the law; she also undermines it by having desires of her own and expressing feelings of bitterness and disappointment with her life. She is addressed as "Mary" or "his [Jesus'] mother" but not as the Virgin, and indeed, she fights her imposed destiny.[38] She seeks common pleasures but is prohibited from doing so, which causes her grief and pain. She is a sufferer who focuses mostly on her own grief and not so much on her son's.

The Last Temptation emphasizes two issues that the Christian tradition has not adequately addressed—Jesus' mother giving birth to a child without sexual contact and her being a mother without having a son. And with her son, she also stands out as a tragic figure, one who invites mercy and pity.[39]

A redefinition of the Virgin and a subversion of her symbol are at stake. This is due to a lack within the order of the symbolic that the phallic Logos considers a sacred untouchable "fullness" outside, which it alternately idolizes, disowns, or mourns as distinctively maternal. Kristeva demonstrates how the phallic logos, unwilling to accept its limits and thus the possibility that it may not be self-sufficient, sets up the figure of Mary, the Mother, outside the "parenthesis" of language. Though disowned as irretrievably other to it—Kristeva draws attention to John 2:4—the Mother is the underhand double of explicit phallic power. Rather than the Virgin Other of the Word, she is its "guardian," the bride who makes her husband's impotence look like fullness. In Kazantzakis, this placement is subverted.

In Christianity the very promise of the excess of the Virgin's presence is inextricable from the necessity of matricide in the order established with the Son of God's coming to the earth. In *The Last Temptation* this excess fights against matricide, constituting a contract of the maternal with the patriarchal economy that opens up the very possibility of a new order. Mary chooses to remain inside the Logos of the Father. She does couple with the Word of God—she speaks—but only in order to undermine it.

Magdalene and Desire

Apart from being the agent of eroticism, Magdalene is also the agent of the desire within narrative to flirt with, but ultimately avoid, closure. Her presence shapes Jesus' decision to acknowledge the divine call and be released from his earthly bonds, by asking for her forgiveness. It was his desire for her that first revealed the prohibition, imposed by God, of lusting after a woman.[40] Magdalene is caught betwixt and between Jesus and God. She awakens in Jesus various drives and impulses—senses, smells, and the need of touch—related to the semiotic. Through Magdalene, the body and the senses are brought to the scene of representation:

> Magdalene lay on her back, stark naked, drenched in sweat, her raven-black hair spread out over the pillow and her arms entwined beneath her head. . . . Her hair, nails and every inch of her body exuded smells of all nations, and her arms, neck and breasts were covered with bites.[41]

According to Kristeva, sexuality includes the death drive. And in my view, Magdalene's death drive relates to Jesus' sexuality. If one remains in the realm of the semiotic, he/she dies, as he/she is unable to become a healthy member of society and obey its laws. However, if one is completely cut off from the semiotic, he/she also dies, because the semiotic realm is the one that nurtures him/her, since the initial stage of the formation of our subjectivity is a stage that is never completely over.

Magdalene's words echo Freud's theories about a boy's dependence on the mother, then on the father, and his eternal quest for a mother's substitute, a nurturer:

> "Mary [Magdalene], try to remember back to when we were still small children. . . ."
> "I don't remember! . . . You never had the courage to stand up by yourself like a man and not rely on anyone. If you're not hanging on to your mother's apron strings, you're hanging on to mine, or God's. You can't stand by yourself, because you're scared."[42]

Scared of what? Castration? If Kristeva is right in saying that humans are always infants who need to be nurtured indeterminately, then Kazantzakis's Magdalene is also right in drawing the reader's attention to a series of nurture-figures to whom Jesus turns. He turns to the Father out of fear of symbolic castration, and he turns to his mother and Magdalene due to the semiotic's persistence within his psyche, which needs care and attention.

The drives of death and life coexist in Kazantzakis's Jesus. He feels pity for his mother, and a part of him wants to respond to her expectations for him. However, he has to renounce her; he needs to sever his filial bonds in order for his new property as the Messiah to come forth and be able to offer the possibility of afterlife to humanity. At the same time, he is sexually attracted to Magdalene. And he is torn between his desire to respond to this attraction and his contradictory desire to ignore it. The contradiction lies in the fact that life can be gained through death, while, during this process, the death drives and life drives shape Jesus' destiny simultaneously. I suggest that the coexistence of these opposing drives is a manifestation of the violent struggle that takes place throughout Jesus' course to crucifixion between the semiotic and the symbolic, which ultimately leads him to a death signaling both a closure and a beginning.

Conclusion: Inscribing a New Beginning within an Economy of Sacrifice

In *The Last Temptation*, the presence and force of the threatening and creatively destructive clash between the semiotic and the symbolic element, and the former's dangerous undermining of the latter, is responsible for the novel's subversive effect.[43] The novel challenges the symbolic by attempting to renarrate a story whose sacredness denies reinterpretation by flirting with the endless possibilities offered via language, through the signifier and its interplay with the signified. This violent clash, which leads to the open-ended close of the novel, constitutes the disruptive properties of Kazantzakis's writing, causing the so-called sacrilege of which he was accused. Questions are crying out for an answer, even so many years after the writing of this novel: What can be defined as sacred? And which approach toward the sacred can be characterized as its violation?

Clement says to Kristeva: "That is what you express so aptly as the 'transitory quality' of the sacred. As long as it is provisional, the sacred is indispensable."[44] Kristeva places her theory of the two modalities in the context of the term *metaphorein*; there is an endless flow of meaning from one to the other. I perceive Kazantzakis's *The Last Temptation* as a successful attempt to transfer—*metaphorei*—a story from a specific context whose semiotic elements have been suppressed to another, where the vital battle between the semiotic and the symbolic is manifested. Kazantzakis manages this by visiting what has not been spoken (of), in order to revisit what has been spoken (of)—the Name of the Father. In this way, he offers the possibility of another reading that not only denies closure of meaning but also challenges the imposed meanings and invites new ones. Echoing Kristeva's theoretical frame, I wonder: Is *The Last Temptation* a literary space where the playfulness of sacredness is manifested, as in the playfulness of a musical ornament?

Notes

1. See Jacque Lacan's work in *Écrits: A Selection*, ed. and trans. Alan Sheridan (London: Tavistock, 1977).

2. Hence the use of the suffix "-ology" to refer to a field of study or discipline. In addition, Aristotle uses *logos* to mean the rational principle or element of the soul, as opposed to the irrational principle of desire.

3. Julia Kristeva, "Stabat Mater," in *The Kristeva Reader*, ed. Toril Moi (New York: Columbia University Press, 1984), 47.

4. Kelly Oliver, *Reading Kristeva* (Bloomington: Indiana University Press, 1993), 21.

5. Julia Kristeva, *Revolution in Poetic Language*, trans. Margaret Waller (New York: Columbia University Press, 1984), 47.

6. Kristeva, *Reader*, 143.

7. Lacan, *Écrits*, 65.

8. Kristeva, *Revolution*, 78–80.

9. Catherine Clement and Julia Kristeva, *The Feminine and the Sacred*, trans. Jane Marie Todd (New York: Columbia University Press, 2001), 15.

10. Ibid., 37.

11. Kristeva, *Revolution*, 16.

12. Julia Kristeva, *Black Sun: Depression and Melancholia*, trans. Leon S. Roudiez (New York: Columbia University Press, 1989), 41–42.

13. Kristeva, *Black Sun*, 33–68.

14. This is another legacy of Bakhtin, as he focused on the way meaning is conveyed rather than on the meaning, the ideology, the plot, and the story itself.

15. Julia Kristeva, *Desire in Language*, trans. Thomas Gora et al. (New York: Columbia University Press, 1980), 281.

16. Clement and Kristeva, *The Feminine and the Sacred*, 1.

17. Kristeva, *Black Sun*, 82.

18. Ibid., 43.

19. Kristeva, *Reader*, 95.

20. Julia Kristeva, *New Maladies of the Soul*, trans. Leon S. Roudiez (New York: Columbia University Press, 1995).

21. Nikos Kazantzakis, *Report to Greco*, trans. Peter Bien (New York: Simon & Schuster, 1965), 17.

22. Nikos Kazantzakis, *The Last Temptation*, trans. Peter Bien (New York: Simon & Schuster, 1960), 69.

23. Ibid., 83.

24. Kristeva, *Reader*, 78.

25. Kazantzakis, *Last Temptation*, 1.

26. Julia Kristeva, *In the Beginning Was Love: Psychoanalysis and Faith*, trans. Arthur Coldhammer (New York: Columbia University Press, 1987), 44–45.

27. Kristeva, *Black Sun*, 27.

28. Kazantzakis, *Last Temptation*, 27–28.

29. Ibid., 27.

30. Kristeva, *Black Sun*, 33.

31. Kazantzakis, *Last Temptation*, 15.

32. Kristeva, *In the Beginning*, 25–26.

33. Ibid., 40–41.

34. Kazantzakis, *Last Temptation*, 69.

35. Kristeva, *In the Beginning*, 47.

36. Kazantzakis, *Last Temptation*, 30–33.

37. Clement and Kristeva, *The Feminine and the Sacred*, 87.

38. *Kazantzakis, Last Temptation*, 63–64.

39. Ibid., 63.

40. Ibid., 25–26.

41. Ibid., 88.

42. Ibid., 91.

43. The subversive effect is from a dialectical interplay between the semiotic and the symbolic dispositions of language.

44. Clement and Kristeva, *The Feminine and the Sacred*, 150.

CHAPTER 10

An Unholy Trinity
Women in Pre-Easter Patriarchy

Jen Harrison

Nikos Kazantzakis justifies his sinning Christ as the perfect model for his disciples—the strength of his triumph over evil underscored through the potent depths of temptation to which he succumbs.[1] Jesus the Christ is able to redeem because as Jesus the man he has shown himself susceptible to the seductive power of sin; most compellingly through his engaging with the sin into which Kazantzakis himself most often descends: misogyny.

As a man of mortal passions, Kazantzakis's pre-Easter Jesus falls within his social expectations—a man within patriarchy. His society elevates men and subordinates women, ascribing woman's value according to her usefulness to men. Such is the backdrop to Kazantzakis's text. The norms surrounding Jesus project women as extensions of men's needs and fears. Less than men, a step between man and beast, women are confined to roles in the service of men. Women are men's sexual partners, the mothers of their children, their comforters and homemakers. And little else.

Woman as Servant

Within their households, women are under the orders of their men. Even Salome, a woman both "saintly"[2] and fearsomely assertive[3]—said to "govern" her house[4]—responds to her husband's commands, providing him on demand with food and drink, companionship and care.[5] In the absence of their brother, the man of the house, Martha and Mary invite the village elders to assess and entertain their guest; such is the incapacity of woman in her own home.[6]

Men dominate within the household despite home life being built on women's labor. Women are the center of the home, in fact and perception. The day begins and ends with woman's work.[7] It is women who keep the house welcoming: clean, warm, cozy.[8] They mark the tides and seasons, in step with the community.[9] Yet servitude to her man is portrayed as a woman's desire[10] and domesticity her source of joy: "to wash, to cook, to go to the fountain for water, to chat merrily with the neighbors; and, in the evening, to sit in my doorway and watch the passers-by."[11]

Woman's world is shallow and small. Her very construction demands a master: "We are not men, to have need of another, an eternal life; we are women, and for us one moment with the man we love is everlasting Paradise, one moment far from the man we love is everlasting hell. It is here on this earth that we women live out eternity."[12]

Outside the home, social structures function on a series of hierarchies, constant in the superior status of men over women. When Simeon leads the march up the hill at the Zealot's crucifixion, he is followed in order by elders, men, then women.[13] We see this pattern again and again—leaving the house of Lazarus,[14] listening to Jesus on the hill.[15] Women in public are the servants of men, epitomized in women's drawing well water for men.[16] This hierarchy is enacted also through the narrative, where women in general are caricatures—the desirable metonymized as makeup,[17] the indomitable unattractive,[18] the old disheveled, indistinguishable from the cripples.[19] Where old men are elders: respected pillars of the community,[20] old women are "crones," malevolent and useless.[21]

As their own masters outside the home and within, men move freely across the domestic threshold. For women, the line between private and public realms is a significant barrier. Chaste women keep indoors; those in the streets are construed as whores.[22] Magdalene's sanctification is evidenced in her return to the domestic sphere, both physically, in that she does not leave the house, and by commitment, in her dreaming every night of serving her husband.[23]

Women's general servitude to men does not, however, entail their impotency. On the contrary, woman is a frighteningly powerful force.[24] Her sexual desirability lures good men into sin,[25] and her capacity to breed lures saints into banality.[26] Such conceptions diminish both women and men, confining both to their biology. But whereas men may soar, transcending their physical restrictions and approaching the numinous, women are irredeemable. A woman is her body.

Woman as Body

As body, woman is essentially a vessel for man's pleasure, illustrated perfectly in Zebedee's pursuing other women once his wife has grown old and in his grouping together of "food, wine, women": means to satisfying appetites.[27] Detached from men, a woman has no value, since the role for which she exists—meeting men's needs—remains unfulfilled. Thus, as a thirty-year-old virgin, Martha's sexuality is of no worth to men, and she is portrayed as bitterly undesirable—over the hill and beyond all attractiveness.[28] Yet Mary Magdalene—four years older—is the epitome of sensual delight: Eve herself.[29] The difference, of course, is sexual availability and utility: Magdalene's door is open, where Martha's is closed; and this is all that really matters.

Equating woman's worth with her servicing of men fundamentally dehumanizes her, divesting her of all potential for agency or autonomy.[30] Her own needs are not only insignificant; they are rendered nonexistent, and her social suppression is justified. Kazantzakis's women are doubly controlled by such ideological means, as they are themselves co-opted into perpetuating the very myths that limit their potential. Required to submit to their own denigration, women are indoctrinated to consider themselves feeble and powerless, to count their needs and desires as insignificant, and to fear their own potential.

It is women's voices that are most prominent in associating woman with body and man with soul: "A woman's soul is her flesh. . . . Woman issued from the body of man. . . . Man was created by God."[31] Far from rejecting the depiction of themselves as weak and inescapably enslaved by the physical, Kazantzakis's women reiterate and reinforce such diminishments: "A woman is a wounded doe. She has no other joy, poor thing, except to lick her wounds. . . . We're women and weak."[32]

Women are pitted against each other. Believing themselves to be nothing without a man, they compete for men. Unmarried women treat each other as rivals for an eligible male partner.[33] Even the bonds of sisterhood are expected to break in the face of a potential master.[34] Chaste women fear the unchaste, exhibiting far more consistent condemnation than any man does. The fallen woman is a threatening temptation for the chaste woman's men,[35] makes a mockery of the hard work entailed in preserving her own virtue, and is probably having more fun—all of which provoke the virtuous to resentful judgmentalism.[36] More profoundly, though, the virtuous woman finds her unchaste sister potentially contaminating.[37] Afraid of her own body and the disastrous consequences of its being unrestrained, women learn to fear as well the bodies of their sisters. Even in her own eyes, woman as body is a fearsome demon.

Kazantzakis's men exhibit much more pragmatic responses to the accessible female body. As they avail themselves of its pleasures, it is "paradise."[38] Denied her services, she becomes "whore"—a social danger that must be checked and controlled.[39] For the man who desires marriage and children, a woman's body is a gift from God.[40] For the ascetic, seeking God in his loneliness, a woman's body is the devil's most clever tool.[41] Woman's moral status is entirely dependent upon the measure to which she is satisfying the particular requirements of men. Such transparent relativism underscores Kazantzakis's own critique of these social inequalities. The patriarchal underlays of his social fabric are clearly arbitrary—their religious justifications nothing more than dominance by ideological opportunism. Of that, the mortal Jesus is as guilty as any other man in his society.

Woman as Sin

Throughout the novel Jesus enacts the struggle between human yearning and divine intent. His own words depict this as desire for Magdalene in opposition to the call to save all of humanity, portraying the woman, with her promises of sexual and familial fulfillment, as the greatest obstruction to man's deification. His sinful weakness is expressed: "I want Magdalene. . . . Not the earth, not the kingdom of this world—it's Magdalene I want to save."[42] Such polarizing of woman against God sits at the heart of misogyny. Far from being a fellow human, equally created in the image of God, woman has become a mere extension of man's isolation from the divine, both demonized and dehumanized.

Misogyny, like all irrational prejudice, stems from fear. Kazantzakis's Jesus fears three aspects of womanhood: her reproductive capabilities, her body, and her emotional nurturing. These are embodied in reducing woman to mother, whore, and housewife, and reducing sin to succumbing to his need for women in such roles.

Jesus' tripartite fear of woman is expressed through his trinity of Marys. A mortal, fractured precursor to the holy Trinity of Father, Son, and Holy Spirit, the pre-Easter Jesus gives us Mary the Virgin Mother, Mary Magdalene the Whore, and Mary and Martha combined to serve as Wife and Housekeeper. These are the sum of the faces of woman, above all else material, immutably rooted in this world.

The Mother

The Mother seeks salvation through breeding. She wants children and grandchildren who are unremarkable, conforming, and content. As Mother, her vision is limited to the narrow concerns of human generation—the health, survival, and successful reproduction of her son.[43] Such aspirations stand directly in the way of her son's holy destiny, driving an impenetrable wedge between them. While he is reaching for God in heroic carelessness, her concerns are all cleanliness and decency.[44]

The Mother's procreative capacity makes her a formidable force. Since she is able to create, it seems intuitive that she is equally able to destroy, endowing her curse with fearsome potency.[45] Jesus' fear of the Mother's awesome power is personified in his companion, the Curse, with whom he replaces his mother.[46] So terrifying are woman's reproductive abilities that they solidify in his imagination as "the savage body of a woman covered head to foot with interlocking scales of thick bronze armor."[47] These are the biological forces that separate the Mother from the rest of humanity,[48] which keep the childless woman up at night.[49] He is so incapable of coming to terms with these forces that he prefers to make peace with his beastly imagination rather than his real-life Mother.

The Whore

The Whore personifies woman as body,[50] communicating with man as body:[51] physically at the service of men[52] but driven by such need of men's attentions[53] that she is even more threatening than she is desirable.[54] Sexually awakened, a woman is at the mercy of her body.[55] In the words of Magdalene: "Woman issued from the body of man and still cannot detach her body from his."[56]

The Whore manipulates men in every possible way: flaunting her body to entice him into sexual sin,[57] keeping her emotions in check to lure him into trusting her,[58] molding her behavior to suit his moods and needs.[59] Her sole intention is to entrap men, to prevent them from achieving their divine purpose. Thus even when the Whore is saved—even after she has been "born again with a virgin body"[60]—she is still no more than body. She still goes on expecting corporeal pleasure—holding on to their nuptial perfume until the very last moment.[61] And she remains in his mind as tempting flesh; she is his greatest temptation in the wilderness and the first of his final temptations, so cogently somatic that only a brutal death can release him from her beguiling presence.[62]

The Housewife

The Housewife builds her life around her man's domestic needs, providing food, love, tenderness—all the comforts of family life. Her aspirations encapsulate the mundane, soothing him into settling for ease rather than achieving greatness: "A tiny house is big enough for me, and a mouthful of bread, and the simple words of a woman. . . . Here is the kingdom of heaven: earth. Here is God: your son."[63]

Above all else, Jesus' trinity of Marys stands between man and God—a deliberate obstacle to glory. Each speaks to fundamental human needs: earthly, tangible, material needs; representing the "weak flesh" of which he is so frightened.[64] Jesus' conception of sin consists of submitting to such needs. Choosing the joys of life with women above the cross marks him in his opinion as spineless and ineffectual: "I'm a traitor, a deserter, a coward. . . . I lost courage and fled."[65] His misogyny reaches to the depths of his vision: woman dehumanized as the ultimate inducement into sin; crystallized in his depiction of women as infinitely interchangeable: "There is only one woman in the world; one, with innumerable faces."[66]

Misogyny as Sin

Yet it is this very misogyny that is the subject of the narrative's condemnation. Jesus' reducing of women to embodiments of temptation and need is the serious sin into which he falls. This is the sin underlying the whole of the narrative: the social iniquity repeatedly characterizing women as united by "pain": His falling is not that he engages in carnal pleasures but that in the process of doing so, he enacts his misogynist fears.[67] The triumph of the novel is that Jesus has been tempted into the traps of misogyny—to dehumanize women by taking away their individuality, their humanness, and for his own ends to appropriate woman's labor, the labor of *any* woman—and yet has, in fact, not done this.

Pre-Easter Jesus is confined to a world of limited vision, where woman's divinity is suppressed and she is excluded even from heaven's liberation: "Poor and rich won't exist any more; they will all be one. . . . Israelites and Romans, Greeks and Chaldeans don't exist—nor do Bedouins. We're all brothers!"[68] Post-Easter Jesus triumphs over patriarchy, elevating woman along with man, resurrecting the whole of humanity: "There is neither male nor female; for you are all one in Christ Jesus."[69]

Kazantzakis's Jesus leaves us on the cross, his patriarchal sojourn ended, the new order just beginning.[70] All of his fears of women belong to the pre-redemption world.[71]

Triumphing over the sin of patriarchy, Kazantzakis's Jesus redeems his society—and Kazantzakis himself—with his narrative misogyny absolved through its assignation to the sinful realm. The novel thus becomes the confession of a man struggling against his own misogynist nature; we may infer that it is this to which the author refers in his prologue, describing himself as "a person who struggled much, was much embittered in his life, and had many hopes."[72] Kazantzakis's sinning Christ embodies the breadth of human hopes, serving as the model for women's genuine liberation, where women and men are all free to achieve their individual potential.[73]

Notes

1. Nikos Kazantzakis, *The Last Temptation of Christ*, trans. Peter Bien (New York: Simon & Schuster, 1960), 4.

2. Ibid., 119.

3. Ibid., 172, 187–88. Here Salome's demand that her men provide the assailed Magdalene with protection fills them with fear, and Salome prevents a riot by telling the crowd to ignore her husband's mad ravings.

4. Ibid., 327.

5. Ibid., 131.

6. Ibid., 267–78.

7. Ibid., 68.

8. Ibid., 77.

9. Ibid., 70.

10. Ibid., 472–73 (Mary the sister of Lazarus).

11. Ibid., 63 (Mary the mother of Jesus).

12. Ibid., 353 (Mary Magdalene).

13. Ibid., 20.

14. Ibid., 278.

15. Ibid., 182.

16. Ibid., 220.

17. Ibid., 7, 76, 232 (literally, "painted").

18. Ibid., 20, 84, 181.

19. Ibid., 23.

20. Ibid., 20 (Simeon).

21. Ibid., 80.

22. Ibid., 213: Magdala's good women welcome Jesus from their thresholds while their men rush into the street. Also see 319: Cana's women hide indoors while their men emerge to speak to Jesus.

23. Ibid., 213–14.

24. Best exemplified by Simeon's desperate appeal to his daughter to use her superior powers to dissuade Jesus from his suicidal intent. See ibid., 374–76: "You are a woman: your tears and caresses have great power."

25. Ibid., 160–63, 170, 230: the young women in the vineyards, Nathanael, and the prostitutes of Jerusalem.

26. Ibid., 39, 91, 147.

27. Ibid., 161–62. Consider also Simon the Cyrenian's words: "Why did God make wine and women, can you tell me? To while away his own time, or for us to while away ours?" (232).

28. Ibid., 267–73. This is reinforced through Jesus' being tempted to have sex with her out of pity (466).

29. Ibid., 170.

30. The most poignant illustration of this is the young man's intended purchasing of Mary Magdalene: "I'm going to buy Mary with a shipment of cinnamon and pepper, put her in a gold cage and take her away" (ibid., 85). Women become merely a commodity to be traded.

31. Ibid., 90, 329–30. For further discussion of the impact of such gendered moral dualism, see Elisabeth Porter, *Women and Moral Identity* (New South Wales, Australia: Allen & Unwin, 1991).

32. Kazantzakis, *Last Temptation*, 90–91 (Mary Magdalene), 484 (Mary the sister of Lazarus).

33. Ibid., 399 (Mary Magdalene and Mary the sister of Lazarus).

34. Ibid., 273.

35. Both the men who are actually hers by right (husbands, brothers, sons) as well as potential suitors.

36. Ibid., 172–73.

37. Ibid., 215. Consider the virgins' disgust at Magdalene's attending the wedding in Magdala—her lack of chastity has "soiled" the occasion. Also observe the Virgin Mary's reaction to Mary Magdalene (171).

38. Ibid., 85–86.

39. Ibid., 90 (Jesus), 169–77 (Barabbas).

40. Ibid., 146 (Simeon), 343–44 (the fisherman in Capernaum), 215–18 (the possible engendering of the Messiah).

41. Ibid., 37–38 (the Zealot), 41 (John the son of Zebedee), 70 (the young girls of Cana).

42. Ibid., 28.

43. Ibid., 64, 461.

44. Ibid., 311.

45. Ibid., 51–52 (the curse of the mother of the Zealot), 189 (Mary's threats), 403 (Jesus' nightmare).

46. Ibid., 311, 442. Having rejected Mary the Mother at Nazareth, Jesus makes peace with the Curse on the cross.

47. Ibid., 79.

48. Ibid., 254.

49. Ibid., 401–2.

50. Ibid., 70, 147.

51. Ibid., 192.

52. Consider the way Magdalene's clients seek her out, demanding that she return to work for their pleasure (ibid., 80–81).

53. Exemplified in Magdalene's devotion to the Zealot, even when he rejects her (ibid., 46–52).

54. Ibid., 172–73. The depth of men's fear of her body is shown most strongly when the men who had used her services triumph over her suffering under Barabbas's judgment (172–73). Such misogynist fear appears elsewhere in the narrative (39).

55. This is illustrated by Jesus' remorse for having made sensual contact with Magdalene as an infant—taking the blame for having driven her into sin (ibid., 145). Having experienced at age four the joys of touching a boy's naked feet, there is obviously no way that Magdalene could go on into chaste adulthood. Further, the only solution Jesus can see to Magdalene's sinning is for her to marry (126). The sexually awakened woman's body cannot be turned off. Her only hope is to have her sexuality channeled into more appropriate expression.

56. Ibid., 329–30.

57. Ibid., 37–46 (the Zealot).

58. Ibid., 93–96 (with Jesus).

59. Ibid., 355.

60. Ibid., 214.

61. Ibid., 416.

62. Ibid., 257, 448–54.

63. Ibid., 460, 466.

64. Ibid., 402.

65. Ibid., 494.

66. Ibid., 466. Such removal of women's right to individuality reaches its climax when Jesus has sex with Martha.

67. Ibid., 63, 168, 171.

68. Ibid., 367–68.

69. Gal 3:28 RSV.

70. Kazantzakis, *Last Temptation*, 496.

71. This view of Christianity as liberation from patriarchy has been well expounded by feminist theologians such as Rosemary Radford Ruether and Elisabeth Schüssler-Fiorenza. There are, of course, many who dispute Christ's liberating potential, holding that Christianity cannot break free from its patriarchal roots; one thinks of Mary Daly and Daphne Hampson.

72. Kazantzakis, *Last Temptation*, 4.

73. Enacting the theologian and New Testament critic Marcus Borg's understanding of salvation as enlightenment and reconciliation: the opening of our eyes to the presence and glory of God in each other. See Borg, *The God We Never Knew: Beyond Dogmatic Religion to a More Authentic Contemporary Faith* (San Francisco: HarperSanFrancisco, 1997), 161.

CHAPTER 11

Distant Flutter of a Butterfly
The Indian Response to *The Last Temptation*
Mini Chandran

Introduction

Published in Greek in 1955, Nikos Kazantzakis's *The Last Temptation* became the focal point of a controversy regarding intellectual freedom in Kerala, India, in 1986. What accounts for this text's turbulent reception in a place so remote in time and culture from Crete, the author's homeland? Generally speaking, various reasons prevail. Some might say, for example, that because the world is like a global village with shifting boundaries, books like *The Last Temptation* travel across time and culture fairly easily. Still others might claim that *The Last Temptation*'s wide-ranging appeal derives from its ideological association with Christianity, an ecumenical or worldwide religion. And a third theory for explaining the novel's power to scandalize others utilizes a certain sense of the writer's general duty "publicly to raise embarrassing questions, to confront orthodoxy and dogma (rather than to produce them), to be someone who cannot easily be co-opted by governments or corporations."[1] In my view, these opinions fail to account completely for the reception accorded to *The Last Temptation* in India. Unfortunately, the repercussions were not exactly benign; demands were made to ban a play and a critical essay based on the novel, raising the issue of creative freedom for writers in India.

I wish to acknowledge the help of Mr. Sanal Edamaruku of the Indian Atheist Publishers in giving me a copy of P. M. Antony's play *Christuvinte Aram Thirumurivu*, and of Mr. K. S. Raman, editor with Mathrubhumi Publications, for giving me access to their archives.

Religiopolitical Realities in India

To understand the nature of the novel's reception in India, it is necessary to understand the religiopolitical realities of this country. Religion here is still a living reality and not just a matter of private faith. The dependence of political parties on religious groups for electoral gains complicates matters further. Though predominantly Hindu, India has Muslims, Christians, Sikhs, Jains, Parsis, and Jews, to name a few prominent religions. Interreligious relations are fragile, and ruling governments are apprehensive of anything that might jeopardize the situation. It is no wonder that Section 253 of the Indian Penal Code, which allows the government to prevent publication of any book that might cause offense through blasphemy, has been a major instrument of censorship in India. Obscenity or subversion pales in comparison to the major offense of blasphemy in a country that has witnessed large-scale destruction in the name of gods.

A majority of Christians are located in the state of Kerala, where they form a formidable force in terms of economic and political power. This is not surprising, given the long history of Christianity in that state. Kerala had Christians long before most countries of the West. It is believed to have welcomed Christianity along with Saint Thomas when he came to the Malabar coast in the first century CE. The religion grew with the efforts of missionaries, who established schools and hospitals and rendered a great service in the development of literacy. Even today, many educational and medical institutions in the state are owned and run by Christian organizations; numerous affluent farmers also belong to the Church. And the political equations in the state usually have a Christian factor when it comes to matters of actual governance. Kerala also has strong communist sympathies, since in 1957 it became the first democratic state in the world to elect a communist government to power.[2] Consequently, the state displays a unique blend of communism and extremely conservative religious groups with political affiliations.

Scandalizing Jesus in Kerala?

Today, Kerala is the most literate state in India and has an enlightened reading public, which peruses most of the major Western literary works in English or through translations in the regional language, Malayalam. *The Last Temptation* was well received on first publication in English, and Kazantzakis became a center of attention for his bold treatment of Christian theology. This is not to say that it was encomiums all the way; some voices expressed dismay and shock, but none went beyond the written or spoken word of protest. The public's gaze focused on the novel again in 1986, when attempts were made to stage a Malayalam play, *Christuvinte Aram Thirumurivu* (*The Sixth Holy Wound of Christ*), based on the novel. The dramatist was P. M. Antony of Suryakanthi Theatres, located in Alapuzha, a small town in Kerala. Even before *Christuvinte Aram Thirumurivu* was staged, Christian leaders claimed it offended their religious sentiments. And so they sought as well as demanded the play's prohibition. Acting on the basis of complaints received after advertisements for *Christuvinte Aram Thirumurivu* were put on display, the police raided the rehearsal camp and confiscated Antony's script.

Christian outcry over *The Last Temptation* intensified in 1987 when some educators assigned P. A. Warrier's book *Anubhavangal* (*Experiences*), which features an essay on Kazantzakis's novel, for undergraduate study at Kerala's Calicut University. Various Christian clergy and political leaders believed Kazantzakis's novel insulted Christianity and that students were not mature enough to read a different version of the life of Christ. The matter was discussed in the legislative assembly, and the current education minister, after much deliberation, removed Warrier's essay from the textbook. Christian leaders therefore were appeased.

But the drama controversy over *Christuvinte Aram Thirumurivu* continued. The play's most trenchant critic, the late Bishop Joseph Kundukulam, leader of the largest Catholic diocese in India, spoke out against the play, Warrier's interpretative essay, and Kazantzakis himself. When asked about his antipathy, the bishop charged: "Christ has been depicted as a debauch, as a person who is promiscuous, in that book [*The Last Temptation*]. It is not at all right to insist that it has to be taught or studied."[3] And the news that American seminary professors both assigned and taught Kazantzakis's novel only antagonized him further:

> Do we have that situation here? They [Americans] don't care for God at all. Women there [in America] wander around in their underclothes. Will it work if we say that everything here should function the way as it is there? They need the Lord only when they are about to die. The Lord is not necessary for material pleasures. Is that the culture we have here?[4]

Most critics who attacked Antony's play and Kazantzakis's novel had read neither. Objections were based on hearsay, and in a country where it is easy to promote strong feelings through propaganda, fervent exhortations by Christian leaders were sufficient to successfully ban *Christuvinte Aram Thirumurivu* as well as the essay based on *The Last Temptation*.

Analyzing *Christuvinte Aram Thirumurivu*

Antony's play faithfully adapts *The Last Temptation* into a concise drama marked by thirteen scenes. Though he follows the novel's sequence of events, he stops short of the notorious crucifixion scene. The temptations do not play a major role here; in fact, the closest that Antony's Jesus ever comes to Mary Magdalene is when he visits her house and apologizes for having led her astray. In my view, it is difficult to see why Christian spiritual leaders were so upset by the play, which appears tame when placed alongside *The Last Temptation*.

Like *The Last Temptation, Christuvinte Aram Thirumurivu* depicts Jesus as the cross-maker who is reviled by Judas and other patriotic Jews. And like Kazantzakis's Jesus, Antony's Jesus is aware of his status as the Chosen One and fights against it by trying to rebel against God. Antony's Jesus desperately tries to be an ordinary man, and his cross-making is a part of that futile attempt. When questioned by Mary as to why he persists in making crosses, he replies: "I have to escape the hands of God, which are hunting me. I want to be a man. . . . I just want to be a man."[5] Humiliated by Jesus' spurning, Mary retorts: "You can do nothing. You do not have a heart. You do not have nerves that feel pain. You are a desert from where even the last spring of love has dried up."[6] Like Kazantzakis's Jesus, Antony's Jesus feels torn between the beguiling placidity of domestic life and the painful divine mission he has been entrusted with.

Antony's Judas is a strong character, perhaps even stronger than Jesus. He is the quintessential revolutionary leader, someone who believes that "power can be answered only in the language of power."[7] And he is caught between his deep love for Jesus and his obligation to the Fraternity, which wants Jesus dead. He stands between Jesus and the mob angered by Jesus' preaching about love and brotherhood, and on many occasions acts as his protector. Judas is sword and love, while Jesus is love alone. In Antony's hands, Judas even seems Marxist, especially when he explains why human beings find it hard to love one another: "Centuries of slavery. The earth and all earthly things have been in the hands of a powerful and wealthy few. The hungry cannot love the well fed, Jesus, neither can the oppressed love the oppressor."[8] He further exhorts Jesus: "If you are Israel's Messiah then you are the axe, as prophesied by John. Rome is the tree that bears no fruit. If you are the Messiah, Rome is the chaff described by John. Jesus, you are the fire that will burn it."[9] In response, Jesus is moved to repeat: "I am the fire. . . . I am the fire. . . . I am the fire, Judas."[10] Judas understands the common people in a way Jesus cannot: "They desire bread and freedom. But you talk about the soul, which nobody understands."[11]

In *Christuvinte Aram Thirumurivu*, Jesus' mission acquires the hue of a revolutionary struggle as its emphasis shifts to the need for Israel to break free from slavery. Barabbas and his Fraternity are like contemporary guerilla fighters, and Mary Magdalene is the prostitute with the golden heart who supports the Fraternity by secretly supplying it with money. But Jesus is never shown as being tortured by the vivid, fleshly temptations that are described in *The Last Temptation*. Whenever his thoughts stray to the sensual, he manages to overcome them almost immediately. However, the play's critics were incensed. Bishop Joseph Kundukulam had this to say:

> The play has facts that are directly in opposition to what Christ taught and lived for. How absurdly has Christ been distorted! Mary Magdalene invites Christ to prostitution, Christ beseeches Mary to allow him to sleep with her—let me ask you, if your God were to be depicted this way, would not your blood boil? Numerous common people complained to me: "Father, we wondered if this was the Christ that we love." The whole play is nothing but a mockery of Christ.[12]

It would not be fair, of course, to imply that the church in Kerala is monolithic, that all its members opposed both Kazantzakis and the play he inspired. There were priests who felt that Antony's drama was religiously sincere. But many commentators, religious and otherwise, were deeply critical. A good example is the contemporary Malayalam writer O. V. Vijayan.

Criticizing Antony and Warrier

Although he affirmed Antony's creative freedom and poetic license, Vijayan also incisively criticized Antony's depiction: "I do not believe that we can be true to Christ's mission by locating him in history and judging him by sociological standards. And that is what the play does. It is not only historicizing, the play is forcing the Son of Man who is also the Son of God to fit into the framework of a particular ideology."[13] What lies beneath this remark, I think, is Vijayan's reaction to Antony's well-known communist sympathies. But to say that Antony forces Jesus into communist ideology is to misread Antony's focus on Christ the Deliverer, the one who liberates Jews from Roman slavery, a focus largely unopposed by mainstream Christian interpretation.

Warrier's essay is a sophisticated plot summary of *The Last Temptation*. And it cites Peter Bien's English translation liberally, electing to see the prologue as the heart of Kazantzakis's novel.[14] Understandably, the vast majority of Kerala writers were unable to see why Warrier's essay, which recognizes the spirit behind Kazantzakis's work, had to be withdrawn from Calicut University's undergraduate syllabus. This prohibition had notable political overtones, since it was a directive from the minister for education that ensured its removal. The issue was discussed at length in the State Legislative Assembly, and the Kerala government did not want an irritant like Warrier's essay to upset the state's Christian voters.

I think this political move was based on the questionable assumption that the "human" face of God or God's messengers is too much for people to bear. It would be appropriate to wonder, though, if such unwillingness to scrutinize aspects of Christian doctrine is unhealthy, particularly if this attitude comes down to average congregants from high-minded Church leaders. More generally, I wonder if theocratic leaders, and not just Christian leaders, appreciate how novelists and novels work. Thus Milan Kundera commenting on the Iranian *fatwa* on Salman Rushdie:

Rushdie did not blaspheme. He did not attack Islam. He wrote a novel. But that, for the theocratic mind, is worse than an attack: if a religion is attacked (by a polemic, a blasphemy, a heresy), the guardians of the temple can easily defend it on their own ground, with their own language; but the novel is a different planet for them; a different universe based on a different ontology; an *infernum* where the unique truth is powerless and where satanic ambiguity turns every certainty into enigma.[15]

Rushdie's example holds relevance here, I think, because like Antony and Kazantza-kis, he found his work banned in India. The same can be said of the writer Aubrey Menen. In the next section, I discuss Aubrey Menen's *Rama Retold* and Salman Rushdie's *The Satanic Verses*, viewing them as secular rereadings of sacred writings. And I claim that *Rama Retold* and *The Satanic Verses* compare favorably with *The Last Temptation* because each offers its own personalized view of revered godheads.

Menen, Rushdie, Kazantzakis

Rama Retold is a secular retelling of the *Ramayana*, the sacred epic of the Hindus. The hero of the epic, Rama, holds a unique position in the Hindu psyche, revered as he is as the ideal person, fusing virtues of man and king alike. He is the *Maryadapu-rushottam*, which means "Sublime among men." It is this Rama whom Menen incorporates into his novel.

Menen's opening passage sets the tone for the rest of the narrative:

> This is the story of Rama, a prince of India, who lived his life according to the best advice. He reverenced his intellectual betters, who were called Brahmins, and did what they told him to do. He took his morals from the best moralists, and his politics from the most experienced politicians. As a result he was ruined, exiled, and disinherited: his wife was stolen from him and when he got her back he very nearly had to burn her alive from the highest of motives.[16]

It is noteworthy that the *maryada purushottam* of the Hindus has become a "prince of India," who learns the practical realities of life the hard way. In effect, Rama ceases to be an incarnation of God and is, instead, a simple, callow youth.

In the Hindu epic, Rama is the king's son who renounces the throne, denies himself material possessions, and then exiles himself in the forest for fourteen years so that his father can keep a promise. But Menen offers an absurd touch to the exile of the original epic by emphasizing Rama's gullibility; he is completely taken in by his father's duplicitous attempts to send him to his exile in the forest. In the forest, he meets Valmiki, the author of the epic and a non-Brahmin, who opposes the nefarious ways of the court as well as the hierarchical caste system. Basically, it is Valmiki who becomes Rama's mentor and the actual hero of the novel.

Menen also departed from the epic in the portrayal of Sita, Rama's wife. Sita is the archetypal wife, as far as Hindus are concerned—the one who goes through fire to demonstrate chastity and fidelity to her husband. In the epic, the ten-headed evil demon king, Ravan, abducts her. Later, her husband, Rama, rescues her and slays the demon in a prolonged war. But Menen transmutes these characters. His Sita, for example, is not the docile wife who accepts all that her husband tells her. Menen hints at the instant attraction that springs up between Sita and Ravan, making her abduction by Ravan seem more like an elopement. Menen also insinuates that Sita was far from chaste during her sojourn in Lanka as Ravan's hostage. Ironically,

Menen's Rama describes Sita as "Most Faithful Wife," even though he questions her fidelity. The epic's trial by fire, the so-called *Agnipareeksha*, becomes a conjuror's trick in Menen's hands as his Rama arranges for Egyptian fire that does not burn.

In my view, Menen challenges Hinduism's basic tenets by striking a blow where it hurts most, at the revered godhead of Rama. And not surprisingly, his novel was burned by a group of priests in Bombay when it was published in 1956. The Indian prime minister Jawaharlal Nehru was not willing to take risks with communal harmony; the riots that followed the India-Pakistan partition were still fresh in memory. The novel was banned, therefore, and continues to be so, though a few have read it.

Thirty-two years later, Salman Rushdie's *The Satanic Verses* experienced a far worse fate. A novel about the immigrant experience in twentieth-century England, *The Satanic Verses* also probes Islam's origin and dissemination, especially in the sections entitled "Mahound" and "Return to Jahilia." (These sections provoked the most outrage among Muslims.) Rushdie's choice of the name Mahound for the Prophet Muḥammad is problematic, largely because it is considered a derogatory term. In his defense, though, Rushdie did not invent the name; it derives from medieval Western scholarship. Even more blasphemous, as far as Muslim believers were concerned, was Rushdie's choice to name the Jahilia prostitutes after Muḥammad's twelve wives.

Irreverence about God and sacred scriptures, like the Koran, is not something that religious leaders take kindly to. And *The Satanic Verses* fallout was immediate. India was the first country to ban the novel after its publication in England in 1988. It even became the topic of political debate when several Muslim parliamentarians demanded its abrupt suppression. In their eyes, *The Satanic Verses* insulted Islam. As usual in such cases, however, many of the book's critics attacked it without reading it. Needless to say, the public outcry led to riots in various parts of India, including Bombay, Rushdie's home city, and a few people were even killed.

In my view, Kazantzakis's Jesus has the same human face that Menen's Rama and Rushdie's Mahound have, but I think Kazantzakis's treatment of Jesus' humanity makes him stand out from the other two characters by comparison. In the agony brought on by the clash of opposites in his soul (flesh and spirit), he is more accessible in human terms. The doubts and despair that tear him apart find an echo in every human heart, and for this reason his victorious surmounting of all temptations becomes a personal victory of sorts for the reader, or the "man who struggles."

The writer's intention should never be the criterion by which one judges a novel, of course, but Kazantzakis's stated intention in his novel's prologue should not be passed over lightly:

> This book was written because I wanted to offer a supreme model to the man who struggles; I wanted to show him that he must not fear pain, temptation or death— because all three can be conquered, all three have already been conquered. Christ suffered pain, and since then pain has been sanctified. Temptation fought until the very

last moment to lead him astray, and Temptation was defeated. Christ died on the Cross, and at that instant death was vanquished forever.[17]

This is Kazantzakis's answer to all allegations of blasphemy, for what he has shown is the transformation of a clod of earth into ethereal sublimity, the truth that "life on earth means: the sprouting of wings."[18] Jesus' passion becomes a role model for all those who aspire to rise up above their human limitations. Jesus feels that it is the devil inside him who cries: "You're not the son of the Carpenter, you're the son of King David! You are not a man, you are the son of man whom Daniel prophesied. And still more: the Son of God! And still more: God!"[19] What he encounters as the ultimate temptation is an exhortation to discover the god that is buried under the layers of fat in our souls.

In my view, Kazantzakis does not treat Jesus with the levity that seems present in Menen's and Rushdie's fictional depictions of Rama and Mahound. Both Menen and Rushdie question the basic tenets of their faiths in a way that Kazantzakis does not. For instance, Rushdie recalls:

> Mahound himself had been a businessman, and a damned successful one at that, a person to whom organization and rules came naturally, so how excessively convenient it was that he should have come up with such a very businesslike archangel, who handed down the management decisions of this highly corporate, if non-corporeal, God.[20]

Mahound is reduced to a laconic corporate executive who ruthlessly sees to the success of his venture. Likewise, *Rama Retold* strips Rama of his divine stature; it shows him bereft of the qualities—leadership, courage, moral tenacity—that the original epic endowed him with. Kazantzakis's Jesus, on the other hand, is a bright beacon for those who toil on their individual, stony paths to Calvary; he has only reinforced the triumph of the victory on the cross, not denigrated it.

Ascent seems to be *The Last Temptation*'s leitmotif, and actually of all of Kazantzakis's works. "Struggle between the flesh and the spirit, rebellion and resistance, reconciliation and submission, and finally—the supreme purpose of the struggle—union with God: this was the ascent taken by Christ, the ascent which he invites us to take as well, following in his bloody tracks."[21] But this appeal was never heard amid all the allegations of blasphemy. Kazantzakis would have been justified if he felt a despair akin to Jesus' on hearing Jacob's determination to preserve his, Jesus', words in new Holy Scriptures, and synagogues, and the selection of high priests, scribes, and Pharisees. Jesus' answer to Jacob is telling: "You crucify the spirit, Jacob!"[22] I think a similar spirit behind Kazantzakis's novel was crucified when some Christian leaders protested against the novel, ignoring his prologue.

After we have assessed the negative reaction to Kazantzakis's novel among some Christian clergy in India, we must acknowledge that Antony's play and Warrier's essay created far more consternation and outrage. One reason for this lies in the audience each writer—Antony and Warrier—envisaged; I suspect the play and the essay, both written in Malayalam, reached out to the masses in a way that an English novel did not. And one cannot discount the impact of the staged play as opposed to words on a printed page. Similarly, an essay prescribed for study in an undergraduate curriculum ensures that the writer's message gets across to impressionable minds, sowing the seeds of a so-called alternative, a potentially dangerous truth.

Theocratic leaders of institutionalized religions are wary of so-called heretics, blasphemers, or proponents of an alternative reality, since the latter allegedly undermine the former's monopoly of wisdom, status, and power, especially over the laity. This would explain why most ecclesiastical circles found it difficult to accept Kazantzakis's depiction of the glorious struggle and victory of Jesus. The novel was banned by the Roman Catholic Church, the author was refused an official burial by the Greek Orthodox Church, and he was opposed by a few Christian leaders in Kerala, India. It seems, therefore, that occupants of Christianity's hierarchical structure, broadly construed, find it hard to brook the flourishing of a faith that needs no intermediaries. The history of the elders of traditional belief persecuting mystics is a testimony to this observation. Mystics appear to prefer a ritual-free spiritual love that encompasses and embraces our imperfect world. Here I include Saint Francis of Assisi's spiritual brotherhood, the Sufi way to God through love and music, and the Indian Bhakti movement, which sings of universal brotherhood before God—all of them accepted no authority but God. Theirs was and is the path of devotion that shuns material circumstances and rewards. In my view, a similar spiritual dedication lies at the heart of Kazantzakis's communion with God. And all the unique beauty and strength of this mystic affinity is captured by his image of the almond tree that flowers in the middle of winter: "I said to the almond tree, 'Sister, speak to me of God.' And the almond tree blossomed."[23]

I suspect that the primary reason for the harsh ecclesiastical reaction against Kazantzakis, Antony, and Warrier lies in established religion's jealous guarding of traditional faith. Many in the Christian Church apparently disfavor independent readings of Scriptures reaching the masses. A play or an essay prescribed for study is a potential danger for precisely this reason. This said, I close my chapter by exploring the intellectual implications of an image, one that is as fully popular as it is Kazantzakian, because he took delight in butterflies.

Scientists tell us that the world is so thoroughly interconnected that the flutter of butterfly wings in a South American rain forest is capable of rousing a storm in Iceland. Likewise, I would say that an unorthodox thought in Europe can spark off an intellectual debate in a country remote from it in language and culture. As I have indicated, the Malayalam dramatic adaptation of a Greek novel exemplifies the concatenated nature of writing. It transcends geolinguistic barriers and, in doing so, contributes to the unbroken realm of free thought, which is beyond artificial control. Writing thus posits the ultimate nightmare before those who wish to homogenize free thought and sanitize free expression. It is surely to the credit of Kazantzakis's creative originality that his agonized cry on the stony, storied island of Crete found an answering echo in tropical India.

Notes

1. Edward Said, *Representations of the Intellectual* (New York: Pantheon, 1994), 11.

2. See http://www.greenglobetourism.com/kerala/kl_generalinfo.htm.

3. Interview with Bishop Joseph Kundukulam, *Mathrubhumi* (weekly), November 30—December 6, 1986, 9.

4. Ibid., 9.

5. P. M. Antony, *Christuvinte Aram Thirumurivu* (New Delhi: Indian Atheist Publishers, 1988), 56.

6. Ibid., 57.

7. Ibid., 71.

8. Ibid., 119.

9. Ibid., 121.

10. Ibid., 121.

11. Ibid., 136.

12. Interview with Bishop Joseph, 7.

13. O. V. Vijayan, "Palliyude Murivukal," *Mathrubhumi* (weekly), January 11—17, 1987, 6.

14. Nikos Kazantzakis, *The Last Temptation of Christ*, trans. Peter Bien (New York: Simon & Schuster, 1960), 3.

15. Milan Kundera, *Testaments Betrayed*, trans. Linda Asher (London: Faber & Faber, 1996), 8–9.

16. Aubrey Menen, *Rama Retold: A Secular Retelling of the Ramayana* (London: Chatto & Windus, 1954), 3.

17. Kazantzakis, *Last Temptation*, 4.

18. Ibid., 493.

19. Ibid., 147.

20. Salman Rushdie, *The Satanic Verses* (New York: Viking, 1989), 364.

21. Kazantzakis, *Last Temptation*, 2.

22. Ibid., 427.

23. Nikos Kazantzakis, *Report to Greco*, trans. Peter Bien (New York: Simon & Schuster, 1965), 234.

PART TWO
Screen Savior

CHAPTER 12

Satan and the Curious
Texas Evangelicals Read *The Last Temptation of Christ*
Elizabeth H. Flowers and Darren J. N. Middleton

Let no publicity draw your curiosity to the profit of Satan. Director Martin Scorsese may have studied for the priesthood, but he has failed, as Satan did at the right hand of God. Let us hope that the investment in this movie is very high, and let us pray that it reaps nothing. May the weight of debt bring all who were with this act of Satan to total failure, and those who see they have wronged the Savior pray for forgiveness with earnest hearts.

Be it done that each time Satan calls on the curious, that the cost to fulfill be sowed in the house of God, to glorify his name through Jesus Christ our Lord. Let the truth be thrust around the world, leaving the act with no place to dwell.

—Jess W. Wood, Mansfield, Texas[1]

Introduction

Reader-oriented approaches to Nikos Kazantzakis's work have recently taken their place alongside more customary biographical studies. This signifies the critical move to emphasize the reading *process*—how we as readers experience a novel as a sequence of responses over time. All texts have various moments of historical reception. There obviously are moments when we feel ourselves confirmed, challenged, or unhinged by what we read. Our individual responses are often shaped by one another, thus coalescing to form a larger, collective response. This process occurs in cinematic as well as in literary art. When we read a novel or view a film, we frequently find ourselves brought—sometimes willingly, sometimes reluctantly—into a new awareness of our assumptions, expectations, and values. Jess W. Wood exemplifies the strong response elicited by Kazantzakis's work, in novel and cinematic form. Though his response proves roundly dismissive, many negative responses can be seen as valuable to Kazantzakis's supporters and critics.

Certain reader-responses to Kazantzakis's novelistic re-creation of Jesus' life and death are well-known. There is hardly any need to rehearse, for instance, that certain Greek Orthodox clergy tried to prosecute Kazantzakis for it, or that the Vatican placed it on its Index of Forbidden Texts.[2] However, more localized receptions of this novel/film are less well-known.[3] Yet such local histories are valuable. They articulate an apprehension of Jesus at the grassroots level, from within the local churches and Christian communities where faith actually lives. Moreover, they illustrate what happens when the fissure between what certain Christians believe and what an artist in his or her artwork poses becomes so wide that such Christians revolt at the alleged pressure to approve or conform. In such cases we find examples of *oppositional readings*—interpretations that proclaim standards, interests, and discernment contrary to those felt to be implied in the artwork.

In Fort Worth, Texas, where we, the coauthors of this chapter, have lived and taught Christian theology and the history of religions for several years, we have discovered many oppositional readers to *The Last Temptation of Christ*. By focusing on newspaper letters, Op-Ed columns, Church petitions, and community newsletters that appeared in Texas during the late 1980s, we outline a particular collective reader-response to Kazantzakis's/Scorsese's artwork.[4] As we argue here, there is much to be gained from examining this oppositional response or reading. Much of the furor surrounding *The Last Temptation of Christ*—certainly the film version—arose in the so-called American evangelical Bible Belt, with Texas being its buckle. Considering Texas evangelicals' opposition to *The Last Temptation of Christ* might help us better comprehend a particular aspect of American Christianity. But it could also help us better understand Kazantzakis, Scorsese, and *The Last Temptation of Christ*. It is often said that American evangelicals did not understand Kazantzakis's/Scorsese's artwork. This might be true in some cases, for several commentators dismissed the film sight unseen. But as we have discovered, many evangelicals understood only too well the issue at stake in Kazantzakis's/Scorsese's artwork. What they opposed was an irresolute, beleaguered Jesus, one who suffered from peculiar visions and breakdowns, one tempted to the point of giving up the call of the cross. The point is, they rejected *The Last Temptation of Christ* because it demanded too much of them by presenting a Jesus just a shade too human.

The "Many Citizens" Protest

In the months before Scorsese's film was released to the general public on August 12, 1988, various transdenominational, parachurch, and ecclesial organizations mounted protests. The National Association of Evangelicals (NAE) urged Christians to boycott the movie.[5] The American Family Association, Billy Graham Ministries, and Campus

Crusade for Christ all denounced *The Last Temptation of Christ* as blasphemous.[6] In Texas, evangelical Christians responded most vehemently.[7] Several concerned Fort Worth residents purchased a full-page advertisement in the August 8 edition of the *Star-Telegram*, the city's daily newspaper. Signed by "many citizens who love the Lord," the ad opened on an anxious note: "It is with heartfelt grief and shock that we feel called to bring to your attention a matter of great concern to all of us." Perceiving themselves as called by God, the "many citizens" pointed to Jesus' fantasies of sex with Mary Magdalene. Such fantasies are "horrible lies," they declared, and the "sordid pictures [of Jesus and Mary Magdalene coupling] will be imprinted upon their [young people's] minds for the rest of their lives." Condemning the film as an "affront to Almighty God," the "many citizens" used biblically and christologically inspired rhetoric to advance their claims:

> We feel that the heart of God is pierced and broken by such an attack upon His beloved Son. We believe He is asking those of us who love Him, "What will you do, now, for my Son, who died for you on the cross and rose again that you and all who believe might have eternal life?" We shall answer this call with a strong determination to stand for our Lord. We do not have to stand by and let Universal Studios and their cohorts treat the one we love with such disrespect and trample upon our faith. We see, in this movie script, the culmination of all the wickedness of pornography which has been spread upon our land, lo, these many years, for there cannot be anything more evil than to attribute such sins to the Holy, pure Son of God.[8]

These Fort Worth citizens typify other Texas evangelicals. For them, Kazantzakis's/Scorsese's Christ veers far too much into the human condition. As we will see, it is particular aspects of this condition that they find most disturbing.

Contrasting Christologies

Evangelical Christians hold specific beliefs about Jesus Christ, which they believe the divinely inspired Bible supports directly. Both the National Association of Evangelicals and the Southern Baptist Convention have faith statements that epitomize basic evangelical christological convictions. They can be summarized in the following way: Jesus existed before all things. He is the same as God, begotten and not made. He is God incarnate, the divine Son, one person of the Holy Trinity, who became flesh and blood and took on human form. He lived a sinless life on earth; performed miracles; and died as a substitutionary sacrifice, or atonement, to bring back people from evil, which had taken hold of the world when the first man, Adam, disobeyed God. On the third day, He rose from the dead. Finally, He is not only a unique historical figure; He is also a living, real presence who shares in the believer's daily life.[9] As we see here, evangelicals draw upon an inerrant reading of the Bible, the traditional doctrines behind the ecumenical creeds, and a strong sense of pietistic revivalism to define their faith.

Kazantzakis's/Scorsese's Christology challenges this faith. Briefly, Kazantzakis questions Jesus' supernatural origins, virgin birth, miracles, substitutionary death on the cross, physical resurrection from the dead, and ascension into heaven.[10] What remains after such questioning is the man from Nazareth, whose exemplary ethical vision, Kazantzakis holds, energizes his followers.

Kazantzakis's novel begins not with the miraculous virgin birth but with Jesus as an adult carpenter. Temptations confront him through dream sequences. In the first, dwarfs and devils declare war on any contentment he feels. Soon he finds his soul a battleground between domestic comfort and spiritual meaningfulness. It is little wonder that Scorsese found Kazantzakis's Jesus an apt symbol for contemporary, middle-class American existence. Scorsese, then, highlights Jesus' struggle with temptations to familial and material fulfillment. Only through spurning the last temptation, the final dream sequence, does he effect his divinity and achieve mystical union with God. Here there is no empty tomb, no final resurrection, no supernatural ending.

It is no surprise, then, for Texas evangelicals to charge that *The Last Temptation of Christ* decenters Jesus' divinity and, instead, portrays him throughout as an uncertain, lust-ridden, wavering whiner.[11] As one Bedford woman wrote to her local newspaper editor, "This film depicts with graphic and blatant lies that Jesus Christ was a sinful, false-prophet man, not at all what Christians know to be true of him—the sinless, perfect son of God who chose to die for the sins of all mankind and purchase their salvation."[12]

The Sacrilege of Sex

Texas evangelical protest, like most oppositional readings, was far from systematic. However, one of the most persistent objections focused on Jesus' sexuality. This takes us to the heart of Kazantzakis's/Scorsese's artwork, the final dream sequence. Nailed to the cross, Jesus cries out to God and then faints. This is an opportune moment in which Satan presents one last temptation—a fantasy in which Jesus is shown not only to lead an ordinary life with marriage and children but to engage in sexual intercourse with Mary Magdalene and then, though only implied, Lazarus's sisters. As one woman, a member of the First Baptist Church of Euless, complained to a regional religion reporter: "It [Scorsese's movie] is a blasphemy against the sinless Jesus. How can they have a scene where Jesus and Mary Magdalene go to bed together I don't know. Those who wrote the script must know nothing about the Bible."[13] Likewise, a Fort Worth man asserted: "The terrible thing about this film is that the minds of people are being contaminated by the out-and-out lies it depicts. The Bible states categorically that Jesus was without sin. He did not go to bed with Mary or Martha or anyone else. If these people who wrote the script had spent as much time in the Bible as they have in defense of their sacrilege, they would have known better."[14] For many, the visual nature of the fantasies went too far. According to this Midland man, "The movie appears to be inconsistent with the way Christ dealt with temptation. Though he was tempted to turn stones to bread while hungry and the kingdoms of the world were offered to him if he would bow to Satan, I don't think he imagined himself doing so. Let's not forget he was God also. Instead he rebuked Satan with Scripture then the devil left him."[15]

It's Not about the Sex

Some might accuse evangelicals of being somewhat prudish here. But their protestations of Jesus' sexuality actually point to something much larger. For Kazantzakis/Scorsese, Jesus served as a model not simply because he fantasized about sex, but also because he demonstrated what it meant to work though our humanity, with all of its temptations and flaws, en route to union with God. Sex, then, became a powerful symbol of Jesus' humanity. Kazantzakis and Scorsese flirted with Jesus' sexuality in order to accentuate the full range of "normal things" with which Jesus must have wrestled. The normal, as they interpreted it according to their twentieth-century contexts, involved the possibility of marriage, the joy of sex, the gift of children, even the rewards of a hard-earned career. Their sense of the normal fed the imaginative what-if moment of the final dream sequence.

Texas evangelicals, however, felt scandalized by the vision of Jesus having sex with women. Evangelicals have certainly focused on more individualized moral issues and "sins," like fornication, drinking, and gambling. Yet their dis-ease here stemmed as much from the way sex indicated an indecisiveness in Jesus' messianic vision as from the sex itself. Furthermore, according to evangelical thinking, indulgence in temptation could lead to the enacting of it. (We all remember Jimmy Carter's *Playboy* confession that he had, indeed, committed adultery—the tempting lust of the heart and mind.) Thus, any temptation posed a danger—so much so that many evangelicals have correlated the temptation with the actual deed itself. When we read evangelical protest in the context of their theology, we find that they indeed recognize the power of the symbol.

Seen through evangelical eyes, the final dream sequence illustrates a wavering, weak-willed, even dangerous Jesus, one who suffers from peculiar visions and breakdowns, one so tempted to give up the cross that He might as well have done so. For evangelicals, this Jesus came across as a human being no better or worse than themselves. Jesus was no longer the innocent Isaac but the wavering Adam, the wayward David, or the doubting Thomas. And that was simply not enough, christologically or devotionally.

Kazantzakis's/Scorsese's Jesus was so demystified, so stripped of his human-divine qualities ("Let's not forget he was God also"), that His holiness and innocence had to be questioned. As evangelicals insisted, Jesus was the eternal Son of God, who honored His Father by living in filial, unbroken obedience, even to the cross, God's particular and unique provision for humankind's redemption. Not once did Jesus falter. Not once did He waver. Texas evangelicals rejected Kazantzakis's/Scorsese's Jesus as unworthy of their following. As stated before, the gap between what Texas evangelicals believed and what *The Last Temptation of Christ* depicted was so wide that evangelicals not only shied away from the novel or movie but also protested any pressure to approve or conform to it. In fact, any participation in such a portrayal was *their* final temptation. Taking her cues from an old-time spiritual, this Farmers Branch woman summarized what was at stake:

> A familiar hymn asks the soul-stirring question, "Were you there when they cruci-fied my Lord?" We've also heard sermons suggesting that had we been at Calvary that day, we, alongside the hysterical masses, would have cried out, "Crucify him! Crucify him!"
>
> And now, the 20th century masses have a unique opportunity to visit the scene at Calvary, this time at a motion picture titled *The Last Temptation of Christ*. In dark-ened movie theaters across the nation, viewers will witness a mocking, shameful, blasphemous crucifixion of Jesus Christ's character and deity. Some will undoubt-edly go to the movie out of curiosity, insisting that they are innocent bystanders. Others will enjoy watching the proclaimed son of God portrayed as a weak, sinful, lustful human being no better or worse than themselves. But for whatever reason one decides to go to such a film, each person should seriously ask himself, "Will I align myself with the masses who support such a film and find myself shouting, 'Crucify him! Crucify him!'"[16]

Conclusion

The nature of evangelicals' opposition helps us to grasp the radical humanity of Kazantzakis's/Scorsese's Jesus. Kazantzakis intended his novel to challenge, provoke, and disturb by giving readers a Jesus who looked much like themselves. He certainly hoped that they would see Jesus' struggle and take spiritual strength from it, strength to endure their own struggle. Scorsese's sexually immodest, even Hollywood-style Jesus was true to Kazantzakis's intent. Indeed, the Jesus of Scorsese's movie repre-sents temptations toward everyday domesticity, material fulfillment, and middle-class mediocrity, real and pressing temptations that have plagued contemporary Western society. But evangelicals cried out in protest: How could such a Jesus point the way to the divine?

In 2004, almost fifty years after *The Last Temptation*'s publication and exactly six-teen years after its cinematic release, evangelicals have responded quite fervently to another Jesus-story, Mel Gibson's movie *The Passion of the Christ*. Yet evangelicals have uniformly celebrated Gibson's Christ. This is hardly surprising. Contrary to popular belief, art has been a central feature of evangelical practice, particularly in the last several decades. But evangelicals are wary of what they might call "extrabiblical" aesthetic renderings that go against the grain of their biblical interpretation, tradi-tion, and born-again experience. In contrast to Kazantzakis's/Scorsese's portrayal,

Gibson's Jesus is unwavering in the face of crucifixion. He gives no hint of temptation and offers no final scandalizing vision. As implied in the movie's opening quotation of Isa 53, Jesus is the Lamb willingly led to the slaughter.

Yet while Gibson's depiction has found evangelical favor, it has also had more than its share of oppositional readers. In fact, those liberal Christians who championed *The Last Temptation of Christ* have largely protested *The Passion of the Christ*. They have called Gibson's flesh-ripped Christ "repulsive" and dismissed his blood-dripping death as an "outmoded" form of substitutionary atonement theology. When protestations of *The Passion of the Christ* are seen alongside those of *The Last Temptation of Christ*, they reveal that no one portrayal could ever satisfy our human imaginations or longings.[17] Depictions of Jesus will inevitably court controversy. Their adherence or their faithfulness to the traditional stories will be debated. They will both fail and fulfill human hopes for a divine Savior. This does not mean that certain responses are not misguided and that no opposition should go unchallenged. But by engaging the passion of its most ardent detractors, we as critics can somewhat ironically better appreciate the artistic vision at hand.

Notes

1. Jess W. Wood, *Fort Worth Star-Telegram*, July, 30, 1988, sec. 1, p. 30.

2. See Michael Antonakes, "Christ, Kazantzakis, and Controversy in Greece," *Modern Greek Studies Yearbook* 6 (1990): 331–43; repr. in *God's Struggler: Religion in the Writings of Nikos Kazantzakis*, ed. Darren J. N. Middleton and Peter Bien (Macon, GA: Mercer University Press, 1996), 23–35. For the videocassette version of Scorsese's film, see *The Last Temptation of Christ* (Universal City, CA: MCA Home Video, 1989), color, 165 minutes. For the DVD version, featuring instructive audio commentary by Scorsese, Willem Dafoe, Paul Schrader, and Jay Cocks, see *The Last Temptation of Christ* (Universal City, CA: Criterion Home Collection, 2000). For criticism of the film, see John Ankerberg and John Weldon, *The Facts on "The Last Temptation of Christ": The True Story behind the Controversial Film* (Eugene, OR: Harvest House, 1988); Michael Medved, *Hollywood vs. America: Popular Culture and the War on Traditional Values* (New York: HarperCollins, 1992), 37–49; and finally, Larry W. Poland, *The Last Temptation of Hollywood* (Highland, CA: Mastermedia International, 1988). For a short defense of the film, see Peter A. Bien, "Scorsese's Spiritual Jesus" (Op-Ed column), *New York Times*, August 11, 1988, A25. Finally, three recent "Jesus in film" book surveys offer informative assessments. See Lloyd Baugh, *Imaging the Divine: Jesus and Christ-Figures in Film* (Kansas City: Sheed & Ward, 1997), 48–71; Richard C. Stern et al., *Savior on the Silver Screen* (New York: Paulist Press, 1999), 265–95; and lastly, W. Barnes Tatum, *Jesus at the Movies: A Guide to the First Hundred Years* (Santa Rosa, CA: Polebridge, 2004), 178–92.

3. For heuristic purposes, we speak in this chapter of "the novel/film" or "Kazantzakis's/Scorsese's artwork." We recognize the obvious caveat that must be made here—the novel and the film have their differences, need not be collapsed together as a single item, and so on. But in analyzing reader-responses to the film, we have discovered little if any distinction in the minds of those inclined toward oppositional readings. Some letters to the press, especially from those who praise the film according to religious persuasion, reference Kazantzakis and

appeal to an understanding of his biography and overall literary output and intention, but these letters are few and far between. Most of the newspaper correspondence we have read, and many of the petitions we have seen, conflate Kazantzakis's novel and Scorsese's film. Kazantzakis scholars will dislike this conflation, and as informed critics they should, but this is the heart of the challenge—for the scholar at least—of coming to terms with reader-oriented approaches to art. Quite frankly, readers will respond as they see fit.

4. We owe a great debt to Middleton's colleague Dr. Joey Jeter. He gave us unrestricted access to his extensive archive of newspaper clippings, pamphlets, and other items related to the local furor surrounding *The Last Temptation of Christ*. In addition, we appreciate the work of Austin S. Lingerfelt, Middleton's former student assistant, who has constructed a Web site detailing some of the salient issues at the heart of this local and national controversy. For additional information see Lingerfelt's site: <http://homepage.mac.com/infestation/site/temptation/index.html>.

5. The NAE represents numerous Christians conservatives: <http://www.nae.net/>. For a historical background to the NAE, see Joel Carpenter, *Revive Us Again: The Reawakening of American Fundamentalism* (New York: Oxford University Press, 1997), 141–60.

6. Full details of the historical developments surrounding this film may be found in Robin Riley's *Film, Faith, and Cultural Conflict: The Case of Martin Scorsese's "The Last Temptation of Christ"* (Westport, CT: Praeger, 2003), 11–34.

7. While Scorsese's movie was released in major East Coast and West Coast American cities on August 12, 1988, it was initially delayed in cities of the American south and southwest. "Movies like 'Last Temptation,' an art film that cost only $6.5 million to make, are usually released in Atlanta, Dallas and Houston as well as Northern cities. But Universal chose not to present the film [initially] in the South because of the high concentration of Christian conservatives." See Diane Winston, "Christians Condemn Jesus Film," in *Dallas Times Herald*, August 13, 1988, A2. Winston's article mentions a 300-plus demonstration at the southwest headquarters of the movie's distributors, located at the corner of Greenville Avenue and Walnut Lane in Dallas, Texas. But Winston does not indicate how many of these protestors had viewed the film before taking to the streets to denounce it. What we do know, though, is that the Texas premiere of Scorsese's film took place at theaters in Austin and Houston, August 19, 1988. *The Last Temptation of Christ* opened in Dallas on August 31, 1988. And it was released in Fort Worth on September 23, 1988.

8. *Fort Worth Star-Telegram*, August 8, 1988, sec. 1, p. 5. Also see Jim Jones, "For Fort Worth Christians, Ad Proclaims Bad News for Film," in *Fort Worth Star-Telegram*, August 9, 1988, part 2, sec. 1. According to Jones, Rev. John Hildebrand, then rector of Fort Worth's St. Andrew's Episcopal Church, and his wife, Betty, initiated the advertisement, which cost $6,546.75 to run. For more information, see *Fort Worth Star-Telegram*, August 18, 1988, sec. 1, p. 24.

9. Compare the faith statements made by two major evangelical groups: the NAE, <http://www.nae.net/index.cfm?FUSEACTION=nae.statement_of_faith>, and the Southern Baptist Convention, <http://www.sbc.net/bfm/bfm2000.asp>.

10. Evangelicals often express their belief in Jesus' divinity by capitalizing pronouns used to refer to him. When we are referencing evangelical views about Jesus, then, we use uppercase letters. Sometimes quotations from evangelical sources go back-and-forth, using upper- and lowercase letters, and so, when we quote, we cite accurately, reproducing the quoted words as they appeared originally. When we are discussing Kazantzakis's Jesus, however, we use lowercase

letters, doing so under advisement. In personal correspondence, Peter Bien informs Middleton that he fought with Kazantzakis's American publisher, Simon & Schuster, to use lowercase letters for "him," "he," and "his" when referring to Jesus. Using capitals when discussing Kazantzakis's Jesus "are really very contrary to Kazantzakis's purpose in the book [*The Last Temptation*], which is to make Jesus totally real *as a human being*" (Bien's emphasis).

11. These are strong words, we know, but many are traceable to the opinions of various evangelical Christians. See the *Fort Worth Star-Telegram*, July 13, 1988, sec. 1, p. 6; *The National Christian Reporter*, July 29, 1988, 4; and finally, *People Magazine*, August 8, 1988, 40–43.

12. See Amy Pittard's letter to the editor of the *Fort Worth Star-Telegram*, July 24, 1988, sec. 3, p. 2.

13. Elaine Shaw is quoted in Jim Jones, "Christian Rage: Conservatives Say Movie about Jesus Is Blasphemous," *Fort Worth Star-Telegram*, July 25, 1988, sec. 1, p. 3.

14. Scottie L. Spurlock's comments appear in his letter to the editor of the *Fort Worth Star-Telegram*, August 14, 1988, sec. 3, p. 2.

15. Consult Timothy C. Powell's letter to the editor of *The National Christian Reporter*, August 12, 1988, 4.

16. See Carol A. Wood's letter to the editor of the *Fort Worth Star-Telegram*, July 31, 1988, sec. 3, p. 2. Additional protests may be found in the *Fort Worth Star-Telegram*, August 9, 1988, sec. 1, p. 14; August 14, 1988, sec. 3, p. 2; and August 20, 1988, sec. 1, p. 31.

17. See Kevin Fauteux, "The Final Portrait of Christ," *Journal of Religion and Health* 28, no. 3 (Fall 1989): 195–206. For an exploration of links between Scorsese's and Gibson's films, see Darren J. N. Middleton, "Celluloid Synoptics: Viewing the Gospels of Marty and Mel Together," in *Re-viewing the Passion: Mel Gibson's Film and Its Critics,* ed. S. Brent Plate (New York: Palgrave, 2004), 71–81.

CHAPTER 13

Battling the Flesh

Sexuality and Spirituality in *The Last Temptation of Christ*

Peter T. Chattaway

One of the most controversial aspects of Martin Scorsese's adaptation of Nikos Kazantzakis's *The Last Temptation of Christ* (1988) was its treatment of sexuality, particularly the sexuality of Jesus. The film not only suggests that Jesus may have had sexual desires; it also depicts Jesus making love to Mary Magdalene and kissing her passionately. This sexual activity takes place in what some have called a "dream sequence," in which Satan tempts Jesus by showing him an alternative reality in which he comes down from the cross and lives an ordinary life—marrying, raising children, and growing old. Ironically, both the protestors who accused the film of blasphemy and the filmmakers who made the actual movie were agreed on at least one core idea: In order to fulfill his divine mission, Jesus could not have known sexual intimacy. But the two sides of this debate came to this conclusion from different premises. The assumptions underlying their respective positions have often gone unexamined, even as the controversy over the sexuality of Jesus continues to flare up with the production of plays like Terence McNally's *Corpus Christi* and the publication of novels like Dan Brown's *The Da Vinci Code*.

Both those who support *The Last Temptation of Christ* and those who oppose it have cautioned against making too much of the sex. Defenders of the film have said that the Jesus of this film is ultimately tempted not by sexuality but by domesticity. Scorsese himself has said that the temptation of the film's title "is not for Christ to have sex, but to get married, make love to his wife and have children like an ordinary man."[1] Scorsese has further emphasized that in the infamous dream sequence, Jesus makes love to Mary Magdalene "for the purpose of having children." He seems to suggest that even the Jesus of his film would not be inclined to engage in sexual intercourse with his spouse simply for the pleasure of it.[2] On the other side of the debate, conservative culture critic Michael Medved observes that Christian leaders identified over twenty other offensive elements in the film, such as the scene in which the apostle Paul says he doesn't care whether the resurrection happened or not. Medved criticizes the media for focusing on the film's sex scene to the exclusion of these other concerns. "By ignoring the issues raised by all other aspects of the film and concentrating exclusively on the sex scene between Magdalene and Christ, the press helped to make the protestors look like narrow-minded prudes."[3]

Nevertheless, sex is a quite significant part of *The Last Temptation of Christ*, both the content of the film and the controversy surrounding it. In certain crucial ways, Scorsese amplifies the sexual content of the story considerably beyond what appears in Kazantzakis's original novel. And when screenwriter Paul Schrader was asked what *The Last Temptation of Christ* has in common with *Taxi Driver* (1976) and *Raging Bull* (1980), the two previous films on which he and Scorsese collaborated, he replied, "They're all of the same cloth: they're about lonely, self-deluded, sexually inactive people." Schrader then added that he is fascinated by celibacy because he was raised in a Calvinist environment, which discouraged having sex for pleasure.[4] Similarly, conservative Christians who protested the film drew specific attention to the sexual elements within it, beginning with the outcry over an early draft of the script in which Jesus tells Mary Magdalene, "God sleeps between your legs."[5] Catholic critic Steven D. Greydanus, in a mostly rational critique of the film written years after the controversy died down, responds more viscerally to the scene of Jesus and Mary in bed together. He asserts that the very "wrongness" of the image of Jesus kissing a woman overpowers whatever the context of the image might be.[6]

Sexuality and Christ in Christian Theology

Certain assumptions tend to lurk behind comments such as these. First, it is assumed that Jesus was never married or sexually active. Second, it is assumed that Jesus was never married or sexually active because it would have been impossible, somehow, for him to be thus. There is a range of reasons *why* it is assumed that Jesus must have been sexually abstinent.

The first assumption, regarding Jesus' celibate status, is rooted in Christian tradition, though it does not go back to the Gospels themselves. One Gospel does attribute a speech to Jesus commending those who have abstained from marriage and become "eunuchs" for the sake of the kingdom of heaven (Matt 19:10–12), but it does not explicitly state that Jesus himself was one of these "eunuchs." Intriguingly, when Paul discusses the pros and cons of marriage in his Epistles, he never mentions the marital status of Christ, though he freely contrasts his own celibacy with the wives whom the "brothers" of Jesus took with them on their journeys (1 Cor 9:5). Thus, any argument one makes about the marital status of the historical Jesus is an argument from silence. William E. Phipps argues it would have been so unusual in the Jewish culture of that time for a man of Jesus' age to be celibate that he must have been married unless the sources state otherwise.[7] However, John P. Meier reports that celibacy was not unknown among marginal Jewish religious groups. Meier makes a compelling case that given the many references to Jesus' relatives and female followers both in the Gospels and in early Christian literature, the most plausible reason the sources never mention whether Jesus had a wife is that none existed, at least not during his public ministry.[8]

As for the second assumption, regarding the reasons for the presumed celibacy of Jesus, it is reasonable to assume that if Jesus did abstain from marriage, then it may have been out of a sense of vocation. Perhaps his commitment to his vision for Israel and to what he called the kingdom of God was so powerful that it overwhelmed all other possible commitments. But one suspects there are deeper reasons why so many Christians have insisted on the celibacy of Jesus, to the point that even thinking that he might have been married is perceived as blasphemous.

Some of this resistance to the notion that Jesus could have been married, and thus sexually active, may stem from a mistrust of the body, a mistrust that has its roots in antiquity. The Gnostics proposed that because God is spirit, the material world must be the product of some other entity; spirit is good because it is divine, but flesh is bad because it is a prison for the soul. Genesis describes God's telling man and woman to be fruitful and multiply *before* they are expelled from the garden of Eden. But the *Secret Book of John* tells a Gnostic version of the creation story. In it, a serpentine deity named Yaldabaoth creates the first woman and plants "the lust for reproduction" within her in order to ensure that the first humans will procreate, and thus create more "bodily tombs" for the spirit.[9] The apostle Paul (or the author who wrote in his name) seems to be taking aim at such attitudes when he says that Christian men must fulfill their marital duties to their wives (1 Cor 7:3–5); He thus gives women a startlingly equal role in determining the frequency of marital relations, highly unusual in the pagan and Jewish cultures of that time.[10] He also says that women will be "saved through childbearing" (1 Tim 2:15).[11]

Nevertheless, suspicion of the body did seep into the early Church. James B. Nelson argues that Christian tradition has long harbored a dualist attitude, inherited from the ancient Greeks. The body is perceived not only as inferior or subordinate to the spirit—not an unreasonable position, if one believes that God himself is spirit (John 4:24) and that the material world is a part of his creation—but also as somehow inherently corrupt as well. The Stoics, Nelson writes, sought a life without passion; the medieval theologians feared the loss of rationality that accompanied orgasm; the Calvinists believed exuberant sexual pleasure was indecent; and the Victorians thought sexual pleasure was animalistic.[12] Jerome asserted that people who had not remained virgins, including those who were married, were "polluted."[13] But this suspicion of the body and its functions was not limited to sexual activity. Augustine argued that eating and drinking, which are necessary for the survival of the individual, and procreation, which is necessary for the survival of the species, were activities to which the "wise and faithful man descends . . . from a sense of duty; he does not fall into them through lust." For Augustine, the ideal state was one in which people could live without food or drink, and have children without marital intercourse.[14]

Other aspects of the Christian tradition have pointed in a rather different direction and have actually affirmed the fact that human beings share their bodily functions with the animals and are thus, in some sense, animals themselves. The Jewish creation story places God's creation of human beings as male and female, along with his command to be fruitful and multiply, on the same day that God creates the other land animals (Gen 1:24–31). In his popular book *The Screwtape Letters*, C. S. Lewis even speculates that the demons, which are pure spirits, rebelled against God precisely because they objected to his plan to create a "revolting hybrid" between animal and spirit. The titular devil scorns the human who is the subject of his letters as a "thing begotten in a bed."[15]

So if it is scandalous that God became human in the person of Jesus, part of the scandal resides in the fact that God, in becoming human, also became an animal. This affinity may be implicit in the stories of the infant Christ being born in a stable and placed in a manger. It is, quite frankly, difficult to believe that Jesus was as embarrassed by his animal functions as Augustine evidently was. The Gospels report that Jesus feasted and drank with such verve that he apparently earned a reputation, however undeservedly, as "a glutton and a drunkard" (Luke 7:34), and he even spoke with frank familiarity about bathroom functions, too (Mark 7:19).[16] As Nelson puts it, it may be "incomprehensible" to think of Jesus as a "laughing, crying, sweating, urinating, defecating, orgasmic, sensuous bundle of flesh." But even by orthodox standards, by which Jesus is believed to be fully human, that is certainly what he was.[17]

However, sexuality is not only physical; it is also psychological and spiritual. If Jesus was indeed fully human, then he did not simply have a physical body; he must have taken on the intellectual, emotional, and spiritual qualities of humanity as well. Some Christians will concede that Jesus "in every respect has been tempted as we are, yet without sinning" (Heb 4:15 RSV), and that this must have included sexual temptations as well. But even this is not as strong an affirmation as it could be. The word "tempted" implies that one feels a desire to do something wrong; it obscures the possibility that sexual desire might itself be a good thing, and that Jesus almost certainly felt this sort of desire the same way he felt hunger and thirst. If Jesus abstained from sexual activity, it was not because he had no sexual feelings or inclinations but because he chose to set these desires aside in favor of his higher calling. Indeed, if the presumed celibacy of Jesus is to serve as any sort of example, we must presuppose that Jesus was a fully sexual being.

Sexuality and Christ in Art and Film

Not surprisingly, artists down through the years have not given this aspect of the incarnation much attention. For the first few centuries of its history, the Church was more interested in proclaiming the divinity of Christ and his lordship over and above that of secular powers such as the Caesars. To underscore this, Jesus was often depicted in religious art performing miracles or assuming the garb and accoutrements of imperial power. There was little perceived need to emphasize the humanity of Christ, much less his sexuality, which in any case would not have been easy to depict, given the traditional belief in Jesus' lifelong celibacy. And yet beginning with the Renaissance, artists did start to assert the humanity of Christ in naturalistic ways that drew specific attention to his genitalia.

In an impressive survey of hundreds of paintings and sculptures from the fourteenth to the sixteenth centuries, Leo Steinberg has argued that religious art in this period generally depicted three major portions of the life of Jesus: his infancy, his adult ministry, and his passion and resurrection. In the middle portion, Jesus is always clothed; his sexuality is kept in check by his conscious commitment to chastity over concupiscence. But at the beginning and end of his life, Jesus is often portrayed in the nude, and his penis is often drawn to the viewer's attention. Persons within the portrait observe it or gesture toward it, or Jesus or another figure, such as his grandmother Saint Anne, actually touches it. In images of the Christ Child, this nudity confirms the incarnation and the fact that "the humanation of God entails, along with mortality, his assumption of sexuality." And in expressions of the crucifixion and resurrection, such as Michelangelo's sculpture *Risen Christ*, this nudity underscores Christ's triumph over the sin and shame of Adam; the "naughty bits," so to speak, are naughty no more but have been restored to their original created innocence.[18]

Filmmakers, working in a medium that originated in the late Victorian age, have been understandably reluctant to explore this sort of thing. Most producers and directors need to ensure that their films will appeal to the broadest possible audience, and this, in turn, has invited the ever-vigilant attention of moral watchdogs. Hence, most films based on the Gospels have steered clear of controversy and thus of sexuality. But filmmakers before and after Scorsese have still found ways to introduce sexuality to the Jesus-movie genre.

Back in the silent era, Cecil B. DeMille—who could never resist turning a biblical story into a love triangle[19]—launched his life-of-Jesus movie, *The King of Kings* (1927), into an unusual start by opening with a scene of Mary Magdalene hosting an opulent banquet. Mary, scantily clad and described in an intertitle as a "beautiful courtesan" who "laughed alike at God and man," taunts her guests by withholding her affections from them while kissing exotic animals in their presence. She is also furious with her absent lover, Judas Iscariot, because she assumes he is off with another woman. When one of her guests tells her that Judas has begun to follow a healer from Nazareth, Mary sets off to retrieve her lover, boldly declaring, "This carpenter shall learn that he cannot hold a man from Mary Magdalene! . . . I have blinded more men than he hath healed!" Of course, Mary's plans are thwarted. When she arrives at the house where Jesus is staying, she is struck with awe, and he casts the seven deadly sins (cf. Luke 8:2, "demons") out of her, the first of which is Lust.[20] Thus exorcised, Mary pulls her robe around her in a more modest fashion, and Jesus states, "Blessed are the pure in heart, for they shall see God" (Matt 5:8 RSV).

DeMille, having titillated his audience with a half-naked woman, thus calls an end to our voyeurism, and presumably also to the entirely fictitious affair between Mary and Judas. In addition, he seems to imply that purity of the heart is a specifically sexual kind of purity; Jesus himself seems to be entirely above sexual matters.

The first mainstream film to suggest an erotic link between Jesus and Mary Magdalene, however sublimated, was Norman Jewison's rock opera *Jesus Christ Superstar* (1973). As in DeMille's film, Judas is once again a political revolutionary. But this time, instead of keeping a lover on the side, he objects to the way Jesus allows himself to be distracted by Mary's attentions as she anoints his feet and head. In this as in so many other things, the Jesus of this film is so passive it is difficult to say whether he actually feels anything sexual for Mary or is simply letting her do what she does. For her part, in a song called "I Don't Know How to Love Him," Mary observes that although she has had "so many men before in very many ways," she does not know what to make of her feelings for Jesus. Does she feel a purer kind of sexual attraction? Or is she on the verge of giving up sexuality for some sort of spirituality? Such ambiguities extend even to Jesus' relationship with Judas, who repeats a key line from Mary's song shortly before committing suicide. Indeed, some critics have inferred that there may be something more than political zeal behind Judas's frustrations. Lloyd Baugh observes that Jesus and Judas exchange "intense looks" and are sometimes framed with Mary in a way that suggests "a rather tense ménage à trois."[21]

More scandalous films were to follow. *Monty Python's Life of Brian* (1979) is a tart spoof of sword-and-sandals epics involving a Jewish man who is mistaken for a messiah during the reign of Pontius Pilate. Throughout the film a running joke is that Brian joins the Jewish revolutionary movement not primarily out of any political conviction but because he's in love with one of the female revolutionaries. However, she does not find him appealing until she becomes convinced that he is some kind of great new leader. When his mother finds them together, the morning after they consummate their relationship, she indignantly tells a crowd waiting outside his window, "He's not the Messiah—he's a very naughty boy!" Brian's sexual activity is just one sign among many that he is anything but the spiritual leader that some people believe him to be.

Perhaps the most scandalous treatment of sexuality in a film based on the Gospels, prior to Scorsese's, was Jean-Luc Godard's *Je vous salue, Marie* (1985), released in the United States as *Hail, Mary* (1985).[22] This film differs from the others, though, in that it is set in modern Switzerland, not in the ancient world. In addition, it is not about the adult Christ but instead concerns his virginal conception and is thus about the sexuality of the Virgin Mary. In this film, Mary is the teenaged daughter of a gas station owner, and her boyfriend, Joseph, drives a taxi. When she is told that she will bear the Son of God, she accepts this. But she then goes on to obsess over the discomforting changes to her body caused by her pregnancy, all the while resisting Joseph's attempts to persuade her to sleep with him. Godard's film was quite controversial at the time, partly because he frequently depicts Mary in the nude. There is nothing particularly exploitative about the nudity. On one level Godard is simply emphasizing that Mary was a human being with breasts and a vagina and complex emotional ties to the people in her life, even as he affirms her traditional ever-virginity. But the film does raise interesting questions about voyeurism, both human and divine.

In one voice-over, Mary says she "rejoiced in giving my body to the eyes of Him who has become my Master forever, and glanced at this wondrous being." In the epilogue, Mary allows the young child Jesus to put his head beneath her housedress and recite a string of euphemisms for the various female body parts. When Joseph grumbles that Jesus is too old to see Mary naked, she replies, "*Quia respexit*, Joseph." Thereby she uses two words from the Latin translation of the Magnificat, in which the biblical Mary says she will praise God "*for he has regarded* the low estate of his handmaiden" (Luke 1:48 RSV). Thus, in Godard's film, God through the incarnation has affirmed and elevated the human body, and specifically the female body. By extension, because all human bodies are filled with soul and animated by soul, the body is good. And yet in being elevated, the sexual form of the body has been cut off from its sexual functions. The film ends with Mary sitting in a car, distractedly lighting a cigarette and putting on lipstick; perhaps she still misses the normal, sexual life that she could have had.

Scorsese's film came soon after Godard's, but it was not the last word on sexuality in Jesus-films. *Jesus* (1999), a two-part TV-movie directed by Roger Young and shown in slightly different versions in Europe and North America, also explores whether Jesus might have had to deal with romantic attraction. This time the object of his affections is not Mary Magdalene but Mary of Bethany, the sister of Martha and Lazarus. Like some of Young's other made-for-TV Bible movies, *Jesus* is a down-to-earth drama that emphasizes the humanity of its protagonist.[23] Jesus and Mary feel a strong affection for one another; in the American version of the film, Jesus even admits to his earthly father, Joseph, that he loves Mary. But he is reluctant to talk openly about his feelings with Mary herself or with either of her siblings. Finally, when Joseph dies, Jesus tells Mary to live her life "without me," emphasizing that the death of his earthly father has "ended my life as I knew it" and that he must now pursue a higher calling.

The film also introduces Mary Magdalene in a way that emphasizes not just her sexuality but also the way she expresses her sexuality in a misguided quest for empowerment. The first time we see Mary, the camera is pointed at her bare back as she rises out of bed and walks behind a fluttering gauze curtain to get dressed. As she crouches in a pose that tastefully obscures her seminudity, a passing breeze pulls the curtain back and exposes her to the viewer one last time before she covers herself. Finally, when her client bids her farewell, Mary makes a point of saying that it is she, not he, who decides when they can have sex. In the European version of the film, this scene is followed by the sequence in which Jesus pardons the adulterous woman. Mary happens to witness this and is surprised by Jesus' compassion and forgiveness. But in the American version, the scene of Mary's leaving her client is moved to a much earlier point in the film, and in its former place, there is a brief scene of Mary engaging in sweaty sexual intercourse with another of her clients. This sequence is fairly tame by the standards of cable or even network television: The camera shows Mary and her partner only from the shoulders up, and she, at least, appears to be partly clad. But it is still a remarkably unusual thing to see in a life-of-Jesus movie, especially one that has enjoyed the qualified support from the evangelical community that this film did. One wonders whether such a scene would have been possible if *The Last Temptation of Christ* had not broken the ice several years before. One also wonders whether it is possible to emphasize Mary's sexuality without somehow making it voyeuristically appealing to the viewer.

Sexuality and Christ in Kazantzakis's Novel

All this brings us back to *The Last Temptation of Christ*. The film's opening titles quote the introduction to Kazantzakis's novel to the effect that this is a story about "the incessant, merciless battle between the spirit and the flesh." In this context, both the novel and the film address the question of human sexuality, both with ambivalent results. The Jesus of this story is quite capable of using a metaphor pregnant with sexual implications, such as a wedding, to describe the kingdom of heaven, but he distances the metaphor from the actual flesh of humanity: "God is the bridegroom and the soul of man is the bride."[24]

Nevertheless, sex—not just marriage, but sex—is a recurring motif in Kazantzakis's novel. Although his treatment of the subject is somewhat ambiguous, some general patterns do emerge. First, nature itself is saturated with sex. An owl begins to "hoot tenderly to its mate" after a whirlwind sent by God has passed.[25] A bull mounts heifers in the distance as Jesus and Mary Magdalene make love for the first time in the dream sequence.[26] And it is not just the animals that know conjugal bliss—even the elements are sexualized. In describing a rainfall, Kazantzakis writes that "the male waters poured out of the skies with a roar and the earth opened its thighs and giggled." And at one point Jesus feels the earth tingle beneath his feet "as though countless mouths were suckling at its breasts."[27] In addition, Kazantzakis frequently links sex with food and drink, and especially wine, all of which are portrayed as the sort of worldly, hedonistic pleasures that threaten to distract Jesus from his spiritual destiny. Fishermen get drunk in a tavern and sing songs about women the night before they witness a Zealot's crucifixion. Zebedee, a philandering businessman who represents the nonspiritual life, likewise sings the praises of wine and women.[28]

Kazantzakis also gives sex a significant role in the Jewish hope for their nation, though here sexual pleasure is subordinated to a sense of religious and political duty. The soul of Israel becomes a nightingale that calls to the single women of Israel and asks why they have not mated and borne children to ensure the survival of their nation.[29] The novel also underscores the role that sexual intercourse might play in bringing about the Messiah. The abbot at the monastery visited by Jesus tells the other monks, "That is why the Scriptures call him the son of man! Why do you think thousands of Israel's men and women have coupled, generation after generation? To rub their backsides and titillate their groins? No! All those thousands and thousands of kisses were needed to produce the Messiah!"[30] Similarly, when Jesus attends the wedding in Cana, the possibility is raised that "the two bodies which would couple that night might engender the Messiah."[31]

And yet sex is still presented as, in some sense, the original sin. When the monk Jeroboam witnesses snakes mating in the middle of the night, he thinks to himself that it was for sexual activity just like this that God banished humans from Paradise.[32] And when Jesus sits in his circle in the middle of the desert and faces his temptations, a snake with the eyes and breasts of a woman approaches. This experience prompts Jesus to recall that just such a serpent "seduced the first man and woman to unite and give birth to sin."[33] (In the film, this serpent even claims to have created the first woman as a companion for Adam, a concept that is intriguingly reminiscent of the Gnostic myth regarding the serpentine deity Yaldabaoth.)

Several characters seem to represent not only the idea that sexual fulfillment and spiritual fulfillment are incompatible but also that the quest for one is often a poor substitute for the other. "When I was young there were times when I got all heated up and twisted and turned on my bed," says Zebedee at one point. "I thought I was looking for God, but I was really looking for a wife—for you, Salome! I got married and calmed down."[34] Similarly, Jesus recalls how his uncle, a rabbi, used to live in a monastery, "praising God and healing men," until one day he "saw a woman, abandoned the holy life, stripped off his white cassock, married—and fathered Magdalene. Served him right! God gave the apostate his just reward."[35] Both Zebedee and the rabbi claim to have found tranquillity since giving in to the flesh, and yet neither man is truly content. Zebedee, despite his mock praise for his wife, spends his nights "playing with the widows."[36] Meanwhile, the rabbi has to live with the shame of having a prostitute for a daughter. In a similar vein, the disciple Peter recalls the death by drowning of his brother Andrew's fiancée. He ponders the possibility that Andrew is now engaged in his spiritual quest mainly because he hopes that where he finds God, he will find his lover: "Obviously, he was seeking his fiancée, not God."[37] And Martha, jealous of the attention that her sister and Jesus lavish on each other, and expressing her own sexual frustration, remarks in a "harsh" voice that "all the unmarried women of the world think of God" when they weave: "We hold him on our knees like a husband."[38]

What's more, the female characters frequently define themselves in ways suggesting that they lack the spiritual substance and inclinations of men. Mary Magdalene, in particular, defines herself in purely physical terms both before and after she becomes one of Jesus' followers. When Jesus visits her in Magdala, she tells him he cannot save her soul unless he takes her into his arms, because "a woman's soul is her flesh."[39] Similarly, when Jesus' mother casts a sympathetic look at Magdalene, she cannot help but regard the woman before her as a "sinful body."[40] Later, after Jesus has saved Magdalene from being stoned, she becomes a follower of his and begins to feel that she has, in a sense, reclaimed her virginity. Even so, she tells Jesus that women have no interest in eternal life because "it is here on this earth that we women live out eternity."[41] Another Mary, the sister of Lazarus, echoes these thoughts at a point in the dream sequence after Magdalene has died and she, Mary, has become Jesus' second wife: "I hug the man I love and have no desire for any other Paradise. Let's leave the eternal joys to the men!"[42]

It is unclear to what degree statements like these are meant positively, as a sacralization of the material world and a mystical recognition that God is somehow present in all things. Or to what degree they are meant negatively, as a sign that women do represent the ultimate temptation that lures men away from the divine. Matters are further confused by the fact that Jesus treats the women in his life as more or less interchangeable. In this, he is spurred on by a guardian angel, ultimately revealed to be Satan in disguise, who tells him, "Only one woman exists in the world, one woman with countless faces."[43] Near the end of the decades-long dream sequence, when Jesus is lying on his deathbed, Judas confronts him. Judas accuses him of giving in to the women and "manufacturing" children for them, children who will become just another set of "morsels" for Charon, the Greek deity who ferries the souls of the dead to the underworld.[44] Jesus, thus rebuked, regrets the life he has lived. And then, suddenly, the dream is over and he finds himself back on the cross.

Sexuality and Christ in Scorsese's Film

In some ways, Scorsese's film entrenches the dualism of the book even deeper. Instead of examining the many pleasures of the flesh, including food and wine, it focuses almost exclusively on sexuality—only to reject it in the end, in favor of a spiritual escape from this world. What's more, Scorsese approaches the sexuality of his characters in a way that can only be described as conventional, even conservative. For one thing, he boldly puts female nudity on display on several occasions, sometimes emphasizing the fact that we are seeing these naked women through the eyes of a male protagonist. But when it comes to male nudity, he is much more coy. Near the beginning of the film, a Zealot is crucified on a cross built by Jesus. His loincloth is ripped from his body immediately before his cross is raised, and the Romans make a point of announcing his nakedness, but we see him only from behind. In a later sequence, we see several monks standing around the naked body of an abbot who has just passed away. Though the monks who venerate his body can see it in its entirety, the camera offers us only a side view, which keeps the abbot's genitals conspicuously hidden. Still later, we see Jesus himself naked, both when he is beaten by the Roman soldiers and when he is nailed to the cross, exposed to the taunts and jeers of the crowd. But on both occasions, the camera and the actor's body are positioned in ways that hide his genitals. For some reason, it is important that the characters should be allowed to look at these naked men, but we in the audience are denied this view.[45]

There is no such reticence in Scorsese's depiction of the naked women, though, and in this he sometimes goes beyond the original novel. This impression is furthered by Scorsese's use of voyeuristic point-of-view shots. When Jesus first arrives in Magdala, he sees a topless woman sitting by a well, her painted breasts in full view and her eyes ultimately looking straight at the camera, and thus at Jesus and at the viewer. However, in the book this woman is smiling at some merchants, and Jesus reacts to the sight of her so negatively that one can imagine other, less voyeuristic ways that such a shot might have been composed.[46] Jesus then proceeds to the home of Mary Magdalene. In the novel, Mary entertains her clients behind closed doors, one at a time, while the other men wait in an open courtyard, eating and joking about the nature of reality. In Scorsese's film, however, the men sit inside and watch in silence as Mary takes her partners to bed, and the film cuts from shots of the men's faces, including the face of Jesus, to close-ups of Mary and her clients in action. Scorsese has said that he wanted this scene to dramatize "the closeness, the proximity, of sin, which is around every human being, every day. . . . If [Jesus] could deal with it, we could deal with it."[47] However, most people are not surrounded by explicit displays of sexual intercourse between strangers every day, and Scorsese's explanation for this revision tends to confirm Margaret R. Miles's charge that the film reflects "a modernist reduction of all sin to sins of the flesh."[48] It is also questionable whether Jesus would have "dealt with" an open display of sin, sexual or otherwise, by becoming one of its spectators.

In addition to these scenes, Scorsese's tendency to insert gratuitous sexual material into the story surfaces in at least one other sequence. When Jesus visits John the Baptist, Scorsese populates the banks of the river Jordan with topless and fully naked women, chanting loudly and swinging their heads back and forth to the drums. Scorsese has said that he wanted this scene to underscore how "dangerously" close to sexual ecstasy some forms of religion can be. But if there are any men chanting in a naked trance on the banks of the river, the film hardly notices them.[49]

To be fair, it does seem that Scorsese wants to boost the role of women in the Gospel story, most notably by putting Martha and the three Marys at the Last Supper, an event that has traditionally been depicted as involving only Jesus and his twelve male disciples.[50] Scorsese has also acknowledged that he had quibbles with some of the elements in Kazantzakis's novel which, of necessity, were incorporated into the film. These include the notion that Mary Magdalene became a prostitute specifically because Jesus turned her down, one of several elements in the story that emphasizes the active role of men versus the passive role of women.[51] But despite Scorsese's good intentions, the film is anything but feminist. Indeed, W. Barnes Tatum has said that the film is marked by a "blatant sexism."[52] And Miles has recognized that the film casts men and women alike in stereotypical roles while reiterating "traditional dualisms" that reinforce "popular caricatures of Christianity: spirit/flesh; suffering/pleasure; spirituality/sexuality; man/woman."[53] These problems can indeed be traced back to elements in the original novel, but they are considerably more pronounced in the film. While Kazantzakis devotes no small number of pages to exploring the internal thought processes of Mary Magdalene and Mary the mother of Jesus, Scorsese effectively reduces these women to ciphers and deprives them of their subjectivity. The only mind Scorsese wishes to get inside, ultimately, is that of Jesus himself.

It may be true that the last temptation faced by Christ is not sex per se, but something more seemingly benign like domesticity or contentment. Nevertheless, the temptation is still expressed in highly sexual terms. As Baugh recognizes, the Jesus of the dream sequence is "not only interested in sex but [also] rather more than usually active therein" as he floats between three different sexual partners and sires a number of children.[54] The highly controversial sex scene between Jesus and Mary Magdalene may be defensible on the basis that the two characters are married to one another at that point in the story. But the film also shows, however discreetly, Jesus embarking on an affair with his second wife's sister. So when Jesus finally rejects his temptation and says he wants to be the Messiah after all, he is effectively rejecting sexuality for spirituality. Sex is one of the things, and perhaps the primary thing, that Jesus must renounce in order to fulfill his spiritual mission.

Surprisingly, those who protested the film in the name of orthodox Christian belief did not dispute the notion, implicit in the film, that sexuality and spirituality are mutually incompatible. Indeed, the protestors seemed to take it as a given that Jesus, being divine and therefore purely spiritual, could not have engaged in sexual intercourse, which is presumably the exclusive domain of the flesh. Throughout the film Jesus is sexually abstinent—apart from the dream sequence, in which Satan tempts him. Hence, the main point of disagreement between the film and its protesters was ultimately not over whether Jesus could or should have had a sexual partner but whether this possibility should even be portrayed.

But the stances taken by both sides in that debate suggest an impoverished imagination on both of their parts. The filmmakers could have found a way to emphasize, as Kazantzakis did, some of the other physical pleasures that make life in the body so enticing. They also could have tried to explore how it might be possible to embrace one's sexuality while also embracing a call to celibacy, though pursuing this last point probably would have taken them far afield from the book. And as for the protestors, it is even more ironic that this dualistic sensibility was presented as the orthodox Christian view. After all, the orthodox Christian belief is that Jesus, rather than choose between humanity and divinity as he does in the film, was and is fully human as well as fully divine. Instead of pouncing on films that explore what it means for God to become an incarnate, human, sexual being, it would be more profitable for all concerned if such protestors would seize the opportunity to consider just what the sexuality of Jesus might mean for the sexuality of us all.

Notes

1. Martin Scorsese, *Scorsese on Scorsese*, ed. David Thompson and Ian Christie (London: Faber & Faber, 1996), 214.

2. Ibid., 124–26.

3. Michael Medved, *Hollywood vs. America: Popular Culture and the War on Traditional Values* (New York: HarperCollins, 1992), 44.

4. Paul Schrader, *Schrader on Schrader*, ed. Kevin Jackson (London: Faber & Faber, 1990), 140. Schrader also says he and Scorsese coined the term DSB (Deadly Sperm Backup) to signify what happens when celibate people go crazy (136). This concept, expressed in the film version of *The Last Temptation of Christ* by one of Jesus' fellow Nazarenes, was probably inspired by the comment an old fisherman makes in the original novel: "This is what happens to those who don't get married. . . . The sperm rises to their heads and attacks their brains." See Nikos Kazantzakis, *The Last Temptation of Christ*, trans. Peter Bien (New York: Simon & Schuster, 1960), 343–44.

5. Robin Riley, *Film, Faith, and Cultural Conflict: The Case of Martin Scorsese's "The Last Temptation of Christ"* (Westport, CT: Praeger, 2003), 15, 75.

6. Steven D. Greydanus, "The Last Temptation of Christ: An Essay in Film Criticism and Faith," 2001; http://www.decentfilms.com/commentary/lasttemptation.html.

7. William E. Phipps, *The Sexuality of Jesus* (Cleveland: Pilgrim, 1996), 44–109. Phipps also devotes a chapter to Kazantzakis's approach to sexuality, both in his novels and in his life, in the similarly titled but much earlier book, *The Sexuality of Jesus: Theological and Literary Perspectives* (New York: Harper & Row, 1973), 121–31.

8. John P. Meier, *A Marginal Jew: Rethinking the Historical Jesus* (New York: Doubleday, 1991), 332–45, 363–70.

9. *Secret Book (Apocryphon) of John*, from Nag Hammadi, 6.6–9; 11.18; 12.1–4; 13.12–14. Cf. Marvin Meyer, *The Secret Teachings of Jesus: Four Gnostic Gospels* (New York: Random House, 1984), 64, 77, 78, 80.

10. Rodney Stark, *The Rise of Christianity: How the Obscure, Marginal Jesus Movement Became the Dominant Religious Force in the Western World in a Few Centuries* (New York: HarperSanFrancisco, 1997), 123.

11. The possibility that the author of 1 Timothy may have Gnostic traditions in mind is also suggested by his admonition against "myths and endless genealogies" (1:4); cf. the many genealogies in the *Secret Book (Ap.) of John*.

12. James B. Nelson, *Between Two Gardens: Reflections on Sexuality and Religious Experience* (New York: Pilgrim, 1983), 36.

13. Jerome, *Jov.* 1.40; quoted in Leo Steinberg, *The Sexuality of Christ in Renaissance Art and in Modern Oblivion*, 2nd ed. (Chicago: University of Chicago Press, 1996), 144.

14. Augustine, *Serm.* 1.23–24; quoted in Steinberg, *Sexuality*, 133.

15. C. S. Lewis, *The Screwtape Letters*, rev. paperback ed. (New York: Collier, 1982), 36, 148.

16. Some Bibles translate the Greek word *aphedron* as "drain" (REB) or "draught" (KJV); others, like the NIV, omit it altogether. Thomas Cahill, *Desire of the Everlasting Hills: The World before and after Jesus* (New York: Nan A. Talese, 1999), 89, translates this word as "shithole" on

the basis that it is "Macedonian slang that would have sounded barbarous to Greek ears." The original words spoken by Jesus were most likely Aramaic.

17. Nelson, *Between Two Gardens*, 17.

18. Steinberg, *Sexuality*, 24.

19. Cf. the love triangles between Samson, Delilah, and her sister Semadar in *Samson and Delilah* (1949), or between Moses, Rameses, and Nefretiri in *The Ten Commandments* (1956).

20. Scorsese, *Scorsese on Scorsese*, 131: "I remember vividly the Casting Out of Devils, with those images coming out of her body: it made quite an impact on us as kids, mainly, I think, because of the sexuality of it."

21. Lloyd Baugh, *Imaging the Divine: Jesus and Christ-Figures in Film* (Kansas City, MO: Sheed & Ward, 1997), 250.

22. Indeed, the controversy over *Je vous salue, Marie* prevented Jack Lang, the French minister of culture, from giving his financial support to *The Last Temptation of Christ*; Baugh, *Imaging the Divine*, 51.

23. Cf. *Joseph* (1995) and *Moses* (1996), both of which were broadcast in the United States on the Turner network. *Jesus* had its North American premiere on CBS in 2000.

24. Kazantzakis, *Last Temptation*, 216.

25. Ibid., 158.

26. Ibid., 447–50.

27. Ibid., 94, 362.

28. Ibid., 39–40, 162.

29. Ibid., 401–2.

30. Ibid., 105.

31. Ibid., 215. Ironically, however, the novel affirms that Jesus has already been born of a virgin. Contrast that with Scorsese's film, which gives one the impression that the doctrine of the virginal conception is one of the "lies" invented by Paul, even though it never appears in any of Paul's writings.

32. Ibid., 150.

33. Ibid., 255.

34. Ibid., 131.

35. Ibid., 67.

36. Ibid., 161.

37. Ibid., 165.

38. Ibid., 270.

39. Ibid., 90.

40. Ibid., 171.

41. Ibid., 353.

42. Ibid., 472.

43. Ibid., 457.

44. Ibid., 491.

45. Cf. Peter Lehman, "Penis-Size Jokes and Their Relation to Hollywood's Unconscious," in *Comedy/Cinema/Theory*, ed. Andrew S. Horton (Berkeley: University of California Press, 1991), 49–50.

46. Kazantzakis, *Last Temptation*, 74–77.

47. *The Last Temptation of Christ*, Criterion Collection, DVD audio commentary (2000).

48. Margaret R. Miles, *Seeing and Believing: Religion and Values in the Movies* (Boston: Beacon, 1996), 36, 37.

49. *Last Temptation*, DVD audio commentary.

50. Some conservative Christians are apparently open to this innovation, too. Philip Saville's *The Gospel of John* (2003), a word-for-word adaptation produced by The Visual Bible and promoted heavily among evangelicals, also places Mary Magdalene at the Last Supper and the "farewell discourse" that follows it.

51. Scorsese, *Scorsese on Scorsese*, 143.

52. W. Barnes Tatum, *Jesus at the Movies: A Guide to the First Hundred Years* (Santa Rosa, CA: Polebridge, 1997), 168.

53. Miles, *Seeing and Believing*, 36, 38.

54. Baugh, *Imagining the Divine*, 68.

CHAPTER 14

Martin Scorsese's *The Last Temptation of Christ*
A Critical Reassessment of Its Sources, Its Theological Problems, and Its Impact on the Public
Lloyd Baugh, S.J.

> Kazantzakis' novel . . . represented . . . also an autobiographical statement. Kazantzakis was using the Jesus story to continue working through his own lifelong struggle *between the flesh and the spirit*—a struggle he considered to be the universal human struggle.
>
> —W. Barnes Tatum[1]

> Scorsese's film is a representation of the existence of the man Jesus conceived as a continuous dramatic temptation, a chain of resistances and hesitations. Scorsese's Jesus is therefore and above all the projection of the conflicts and emotions of the director.
>
> —Luigi Bini[2]

> "This film is not based on the Gospels but upon the fictional exploration of the eternal spiritual conflict." These latter words [of Scorsese], of course, disclaim too much. As with the Kazantzakis novel, the film is based in some sense on the story of Jesus as narrated in the four gospels.
>
> —W. Barnes Tatum[3]

Introduction

When he took on *The Last Temptation of Christ* project, Martin Scorsese was a well-established and internationally respected filmmaker, an auteur in the full sense. That reputation and the seriousness and tenacious dedication he devoted to the project oblige us to treat the film seriously. Already as a child, growing up a Catholic in New York, Scorsese dreamed of this project: "At age ten he had drawn the storyboards for a movie he wanted to make on the life of Christ."[4] As a film student at New York

173

University, Scorsese studied "previous biblical films based on the gospels,"[5] and he himself reveals his early hopes to do a Jesus-film: "This desire is evident in *Jerusalem, Jerusalem!* a script I wrote in the mid-sixties, where the Passion of Christ is played out against a background of the Lower East Side of Manhattan."[6]

Scorsese's interest in Kazantzakis's novel spanned more than thirty years of his life: "In 1961 a Greek friend, John Mabros, told me about *The Last Temptation,* . . . but it really started when Barbara Hershey gave me the book in 1972."[7] Sixteen years later, the film came out, and although it has always been associated quite closely with Kazantzakis's novel, Scorsese actually shifts much of the material and the significance of the novel in original and often troubling directions.

In this chapter, after some further introductory comments, I analyze some of the many shifts and changes Scorsese made in his film. I will suggest how the overall effect of these changes creates a representation of Jesus radically different from that of Kazantzakis, a very different implicit Christology. I also discuss the originality of both Kazantzakis's and Scorsese's subjective representations of Jesus.[8]

Developing Christologies in the Tradition of the Jesus-Film

Whenever filmmakers approach the character of Jesus Christ, as many have done in the short history of cinema, inevitably there is a Christology discernible and operative in the image they create. The works of these artists reveal an implicit Christology: they assume a position in reference to Jesus as a historical figure and as the Christ. Some tend to privilege more the dimension of his divinity, what is popularly referred to as a "high" Christology. Others tend to privilege especially his humanity, what is popularly referred to as a "low" Christology.[9] The former does not necessarily exclude the latter, and vice versa; a filmmaker can emphasize Jesus' humanity while at the same time admitting or allowing his divinity. However, some directors, often those with a "low" Christology, go so far in their chosen emphasis that the divinity of the resulting Jesus is either denied outright or is so obscured that in effect it is denied.[10]

D. W. Griffith in the Jesus of *Intolerance* (1916) and Cecil B. DeMille in the Jesus of *The King of Kings* (1927) manifest a very "high" Christology, creating remote, untouchable figures, distant from all who come into contact with them. Nicholas Ray in *The King of Kings* (1961), in the "California-surfer"[11] Jesus played by teen-idol Jeffrey Hunter, clearly opts for a quite "low" Christology. It was opposed that same year by George Stevens's Jesus in *The Greatest Story Ever Told* (1965), whose stiff, cold formality makes for a relatively "high" Christology. The two Jesus musicals are opposed in their operative Christologies. The whining, neurotic protagonist of *Jesus Christ Superstar* (1973), who inspires no one, clearly exemplifies a "low" Christology. The strong, patient, and generous Jesus of *Godspell* (1973) manifests a "higher" Christology.

The three classic Jesus-films from Italy tend toward a "high" Christology. The aloof intellectual pedagogue-master of Rossellini's *Messiah* (1975) is matched by the strong, iconic Jesus of Zeffirelli's *Jesus of Nazareth* (1977). Paradoxically, for the protagonist of a film by a declared atheist, the Jesus of Pier Paolo Pasolini in *The Gospel according to St. Matthew* (1964) clearly displays dimensions of a "high" Christology. This is evident in Jesus' self-assured and strong approach to preaching, performing miracles, and dealing with his apostles and with the temple authorities.

From Kazantzakis to Scorsese: Two Versions of a Reluctant Messiah

Beyond the shifting "high" and "low" Christologies in the classical Jesus-films, the *Last Temptation of Christ* phenomenon provides a unique and fascinating case study of a shifting understanding and representation of Jesus, a shifting Christology between the original novel, the explicit source of the film, and the film itself. In this case, the shift is "downward" from the "low" Christology of Kazantzakis to the even "lower" Christology of Scorsese's film. As attested by much scholarship, both Kazantzakis and Scorsese deviate from the representation of Jesus in the New Testament, in effect creating a "'symbolic Jesus' . . . in their own images."[12] What interests us in this chapter is precisely how, in his filmic version of *The Last Temptation of Christ*, in his "symbolic" Jesus, Scorsese shifts his representation of Jesus and of the human-divine tension discernible in him away from the "symbolic" Jesus proposed by the novel. One critic recognizes the novel as the main source of the film and yet insists also on the biblical connection in the Catholic Scorsese. He refers to two other film adaptations of the biblical Jesus-story and speculates on how the process might have gone in Scorsese: "Pasolini and Rossellini go from the history [the Gospels] to the character [of Jesus]. . . . Scorsese goes from the character to the history. He develops in his mind a certain notion of Jesus, which he then uses as a hermeneutical key for those chapters of the Gospel that interest him."[13]

One of the strategies that Scorsese operates in reducing Kazantzakis's five-hundred-page novel for the screen is surprisingly that of adding elements, even entire episodes, that are not in the novel. Going beyond anything in Kazantzakis, these additions do much to raise the overall tone of violence in the film and to shift the story toward spiritual and psychological imbalance in the character of Jesus, creating a much "lower" Christology.

Certainly the most obvious and in a sense the most violent of these additions is the infamous "Sacred Heart" scene, a macabre episode totally original to the film. Scorsese gathers the disciples in an eerie cave, as if they are seeking refuge. He has Jesus arrive, speaking violent words about the war they now have to fight. And then he shows Jesus plunging his hand into his chest and pulling out his heart. The density of the bizarre gesture—augmented by strange red lighting in the expressionist manner and by the blood dripping into a pool of water, causing it to boil—is nonevangelical and non-Kazantzakis. The awkward materialism of the scene not only betrays Scorsese's own subversive misunderstanding of this traditional Catholic icon, meant to represent Jesus' redeeming and integrating love—a devotion popular in the Church since the seventeenth century. It also makes of his Jesus an unbalanced and masochistic refugee from a Cronenberg horror movie.

A second episode, more or less original with Scorsese, is the raising of Lazarus. Kazantzakis represents the event briefly and indirectly in the narrative account of an eyewitness. Scorsese, however, puts it directly on screen in a remarkable set piece that illustrates well how the filmmaker "reads" Kazantzakis in his own idiosyncratic way, subverting the Jesus of both Kazantzakis and the Gospels. Scorsese begins the scene, one of the longest in the film, with Jesus' rejecting his own mother in a particularly brutal way. The area around the tomb is besieged by mourning women, whose shrill staccato crying creates a chilling effect. Jesus slowly moves down to the tomb, and when the stone sealing it is moved back, Scorsese cannot resist the melodramatic effect of having Jesus and everyone else clap their hands over their noses for the stench apparently exploding out of the tomb.[14] The camera makes a very slow and eerie movement into the pitch dark of the tomb and then turns around to show Jesus. When Lazarus does not respond to the first summons, Jesus sits Buddha-like in the opening. Then, in a gratuitous shot straight out of a Hollywood horror movie—*Night of the Living Dead* comes to mind—Lazarus's scabby, decomposing hand suddenly reaches up.[15] Accompanied on the sound track by the horrifying buzzing of flies, the hand grabs Jesus and begins to pull him into the tomb in a gruesome metaphor of the struggle of life against death that Jesus is facing here.

Jesus is barely able to resist, so when Scorsese finally shifts his camera outside the tomb, we may hope for some respite, some sign—clearly present in Kazantzakis's novel—that this miracle is an important victory for Jesus, a prelude of his own resurrection. But Scorsese provides no such victory. In editing, he offers two disturbing close-ups of Jesus' terrified face as the newly raised Lazarus—more a zombie than a man—embraces him, and photographs Jesus in a high-angle shot, making Lazarus taller than Jesus and thereby diminishing his authority. Thus Scorsese represents a Jesus who, in this dramatic manifestation of his divine power over death, demonstrates not joy at this sign of God's and his victory over death, but only the terror and confusion of a man deeply divided within himself.

One of the strangest and dramatically most unjustified choices that Scorsese makes in adapting Kazantzakis's novel for the screen is to double the scenes of the cleansing of the temple precincts by Jesus. The novel represents the event once, but Scorsese dramatizes it twice and both times makes Jesus' violent actions more the fruit of schizoid mood shifts than of clear prophetic decision.

A well-recognized stylistic hallmark of Martin Scorsese's cinema is the leitmotif of blood. From the early *Taxi Driver* (1976) to the most recent *Gangs of New York* (2002),[16] the filmmaker's fascination with blood results regularly in dramatic and violent effects. In *Raging Bull* (1980), a film mostly in black and white, splatters of "black" blood fly through the air regularly. This motif is announced in the film's opening when its title appears in bold red letters against a gray, black, and white background, with Robert De Niro as the boxer Jake LaMotta dancing in the boxing ring in abstract, poetic slow motion. Though there are few references to blood in Kazantzakis, Scorsese finds the Jesus subject matter more than apt for a feast of blood. He argues rather ingenuously: "Blood is very important in the church. Blood is the life force, the essence, the sacrifice. And in a movie you have to see it."[17] Scorsese creates a thick network of blood images, the first of which is in the opening frames of the film, preparing for the title: we see a series of abstract patterns of a black crown of thorns against a blood-red background. Then, early in the narrative, Scorsese has Jesus, who builds crosses for Roman executions, actually help nail a victim to a cross. In a tight close-up, Scorsese shows blood from the victim's foot splatter on Jesus' face. In the novel, there is this reference to blood but with one significant difference: Jesus is standing close by as a gypsy does the nailing. The blood leitmotif is a constant throughout the film, dramatically marking a number of events—the slaughter of the lamb in the Cana scene, the Sacred Heart image, the Last Supper, and the crucifixion—and inevitably modulating them in the direction of physical violence.

Changes and Adaptations in Scorsese

A second strategy that Scorsese operates on Kazantzakis is to represent events in the novel by shifting and changing them in quite significant ways, with the effect, direct or indirect, of diminishing the character of Jesus and especially his divine dimension. For example, in Kazantzakis, Jesus' meeting with John the Baptist at the Jordan is relatively low-key and develops over time. Scorsese dramatically raises the visual-aural pressure of his meeting with disturbing zooms and oblique camera angles, aggressive editing, and pounding, hypnotic Hare Krishna–like music. He gives the role of the Baptist to a wild-looking and far-too-old André Gregory,[18] who strides "maniacally about spouting dark Old Testament apocalyptic (nothing of the Baptist's actual themes of repentance or the kingdom of heaven)."[19] In this scene, visually and aurally one of the densest in the film, the Baptist's redemptive ministry becomes "a hysterical-ecstatic Pentecostal revival meeting."[20] He is transformed into a "seducer and rapist of spirits," and the penitent faithful become his "groupies, literally shaking with the rhythms of 'transcendental mediation.'"[21] And in all this high confusion, the crucial spiritual significance of Jesus' submission to John's baptism fades into the background.

Kazantzakis devotes a major part of his narrative to Jesus' disciples, much amplifying the individual and varied vocation narratives of the Gospels, carefully developing the personalities of each of them and representing how Jesus relates to them individually with care and respect. In the extended vocation narratives, there is much rich dialogue, very human but also pointing to God. The disciples form a community and learn from Jesus the Master. For example, in one memorable scene Kazantzakis has the disciples recall Jesus' baptism and speculate about the possibility of his being the Messiah, and he has Peter identify the descending dove as the

Holy Spirit. Later, Jesus commissions the disciples to preach the good news, and when they return, Jesus welcomes and reassures them.[22]

Scorsese radically shifts Jesus' relationship with his disciples. First of all, Jesus does not call the disciples individually by name. On the shore of a lake, Jesus, flanked by Judas, who, in a bizarre reversal of the biblical protocol, has already chosen him, stares intensely at the sons of Zebedee as they clean their nets. They immediately leave everything and follow him. This group vocation by hypnosis is humanly and theologically unacceptable. Then, as Jesus and the first disciples walk across the countryside, Scorsese, clearly wanting to telescope time, edits in a series of lap dissolves to demonstrate the power of Jesus to attract followers. Scorsese might better have saved time elsewhere. The result of his lap dissolves is to shift the critical biblical representation of the call to discipleship into evangelization by magic and cinematic effects. Here there is no question of personal call and response, no question of human liberty, and certainly no question of grace. Then for the entire film, Scorsese's disciples—"small-minded, spineless men, . . . insubstantial"[23]—remain an almost indistinct mass, with apparently little contact among themselves and no significant contact with Jesus. The interior conflict that Scorsese gives Jesus is "a solitary struggle that never goes beyond self-scrutiny, not a communal experience to be shared."[24]

One of the passages of dialogue in Kazantzakis's novel that Scorsese maintains in the film is a phrase spoken by the tempting angel in the last-temptation sequence. It is meant to reassure Jesus as he passes from his marriage to Mary Magdalene to a rather looser rapport with Mary and Martha: "Only one woman exists in the world, one woman with countless faces." A blatantly sexist statement, unjustly replacing the uniqueness and individuality of women with their common sexuality, the declaration characterizes to some extent Kazantzakis's treatment of women in the novel. He sees woman as primarily sexual, woman as temptress, woman as a distraction to men and to the man Jesus. At the same time, he offers some exceptions to this caricature, including some quite beautiful moments of Jesus' relating to women in a respectful and healthy way. An example is the conversation he has with the Samaritan woman at the well.[25]

Scorsese, on the other hand, removes the episode of the Samaritan woman and buys wholeheartedly into Kazantzakis's tempting angel's statement, though at first it might not seem so. Reacting against the limited and stereotypical role of women in the previous Jesus-films, Scorsese wants to give his Jesus-film a significant presence of women. Mary Magdalene is portrayed as one of Jesus' disciples, and she and Martha and Mary participate in the Last Supper. *The Last Temptation of Christ* is the only serious Jesus-film to allow this. A closer study of these strong characters, however, reveals that in them there is little new. Scorsese certainly keeps them within the limits of "traditional conceptions of women" and within the strict limits he gives to women in his earlier films, as with both the wife and mistress/second wife of Jake LaMotta in *Raging Bull*. In *The Last Temptation of Christ*, even in the mind of its Jesus, woman is still "the earthly other to spiritual man," and her role is limited to that of embodying "sexuality and domesticity."[26] It is not by chance that Martha's words to Jesus when she first meets him are, "You got a wife?" Scorsese seems not to appreciate that the Jesus of the Gospels has an infinitely more enlightened view of woman and gives her a determining role to play in the establishment of the kingdom of God.

In Kazantzakis, Judas, a thoroughgoing Zealot, encourages Jesus toward the Zealot cause at the beginning. Then, much later, as Jesus enters his passion, Judas assumes an important role again. But for most of the novel, Judas is treated as one of the disciples and, in fact, often slips into the background as Jesus relates to Peter, John, Jacob, Matthew, and the others. Scorsese, however, changes Judas's role dramatically. He reduces the other disciples to an amorphous mass of weak and largely inconsequential men and makes Judas almost omnipresent on the screen. "Almost invariably at Jesus' side, Jesus's symbiotic second self," this Judas, different from that of Kazantzakis, replaces Peter as leader and John as the disciple Jesus loved. Scorsese's Jesus relates only to Judas and almost always in a dependent-submissive and at times sexually ambiguous manner. "The boldest . . . image of their affinity . . . comes when the camera looks down on Jesus asleep in the protective embrace of his friend 'my brother.'"[27] Judas is the first disciple-companion of Jesus. Repeatedly he stalks Jesus, and with brutal words and actions he criticizes the fear and uncertainty that characterize Jesus: "Throughout the movie Judas acts almost as Jesus' conscience."[28]

Theirs is a "combative relationship,"[29] often violent verbally, physically, and especially psychologically: "Judas and Jesus together, moreover, constitute a psycho-drama [that is] bloody and self-destructive."[30] From the outset, Scorsese provides extradiegetical evidence of Judas's domination: Harvey Keitel's physique—thick, muscular body, red Afro-style hair and beard—easily overpowers a rather wimpy-looking Dafoe, as does his strong voice and tough-guy New York accent. Repeatedly Scorsese places Keitel-Judas in the dominant position in compositions, as in the episode of the call of the sons of Zebedee, with Dafoe-Jesus below or to the side. Often Scorsese has Judas precede Jesus and walk with more determined strides than he. The outcome of the Jesus-Judas psychodrama evidently is the further diminishment, the moral and spiritual destruction, of the character of Jesus.

The motivation for these major changes of the Kazantzakis text lies in Scorsese's human and artistic sensibilities and preoccupations. *The Last Temptation of Christ* repeats one of the classic dynamics of the Scorsese canon, as the filmmaker recognizes in Kazantzakis's novel "the ultimate buddy movie. For 15 years Scorsese has been directing secular drafts of it. Two men, closer than brothers, with complementary abilities and obsessions, who must connive in each other's destiny."[31] As in most films in the Scorsese canon in which the male-male bonding is the most profound and dynamic, so also in *The Last Temptation of Christ*. "Passion principally exists between men, whether expressed through love or brutality; here it is basically the love that passes between Jesus and Judas."[32] Hence, it ought to be no surprise that the betrayer's kiss in Gethsemane is "a desperate kiss of love."[33]

A classic example of Scorsese's shifting the tone and meaning of Kazantzakis can be seen in the episode of the wedding at Cana. In the novel, the scene is quite low-key. Jesus and the disciples arrive at the feast, meeting the virgins with their lamps, and Jesus uses that occasion to speak of the "kingdom of heaven," offering an original version of the parable of the wise and foolish virgins.[34] Here Jesus performs no miracle but sings and dances with the guests. Scorsese makes an interesting adaptation of this scene, which well illustrates how his intuitions often are good. But then in the development of the scene, other considerations get in the way and ruin the overall effect. Scorsese shows Jesus arriving with his disciples, including his following of women. Then he dances with the men, an original and credible first-century Palestinian touch, and finally transforms the water into wine. But three elements disrupt the respectful tone of the episode: Once again tempted by his penchant for blood, Scorsese introduces the wedding with close-up shots of the bloody slaughter and disembowelment of the lamb for the meal. A close examination shows that the wedding ritual, costumes, music, and dance are not Hebrew but perhaps reflect more the culture of North Africa and Islam. And Jesus follows up the miracle of the water-into-wine with an ironic, knowing grin and toast to the surprised servants, reflecting more late-twentieth-century and Western practice than that of first-century Palestine.

Jesus' Preaching and His Healing Miracles: Confusion and Fear

Much of the text of the Gospels is taken up with Jesus' preaching and teaching, something Kazantzakis reflects in his novel as Jesus preaches with power and authority. At least four parables are narrated, as is Jesus' redeeming conversation with the Samaritan woman at the well. Jesus spends much time teaching his disciples. He reads the passage from Isaiah at the synagogue in Nazareth and proclaims that "the prophesied day has come." Jesus identifies himself to the elder Simeon as "the Son of man." And elsewhere, in insisting that he has come not "to abolish the commandments but to extend them, he proclaims he is the new Moses; and toward the end of his mission, Kazantzakis has Jesus preach eloquently at the Temple. Consistently, Jesus' preaching is clear and authoritative such that the people, filled with hope, joy, and comfort, call him "the new Comforter."[35]

In Scorsese there is little of this preaching and none of this authority and comfort. He gives the early scene of the first parable a certain freshness: Jesus, finding himself with a group of people, simply begins to talk. Speaking awkwardly, uncertainly at first, the parable seems to take shape as he speaks it. The problem, however, is that Jesus does not complete this parable, and the few times he does preach afterward, he is always awkward and uncertain, looking to Judas for support, never developing any self-confidence or skill, never speaking with authority.

In Kazantzakis, the healing miracles are spread throughout the ministerial activity of Jesus. They are personal gestures that express the loving mercy of God and

Jesus, and they are based on the sincere faith of the people asking for them. Scorsese collapses all the healing miracles in one surreal, apocalyptic scene. He has Jesus descend alone into a dusty valley. There he is quite literally attacked by a mob of strange creatures, presumably in need of healing, who pour out of a tower and rise out of holes in the ground. Like zombies escaped from *Night of the Living Dead*, they grab and tear at Jesus—this *Grand Guignol* ballet is filmed in agonizing slow motion—and only the arrival of the disciples, in the nick of time, assures Jesus' survival. This resistance and struggle on Jesus' part flies in the face of overwhelming evidence in the Gospels and even in Kazantzakis. Scorsese's explanation is quite strange: "Every miracle, everything that gets him closer to his destination, also brings him closer to his death, closer to the Crucifixion, and that is something he doesn't want."[36] Distancing himself from Kazantzakis's approach, Scorsese's representation of this one miracle scene manifests not the least sense of Jesus' thaumaturgical gestures as an authoritative offering of healing made out of love for the afflicted and as an efficacious sign of the irruption of the kingdom of God.

The Passion of Jesus: From Passover to Grotesque

In his Last Supper scene, Kazantzakis remains rather faithful to the text and spirit of the Gospels. Jesus sends disciples to prepare the Passover meal; Martha and Mary are left in Bethany. Jesus, very much the Master, calm, in control of himself, washes the feet of the disciples, and during the traditional Passover ritual meal—celebrated with unleavened bread, salt water, lamb, and bitter herbs—he blesses the bread and wine and pronounces them as his body and blood. Then, out of loving concern for his disciples, he explains what is about to happen and reassures them that he will send the Comforter, the Spirit of Truth.

Scorsese, perhaps not satisfied with the respectful tone and content of the novel, takes his viewers on an emotional roller-coaster ride that drastically changes the significance of this most crucial experience of Jesus. First, he adds new content to the episode with two scenes preceding the Last Supper proper. One is a horrific scene of the animal sacrifices in the dark and foggy interior of the temple, exaggeratedly gory with blood. The other is of Jesus, barely visible through the dense mist, descending into a ritual bath. Then, in the Last Supper scene proper, Scorsese includes four women, Jesus' mother, Mary Magdalene, and Martha and Mary, Lazarus's sisters,[37] and he represents a more or less silent, sullen, and withdrawn Jesus. When Jesus nervously pronounces the words, "This is my body. . . . This is my blood," he glances furtively from side to side as if seeking confirmation from the disciples. Finally, in another bizarre manifestation of the blood leitmotif, Scorsese has the wine transform into physiological blood, forming a blood clot in Peter's mouth.[38] Typical of Scorsese in this film, by doing an exaggeratedly literal reading of the sacramental symbol, he transforms what in the Gospel and in Kazantzakis is the Passover ritual meal into a "Eucharistic river of blood."[39]

In further contrast to Kazantzakis's low-key Last Supper, the dizzying visual intensity of Scorsese's version is augmented by fast, aggressive editing and unusual camera angles. The high-angle close-ups of Jesus as he says, "This is my body," make him look weak, and the dense sound track at one point becomes grotesque. The music is clearly Arabic and not Hebrew. Heard during the most solemn part of the Last Supper scene, as Jesus institutes the sacrament of the Eucharist, it is a quite incredible juxtaposition, inappropriate and offensive to both Christians and Muslims. Peter Gabriel, the film's music editor, identifies the piece: "Baaba Maal, a Senegalese singer, did the traditional Moslem call to prayer."[40] It is not, in fact, the classical Muslim call to prayer but rather an Islamic profession of faith, which says textually: "I believe that there is no God [Allah] but God [Allah] and that Muḥammad is the One sent by God [Allah]." In the song, here in Arabic, this phrase is repeated, as are other words in praise of Muḥammad as the Prophet and the Beloved of God.

Visually, Scorsese's *via crucis* is an exceptional piece of filmmaking, and it illustrates well how, often in his film, he seeks an original solution rather than depending on Kazantzakis. In the novel, Kazantzakis attenuates the dramatic horror of Jesus' climbing to his death by representing the disciples gathered in hiding at Simon the Cyrenean's tavern and then bringing in Simon, who, after criticizing the disloyal cowardice of the disciples, goes to Jesus, encourages him, and carries the cross. Scorsese completely bypasses this version with a human touch and represents the *via crucis* in a very long, sixty-second shot, in deliberate, painful slow motion, which manifestly imitates the sixteenth-century painting of Hieronymous Bosch, *Christ Carrying the Cross*.[41] Already Bosch's image is violent: "Christ almost suffocated in the middle of the frame by the faces of the mob, . . . overwhelmingly sadistic, the facial expressions of those characters."[42] But the violence of the painting is somewhat lessened by the inclusion of two more positive figures, the good thief and Veronica, both sympathetic to Jesus. Typically, Scorsese, wanting to create a "more extreme" image of the terrible solitude, social and psychological, of Jesus, omits these two.[43]

Scorsese's Deletions: A Messiah Much Diminished

As already mentioned, Scorsese applies radical reductions to the Kazantzakis text, presenting a drastically subdued dynamic between Jesus and the disciples and eliminating almost all of his preaching and teaching and most of his miracles. Beyond these reductions, Scorsese makes outright cuts of a number of specific elements in the novel.

Some of these deletions are inevitable in the operation of reducing such a long novel to a two-and-a-half-hour film. Examples are the subplot of the meeting of Jesus and the centurion, their subsequent friendship, and Jesus' meeting with Pilate and Caiaphas sometime before the passion. Other deletions Scorsese seems to make, perhaps uncharacteristically, out of prudence. For example, he suppresses the many passages that in Kazantzakis identify the disciple Matthew with the evangelist and represent his keeping records of Jesus' preaching and actions, in effect his Gospel in the making. This leitmotif, especially in the way Kazantzakis has Matthew shift and adapt what Jesus says and does, would certainly be surprising and shocking to most mainline Christians.[44]

In the same vein, Scorsese also suppresses the references to Jesus' dictating the text of the Apocalypse to John the beloved disciple, who, briefly, is transformed into the ancient elder of Patmos. Perhaps Scorsese intuited that his representation of Saul/Paul in the last-temptation scene would be about as much as his audience could take, and so he prudently cuts the analogous references to Matthew and John.

Further, and as a direct result of his cutting much of Jesus' preaching, Scorsese removes most of the indications given in Kazantzakis that point to Jesus as the Messiah, as the Son of God, indications recognized by others and by Jesus himself. In Scorsese, there is no reference to the particular circumstances of Jesus' birth or to the visit of the Magi, nor to his redemptive meeting with the Samaritan woman at the well, nor to Jesus' transfiguration, nor to his being the new Moses—all of them elements in Kazantzakis. Also missing in the film is much of the speculation regarding the divine identity of Jesus on the part of his mother, Mary Magdalene, the disciples, the centurion, and others. Though in interviews Scorsese insists, "I believe that Jesus is divine,"[45] the result of his operation of editing and of many other content and stylistic choices in the film is the considerable diminishment of the person and identity of Jesus as the Christ.

The Controversial Last-Temptation Episode

The last-temptation episode in Scorsese's film reveals itself as a microcosm of how the director adapts Kazantzakis's entire novel to the screen. Overall, Scorsese maintains the structure of Kazantzakis, beginning the episode with a break from the narrative of the crucifixion and then returning to the crucifixion at the end. Jesus comes down from the cross, marries Mary Magdalene, and later cohabits with Mary and Martha, producing many children. He encounters Saul/Paul, he ages, and at the end of his life, Judas shames him into returning to the cross and completing his mission of redemption.

Though Scorsese streamlines the Kazantzakis episode, it is still relatively longer in the film. In the novel, the last-temptation chapters are fifty-two pages long, roughly one-tenth of the book, while the same episode takes up one-fifth of the total time of the film. Clearly, the scandalous, polemical content of the episode interested Scorsese, so he gives it much more weight in his film. Perhaps the greatest similarity between the two versions of the last temptation results from Scorsese's maintaining the dominant domestic quality of the temptation. Though the coupling of Jesus with Mary Magdalene is more graphic and shocking in the film version than in

Kazantzakis, in fact, the temptation Jesus dreams through is primarily that of the quiet domestic life with wife and children and nature all benevolent.

One controversial detail from Kazantzakis that Scorsese imports directly into his film is, as already mentioned, the statement of the angel/tempter: "Only one woman exists in the world, one woman with countless faces." This is in contradiction to the prophetic, liberating manner in which the Jesus of the Gospels relates to women. Further regarding women, one major shift that Scorsese makes away from Kazantzakis is to alter the disguise of the guardian angel/tempter who accompanies Jesus in this episode. In Kazantzakis, the tempting angel is male and much of the time appears as a "Negro boy." In Scorsese, he becomes a sweet and seductive young girl, further strengthening the film's proposal of woman as temptress.[46]

Scorsese also imports from the novel the episode of Jesus' meeting with Saul/Paul. For the typical mainline Christian, this episode is perhaps the most problematical of the film. The basic point of Saul/Paul's argument is the questionable theological principle that "'faith' is more important than Jesus' resurrection."[47] This episode explicitly and in very concrete terms raises "the possibility that belief in the resurrection had been fabricated."[48] In Scorsese, the suggestion of fraud is much strengthened when he makes the meeting a violent public confrontation in the precincts of the synagogue. He directs a scrawny and rather sleazy Harry Dean Stanton to do the scene as a ranting TV evangelist, a category of media personality well-known for fraudulent claims and practices.

As in the main part of the film, also in the dream/temptation episode, Scorsese cuts much material as a necessary operation. But in the case of the last-temptation episode, Scorsese's exercise offers some quite telling results insofar as it further delineates the character of Jesus. For example, in the novel's temptation episode, Jesus engages in elaborate conversations with his "guardian angel," with his three women, and with his disciples. In the film, these conversations are truncated or deleted; the operation suggests a Jesus who is oddly out of touch, almost autistic. This sense is increased when Scorsese suppresses the voice-over interior monologue of Jesus in the entire episode. In Kazantzakis's dream episode, Jesus repeatedly experiences real happiness, but Scorsese removes most of this, and the remaining Jesus seems to be an empty, emotionless zombie, going through the motions of living and loving but deriving no real joy from them.

Some of the novel's details that Scorsese cuts actually reduce the shock effect of the episode. For example, early in the episode, Kazantzakis has the angel/tempter point out to Jesus a virile virgin bull eyeing the heifers in the adjacent field and then enthusiastically going after them, as if to prepare Jesus for his encounter with Mary Magdalene.[49] Mercifully but surprisingly, Scorsese suppresses that detail. The presence of Matthew the evangelist is also cut from the episode—and from the entire film—probably because dramatically his presence would have clashed with that of Paul and confused the situation even more. Scorsese has the bizarre detail of God's taking the life of Mary Magdalene quickly and neatly, with a mysterious flash of light. This is opposed to the extended scene in Kazantzakis, where God dialogues with Mary before consigning her to death as a prostitute, being stoned at the hands of Saul and the crowd.

Scorsese adds some new elements to the episode. For example, instead of having Jesus enter and exit the dream/temptation immediately, as if it lasts only one second between the words "Eli, Eli" and "Lama sabachthani?" Scorsese makes the transition gradual both times. He has the girl-angel/tempter remove the nails from Jesus' bloodied body, one by one. Then, in a gesture perhaps meant to convince a bewildered Jesus that she is his guardian angel, she kisses his sacred wounds and leads him through the crowd of onlookers deriding him, whom they still see on the cross. At the end of the temptation episode, Scorsese has Jesus crawl reptile-like across the room, out of the house, and up Calvary. This ignoble gesture, compounded by the close-ups of Jesus' masochistically grimacing face as he repeatedly screams to God, "I want to die! . . . Make me die!" effectively makes Jesus' decision a narcissistic act of self-indulgence, a sort of personal victory over self in a bizarre "extreme sport" instead of an outward-looking loving act of self-giving for the redemption of God's people.

In one sense, the major problem with the episode of the last temptation in Scorsese has to do not so much with the reality it represents, a reality more clearly introduced as a dream/temptation in the film than in Kazantzakis's novel. Instead, the problem is with its reception by almost any audience. The concreteness and specificity of the film medium, the great power of its visual/aural images to evoke reality, and the sheer length of the episode—all conspire to convince all but the most seasoned and experienced spectators that what they are seeing is real. And clearly, the screen reality of seeing Jesus the Christ, the Son of God, effecting the redemption of the world under coercion by Judas, or consummating his marriage with Mary Magdalene in vivid close-up, is extremely disconcerting. That the latter image is part of a "'temptation' doesn't mend matters at all; the sheer force of the image is greater than its context" or than its literal meaning.[50] One critic expresses succinctly the problem of the episode and, in a sense, of the entire film: "True, it is only a dream, a dream from which the Savior awakes victorious. But cinema is enchantment and magic: the images change dream into reality and reality into dream."[51]

The Originality and Significance of a Subjective Jesus

Returning to the Kazantzakis/Scorsese nexus, let us move beyond the criticism that can be, and has been, justly leveled at their respective portraits of Jesus by orthodox theology and Christology. Both the novel and the film do make an important contribution to the contemporary christological debate in an element that few of the critics notice. This is the careful attention both of them devote to the self-consciousness of Jesus, to Jesus' own reflections and developing understanding of who he is, what he is about, and his relationship to the Father, and to the significance of this relationship.

Repeatedly in his novel, Kazantzakis represents a subjective Jesus, offering the reader fascinating glimpses into his innermost thoughts and feelings, his soul. Sometimes the omniscient speaker of the narrative suggests Jesus' self-consciousness by, for example, the repeated, powerful descriptions of Jesus' dreams and in the representations of Jesus' thoughts in the garden of Gethsemane. Other times Jesus' own thoughts and words suggest it. For example, when left alone after a tiring day of proclaiming parables, the Beatitudes, and the commandment to love, he thinks of God and speaks directly to him. Also in the passage analogous to Luke 4, in the synagogue Jesus proclaims the words of Isaiah and then adds, "The prophesied day has come, brothers. The God of Israel has sent me to bring the good tidings."[52]

The single element that most distinguishes the Jesus of *The Last Temptation of Christ* from the Jesus characters of all the other Jesus-films is his subjectivity: "Only the Scorsese film offers a subjective Jesus."[53] Repeatedly, Scorsese represents the reality of events as Jesus himself perceives them—the viewer sees and hears things with the eyes and ears of Jesus, privy to his innermost thoughts and feelings. Scorsese creates this high subjectivity of Jesus—evident from the opening of the film—through his interior monologue but also by having his physical presence dominate the screen: "This almost total occupation of the screen is the precondition of the film's intensely subjective feel."[54] Jesus' dominating presence is supported by a photographic technique indicating interiorization—many subjective point-of-view shots, including some filmed with a shaky, handheld camera—clearly dramatizing his subjectivity. With consummate skill, Scorsese even creates instances of aural subjectivity, for example, in "the sounds of everything but the water bleeding away when Jesus meets the Baptist."[55] There also is the sudden silence on Calvary to indicate the beginning of Jesus' last temptation, and the shocking return of the violent noise when Jesus conquers the temptation.

The Jesus-film tradition, even in its finest creations, limits itself almost exclusively to objective portrayals of Jesus, to seeing and hearing him as others see him, as fascinating and challenging as that can be. This tradition often wants to portray only the divinity of Jesus, even if in a reductionistic way, by interpreting this divine dimension as material power and majesty, aloofness and distance, human perfection. By doing so, it typically avoids dealing seriously with the incarnation of God, with Jesus' humanity in all the limitations of that humanity. Suppose that "to subjectivize Christ is to release questions, . . . disrupting traditional representations in which the primary question is how others relate to Christ [and] not how he related to himself."[56] If so, then inspired by Kazantzakis's subjective Jesus and by his own history of representing his protagonists subjectively, Scorsese takes up this considerable challenge. Viewers may consider that he offers discerning film viewers a significant model against which to measure their own developing and maturing understanding of and faith in Jesus.

Unfortunately, however, this profoundly dualistic Jesus, neurotically and perhaps psychotically divided within himself, with his spirit constantly struggling against his flesh, is a fictional Jesus. He projects more the autobiographical experiences and concerns of the authors than anything in the historical or biblical Jesus. Scorsese, and to a lesser extent Kazantzakis, in effect deny the incarnation, the essential Christian belief in which flesh is enspirited and spirit is enfleshed, in the only divine-human harmony that can bring redemption.[57]

Conclusion: Scorsese's "Low" Christology and "Low" Anthropology

The negative reactions of the Orthodox and the Roman Catholic Churches to Kazantzakis's novel are well documented. Even better documented are the negative reactions of the Catholic and Protestant Churches to Scorsese's film.[58] Some of these reactions are clearly exaggerated, especially when the people voicing them have not seen the film. Some are based on evident misinterpretation of the film. One example is the inability to recognize language signaling the beginning and the end of the last-temptation sequence in the film, the obvious signs that what is on the screen is a dream or fantasy experience. Some reactions, too, mistakenly focus on the issue of Jesus' sexuality and his contact with women as if that were the only theme of the film.

Many, however, are reasoned, reasonable, and justified critiques, such as those quoted at the beginning of this chapter. Citing many of the points I have made here, they point to the extremely "low" Christology of Scorsese's film, of his exaggerations in depicting Jesus' humanity, which in effect exclude his divinity. One critic says succinctly: "It is as heretical to deny Christ's humanity as it is to deny his divinity. But the markers of Christ's humanity in the Gospels . . . don't come close to the prolonged identity crisis of the film."[59] Scorsese's disclaimer is inserted before the opening credits of the film: "This film is not based on the Gospels but upon the fictional exploration of the eternal spiritual conflict." Against this, several critics argue that in some sense Scorsese's Jesus, and Kazantzakis's Jesus before him, are in fact based on the Jesus of the Gospels. They maintain that it is "insufficient to insist that the work is not meant to show the gospel story itself. . . . Clearly some of the plot is fabrication, but there is more than enough dialogue and connection with the gospels to bring the thrill, or shock, of recognition."[60]

The major problem with Scorsese's Jesus is not only that, as I have proposed, he is a projection of the director's issues and conflicts, leading the filmmaker to very debatable conclusions, as where he misinterprets both Kazantzakis's Jesus and the Jesus of the Gospels: "This neurotic—even psychotic—Jesus [of Kazantzakis] was not very different from the shifts of mood and psychology that you find glimpses of in the Gospels."[61] The problem is also that in this film Scorsese cannot liberate himself from the antiheroic protagonists he has created in his earlier films. "Scorsese's interpretation of Christ coalesces images that haunt all his earlier films—disorienting, disturbing, and evocative archetypes of fear, guilt, and desperation; overpowering, unsettling, and visceral visions of blood, sexuality, pain, suffering, and ecstasy."[62]

In his desire to create a human Jesus, Scorsese makes him an embodiment of Kazantzakis's eternal "struggle between the flesh and the spirit."[63] But behind this eternal conflict, a conflict Scorsese embodies in the protagonists of many of his films—the deeply troubled Travis Bickle of *Taxi Driver* is the obvious example—lurks an erroneous and radically anti-Christian philosophical-theological principle. This anti-Christian principle holds that in human nature there is a sharp and irreconcilable dualism between the flesh and the spirit, a dualism that "condemns the flesh but exalts the spirit."[64] A Protestant critic speaks of this exaltation of dualism as "the most dangerous and most deeply misleading thing about this film." He concludes that the film, therefore, fails "in its central purpose—to affirm the humanity of Jesus."[65]

Scorsese's Jesus shifts repeatedly in his understanding and acceptance of his divine identity, as if there were a profound and unbridgeable gap between his humanity and his being the Son of God. This creates an insurmountable theological problem. While it is theologically acceptable to say that at some point Jesus of Nazareth struggled with his identity, I believe it is theologically unacceptable to represent him as having never arrived at a point of self-understanding and integration. And it is theologically unacceptable for this Jesus to continuously imagine God as a violent, rapacious bird of prey that pursues and attacks him, obliging him to do and to be something he does not want. Hence, Scorsese's Jesus cannot possibly be God, for God cannot work against, or oppose, God's own self.

After all is said and done, it seems clear that the fatal weakness of the Jesus of Scorsese's *The Last Temptation of Christ* is the filmmaker's anthropology, more skewed and unbalanced than that of Kazantzakis. Scorsese's Jesus is weak, uncertain, and riddled by guilt. He is fascinated and even pleased by his own suffering, at times seeking it out, clearly indicating dimensions of neurotic masochism. He moves with high energy through phases of frenetic activity, aggressive preaching, and violent criticism of the authorities, and then he falls into periods of passivity, impotence, depression, clearly symptoms of a manic-depressive psychosis. His human relationships are without freedom and strangely unbalanced. He dominates all the apostles except Judas, by whom he lets himself be dominated. His relationships with women are marked by confused feelings of guilt and desire that in the end are not resolved. Perhaps the most tragic human flaw of Scorsese's Jesus—a conspicuous shift away from Kazantzakis—is that, narcissistically closed into himself, he is incapable of being gracious toward others, incapable of loving, which after all is the most fundamental trait of a normal human personality.

For the Christian—and thus for Scorsese, who insists on his Catholic faith—Jesus cannot be just another historical figure. As the Christian creeds proclaim, he is the Son of God, who died and rose from the dead, and he lives here and now, dynamic and efficacious, in every human being and in every dimension of human culture and civilization. In *The Last Temptation of Christ*, Scorsese represents Jesus the Christ with an anthropology so diminished that he ceases to be a normal human being. Scorsese's anthropology, "applied to a figure who, for the

Christian world, represents the Son of God, the apex of the religious impulse, is absolutely unacceptable."[66]

Notes

1. W. Barnes Tatum, *Jesus at the Movies: A Guide to the First Hundred Years* (Santa Rosa, CA: Polebridge, 1997), 161.

2. Luigi Bini, "*L'ultima tentazione di Cristo* di Martin Scorsese," *Letture* 44, no. 453 (January 1989): 65.

3. Tatum, *Jesus at the Movies*, 165.

4. Mary Pat Kelly, *Martin Scorsese: A Journey* (New York: Thunder's Mouth, 1991), 161.

5. Marie Katheryn Connelly, *Martin Scorsese: An Analysis of His Feature Films with a Filmography of His Whole Career* (Jefferson, NC: McFarland, 1993), 125.

6. Michael Henry, "Entretien avec Martin Scorsese sur *La dernipre tentation du Christ*," *Positif* 332 (October 1988): 7.

7. Kelly, *Martin Scorsese*, 169. Rather significantly, Scorsese adds that at the time "I was thinking of making a movie from a different novel, *King Jesus* by Robert Graves" (ibid.).

8. My first analysis of Scorsese's film and of its source in Kazantzakis's novel is in a chapter of my book *Imaging the Divine: Jesus and Christ-Figures in Film* (Kansas City, MO: Sheed & Ward, 1997), 48–71.

9. In using the terms "high" and "low" Christology, my intention is not to dismiss the theological complexity of the traditional Antiochene/Alexandrian debate in the West and of the Monophysite issue in the East, nor to refer to the quite different theological distinctions between a Christology from above and a Christology from below. My basic position in this chapter is that of a mainline Roman Catholic Christian living and reflecting, in a theological space transformed and liberated by Vatican II, on who Jesus the Christ is for me and for the world. More fundamentally, my starting point is the commitment to explore creatively and critically but also faithfully how this human being, Jesus, a Jew who lived, preached, healed, and died in Roman-occupied Palestine twenty-one centuries ago, is at the same time, as John Macquarrie says, "the focus where the mystery of Being is disclosed, . . . the supreme miracle, the culmination of God's providential and revealing activity" (*Principles of Christian Theology* [New York: Scribner, 1966]), 249, 251). For me, the image of Jesus in a work of art—whether painting, prose, poetry, drama, or film—is valid and valuable insofar as its creator has succeeded in holding in balanced tension these two necessary dimensions of Jesus the Christ, his humanity and his divinity. I do not consider this tension in sacred images of Jesus a static or fixed reality; instead, it shifts back and forth within a range of acceptable possibilities, sometimes privileging more the human dimension of his reality, sometimes privileging more the divine. To use the terms I propose above, it moves between "high" and "low" Christologies. The Greek Orthodox Church chastised Kazantzakis because his image of Jesus was judged heretical, un-Orthodox. The Roman Catholic Church condemned Scorsese's film because its image of Jesus was deemed unbalanced, unacceptable. In both cases, from the point of view of the institutional Church in question, whose responsibility is to teach the true doctrine, the "ortho-doxy" about Jesus the Christ, the images of Jesus developed in the novel and the film

diverge too much from that range of tension between "high" and "low" Christologies. They veer in the direction of a Jesus in whom the deeply troubled human dimension—in eternal conflict within itself—overshadows in an exaggerated way the divine. In this chapter, my interest clearly is not to evaluate the merits or demerits of the ecclesiastical-institutional condemnations of both works, but rather to consider how in his film Scorsese develops themes and details of Kazantzakis's novel in directions of his own interest. I use the popular-theological terms "high" and "low" Christologies as linguistic tools in order to render more clearly the divergences between the novel and the film, and between both of those works of art and the traditional biblical-theological images of Jesus the Christ as proposed in mainline Christian belief.

10. Clearly, it is also theoretically possible for a film to have such a "high" Christology that the humanity of Jesus is effectively denied.

11. Baugh, *Imaging the Divine*, 22.

12. Tatum, *Jesus at the Movies*, 172. Tatum is quoting David Neff in an editorial in *Christianity Today*, October 7, 1988.

13. Bini, "*L'ultima tentazione*," 65.

14. In a dramatically effective but illogical move, Scorsese has the smell arrive simultaneously to Jesus and to the disciples and others who are much farther away than he from the tomb.

15. An American production, directed by George A. Romero and released in 1968, this bizarre film has become a cult classic.

16. During the filming of the most gruesome scenes of this extremely violent film, some blood accidentally splattered on the lens of the camera. Normally this would be a technical problem and the unacceptable footage would be discarded, but Scorsese liked the shot so much that he edited it into the final film.

17. Richard Corliss, ". . . and Blood: An Interview with Martin Scorsese," *Film Comment* 24, no. 5 (September–October 1988): 42.

18. According to Luke's Gospel (1:36, 57), John the Baptist is related to Jesus and is born only six months before him. And in Medieval and Renaissance art, they are represented as babies together. Willem Dafoe, born in 1955, was thirty-four years old when the film was released; André Gregory, born in 1934, is fifty-four, so this John the Baptist was more than twenty years Jesus' senior.

19. Steven D. Greydanus, "*The Last Temptation of Christ*: An Essay in Film Criticism and Faith"; <http://www.decentfilms.com/commentary/lasttemptation.html>.

20. Ibid.

21. Leandro Castellani, *Temi e figure del film religioso* (Leumann [Torino]: Editrice Elle Di Ci, 1994), 161.

22. Nikos Kazantzakis, *The Last Temptation of Christ*, trans. Peter Bien (New York: Simon & Schuster, 1960), 287, 348, 360–61.

23. Connelly, *Scorsese: An Analysis*, 130.

24. Jonathan Rosenbaum, "Raging Messiah: *The Last Temptation of Christ*," *Sight and Sound* 57, no. 4 (Autumn 1958): 282.

25. Kazantzakis, *Last Temptation*, 457 (tempting angel), 220–22 (Samaritan woman).

26. Bruce Babington and Peter William Evans, *Biblical Epics: Sacred Narrative in the Hollywood Cinema* (Manchester: Manchester University Press, 1993), 109.

27. Castellani, *Temi e figure*, 161, 162.

28. Greydanus, "Essay in Film Criticism."

29. Cart., "Film Reviews: *The Last Temptation of Christ*," *Variety*, August 10, 1988, 12.

30. Leo Lourdeaux, *Irish and Italian Filmmakers in America: Ford, Capra, Coppola, and Scorsese* (Philadelphia: Temple University Press, 1990), 260.

31. Richard Corliss, "Body . . . ," *Film Comment* 24, no. 5 (September–October): 43.

32. Rosenbaum, "Raging Messiah," 281.

33. Castellani, *Temi e figure*, 161.

34. Kazantzakis, *Last Temptation*, 216–17.

35. Ibid., 220–22, 307, 317, 345, 351.

36. Kelly, *Martin Scorsese*, 230.

37. Forgetting that the disciples had prepared the Passover meal, Scorsese justifies his daring move with characteristic ingenuousness and a somewhat limited Eucharistic theology: "Jesus was so great, I just couldn't see him telling the women at the Last Supper, 'Wait in the kitchen.' . . . He would have them take part in the first Mass." Kelly, *Martin Scorsese*, 224.

38. If this detail makes the Last Supper seem to verge on cannibalism (Les Keyser, *Martin Scorsese* [New York: Twayne, 1992], 183), we might consider how it could have gone. The original scriptwriter of *Last Temptation*, Paul Schrader, had a "literal version of the Last Supper in terms of swallowing the flesh and blood of Jesus" (Martin Scorsese, *Scorsese on Scorsese*, ed. David Thompson and Ian Christie [Boston: Faber & Faber, 1989], 118.) Mercifully for the viewer but logically inconsistent, Scorsese keeps only half of Schrader's idea—the wine becomes blood, the bread remains bread—which might lead the theologically astute viewer to conclude that in this film, the miracle of transubstantiation is only half-successful.

39. Keyser, *Martin Scorsese*, 184.

40. Kelly, *Martin Scorsese*, 223.

41. Scorsese explains how he translated the meaning and feeling of the painting into the film medium: in the "painting by Bosch . . . the surrounding faces gave no sense of three dimensions. It took all morning to do that scene, at 120 frames per second [for slow motion]. To keep the people around him, some of them laughing or pointing at him, we had to tie them together with ropes, so they could move only one step at a time" (Scorsese, *Scorsese on Scorsese*, 138).

42. Babington and Evans, *Biblical Epics*, 163.

43. Ibid.

44. Here I do not wish to dispute Kazantzakis's reliance on Ernest Renan, whose *Life of Jesus* (1863) gives priority to Matthew. But I want to make a couple of points. I really wonder if Scorsese, in preparing his film, delved into the rather complex biblical-theological implications of Renan's work. We know that Scorsese makes a point of insisting that he is a Catholic and that he believes in the divinity of Jesus, in contrast to Renan's denial of the divinity of Jesus and of the existence of God. Hence, I suspect that Scorsese would in any case not have incorporated Renan's conclusions into his film. I think that he suppresses Kazantzakis's more

elaborate treatment of Matthew because, in order to create and maintain the absolute priority of the Jesus-Judas relationship, he has to reduce the importance of all the other disciples.

45 Kelly, *Martin Scorsese*, 243.

46. Kazantzakis, *Last Temptation*, 457, 479.

47. Greydanus, "Essay in Film Criticism." There seems to be a logical contradiction in this scene. Suppose, as both novel and film maintain, the last temptation is conjured up by Satan to stop Jesus from dying on the cross and redeeming the world. Then surely Satan should not have him meet Saul/Paul, an event that disturbs Jesus's quiet domesticity and his submission to the spell of the temptation.

48. Tatum, *Jesus at the Movies*, 166. The idea is certainly not original to Kazantzakis or Scorsese. It was raised more than two hundred years ago by H. S. Reimarus and later scholars of the "quest for the historical Jesus" school. Also see Tatum's essay in this volume.

49. Kazantzakis, *Last Temptation*, 448.

50. Greydanus, "Essay in Film Criticism."

51. Bini, "*L'ultima tentazione*," 69.

52. Kazantzakis, *Last Temptation*, 431–32 (garden of Gethsemane), 192–93 (Jesus speaks to God), 307 (Jesus and Isaiah).

53. Babington and Evans, *Biblical Epics*, 128.

54. Ibid., 151.

55. Ibid., 152.

56. Ibid., 151.

57. Biblical scholarship demonstrates how the Gospels themselves—and so also the image of Jesus created in those Gospels—reflect personal and social experiences and concerns of their writers. For mainline Christians, however, the Gospels are the Spirit-inspired Word of God, while the texts of Kazantzakis and Scorsese are not.

58. David Ehrenstein gives a detailed account of the varied positions of those who objected to the film. See Ehrenstein, *The Scorsese Picture: The Art and Life of Martin Scorsese* (New York: Birchlane-Carol, 1992), 112–13. Les Keyser, *Martin Scorsese*, 184–86, provides further information on the protest.

59. Carol Iannone, "*The Last Temptation* Reconsidered," *First Things* 60 (February 1996): 51.

60. Ibid.

61. Scorsese, *Scorsese on Scorsese*, 116–17.

62. Keyser, *Martin Scorsese*, 182.

63. Kazantzakis, *Last Temptation*, 2.

64. Neff, in Tatum, *Jesus at the Movies*, 172.

65. Ibid.

66. Castellani, *Temi e figure*, 160.

CHAPTER 15

Teaching the *Temptation*
Seminarians Viewing *The Last Temptation of Christ*
Melody D. Knowles and Allison Whitney

Introduction

How do present-day seminarians with sophisticated skills in biblical exegesis and a commitment to their religious communities interact with *The Last Temptation of Christ*? How is Martin Scorsese's adaptation of Nikos Kazantzakis's Christ analyzed by students schooled to distinguish the historical Jesus from the portrayal of Christ canonized by the early Church in the Gospel narratives? How do students and teachers study films without prior training in formal film analysis? This chapter offers a reflection on the fruitfulness of incorporating the film of *The Last Temptation of Christ* into seminary curricula, documents the responses of seminary students to Scorsese's movie, and demonstrates its pedagogical potential in raising issues that are often left unaddressed in the training of clergy.

The film was screened in the context of a master's-level course entitled "Film and the Bible," cotaught by a biblical scholar and a film studies scholar at McCormick Theological Seminary in Chicago.[1] The school is a fairly liberal Presbyterian institution, although our class included a number of Baptists and Pentecostals, and the students held theological viewpoints ranging from liberal to conservative. A majority of the students were preparing to be full-time ministers in the Church, and most of them entered the class with fairly sophisticated exegetical skills, including knowledge of biblical Hebrew and/or Greek, as well as extensive coursework emphasizing careful analysis of biblical texts. However, few if any of the students were well versed in film studies. The course was designed to examine and critique the use of biblical stories in an international selection of films and to give seminarians practical skills for the analysis and interpretation of film and popular media so that they might bring this consciousness into their ministries. The goals of the class included a sustained and critical engagement with the ways film artists interpret biblical texts, exposing students to a variety of visual exegetical projects, and an expansion of students' ability to discuss biblical themes in reference to popular culture. The format of the class included a weekly plenary session and screening, weekly small-group discussions led by students, and weekly reflection papers that combined a short synopsis with a critical evaluation of the film vis-à-vis the biblical text. In the case of *The Last Temptation of Christ*, we asked the students to address four main issues: the portrayal of the divine in the film, Jesus' psychology, the film's relationship both to the biblical text and to the Church's traditions about Jesus, and the controversy surrounding the film's release.

Scorsese's film might seem out of place in a course on biblical adaptation, since it is really an adaptation of a novel that is itself a sometimes radical departure from the Gospels, or, as one student described it, a "midrash"—an interpretative exercise based on scriptural people and events. Nonetheless, our inclusion of this film stems from a strategic effort to break down a significant barrier to the discussion of film in the context of a Protestant seminary, where the typical response to religious art of any kind is to comment solely on its fidelity to its biblical source. While it may be fruitful to contemplate this element of the adaptation process, it is here that the debate generally stops, almost always with a conclusion that characterizes the adaptation as inferior to, or a distortion of, Scripture. Further debate is often curtailed by an underexamined notion of "accuracy" that fails to recognize the unique powers of film as an exegetical tool. It was our purpose to encourage seminarians to look at films not as would-be substitutes for Scripture but as a vital component in the larger culture's attempts to grapple with issues ranging from the intensely political to the intimately personal, many of which are encoded in Scorsese's imaginative project. We wanted to explore how seminarians, working with contemporary distinctions between the Jesus of history and the Christ of the Church, would respond to *The Last Temptation of Christ*'s complex Jesus.

Scorsese's Jesus, the Historical Jesus, and the Church's Christ

In their seminary education, students interact with current scholarship on the historical Jesus that emphasizes his Jewishness and the influence of the later Christian communities to rework the historical tradition.[2] In viewing *The Last Temptation of Christ*, the class was able to wrestle with a singular interpretation of Jesus that is formed both by historical scholarship and by the particular concerns of the Western tradition and modern sensibilities. Many other films about the life of Christ make claims to historical validity by calling on archaeological evidence or other historical sources. On the other hand, Scorsese's film is particularly effective in encouraging students to scrutinize the practical implications of the historical Jesus. We think that this power stems from the film's intense focus on Jesus' internal psychological life. While it might seem strange to link the film's debt to historical research with Willem Dafoe's performance of Jesus, the method acting used in this film forces the viewer to consider the Jesus story in terms of psychological realism. The majority of Jesus-films and indeed the Gospels themselves, devote little attention to Jesus' personal psychology; we observe his actions and hear his words, but we are rarely led to consider Jesus' emotional motivation. Any actor playing Jesus is thus presented with a mighty challenge, since the implied realism of the film medium demands that he provide some kind of emotional logic to support his facial expressions, movements, posture, and diction. Thus, every element of an actor's performance becomes an exegetical act. Watching Dafoe's heavily psychologized Jesus, one is forced to contemplate what a fully human Jesus would have plausibly said, thought, felt, and done at any given moment—precisely the kind of questioning that underlies much historical Jesus research.

We can best illustrate the connection between psychological and historical realism by examining students' reaction to Dafoe's use of language in his performance. His Jesus is often halting and inarticulate, introducing his parables thus: "Ah . . . Um, I'm sorry, but . . . the easiest way to make myself clear is to tell you a story." Students agreed that this was not as impressive as the assured pronouncements of the New Testament, and many found it hard to believe that people would listen to or follow a man with such limited rhetorical skills. Others found it jarring and anachronistic to hear a variety of identifiably American and particularly New York accents coming from biblical characters, and some criticized the film's use of contemporary language as "contrived." Meanwhile, others supported the filmmakers' linguistic choices, stating that the historical Jesus would have spoken to people in accessible and familiar terms, and that our conception of Jesus' interactions with people is distorted by formalized notions of biblical language.

One student pointed out that this deviation from the generally lofty discourse of most Jesus films allows one to hear Jesus' words in a new way and also marks Jesus as a member of the working class. Although this statement might suggest an imposition of modern class structures onto the ancient world, it is nonetheless relatively rare for us to see or even think about Jesus as a "worker." Yet for most of his life he would have been just that, and his social standing would have certainly been a factor in his everyday interactions. Furthermore, in films made in English, Jesus is often played by actors trained in a Shakespearean tradition, whose diction evokes an upper-class British accent. Meanwhile, Scorsese's actors employ easily identifiable American accents, none of which are associated with upper-class society. Students argued that by using contemporary American speech that "comes naturally" to American actors, the film paradoxically represents Jesus' voice with greater historical accuracy than a contemporary hearing of the King James Version, and positions him as one of "the people" to an extent that is often overlooked.

Students continually remarked on the film's emphasis on Jesus' humanness. Some found it refreshing to see Jesus portrayed in this manner, while others found it disturbing, but they consistently related Jesus' human qualities to theories of the historical Jesus. For example, in the film, Jesus' confusion about God's call and the lack of clarity or consistency in his evolving message point to his human limitations. Judas finds this lack of a grand plan frustrating and angrily confronts Jesus: "Every day you have a different plan. First it's love, then it's the ax, and now you have to die!" Jesus can only explain: "God only talks to me a little at a time. He only tells me as much as I need to know." One student dismissed this Jesus as a "wishy-washy waffler who lacks confidence in, or even a well-defined vision of, his own ministry." Another felt that it was historically likely that God only "parcels out as much information as Jesus can handle at one time," suggesting that there were limits on how much Jesus could process psychologically, and therefore that Jesus' psyche was as fragile and slow to change as any human's. Many contemporary historical Jesus scholars agree that an uncertain and evolving Jesus is more probable than a Jesus self-assured of his divinity and ministry, but the class was clearly divided on this point. What was interesting was that whether defending or criticizing Scorsese's very human Jesus, the students called on both historical and theological discourse.

For instance, one student praised this interpretation of Jesus as a historical plausibility that was later de-emphasized by the Church: "I was particularly struck by the possibility that Jesus hadn't understood what God expected of him all of his life. I think that the way we learn about Jesus in a traditional Sunday school setting implies that Jesus and his mother, Mary, know that he's headed for the cross as soon as he's conceived." Other students presented theological defenses of Scorsese's Jesus based on the humanity that Jesus shared with all creation. "If I were Jesus, . . . I would not know how to interpret God's messages to me; I would struggle with what God is asking me to do and say; and I'm sure I would appear weak, confused, [and] mentally ill."

The film's emphasis on Jesus' humanity was criticized by other students who echoed Judas's frustration with Jesus' lack of a clear plan from God, and again, their critique stemmed from both theological and historical arguments. For instance, one student felt that while emphasizing the human nature of Jesus was a legitimate theological move, the type of person Jesus was in the film led to some jumps of historical plausibility: "Jesus is confused and scared of life. . . . He's not even a convincing leader, to the film's fault—I never did understand why it was that anybody would have followed someone like this Jesus." Similarly, another student commented, "I thought it was hard to believe that people would have followed this Jesus, or would have kept telling the story; there had to be something compelling about this person, or the story wouldn't have been told and spread." Other students argued that the film did not meet the historical challenge of balancing the two natures of Christ: "I felt cheated by this portrayal of Jesus, not by the display of his humanity, but rather the lack of his portrayal as divine."

From their comments, it is clear that present-day seminarians come down on both sides of Paul's statement in the film's temptation sequence that "my Jesus is much more important and much more powerful" than the historical specificities of the man standing before him. While some students wanted a confident and divine Jesus, others were attracted to a portrait of Jesus whose persuasive power is found in his human weakness. Regardless of their individual responses, students consistently reported that watching the film made them contemplate the precise nature of their beliefs and doubts about the Christ-story on both historical and theological grounds, about the role of the Church in retelling that story, and about the mystery of Christ's dual nature.

Much of the discussion of the historical Jesus does seem to stem from contemplation of Jesus' personal psychology. Nevertheless, the students also noticed that the film's post-first-century sensibilities eclipsed the historically valid notion of Jesus as a man full of love for the community, "one who exhibits compassion, love for his neighbor, and ultimately gives his life." According to one student, this Jesus' individualistic focus made him "antisocial." Another student granted that while the emphasis on Jesus' "personal internal battles with self-esteem, anger, and fear" and "individual commitment and destiny" may resonate with a contemporary audience, it is nevertheless at odds with "the radical communal love ethic" that defined the ministry of the historical Jesus. "Throughout the film Jesus exhibits little compassion for the people he heals and seems oblivious to the struggles and suffering of others." For example, he pushes his way through a crowd of people with physical deformities "with a look of terror on his face" and "exhibits no connection or love for [Lazarus] . . . and appears aghast at the monster he has pulled from the tomb." The same student thought that the film's use of Magdalene weakened our sense of Jesus' communal ethic. In the biblical text, Jesus saves a woman whom he does not know from being stoned for adultery (John 8:1–11) and in so doing "presents a powerful communal ethic to the community about sin." In the film, however, it is Magdalene who is being stoned, and Jesus' personal history with her obliges the audience to interpret the scene as Jesus' "mak[ing] up for his previous missteps in their relationship" rather than a bold statement of communal ethics. For the student, this interpretative move "cheapens" the struggle of Jesus "and simplifies it to an individual's fulfilling his personal calling."

Another element of the film that aroused historical debate was the degree to which the film addresses Jesus' Jewishness. Though the film does make clear that he is a Jew, the students remarked on the abundance of Catholic themes and imagery, including his stigmata at the temple and his removing his bleeding heart from his own chest. They found that such features tended to distance this Jesus from his historical context. Having said this, there is still a complex balance in the film between historical research and Church tradition—a point that is perhaps best understood in the students' responses to the crucifixion scene. Scorsese consulted both archaeological and art historical sources for his depiction of the crucifixion. Hence, Scorsese's Jesus is naked, somewhat crouched with his knees raised, and the nails pierce his wrists rather than his palms, while the composition of the scene is based on religious art of the fifteenth century.[3] One student praised this as "a nonsanitized portrayal," the "first realistic depiction of the crucifixion" she had seen in a Jesus film. Further discussion revealed that this notion of realism has as much to do with the brutality of the depiction, our psychological identification with Jesus, and the effectual power of Church traditions of representation as it has to do with the archaeological record.

The Sex Lives of Jesus and Seminarians

Given that this film devotes so much attention to Jesus' psychology, it is inevitable that his psychological profile includes sexuality. We asked students to contemplate the controversy that surrounded this film at the time of its release, particularly concerning its sexual content. Students' reactions to the portrayal of Jesus' potential sex life ranged from approving to appalled. However, most thought it was a legitimate exploration of Jesus' human side wrestling with questions that the Church, in portraying Jesus as sexually disinterested, has effectively denied and/or ignored.

In the students' discussions of Jesus' sexuality and his interactions with women, it became clear that they considered the relationship between sexuality and spirituality as not solely a theological issue but one that carries implications for their own professional ethics as well. According to Margaret R. Miles, "Liberal theologians have recognized the unacceptability of posing sexuality and spirituality as contradictory attractions, so many or most liberal Christians are no longer gripped by guilt over sex because of their religion."[4] However, the experiences of the seminarians in our class do not necessarily attest to Miles's observation, for even in liberal denominations, seminarians must adhere to a moral code that is more stringent than what many of the laity enact in their own lives. The provision is fought over with great vigor in the Presbyterian Church (USA). Yet people wishing to be ordained are obliged to "live either in fidelity within the covenant of marriage between a man and a woman . . . or chastity in singleness," a statement that is generally interpreted as prohibiting all sex outside of heterosexual marriage.[5] While Church officials, including those who ordain and those who form search committees, might themselves be "no longer gripped by guilt over sex because of their religion," they nevertheless demand strict sexual standards from ordinands. In exploring Jesus' humanity on the sexual plane, it seemed as if the class could identify with a portrayal of Jesus whose sexuality the Church would prefer to deny. The reaction that was heard so often in response to the movie when it originally came out ("Jesus was human, but I don't want to see him as *that* human") is a sentiment that seminarians themselves have to negotiate in their own professional lives.

Identification and the Politics of Bodies on Film

Not only did the film open the door to discussion of sexual politics in ministry; it also highlighted the complexity of identity politics in the presentation and interpretation of both the Bible and the traditions of the Church. One of the surprising responses from students was the degree to which they identified with characters in the film and how their responses emerged in gendered and racialized terms. This was particularly evident in reference to the scene in which Jesus watches Magdalene having sex with her clients. One student talked about how she kept thinking about Magdalene's physical and psychological experience, being tired, sore, sweaty, fearful of pregnancy, and emotionally exhausted. A male classmate said that he found her account enlightening, as his experience was to identify more with the male figures in the scene, admitting that his "crude" response was to think, "Why would I want used goods?"

In another discussion, an African-American student stated that she was disturbed by the racial dynamics of this scene, in which dark-skinned men form the majority of Magdalene's clients, generating an excessive association of black masculinity with Magdalene's degradation. She also noticed that the color scheme in this sequence tended to emphasize the contrast of Magdalene's skin tone with her clients'—an example of how the formal qualities of the scene relate to its ideological interpretation. In pursuing this discussion, classmates recognized that few if any films about Jesus fare very well in representing racial diversity, or even in admitting that neither Jesus nor his disciples would have been white Anglo-Europeans. Though we are not trying to make a facile argument about audience-character identification, we report that students found the diversity of responses among their classmates enlightening, and it sensitized them to the responses they may encounter among their parishioners. We also used this as an opportunity to examine the importance of diversity and inclusivity in religious iconography and language. After all, parishioners will to some degree want to see themselves represented in the multiple texts and images that form their experience of Christianity.

Specificities of the Medium

One of our goals in teaching this course was to help students learn to think about films as films—to appreciate the specific properties of cinema and its unique formal qualities. We found that as the course progressed, the students started to notice how film's representational powers offer unique ways of contemplating the mystery of faith. For example, a recurring question throughout the course was "How is God represented in the film?" In the case of films about Jesus, this question pertains specifically to God the Father and the Holy Spirit, both of whom have a complicated relationship with visual representation. Of course, Jesus can be represented because he was a historical figure with a body (although the Gospel writers themselves prioritize believing in Jesus over seeing his physical form). The Holy Spirit has a tradition of symbolic representation (tongues of flame, the dove) that could be employed in a film, partly because films routinely employ symbolic and narrative structures operating on a synchronistic logic that might be suitable for representation of the kind of mystery we associate with that part of the Trinity.

However, the strong aniconic tradition for God the Father within the biblical text presents a major challenge for artists working in a photographic medium. Although God is sometimes described as a warrior or king or father, there is a strong prohibition of images in the Hebrew Bible: "You shall not make for yourself an idol, whether in the form of anything that is in heaven above, or that is on the earth beneath"

(Exod 20:4). The prohibition stems variously from God's jealousy (20:5) or God's formlessness ("You saw no form," Deut 4:15–19). The repeated denunciations of idol worship in the Prophets indicate that figures *were* used to represent the divine, and depictions of divinities are found in the archaeological strata of Israelite sites.[6] Yet the later biblical tradition was strongly averse to such representation, and so, in depicting the First Person of the Trinity, filmmakers are perhaps wise in depicting God via the nonanthropomorphic images of wind, fire, thunder, or only a voice. The students noticed that Scorsese avoids pictorial representations of the First Person of the Trinity (one remarked, "We don't have an image of God [in the film]"), preferring audible sounds (which may or may not exist solely in Jesus' mind) and descriptions of a bird with claws.

Curiously, some students also pointed out that this leads to a representation gap between God and Satan in the film. While God is only heard, Satan assumes many visual representations in the form of a lion, snake, flame, or child. In visually representing the realm of "principalities and powers," Satan is recorded photographically with greater ease.

This tension in representing the divine and transcendent is also felt in the Last Supper sequence, in which the wine visibly transforms into blood—a point emphasized when Jesus' followers pour it out and feel its texture between their fingers. This image addresses the mystery of transubstantiation in a way that is specific to a photographic medium. In transubstantiation, the bread and wine become the body and blood of Christ in essence but not in appearance. But if this process is not visible, how is one to represent it in the film medium? One could read the apostles' reaction and handling of the wine/blood as metaphorical or symbolic of their realization of Jesus' status as divine, but the point of transubstantiation is precisely that it is not solely metaphorical. Here is an excellent example of how film is ambiguous in its "literalness." It uses images of the material world, but it can do so in a way that may represent interior vision, hallucination, fantasy, dream, or indeed, spiritual revelation. In the case of the wine/blood, film possesses a unique capacity to meditate on this mystery of transubstantiation and to visualize explicitly what many Christians believe but never actually see.

Scorsese's film further advances this discussion in its final shot, where the representational abilities of cinema appear literally to break down before the viewer's eyes. The image of Christ dying on the cross vanishes into a brief sequence of flickering: light spills into the image from the sprocket holes until the image disappears in what seems to be overexposure, followed by a series of varying colors and abstract forms. Immediately after viewing the film, we asked students what they made of this representational breakdown. They said either that they thought something was wrong with the projection or that they thought the change in image was motivated by the corresponding change in sound, whereby the women's ululations dissolve into church bells. Several students read this sound transition as an indication of the Church's taking over the story after Christ's death, and of Scorsese's indication that his meditation on Christ's life is similarly detached from Church history.

In pursuit of a fuller understanding of this scene, we highlighted its relationship to the traditions of experimental filmmakers whose works are in many ways "about" the materiality of film and the limits of its representational qualities.[7] By using techniques like scratching or painting directly on film, exploring the visual possibilities of "mistakes" like flaring and overexposure, or alternating abstract colors and forms, the filmmakers highlight the viewer's relationship to the film material and the technology of film production and exhibition. Once the students came to understand this element of *The Last Temptation of Christ* as a form of metacinema, their interpretations of its theological implications became considerably more complex. For example, some speculated that since the film focuses so intently on Jesus' psychology, and uses God's and Satan's respective invisibility and visibility literally to flesh out this meditation, then it follows that the film itself transforms into a different mode at the moment of Jesus' human death—the end of his life as a psychological being. Regardless of which historical Jesus narrative you find plausible, or the degree to which you believe in a "literal" resurrection, the human Jesus has died, and the film literally breaks down under the pressure of trying to represent what happens next.

One student speculated that the "end" of the film, both as a narrative and as a strictly representational medium, was Scorsese's way of saying that the story is not over. "With his use of film images cutting across the screen (as well as the music), the viewer knows that something else, something hopeful, is going to happen. It is as if the film imagery signaled the end of one reel (i.e., Jesus' earthly ministry) and the time to put on the next one (i.e., the ministry of the Church under the guidance of the Holy Spirit). These stories are separated in the Bible; why shouldn't they be here?" Another student commented: "While we do not see the resurrection in this film, the ending leads one to believe that the world is turned upside down by Jesus' death and that the resurrection is the redeeming grace of God, through music and color." Other students found that the emphasis on the film's materiality made them think about the implications of this being "only a movie" and the degree to which one tends to believe what one sees in the cinema as having a privileged relationship to "the truth."

Conclusion

Our teaching *The Last Temptation of Christ* demonstrated some ways in which education in media literacy allows for more nuanced interpretations of religious themes in cinema, and the ways in which these interpretations can stimulate theological debate among seminarians. By sharing the teaching responsibilities between a biblical scholar and a film scholar, we were able to retain a high level of discourse on both fronts, and thereby give a fairly nontraditional field of studies an entrée into the seminary curriculum. As students learned more about film history and analysis, they were able to engage with both filmic texts and their biblical sources in new and surprising ways. They became freshly conscious of the interpretive possibilities of the written word, more cognizant of its depiction in the Western artistic tradition, and more aware of the role of visual culture in contemporary spirituality. In understanding this and other films "as films," we hope that seminarians will be better equipped to encourage their congregations to form thoughtful and informed opinions and responses to future films and to appreciate filmmakers' attempts to grapple with the mysteries of faith.

Notes

1. The students in the class were Rhohemia Algee, Thomas Baik, David Barnhart, Nicole Bates, Mark Bedford, Stephanie Downey, Beth Hamilton, Rebecca Hancock, Anthony Hoshaw, Jin Yang Kim, Jacquelina Marquez, James Nelson, Sasa Radmilov, Jennifer Rund, Charles Schantz, Mary Scott-Boria, Sooil Shim, Margaret Shreve, Josie Smith, and Terrill Stumpf. Many thanks to them for their thoughtful engagement with the film and their permission to use their reflections in this chapter.

2. Scholars who emphasize the Jewishness of Jesus include Géza Vermès, *Jesus the Jew: A Historian's Reading of the Gospels* (London: William Collins, 1973); E. P. Sanders, *Jesus and Judaism* (Philadelphia: Fortress, 1985); idem, *The Historical Figure of Jesus* (London: Allen Lane, 1993); John Dominic Crossan, *The Historical Jesus: The Life of a Mediterranean Jewish Peasant* (San Francisco: HarperSanFrancisco, 1991); and John P. Meier, *A Marginal Jew: Rethinking the Historical Jesus*, 3 vols. (New York: Doubleday, 1991–2001). For an account of the distorting hand of the Church on the portrayal of the historical Jesus, see Gerd Lüdemann, *The Great Deception: And What Jesus Really Said and Did* (London: SCM Press, 1998).

3. For details on the archaeological and artistic inspiration for this sequence, see "Scorsese's Visual Research" on *The Last Temptation of Christ*, Criterion Collection, DVD audio commentary (2000). For example, Antonello da Massina's 1475 painting *Crucifixion* was a source for the portrayal of the thieves' crucifixion on trees.

4. Margaret R. Miles, *Seeing and Believing: Religion and Values in the Movies* (Boston: Beacon, 1996), 38.

5. This quote comes from the 2001–02 *Book of Order* of the Presbyterian Church (USA), G-6.106b. The paragraph continues as follows, "Persons refusing to repent of any self-acknowledged practice which the confessions call sin shall not be ordained and/or installed as deacons, elders, or ministers of the Word and Sacrament."

6. Although the interpretations of the finds are disputed, see especially the objects associated with the "Bull Site," Kuntillet Ajrud, and Taanach. For a discussion about the date of aniconism in ancient Israel, see Karel van der Toorn, "Israelite Figurines: A View from the Texts," in *Sacred Time, Sacred Place: Archaeology and the Religion of Israel*, ed. Barry M. Gittlen (Winona Lake, IN: Eisenbrauns, 2002), 45–62; and Jack Sasson, "On the Use of Images in Israel and the Ancient Near East: A Response to Karel van der Toorn," in *Sacred Time, Sacred Place*, 63–70.

7. Examples include Peter Kubelka's "flicker film" *Arnulf Rainer* (1960), Norman McLaren and Evelyn Lambart's hand-drawn films such as *Lines Horizontal* (1961), or Stan Brakhage's use of superimpositions in *Dog Star Man* (1961–64) or placement of natural materials placed between strips of film in *Mothlight* (1963). These filmmakers are by no means identical in their techniques, but their work is useful in informing students about practices outside of conventional narrative and photographic filmmaking.

CHAPTER 16

The Dual Substance of Cinema
What Kazantzakis's Christ Can Teach Us about Sound/Image Relationships in Film
Randolph Jordan

> I have fought to reconcile these two primordial forces which are so contrary to each other, to make them realize that they are not enemies but, rather, fellow workers, so that they might rejoice in their harmony—and so that I might rejoice with them.
>
> —Nikos Kazantzakis, *The Last Temptation of Christ*

In the last of fourteen koans on Martin Scorsese's *The Last Temptation of Christ*, film scholar Phillip Lopate suggests that the double ending of Christ's narrative amounts to both he and the audience having their cake and eating it too. In Lopate's words: "If Jesus has already enjoyed a normal full life, including the pleasures of the flesh, *even if only in his imagination,* . . . can he be said to be sacrificing quite so much in going back to the cross?"[1] The contradiction inherent in the idea of Christ (and the witnesses to his representation) having the best of two worlds is central to the primary conflict between flesh and spirit. This conflict lies at the heart of Nikos Kazantzakis's depiction of the Messiah and lays the foundation for Scorsese's cinematic adaptation. Appropriately enough, having the best of two worlds is no less than exactly what I expect from the cinema, a medium founded upon two main channels of transmission: sound and image.

Having one's cake and eating it too amounts to what might seem like an insurmountable contradiction, one in which no amount of struggle between the two options might reconcile. As with all koans, though, the benefit comes not from its resolution but rather from the process of mulling over the problem. Dwelling upon the myriad contradictions found in the story of Christ's life and death is precisely Kazantzakis's objective, a dwelling that yields plenty without need for concrete resolution. So it is as well in the ongoing struggle between sound and image in the cinema. A reconciliation of sound and image, understood as two parts of the same thing, may never be embraced in the way that Christians are called upon to accept Jesus as being both human and divine. Nevertheless, their interactions with one another make up the substance of what we know as the cinema, and they have tremendous potential as such. It is in acknowledgement of the struggle between sound and image that the deeper nature of their interaction might be revealed, just as Kazantzakis suggests that the struggle between the spirit and the flesh is revealed to be, in the story of Christ's life, a productive and necessary collaboration.

In the prologue to Kazantzakis's novel *The Last Temptation of Christ*, the author describes his own "incessant, merciless battle between the spirit and the flesh," and his belief that the key to the reconciliation of these two forces is an understanding of the nature of this struggle.[2] Kazantzakis posits Christ as the ultimate model for the battleground between these forces and their final resolution, and that to follow the Messiah's example, "we must have a profound knowledge of his conflict."[3] Essentially, Kazantzakis's project seeks to illuminate just exactly what it is that Christ would have had to experience, in human terms, in order to make his struggle of such importance to the rest of humanity. Finally, in Kazantzakis's point, the struggle itself is the key to its own reconciliation, a contradiction worthy of finding a place within a belief system that posits the human and the divine as being, in the figure of Christ, one and the same thing.

A similar belief in the need for exposing the struggle between opposing forces is expressed by leading film sound theorist Michel Chion. In *Audio-Vision: Sound on Screen*, the author discusses the struggle that sound faces against the image in the cinema and the need for awareness of this struggle if sound and image are to find a better balance with one another in a world that privileges sight over all other senses.[4] The purpose of his project is to foster an understanding of how sound has been treated in the cinema over the years in order to illustrate the role it has had in relation to the image. In this way, Chion's project can be likened to that of Kazantzakis's: Each understands his subject as the product of a struggle between opposing and often contradictory forces, a struggle that can be transformed into productive collaboration through knowledge and understanding.

Not surprisingly, the environment in which Kazantzakis places his Christ is one rife with sensory information, not the least of which is sound. Indeed, it is through descriptions of sound that much of Christ's psychological environment is represented in both the novel and the film. My purpose here is to demonstrate how Kazantzakis's Christ makes an excellent foundation on which to base a cinematic adaptation that blends this content with a formal approach seeking to illustrate some of the key issues found in film sound theory today.

As a point of departure, I examine issues pertaining to R. Murray Schafer's concept of *schizophonia*.[5] Within the concept of schizophonia, I show that the separation of a sound from its source constitutes in equal parts a transgression of both time and space. Schafer feels that this transgression is responsible for a psychological malaise, or perhaps separation anxiety, pervading the world in the age of recording technology. In the context of cinema, I consider the separation of a sound from its source in terms of Michel Chion's discussion of *acousmatic* sound, whereby sounds are heard whose sources are not visible on screen.[6] Chion gives the term "active offscreen sound" to the category of acousmatic sound that can create tension by causing us to question the source of a sound, a questioning often reflected in a character's psychological unease, as with Christ in Scorsese's film.[7] The notion of separation anxiety is then discussed in terms of the birth of cinema itself. As Tom Gunning suggests, the cinema might best be understood as having originated as a medium founded on the separation of the senses both from each other and from their grounding within the human body.[8] Finally, the anxiety that Gunning discusses surrounding this separation of the senses is considered in light of Chion's model of *transsensoriality*. Thereby the cinema offers the means for reconciling sound and image by acknowledging their points of intersection within human perception and the potential for these intersections to be exploited creatively.[9]

Schizophonia, acousmatic sound, and cinema's emergence out of anxieties surrounding the technological separation of the senses yield points of entry into some of the basic questions facing film sound theory today, questions that can readily be applied to Kazantzakis's Christ and his cinematic representation in Scorsese's film. Ultimately, the notion of cinema being based on a separation anxiety borne of technologies of representation is seen as emblematic of the schizophonic state that Schafer believes to be prevalent in contemporary society. Through a discussion of Kazantzakis's Christ as represented in Scorsese's film, I suggest that, though taking place two thousand years before the invention of the phonograph, Christ's experience is much in line with Schafer's idea of the schizophonic. As such, Christ's experience can be understood as being relevant today, especially when represented through the medium of film.

Twenty-First-Century Schizoid Man

To begin, let us consider the fact that through sound's relationship to the image (or absence thereof), one of Christ's biggest struggles is illustrated, most notably in the narrative's first third. Here we have his separation from God, a separation that is the source of the uncertainty regarding his destiny, and thus the very substance of his struggle between the flesh and the spirit. This separation plagues Christ in the form of a paranoia specifically related to his hearing of things unseen, leading him to believe that he is being observed and followed by a potentially malicious force. This paranoia is represented through the separation of sound from source. It is of great significance when considering how Christ's own dual substance might be understood as a metaphor for the struggle that sound faces with respect to the moving image. As we explore, this separation of sound from source can be understood in terms of a deeper separation anxiety, one related to contemporary metaphors of the schizophrenic.

R. Murray Schafer, founder of the World Soundscape Project, coined the term schizophonia, which he describes as "the split between an original sound and its electroacoustical transmission or reproduction."[10] In *The Tuning of the World*, Schafer discusses the role of reproduction technologies in creating a disjunction between original sounds and their propagation through space, and the effect this disjunction has on humans within their sonic environments. Schafer suggests that the technological enhancement of the spatial characteristics of sound is characteristic of late-twentieth-century attempts to "transcend the present tense," again a symptom of the schizophonic mind-set.[11] Schafer's point is that with the artificial creation of sonic environments, any environment can stand in for any other, thus removing the natural context (both temporal and spatial) for the sound's original propagation.

Schafer's argument is echoed by Frederic Jameson's description of the negative connotations of symptoms associated with schizophrenia. In *The Cultural Logic of Late Capitalism*, Jameson argues that the fragmentation, isolation, and surface reassemblage of experience characteristic of postmodernism amount to a loss of historical context. He likens this loss of context to a breakdown in the signifying chain of memory that schizophrenics exhibit in the form of "a series of pure and unrelated presents in time."[12] The crucial point of joining Schafer's thought with that of Jameson is to recognize the role of technologies of sound representation in the breaking down of linear time through acts of recontextualization. By using recording technology to document a moment of both time and space, this time and space can be resituated and reexperienced outside of their original context. In so doing, a layering and often disorientation of one's immediate environment can result. This disorientation can lead to a feeling of separation and anxiety surrounding a lack of stable context.

For Schafer, the negative connotations of the prefix "schizo" are used intentionally to describe a world that he feels has been drastically altered by the invention of technologies capable of pushing a sound well beyond the limits of its original source. Interestingly, Christ's final struggle, the last temptation, is one in which the flow of time is halted, and he is allowed to live out an entire lifetime in the space of a microsecond. His last temptation is, precisely, a moment of existence outside the time of humanity and within the time of God: the living of a lifetime in what Kazantzakis describes as a "lightning flash."[13] In so doing, Kazantzakis's Christ illustrates a key symptom associated with schizophrenia: a breakdown in the mind's ability to manage time in a linear fashion, giving way to memory or hallucination being as central an experience as the lived present. This is a highly Bergsonian idea, and it is well-known that Kazantzakis studied under the renowned French philosopher and would have undoubtedly been exposed to similar ideas about memory and the experience of time's passage. As demonstrated shortly, this last temptation is the culmination of various manifestations of Christ's separation from God, the majority of which have been suggested by both Kazantzakis and Scorsese through the use of acousmatic sound, a use that foregrounds spatial/temporal disjunctions between the seen and the heard.

The Call of the Faithful—Questions of Sonic Fidelity

For the moment, however, let us consider the concepts of separation and reconciliation as they relate more specifically to the cinema as a medium. Cinema can be understood as having been borne of the separation of hearing and sight followed closely by a need to bring them back together again. Tom Gunning suggests that Thomas Edison's stated goal for the Kinetoscope, to "[do] for the eye what the phonograph does for the ear," is indicative of two concerns in early-twentieth-century life. These concerns were the separation of the senses popular for studies of perception and "a desire to heal the breach" resulting from anxiety surrounding this separation.[14] Gunning holds that in the context of the spiritualist traditions alive and well at the time, the technological separation of the human voice from the body was often considered to be unnatural. For many, this separation was akin to the work of the devil and demanded a restitching of the isolated elements to undo the unholy influence. This situation illustrates people's anxiety over having one sense suddenly ripped from its dependence on the body, an anxiety matched by a desire to counter the imbalance.

Thus, cinema can be understood as having been borne of a technological trend toward breaking down the components of human experience into their constituent elements, a trend that made for much popular uneasiness. The bringing of sound and image together in the cinema, it seems, might have been an attempt at reconciliation between the two, a reconciliation as yet incomplete. Sound and image are still separated technologically from one another in film, and they are still removed from their origination in the human senses of hearing and sight through the cinema's technologies of representation. This separation might well be considered analogous to humanity's Babylonian condemnation to eternal translation between the fragments of the original and once universal language. However, the space of linguistic translation is rich with productive struggle, just as it is with translations between sound and image in the cinema. The fall of the great tower need not be considered a condemnation after all and may well have been the originator of new and stimulating negotiations of meaning within human experience.

On this note, one of the key issues raised by the notion of sound being separated from its source in both space and time, a basic tenet of the cinema, is that of the fidelity of transmitted sound to the original it purports to represent. Evoking the "proverbial tree falling in a forest," Rick Altman suggests: "By offering itself up to be heard, every sound event loses its autonomy, surrendering the power and meaning of its own structure to the various contexts in which it might be heard, to the varying narratives that it might construct."[15] Here Altman focuses on the role of perception of sound within space, perception that depends upon the context of a sound's transmission. As James Lastra elaborates: "Even the original itself is intrinsically multiple and internally differentiated—a fact we recognize every time we choose between 'good' and 'bad' seats in an auditorium."[16] Indeed, wherein lies the coveted original sound at a concert consisting of multiple sound sources playing to potentially thousands of different points of audition in the space of the hall? The specter of subjective experience looms large, dampening notions that any given sound might have a tangible original that can be compared to all manifestations of its perceptions.

Sound is dependent upon space, and a given point of audition cannot be occupied by more than one perceiver at a time. In light of this fact, Altman describes the need for a kind of narrative analysis of a sound's "spatial signature," close attention to the translation of a sound within a given space, and an understanding of how this space is an integral part of the sound itself.[17] He refers to the notion of multiple perspectives in sound reception as the *Rashomon* phenomenon, invoking the ubiquitous 1950 Kurosawa film and its play on the idea of subjective realities.[18] Altman's conclusion is that every sound is effectively a heterogeneous event that can never be heard by any two listeners in the same way. Thus, when analyzing sound, one must take great care to pay attention to every little nuance, since it is in the nuances that key information about the sound's production and propagation through space will be found. God is in the details, if you will.

As examined below, the theme of infinite subjectivities inherent in Altman's understanding of recorded sound can be applied to Christ's disorientation in the early part of Kazantzakis's narrative. Experiencing a disjunction between his visible world and its sonic counterpart, Christ suffers from an identity crisis commonly associated with the postmodern breakdown in objective grounding and its yield to endless subjective interpretations. In the early phase of the story, he cannot situate himself in relation to the original sources of the sounds that plague him, and this creates a severe anxiety that often finds him writhing on the ground in agony. As also to be examined, this agony gives way to a measure of peace when Christ embraces the disjunctions in his experience and turns them into productive collaborations.

Transcendent Collaboration

Just as there is increasing acknowledgement of the separation of the senses in the cinema, so, too, is there increasing interest in how the brain itself might process information initially broken down by our five sensory channels. Michel Chion's concept of *transsensoriality* will be useful to consider here. "In the transsensorial model," he says, "there is no sensory given that is demarcated and isolated from the outset. Rather, the senses are channels, highways more than territories or domains."[19] He gives rhythm as an example of an element found in cinema that is neither specifically auditory nor visual:

> When a rhythmic phenomenon reaches us via a given sensory path, this path, eye or ear, is perhaps nothing more than the channel through which rhythm reaches us. Once it has entered the ear or eye, the phenomenon strikes us in some region of the brain connected to the motor functions, and it is solely at this level that it is decoded as rhythm.[20]

This transsensorial model for understanding cinematic experience suggests that there are more fundamental levels of the cinema than simply sight and sound, levels that do not differentiate between the auditory and the visual but that cut through both to a deeper and more holistic understanding of experience.

So what we have here are the makings for a "vision" of cinema that addresses it from a holistic perspective, one in which we need not necessarily differentiate between sound and image but rather respect them as being parts of one and the same thing: human experience. This is akin to the ultimate understanding of the dual substance of Christ himself, a removal of the separation between him and God in favor of the revelation that they are both one, housed in the body of a human being.

However, as both Kazantzakis and Chion suggest, it is through an understanding of the struggle between these separated elements that we may begin to move toward their reconciliation. In the case of cinema in particular, so much of what it has to offer comes in the way of tension in the translation from sound to image and back again. Sound designer and editor Walter Murch describes the relationship elegantly:

> Image and sound are linked together in a dance. And like some kinds of dance, they do not always have to be clasping each other around the waist: they can go off and dance on their own, in a kind of ballet. There are times when they must touch, there must be moments when they make some sort of contact, but then they can be off again. . . . Out of the juxtaposition of what the sound is telling you and what the picture is telling you, you (the audience) come up with a third idea which is composed of both picture and sound and resolves their superficial differences.[21]

Thus the potential for cinema's two basic elements to be understood as being two parts of a unified whole exists within us as a function of our humanity and its attendant perceptual apparatus. We reconcile the juxtaposition and superimposition of sound and image through our processing of them. In terms of the schizophonia that Schafer suggests is so commonplace in contemporary society, this internal reconciliation would amount to facing the disjunction of sound and source through an awareness of our inherent ability to create meaning out of discordance. It would be an embracing of dissonant elements rather than a breakdown in their presence. Schafer suggests that we need to do away with the circumstances that lead to schizophonia. Kazantzakis's Christ, on the other hand, may well be an illustration that these circumstances exist to be dealt with through the power of humanity's ability to process disparate elements of experience within a unified structure.

The cinema's job, it seems to me, is to present us with an entryway to an appreciation of the interaction between its two channels of transmission. It is here that most cinema fails utterly, wanting us to assume that sound is an accompaniment to the image, a complement that rarely calls into question what is presented visually. But Christ's struggle revolves around questioning, and so should that of the cinema, as it does in Scorsese's treatment of Kazantzakis's novel. With this in mind, let us now turn to an examination of Scorsese's film in order to see how, through various strategies, the filmmaker addresses the dual substance of cinema and its relevance to the story of the Messiah's own struggle.

Seeing Is Believing

The role of sound in relation to Christ's struggle with his dual substance is set up immediately within the film's opening moments. First we find him lying on the ground, eyes closed, the sound of the opening credit music fading out as the sound of an eagle cry cuts through the air, followed by the wind, trees, and crickets. Christ's voice in narration describes a feeling of pain, and we see him stir in his sleep, raising his right hand to cover his ear as an unidentifiable ringing sound emerges. Shortly afterward, Christ's narration tells us that he has been plagued by hearing voices, at which point another unidentifiable, though decidedly choral, sound is heard. Finally, Judas confronts Jesus about the ethics of his cross-making. When frustrated that his words are falling on deaf ears, Judas asks: "Do you hear? Where is your mind? Do you hear me?" Each of these auditory strategies or suggestions of sound implies a distance of one kind or another. This may be the distance between the ringing or choral sounds from their invisible sources, or the distance of Jesus' mind from its grounding in the world as evidenced by his inability to hear what is right in front of him. Jesus is being tormented by Chion's category of acousmatic sound known as "active offscreen sound," a cinematic strategy that evokes tension and uncertainty through its lack of resolution between sound and image, sound and source.[22]

These opening moments of the film set up an environment rife with elements that might be understood as symptoms of schizophonia. Christ exhibits an unstable relationship with the world, one that suggests the primacy of subjective experience over an objective understanding of his surroundings. Certain of these sonic elements, notably the sound of the eagle cry, become motifs for the pain that Jesus suffers as a result of his separation anxiety, an anxiety later revealed to be the product of his separation from God. For example, the eagle cry is associated with Christ's feeling that something from outside is trying to enter his mind. It is heard as he is shown writhing on the floor in the arms of his mother, and later when Magdalene is taken from him during his last temptation. The eagle cry comes a final time as he is pulled out of this temptation and returns to his place on the cross—the final and successful infiltration of Christ's mind by that of God, an end to their separation once and for all.

Most notably, however, is the eagle cry early in the film when Christ walks on the beach and hears the sound of footsteps behind him. He calls out: "Who's that? Who's following me? Is that you?" The eagle is heard, and he drops to the ground and writhes again. This instance is particularly interesting because both the sound of the eagle and the sound of the footsteps suggest a presence that cannot be seen, and it is this lack of sight that induces the agony Christ suffers. If he could see what lay at the sources of these sounds, he would understand what was happening to him. The uncertainty is the source of his struggle in this first third of the narrative, an uncertainty associated with a lack of sight. This is a telling situation. As humans we do indeed place sight at the top of our senses and rely on it for establishing many of our beliefs about the world. Christ can hear what follows him, but this hearing is not sufficient to move him from the realm of speculation to the realm of conviction. Like most humans, he has trouble with his faith because it goes against that most basic of tenets: "Seeing is believing."

The case of the footsteps on the beach is especially interesting in establishing the role of sight in Christ's quest for belief in himself. Their sound is highly reverberated, almost unrecognizable, perhaps even a function of Peter Gabriel's score, also heard in this scene. The otherworldly quality of these sounds indicates that they may, in fact, exist in another space and time. The fact that Jesus is aware of the sounds suggests his own separation from the environment that surrounds him. What ultimately distinguishes these sounds from Gabriel's score, and places them within Christ's range of hearing, is the act of looking. The sounds stop when Jesus turns to see where they come from. So much as a glance in their direction causes them to cease, demonstrating their commitment to remaining completely within the auditory realm as a function of Christ's psychological unrest. He quite literally cannot reconcile the sounds with their source, and so he remains separated from God.

Peace in Multiplicity

Christ's first sign of peace in the film comes when he is blessed by the appearance of dual serpents. Here he comes to understand that "everything is from God, everything has two meanings." The struggle between two things is at the heart of his communion with God. The snakes are intertwined, two beings mingled with one another, as Christ is with God. This image of the dual serpents also suggests that all humans are intertwined with the divine, if only we could embrace the duality. At this moment Jesus understands that he will open his mouth and God will speak through him. He becomes, in a sense, God's medium of sound representation, the site of mediation between the source and the listener.

This idea posits Christ as an embodiment of the problem of original versus copy in the propagation of sound through space. How mediated is Jesus' message from the true word of God? Can this mediation be trusted? How many possible subjective interpretations of the message might there be? Such questions, asked by those in hearing range of Christ's words, are quite similar to those asked by theorists like Rick Altman, concerned with the multiplicities inherent in a sound's transmission from source to perceiver. Christ asks people to believe, however, not that he is a copy of some mysterious original that nobody can see but that he *is* God; he *is* the original finally visible, finally tangible. The problem of fidelity is dealt with through Christ's embodiment of God on earth. There is no separation between the two; he transmits God's voice from God's own mouth. This is made possible by the collaboration of the human and the divine within Christ, an embracing of a duality, revealed to him in the idea that "all things have two meanings." The trick, ultimately, is to appreciate the relationship between the two meanings so that they may no longer seem to be at odds with one another, the struggle turned collaboration.

Revelations

The final stage in Christ's self-recognition comes when John the Baptist confirms this recognition. The baptism scene raises some interesting questions. To begin with, it is one of the first instances of diegetic music whose source is clearly visible. We see people dancing by the water to the rhythm of the music, our first indication that the sound comes from within the space of the narrative. Jesus approaches the crowd, and a voice-over is heard while the rest of the sound track, music, and environmental noise alike is lowered to facilitate greater dialogue intelligibility. However, a different strategy is used when Jesus confronts John face-to-face. The sounds of the music are gradually faded out while the sound of the running stream remains constant. John looks around, and in a point-of-view shot we see the musicians playing but with no correlating sound.

This is a clear revelation of cinema's power to offer a disjunction between sound and image, and it is an extension of the tension that Jesus himself has been feeling as a result of the separation of sounds from their sources. The isolation of the sound of the water comes at precisely the moment when Jesus is about to come into his full identity as the Son of God through recognition and baptism by John. The sonic isolation may even be an indication of Jesus and John stepping into another time frame, occupying the same space but at a time when the musicians and dancers are not present. This would suggest a discontinuity not only between sound and image but also between space and time, an idea in keeping with the notion that Christ exhibits symptoms of schizophonia. As soon as Jesus is baptized, however, the sound of the music returns and with it a full synchronization of sound and image suggesting a removal of the acousmatic separation that has plagued him since the beginning of the story.

The baptism scene is the clearest revelation in the film that sound and image can contradict one another. The isolation of the sound of the river is an illustration of the potential struggle between sound and image that mainstream cinema so often seeks to keep invisible. This approach serves to heighten the drama of the moment by concentrating our attention on Jesus and John rather than the people around them. It is also clearly intended to be an extension of the acousmatic sound that Jesus has been experiencing throughout the film. Awareness of such potential disjunction is what is most important here. Christ's mission is one of creating awareness, as is the use of sound in this scene. The idea that "everything has two meanings" is an acknowledgment of the fact that dualities exist and must be embraced if they are to be reconciled. This scene foregrounds

212

cinema's potential creation of dual meanings and the power of reconciliation through their recognition.

Satan's Call, Satan's Fall

It is interesting to consider God's strategies for the embracing of dual meaning in relation to Satan's presence in the film. As the saying goes, the devil's greatest strength is that people don't believe he exists. Satan's method is to remain invisible so that he may go about his work unnoticed, much in keeping with mainstream cinema's desire to hide the processes of its own creation lest we be distracted from the illusionist spectacle it presents. God's way, that of dual meaning, is more in line with what is sorely needed in the cinema. It needs to move away from invisibility and toward a cinema that does justice to its dual nature, embracing the potential for multiple meanings to be created through the combination of sound with image.

Satan's role of deceiver is most clearly illustrated in the narrative when he appears as a young girl to lead Christ down from the cross and into the space and time of the last temptation. As Magdalene is bathed in light before she is taken, we hear the return of the eagle cry, harkening back to the time when Christ was caught in a separation from God just as he is again here. However, a subtler indication that all is not quite what it should be within the last temptation comes after Magdalene's death. Jesus runs outside with his ax and begins pummeling the ground in frustration that his wife has been taken from him. The sound of each blow reverberates in a manner inconsistent with the wooded outdoor environment in which he finds himself. This is partly a simple punctuation technique to emphasize the power of his anger. Yet this could also be a suggestion of the hollowness of the world he inhabits, the way that pounding on the thin wall of a film set might reverberate through the large space of the soundstage on which it is built. The discordant sound of the ax blows is a classic example of the kind of displacement of spatial signature that Schafer suggests is at the heart of schizophonia. Interestingly, this example falls in the midst of Christ's journey into the altered time frame of his last temptation. As suggested, such an existence outside of the normal flow of time is also a product of schizophonia, and it is certainly related to Christ's ongoing struggle with his separation from God.

It is in the treatment of Satan's voice in the film, however, that he is revealed as an apparently singular being that, upon closer inspection, is found to be in constant separation from himself. He is first called by name in the desert, appearing as a flame and with a voice that has a distinctly different spatial signature than the other voices Jesus speaks with. Its level of reverberation suggests a displacement indicating a potential spatial/temporal disjunction. This abnormal level of reverb turns into an almost complete separation from itself, becoming multiple voices at different pitches yet speaking in unison. This vocal separation effect is finally most pronounced at the end of the last-temptation sequence. Jesus, lying on his deathbed after a long and comfortable life, is confronted by Judas about his succumbing to the pleasures of the flesh. Realizing what has happened, Jesus starts crawling outside to speak with God. Here, as Satan tells Jesus that he must "die like a man," the separation in Satan's voice is more pronounced than before, clearly revealing a multilayering indicative of his true identity.

This multivoicedness is a clever but telling inversion of God's use of multiple meanings. Satan is double-voiced but does not offer double meanings. He does not seek to illustrate duality in the world so that it can be embraced. Rather, he seeks to offer the illusion of comfort to human beings so that he may betray them. God's way is more painful, filled with uncertainty but also with productive struggle.

Shadow of the Cross

In conversation with Judas, Jesus says, "All my life I've been followed—by voices, by footsteps, by shadows. And do you know what the shadow is? The cross." In saying this, Jesus acknowledges his reconciliation of the shadow of the cross with the source of this shadow. It is significant that he does this with reference to acousmatic sound. Voices and footsteps of unknown origin are now understood to be those of God. To this he adds the notion of shadow, which is the absence of light, the indexical marker of a visible object. Just as a sound must have a source, so, too, must a shadow. In many ways, sound in film is like the shadow of the image. Here Jesus finally understands that it is on the cross that the shadow will give way to the light, a reconciliation of source and representation. Christ's journey, then, can truly be understood through the metaphor of the de-acousmatization of sound, the revelation of the sources of unidentified auditory stimuli.

Now Jesus seems to openly acknowledge an understanding of the relationship between the seen and the heard in the context of transsensoriality. By effectively drawing a metaphor between shadow and acousmatic sound, Christ seems to be offering a way of understanding their relationship on equal terms. The form of the cross that caps off this metaphor can be understood as the final and most perfect metaphor of them all: a single shape made up of two distinct elements. Taken on their own, these elements would reduce the cross to the meaninglessness of two simple lines. Together, joined at precisely the point at which they are, these two lines become one of the most powerful indicators of meaning in the world (different though the meaning may be from one person to the next). The cross is a wonderful metaphor for sound/image relationships in the cinema: two elements with a secure point of connection that allows much branching out beyond the confines of this point. This is the ultimate lesson of Kazantzakis's Christ: acknowledge the points of unity between flesh and spirit while understanding the form that takes shape around their separation.

Finally, in this very conversation with Judas, Jesus concludes that he must die, and that to do so Judas must betray him. Judas is unwilling, and this is one of the most interesting elements of the reinterpretation of Christ's journey by Kazantzakis. Revising Judas' role in relation to Jesus is an excellent metaphor for revising our understanding of the role of sound in film. Judas once said to Jesus: "I struggle, you collaborate." What Kazantzakis wants to illustrate is that both of these are one and the same thing, that a struggle is a collaboration. Few would argue that sound and image are collaborators in the cinema. What needs to be exposed is that this collaboration is more of a struggle than is usually acknowledged. In a vision-oriented society, it is only natural that cinema has evolved as a predominantly image-oriented medium. However, sound is here to stay, and few would argue that the great potential for sound to rise to equal status with the image is a long way from being achieved. Sound must be reimagined as a collaborator with image through struggle, an exposition of tension between the elements that can yield a harmony impossible if sound is always to remain little more than support for the seen. The purpose of Kazantzakis's Christ is to illuminate the dual nature of all things and to show that when this dual nature is embraced, a more holistic existence can be achieved. Much of Christ's struggle is represented through the use of sound by both Kazantzakis and Scorsese. Because of this, *The Last Temptation of Christ* provides us a great place to indulge in pondering relationships between sound and image in the cinema. It becomes a place to stimulate my hope for a time when all of cinema truly offers the best of its two fundamental worlds.

Notes

1. Phillip Lopate, "Fourteen Koans by a Levite on Scorsese's *The Last Temptation of Christ*," in Lopate, *Totally, Tenderly, Tragically* (New York: Doubleday Anchor, 1998), 123–37.

2. Nikos Kazantzakis, *The Last Temptation of Christ*, trans. Peter Bien (New York: Simon & Schuster, 1960), 1.

3. Ibid., 2.

4. Michel Chion, *Audio-Vision: Sound on Screen*, trans. Claudia Gorbman (New York: Columbia University Press, 1994).

5. R. Murray Schafer, *The Tuning of the World* (Toronto: McLelland & Stewart, 1977), 90.

6. Chion, *Audio-Vision*, 71.

7. Ibid., 85.

8. Tom Gunning, "Doing for the Eye What the Phonograph Does for the Ear," in *The Sounds of Early Cinema*, ed. Richard Abel and Rick Altman (Bloomington: Indiana University Press, 2001).

9. Chion, *Audio-Vision*, 137.

10. Schafer, *Tuning of the World*, 90.

11. Ibid., 91.

12. Frederic Jameson, *Postmodernism, or, The Cultural Logic of Late Capitalism* (Durham, NC: Duke University Press, 1991), 27.

13. Kazantzakis, *Last Temptation*, 3.

14. Gunning, "Doing for the Eye," 16.

15. Rick Altman, "The Material Heterogeneity of Recorded Sound," in *Sound Theory, Sound Practice*, ed. Rick Altman (New York: Routledge, 1992), 19.

16. James Lastra, *Sound Technology and the American Cinema* (New York: Columbia University Press, 2001), 125.

17. Altman, "Material Heterogeneity," 24.

18. Ibid.

19. Chion, *Audio-Vision*, 137.

20. Ibid., 136.

21. Frank Paine, "Sound Mixing in *Apocalypse Now*: An Interview with Walter Murch," in *Film Sound: Theory and Practice*, ed. Elizabeth Weis and John Belton (New York: Columbia University Press, 1985), 356.

22. Chion, *Audio-Vision*, 85.

CHAPTER 17

Identity and Ethnicity in Peter Gabriel's Sound Track for *The Last Temptation of Christ*

Eftychia Papanikolaou

Introduction

Music aesthetics assiduously wrestle with questions regarding the nature and content of music: Is music an autonomous art, or is it capable of bearing or even constructing meaning? Centuries of philosophical thinking had situated the content of music in its capacity to generate meaning. At least until the end of the eighteenth century, writers of aesthetics privileged emotion and expression as music's primary aesthetic category. In his *Les beaux-arts réduits à un même principe* (Paris, 1746), one of the first systematic explorations into the categorization of fine arts, Charles Batteux (1713–80) identified music and dance as arts that "must have a meaning and a sense." In particular, he asserted that "musical sounds and dance steps have meaning, just as words have meaning in poetry; expression in music and the dance then must have natural qualities similar to those of eloquence in speech."[1] And at the end of the eighteenth century, Johann Georg Sulzer (1720–79) unequivocally endowed music with meaning: "The principal, if not indeed the sole function of a perfect musical composition is the accurate expression of emotions and passions in all their varying and individual nuances."[2]

In a critical reversal, the nineteenth century saw the most famous pronouncement of musical formalism. In his *Vom Musikalisch-Schönen* (Vienna, 1854), music critic Eduard Hanslick famously claimed that music is not capable of representing specific emotions and that its content is "tonally moving forms [*tönend bewegte Formen*]."[3] Thus he located music's content in its theoretically and scientifically oriented properties. Hanslick's aesthetics would have immense impact on the way theorists and composers responded to the controversy surrounding absolute versus program music in the middle of the nineteenth century, and vast implications for the music of the twentieth century.

If any genre of music has been able to shed any intimation of music's status as an autonomous art, that is certainly film music.[4] In her pioneering work on film music, Claudia Gorbman has emphasized—in her categorization of the seven "principles of composition, mixing, and editing" that underlie film music—the importance of music as a "signifier of emotion." According to Gorbman, "Soundtrack music may set specific moods and emphasize particular emotions suggested in the narrative, but first and foremost, it is a signifier of emotion itself."[5] Numerous recent studies concur on that issue and have come to further illustrate Gorbman's early assertion that music signification does not depend on abstract codes. On the contrary, "music signifies in films not only according to pure musical codes, but also according to *cultural* musical codes."[6] It is the latter category that will enable us to "read" the music for Martin Scorsese's *The Last Temptation of Christ* not only as sound that parallels the film's narrative. It also presents a musical hybrid that defies clear representation of ethnicity through its constant negation of specific "cultural musical codes." Traditional Hollywood film scores tend to "render the individual an untroublesome viewing subject: less critical, less 'awake.'"[7] But Peter Gabriel's sound track for *The Last Temptation of Christ* is not subordinate to the narrative. It is not used in order to create a mood or heighten emotions or provide continuity or promote a passive response from the perceiver.[8] On the contrary, the musical discourse demands the perceiver's constant attention as it fluidly crosses ethnic lines and musical borders.[9] Like Kazantzakis's novelistic and Scorsese's filmic narratives, the music for *The Last Temptation of Christ* does not attempt to reproduce meanings and ideologies but instead attempts to create new ones.

Sending Gabriel

Peter Gabriel may initially seem to be an unlikely choice for the creation of a sound track for a film based on the story of Jesus. But for those who have followed the artist's career beyond his groundbreaking collaboration with the rock group *Genesis* and his remarkable work as a solo artist through the early part of the 1980s, Gabriel was actually the perfect candidate. By that time, he had already started experimenting with new aesthetic approaches through electronic media by mixing recordings of music he had collected from around the world with electronic sounds. As his interest in the world's music heightened, Gabriel started writing pieces that included exotic elements, incorporating sounds, techniques, structures, and even instruments characteristic of non-Western music. The result of those revolutionary ideas is partially seen in his 1982 album *Peter Gabriel [IV]*, in which rhythms, drones, and chants from Africa, Bali, and Australian aborigines are fused with electronic sounds to create, at times, a hypnotic, mysterious, even otherworldly effect. The same year, which also saw the creation of WOMAD (World of Music, Arts and Dance), Gabriel prophesied that "an important influence on music over the next few years will be ethnic in origin and I can hear it being combined with electronics and a more expressive, emotive use of the synthesizer."[10] The eruption of interest in ethnic music during the 1990s proved Gabriel's claim to be true. His own idiosyncratic fusion of electronic and world music pioneered an entire new field of music composition. It was only natural that Scorsese would recruit Gabriel early on to write the sound track for *The Last Temptation of Christ*. *Passion*, as the sound-track album was renamed, came out in 1988; it received an Oscar nomination for best original score, and two years later won a Grammy for best New Age recording.

Music, Identity, Ethnicity

To lay the groundwork for the sound track, Gabriel started by searching the National Sound Archive: Pakistan, Morocco, Senegal, Egypt, Turkey, and India are only a few of the countries whose unique musical idioms are represented by indigenous in-strumentalists and vocalists on the sound track's recordings. In addition, he recruited and worked with musicians from around the world. Says Gabriel about this collaboration:

> We recorded some of the finest singers and soloists in the field of world music and set the score on a backdrop of traditional North African rhythms and sounds. It was a wonderful experience working with such different and idiosyncratic musicians. . . . For many of them working with this material was something quite new and they were very enthusiastic. The soundtrack is full of the spirit of their performances.[11]

Passion Sources, a CD with additional original recordings not included in the sound track, came out the following year.[12] Unlike the film's controversial reception, Gabriel's sound track became an immediate success. Today it is considered to be a pioneering work of eclecticism, versatility, and diversity, a model of the harmonious fusion that may be achieved through two apparently contradictory elements of sound: electronic and natural.

In the long tradition of music specifically written for biblical stories on film, composers have summarily favored music that underscored the epic nature of those films. Composers such as Miklos Rozsa (*Ben-Hur*, *The King of Kings*), Alfred Newman (*The Greatest Story Ever Told*), and Maurice Jarre (*Jesus of Nazareth*) were largely responsible for creating music that eschewed ethnicity identifiers in favor of sweep-ing epic sounds that rivaled the majestic images shown on the screen. Such music allowed the perceiver of those films to bring external experiences to them, since the combination of sounds and images presented aural and cultural signifiers (the per-ceiver is used to identifying the fanfare-like passages with the Romans, for example, and string-based symphonic music with biblical epics). In other words, traditional Hollywood musical practices aimed to satisfy the audience's expectations, through a fixed and tightly controlled—and controlling—system of musical significations. During the 1980s and 1990s, under "the changing pressures of identity formations such as race, ethnicity, sexuality, and gender,"[13] the role of film music came into question. Gabriel's sound track constitutes a comprehensive response to those new challenges within a filmic genre that is loaded with traditions and clichés.

Using their directorial authority as auteurs, filmmakers essentially set the tone by which a film is going to unfold. *The Last Temptation of Christ* is generally categorized as a Jesus-film, but its structure and modes of narrative set it apart from other films that earlier dealt with the story of Jesus. The trepidation directors experience when taking on a story that has seen numerous cinematic incarnations only amplifies the struggle to avoid familiar depictions of Jesus on film.[14] For his part, Scorsese did not set out to be an exegete of the Jesus story—a common approach by filmmakers who adhere to Hollywood's traditional standards. He admitted that films such as *The King of Kings* and *The Greatest Story Ever Told* contained an "antiseptic quality, . . . a hermetically sealed holiness that didn't teach us anything new about Jesus."[15] Adhering to what Lloyd Baugh calls an "academic approach," Scorsese demonstrated his knowledge of the tradition and a conscious desire to break with it on several levels. In Kazantzakis's novel, Scorsese found the perfect vehicle to help fight decades of misconceptions and clichés: "I wanted to use Kazantzakis's concepts to tear away at all those old Hollywood films . . . and create a Jesus you could maybe talk to, question, get to know."[16] The Jesus of history, therefore, became Scorsese's focus, not the Christ of faith.

Composers have also been presented with similar challenges regarding whether or not to "duplicate" familiar sounds associated with past portrayals of Jesus on film. Following Scorsese's lead, Gabriel also broke with traditional constructions of the story of Jesus on film. The film's nondiegetic music employs the agency of modern pop sounds to ground the narrative in the everyday. By combining original recordings with rock musical elements (such as synthesizers and electric guitars), Scorsese and Gabriel help reinforce the diachronic element of the story. At times it may be tempting to indulge in the soothing sounds and repetitive rhythmic patterns and to exalt the entire aural palette as a fine essay in exoticism—or, alas, New Age sensibility.[17] Yet Gabriel aurally synthesizes an aesthetic that, from Kazantzakis's iconoclastic narrative to Scorsese's nonconformist interpretation, has the earmarks of stunning originality. The result is a film that both visually and aurally departs from the norm that Hollywood movies have established and offers a sophisticated alternative. Sonic landscapes from the Middle East and Africa are not juxtaposed but fused with the visual narrative.

Naturally, skeptics and purists often voiced their dissatisfaction with some of the choices for the film's music. The presence of indigenous and other landmark recordings, especially those featured in *Passion Sources*, do not even come close to doing justice to the uncharted waters that both Scorsese and Gabriel were testing in the 1980s. Because of the changed role of Hollywood moviemaking, Scorsese and Gabriel were able to consider and work under a different set of race and ethnicity identifiers. Visually and aurally, *The Last Temptation of Christ* was new.

In order for the film to emphasize the historical aspect of Jesus' life, the music should be able to signify ethnicity beyond the perceiver's auditory experiences.

Signifying the "exotic" in music has traditionally involved a standardized musical vocabulary of ethnic sounds: a gong to evoke Chinese music or nontraditional musical scales to create a non-Western ambience. Interestingly enough, the music of the "other" has always been seen through the lens of the dominant culture that tries to use it as an ethnicity marker. As film composer Jerry Goldsmith has remarked, "What is ethnic is what Hollywood has made ethnic. . . . [It is] ethnic-Oriental."[18] By largely avoiding music that signifies ethnicity in favor of a uniform symphonic sound, traditional Jesus-films reinforce a dominant culture that allows for no juxtaposition with the "other." Ultimately, such stereotypical musical features, in essence, say more about the culture that exploits them and less about the culture they ostensibly signify.

On the surface, Gabriel's nondiegetic background music seems to serve as a typical auditory invocation to supplement the visual representation of a biblical landscape. In a memorable opening, and while the now-famous excerpt from Kazantzakis's prologue to the novel appears on the screen, the first nondiegetic sound is heard. It is a synthesizer's eerie ostinato, which will serve as a repeated drone throughout the film. Together with the melody of a wailing duduk, introduced as the film's credits appear, the two sounds dominate the aural landscape of the film from the start. With the appearance of the film's title on the screen, the addition of drumming and electric guitar make the music seem charged. Propulsive rhythms rush the perceiver through the image of an olive grove, only to find Jesus on the ground (in an overhead shot commonly found in Scorsese's films). Jesus' face, wrought with anguish, is as unconventional as the music that has introduced us to the first scene, music using a wide array of electronically manipulated percussive sounds and producing novel rhythmic and aural effects.

On the other end of the aural spectrum stands the solo duduk, a type of double-reed aerophone and an inherently melodious instrument. It occasionally sounds oblivious to the background ostinato, while at times it participates in a musical interplay that evokes emotions of sadness, a common attribute of the sound of the Armenian duduk. Ironically, the duduk's "velvety and deeply evocative sound . . . has become strongly associated with notions of national identity, for many Armenians,"[19] associations probably not lost on the perceiver of this film. As Andy Nercessian has pointed out, solo duduk songs primarily include sad songs; because of the instrument's "melancholy" sound, "funerals are much more the perceived home of the duduk than are weddings."[20] An inquiry into what constitutes sad or happy music, as constructions of culture-specific signifiers, requires a lengthier study. Suffice it to say that nondiegetic duduks draw several scenes together by recurring in an almost leitmotivic fashion. Duduks will accompany Jesus in his encounter with Judas the night before his baptism, when he heals the lepers, during the mourning scene for Lazarus's death, and in a most memorable manner toward the film's ending, in the scene with Mary Magdalene.

By borrowing music from other cultures, Gabriel has the courage to focus musically on the "other." The film's diegetic music (music whose source is implied by either script or action) avoids ethnic signification at all times, in spite of the perceiver's natural tendency to construct such meanings (the sound of the duduk may be one such obvious example of a musical instrument's unequivocal ethnic signification). During the wedding at Cana, diegetic music of ambiguous origin floods the scene. In spite of the fact that the perceiver is aware of the scene's culture-specific implications—after all, this is a Jewish wedding—the music does not act as a mediator of that tradition. In fact, from the chanting to the wedding's dance music (with Jesus himself participating in the dancing), the diegetic music is of Arabic—specifically Moroccan—origin, recorded on location during the filming in Morocco. (The percussion was a studio addition.)

Answering Gabriel's Critics

Many critics have frowned upon the use of music that so blatantly mixes racial, ethnic, and cultural borders. To be sure, both the background and source music utilized in the film make no pretensions to authenticity: Gabriel manipulates original recordings in his studio and makes noncontextual use of music with corresponding scenes. Scorsese and Gabriel are not concerned with ethnomusicological accuracy, which probably would have produced *authentic* music, in the strictest sense of the word, of distinctly biblical or Jewish origin. Actually, such music is virtually (and conspicuously) absent from the entire sound track. When Jesus is seen approaching Magdalene's house in the beginning of the film, diegetic noises from the open market mix with chanting and instrumental sounds of an Arabic, probably Egyptian, song. The music that accompanies the raising of Lazarus uses a traditional melody from Kurdistan. African rhythms are incorporated and amplified throughout the sound track. At the monastery scene, the singing is done by pearl divers from Bahrain.[21] And finally, Qawwali singer Nusrat Fateh Ali Khan from Pakistan lends his wailing voice during "Road to Golgotha," a scene remarkable in its slow-motion cinematography and total absence of any diegetic sound.

The combination of diegetic silence and nondiegetic music of the Sufi tradition, in which Qawwali songs carry the most powerful messages of a Sufi's spiritual and mystical union with God, puts emphasis on the aural dimension of the scene. In her exemplary study of Sufi music, Regula Qureshi observes that it is actually "through the act of listening—*sama'*—[that] the Sufi seeks to activate his link with his living spiritual guide, with saints departed, and ultimately with God."[22] Much like a true Sufi spiritual leader (a *sheikh*), Khan with his song epitomizes one of the main functions of Qawwali: to "present in song a vast treasure of poems which articulate and evoke the gamut of mystical experience for the spiritual benefit of their audience."[23] Consequently, the spirituality of the visual narrative is encapsulated in the aural component of the scene. As in a Sufi assembly, the Qawwali song acts as a mediator of a powerful spiritual experience by diminishing the perceiver's awareness of the film's surrounding world, in defiance of the *inauthentic* use of the music for that particular scene. But as Richard Taruskin reminds us, the "drive toward authenticity" has often been viewed as "a function of modernism."[24] In our postmodern world, where fragmentation is valued over unity, a mosaic may prove to be more stunning than the most perfectly executed painting.

Criticized the most for its inclusion in the film, however, is the music that accompanies the scene of the Last Supper. Among others, Lloyd Baugh has disparaged Gabriel's choice to have Senegalese singer Baaba Maal intone the Muslim "Call to Prayer" during Jesus' institution of the Eucharist. He considers it to be "totally inappropriate, if not downright offensive and blasphemous, both to Christians and Muslims."[25] Baugh, who made it his mission to uncover all the "theological misunderstandings and errors" in Scorsese's film, is quick to point out that Maal's is not the traditional "Call to Prayer" but rather "a song in Arabic based on the Islamic profession of faith or creed."[26] To be sure, all the major components of the Islamic creed are there: "God is great. I testify that there is no god but God [Allah]. I testify that Muḥammad is the prophet of God. Come to prayer. Come to salvation."[27] Baaba Maal's rendition musically adheres to Muslim traditional performance practice: like a *muezzin*'s (*mu'adhdhin*'s) call, it is highly melismatic, virtuosic, and complex, as required by the occasion.[28]

If this were an isolated occurrence of ethnic crossing in the film, an anomaly, then Baugh's severe objection would sustain. It constitutes one more instance, however, in which Gabriel underscores the hybridity of the aural landscape. The various cultures, religions, and ethnicities represented on the film's sound track form an analogue to the novel and the film's multiethnically oriented narrative. Kazantzakis relates the story of Jesus via a predominantly Greek locale and aesthetic, and Scorsese punctuates it cinematically with his own Italian-American sensitivities (the latter unequivocally corroborated by the director himself).[29] The result is a film that differs from the traditional cinematic models of Jesus, and its novelty operates on many levels. Both Kazantzakis and Scorsese offer an iconoclastic view of the Bible. The former does so through his deeply spiritual interpretation of the life of Jesus, whereby the human and the divine clash. Scorsese does so through a cinematic lens that highlights Jesus' humanity with unforeseen and almost unsettling honesty. Consequently, the music also becomes an agent of changes of traditional constructions. Gabriel marshaled music of diverse cultural, religious, and ethnic backgrounds to punctuate the film's separation from conventional clichés. The sound track's lack of any particular cultural identification possibly offers the ideal solution to Hollywood stereotypes and to a story whose appeal transcends boundaries.[30] It is precisely this lack of emotional (or other) identification with the perceiver that makes the narrative's many layers work. The at-times uneasy coexistence of Christianity, Judaism, and Islam is only a testimony to our complex cultural present.

Music as a Third Voice

Ultimately, the music here becomes a third voice that acts as a bridge between Kazantzakis and Scorsese. It not only comments on the drama; it also acts as an interpretive voice. One way that the music becomes an agent of synthesis between the book and the film may be found in the film's final scenes. Often referred to as a "dream sequence," these final thirty minutes of the film problematize the narrative on several levels. Scorsese and Paul Schrader, the film's scriptwriter, made several changes to Kazantzakis's novelistic narrative, chief among them the change of the image of devil from that of a "Negro boy" to that of a blond girl, obviously "to escape charges of prejudice," as Schrader related to Peter Bien.[31] Magdalene's death is also not shown in the film but rather only reported. And most important, the intense vacillation in the novel between images of dream and reality is lost on the viewer. For instance, the novel's guardian angel affirms that Jesus "lived [his] entire Passion in a dream" and he now promises a life full of earthly pleasures.[32] The ambiguous nature of Jesus' earthly existence is constantly punctuated by dream allusions in the novel's final pages. "Life has become a dream," Jesus declares, and wonders, "Can this be the meaning of Paradise?"[33] When Mary has a "horrible dream" that "all this is a dream," she is afraid that the reality she is living with Jesus is otherwise only constructed within a dream.[34] Scorsese manages to highlight this *other* reality by using the cinematic technique of the dream sequence. He wants us to believe that this *is* the dream, unlike what the angel claims.

Up until that point the entire film reads as a cinematic analogue to Jesus' response to "the divine lure or Cry forward," that vital element that in Darren Middleton's interpretation is crucial for the evolution of Jesus into the "Son of God."[35] The raw cinematography and unconventional approach to music in the first two hours of the film resonate with the struggle inherent in the gradual transformation of "matter into spirit." The angel's promised land, however, looks and sounds different. Green vistas predominate over the previously barren biblical landscape. The amalgamated sounds of indigenous music from before have given their place to a sole synthesizer, a sound rather alien to the rest of the film. After Magdalene's death, Jesus visits Lazarus's sisters, Mary and Martha. The sound of the synthesizer, reminiscent of an organ, evokes church music of the chorale style. The music intensifies as Jesus and Mary embrace, and it conveniently helps us transition into the next scene, where two children are seen playing while an old Jesus converses with the angel.

The entire scene projects intense isolation on two levels. Visually, the scene is isolated within a dream sequence. Aurally, it evokes a musical topos that is frozen in time. The filmic narrative has appropriated a specific historical musical style whose aesthetic values are readily identifiable to the perceiver. (Chorale-like music provides unmistakable identification markers to modern-day listeners, unlike the indigenous, multiethnic musical approach from the rest of the film.) It is almost ironic that the dream sequence, which contains the most controversial part of Kazantzakis's novel, is the only part of the film cinematically comparable to Hollywood's images of Jesus and that it is accompanied with the only nondiegetic music in the entire film that comes close to the religious music commonly used in traditional Jesus films. This new, idealized world that Jesus encounters looks and sounds peaceful, with promptly recognizable sounds.[36] The tragic irony lies in the fact that we know this to be the world that the devil has created. One might even be tempted to equate the devil with the very image of Hollywood and everything it represents. In this case, the dream sequence acts as a self-referential artwork, whose meaning lies in the critique of the very image it attempts to represent. Scorsese and Gabriel play on our memories and ability as perceivers to take in these scenes of undeniably prosaic nature and identify them with Hollywood.[37]

Only Jesus' encounter with Magdalene during the dream sequence eludes this process. Scorsese again slightly alters the scene with Magdalene and Jesus. In the novel, their intimate encounter is short, passionate, but for the most part symbolically described. The film's added elements, however, do not betray the spirit of the original source: Magdalene's image as a bride, cleaning the blood from Jesus' wounds in a slow, almost ritualistic manner, is followed by an equally ceremonial lovemaking scene. The sound of the solo duduk accompanies this entire scene, an aural allusion to the *dream*—according to the novel's angel—of Jesus' past life. Actually, this is the only instance in the entire dream sequence in which nondiegetic music that had been previously associated with Jesus' real life appears again. Otherwise, from Jesus' descent from the cross to his entrance to the world of the earth to his future encounter with Martha and Mary, the sound world of the film has changed to accommodate the visual transformation. The crisis in the narrative is objectified in the images, with music providing a counterpoint to that disruption.

Conclusion

The burden of this essay has been to clarify several misconceptions surrounding the sound track and the choices of diegetic music for *The Last Temptation of Christ*. Peter Gabriel's nondiegetic score demands the perceivers' visceral reaction, and the film's diegetic music challenges the audience's perception of the very role of music in film. Indeed, the term "music score" in this case may itself be a misnomer. Kassabian has insightfully remarked on the ambiguity of the term: "Many Western musicians think of a piece of music not in terms of musical sounds but in terms of a musical *score*."[38] By recording music sessions with local musicians in Morocco and electronically manipulating music that exists only as an orally transmitted sound, Gabriel goes against the norm, not only by experimenting with different ways to produce film music, but also by questioning the very nature of what film music is. The music resonates with the novel and film's emphasis on the struggle both of the psyche and of the worlds and cultures that collide within.

Art as a medium has the power to manipulate or persuade the perceiver of an underlying ideology. If any one such ideology exists in the film, I trust that all the previous chapters in this commemorative volume have already unraveled it. The music for the film, however implicitly, imparts an aura of signification that encodes the cinematic discourse with meanings that may or may not be immediately understood by the perceiver—and therein lies the challenge. As we recently became aware once again, cinematic narrations of the life of Jesus will perpetually be entangled in a web of controversy. If the music for *The Last Temptation of Christ* can prove anything, beyond the music's inherent emotional power to signify, it may be that where texts and images tend to divide, music's communicative abilities help to unify.

Notes

1. Peter Le Huray and James Day, eds., *Music and Aesthetics in the Eighteenth and Early-Nineteenth Centuries* (Cambridge: Cambridge University Press, 1988), 39, 41.

2. Ibid., 99; in Johann Georg Sulzer, *Allgemeine Theorie der schönen Künste* (1771; 2nd ed., Leipzig, 1792–94).

3. Eduard Hanslick, *On the Musically Beautiful: A Contribution towards the Revision of the Aesthetics of Music*, trans. and ed. Geoffrey Payzant (Indianapolis: Hackett, 1986), 29.

4. On the other hand, Hanns Eisler and Theodor Adorno's *Composing for the Films* (New York: Oxford University Press, 1947), represents good examples of how nineteenth-century ideologies persevered in the world of music aesthetics in the twentieth century. Both Eisler and Adorno, (*Composing for the Films*, new ed. [London: Athlone, 1994]), viewed music as nonrepresentational and nonreferential. Their music aesthetics had a different point of departure, but they continued not to recognize in film music the existence of meaning. For a brief discussion, see Anahid Kassabian, *Hearing Film: Tracking Identifications in Contemporary Hollywood Film Music* (New York: Routledge, 2001), 37–39.

5. Claudia Gorbman, *Unheard Melodies: Narrative Film Music* (Bloomington: Indiana University Press, 1987), 72.

6. Ibid., 2–3.

7. Ibid., 5.

8. See ibid., 72. The allusion is to traditional Hollywood clichés, as partially outlined in Gorbman's model of principles of composing film music.

9. Some film scholars have used the term "perceiver" in an attempt to fuse the visual and aural aspects of a film. In this essay I embrace Kassabian's preference for this term and use it in place of "viewer" or "listener" because "it does not privilege one sense over others, and because it is slightly more active in tone than 'spectator' or 'auditor.'" See Kassabian, *Hearing Film*, 173n1.

10. Chris Welch, *The Secret Life of Peter Gabriel* (London: Omnibus, 1998), 140. Gabriel has admitted to having enormous respect for musicians from other cultures. In cases of collaboration, their non-Western practices and sensibilities fill in the spaces Gabriel creates with unexpected results. Gabriel's advocacy of world musics and continuing humanitarian efforts have been aptly documented.

11. Ibid., 154; see also Gabriel's commentary in the liner notes for the reissue of *Passion* (Geffen Records, USA; 069 493 273-2, 2002).

12. Quite serendipitously, this became the first album of world music released on Gabriel's Real World label (01704-62301-2-4, 1989), which has since given numerous musicians from around the world the opportunity to record and promote their music.

13. Kassabian, *Hearing Film*, 4.

14. W. Barnes Tatum points out this problem in relation to a reviewer's negative comments for the familiar images of Jesus in DeMille's *The King of Kings* (1927) in the introduction to his *Jesus at the Movies: A Guide to the First Hundred Years* (Santa Rosa, CA: Polebridge, 1997), 7.

15. Martin Scorsese, *Scorsese on Scorsese*, ed. David Thompson and Ian Christie (1989; London: Faber & Faber, 1996), 133.

16. David Ehrenstein, *The Scorsese Picture* (New York: Carol Publications, 1992), 109.

17. Apparently, the sound track's progressive rock and fusion elements made it hard to categorize when nominated for a Grammy. Ironically, *Passion* was awarded a Grammy in the New Age music category, another marker of distortion in our complex musical culture. The sound track testifies to Gabriel's diverse musical interests but also abundant talent that defies classification.

18. Kassabian, *Hearing Film*, 58.

19. Andy Nercessian, *The Duduk and National Identity in Armenia* (Lanham, MD: Scarecrow, 2001), 3.

20. Ibid., 56–57.

21. Mary Pat Kelly, *Martin Scorsese: A Journey* (1991; New York: Thunder's Mouth, 1996), 233.

22. Regula Burckhardt Qureshi, *Sufi Music of India and Pakistan: Sounds, Context and Meaning in Qawwali* (Cambridge: Cambridge University Press, 1986), 1.

23. Ibid.

24. Richard Taruskin, "The Pastness of the Present," in *Authenticity and Early Music*, ed. Nicholas Kenyon (London: Oxford University Press, 1988). Cited in Caryl Flinn, *Strains of Utopia: Gender, Nostalgia, and Hollywood Film Music* (Princeton, NJ: Princeton University Press, 1992), 23.

25. Lloyd Baugh, *Imaging the Divine: Jesus and Christ-Figures in Film* (Kansas City, MO: Sheed & Ward, 1997), 59. In a similar vein, the 1996 film *The English Patient* by Anthony Minghella was rereleased in the United Arab Emirates after its initial ban, only after "five scenes had been cut, one of which featured Almásy and Katharine making love against the backdrop of 'the sound of the Muslim call to prayer.'" Cited in Heather Laing, *Gabriel Yared's "The English Patient": A Film Score Guide* (Lanham, MD: Scarecrow, 2004), 176n101.

26. Baugh, *Imaging the Divine*, 60.

27. Original and translation in Scott Marcus, "The Muslim Call to Prayer," in *The Garland Encyclopedia of World Music*, vol. 6, *The Middle East*, ed. Virginia Danielson, Scott Marcus, and Dwight Reynolds (New York: Routledge, 2000), 153.

28. Moreover, while the "text of the call is fixed, . . . the melodic component [of the prayer] is left to the individual caller." Maal's call does not follow any of the three normative melodic modes singled out by Marcus (ibid., 154).

29. Lawrence S. Friedman, *The Cinema of Martin Scorsese* (New York: Continuum, 1998), 152ff.

30. Andrew Killick, for example, makes a case of the use of "illicit anti-Semitic stereotypes . . . buried in popular film music." Although his essay deals specifically with films whose themes contribute to a particular aural identification with Jewish music, his analysis helps us realize how wise Scorsese and Gabriel were to steer away from any such possible identity markers. See Andrew P. Killick, "Music as Ethnic Marker in Film: The 'Jewish' Case," in *Soundtrack Available: Essays on Film and Popular Music*, ed. Pamela Robertson Wojcik and Arthur Knight (Durham, NC: Duke University Press, 2001), 185–201.

31. Peter Bien, "Nikos Kazantzakis's Novels on Film," *Journal of Modern Greek Studies* 18 (2000): 169n5.

32. Nikos Kazantzakis, *The Last Temptation of Christ*, trans. Peter Bien (New York: Simon & Schuster, 1960), 446.

33. Ibid., 458.

34. Ibid., 467–68. Jesus is asked to placate the irate Mary, and he himself wonders about the reality of his life.

35. Darren J. N. Middleton, *Novel Theology: Nikos Kazantzakis's Encounter with Whiteheadian Process Theism* (Macon, GA: Mercer University Press, 2000), 73.

36. Peter Gabriel described his desire to extend this dichotomy to include the angel/devil image. He explained how he and Scorsese "tried using [a piece with a boys' choir] for the scene when the angel/devil takes Jesus off the cross. It was the only religious music in the entire film. I liked it—I loved it, in fact—and I was disappointed that Marty didn't want to use it. It would have been the only time we used traditional church music. The devil's music, if you like, would have been religious. There would have been that paradox." I believe that the evocation of religious music through the sound of the synthesizer achieves the same effect, nonetheless. Kelly, *Journey*, 235. In the same vein, Paul Schrader concurs that "Scorsese's point in choosing a sweet blond girl [instead of a Negro boy] was that the devil ought to be the very image of an innocent angel" (Bien, "Kazantzakis's Novels on Film," 169n5). The paradox doubles: the devil is masked in visual innocence *and* musically religious aura.

37. As Gorbman (*Unheard Melodies*, 3) has put it, "Any music bears cultural associations, and most of these associations have been further codified and exploited by the music industry. Properties of instrumentation, rhythm, melody, and harmony form a veritable language." This language is known to the perceiver, and the cultural associations implied work on several levels of memory and identification. It would be almost impossible for the perceiver of this dream sequence not to associate it with classical Hollywood.

38. Peter Winkler argues that Western culture has placed a lot of value on musicianship and has made it synonymous with "musical literacy." As a consequence, "music that does not rely on a notated score for its transmissions tends to be seen as an abnormality." Cited in Kassabian, *Hearing Film*, 21–22.

CHAPTER 18

On Reappreciating Kazantzakis

Martin Scorsese

It was my friend Barbara Hershey who recommended that I read Nikos Kazantza-kis's novel. She mentioned it for the first time in Arkansas, when we were shooting my film *Boxcar Bertha*, and then she brought it up again in Los Angeles. I'll never be able to thank her enough. I took my time reading the book. And as I always do whenever I get excited about a novel, I started to make notes. I realized, quickly, that I wanted to make a film based on *The Last Temptation of Christ*.

I had dreamed of filming the story of Christ in a contemporary setting—down-town New York, to be exact, where I grew up. When I saw Pasolini's *The Gospel according to St. Matthew* (1964), I felt that he had basically made that film fit the present: *Gospel* may have been set during the time of Jesus' life on earth, but it felt com-pletely contemporary, from the casting to the point of view to the music.

When I read the Kazantzakis novel, with its magnificent language and its rest-lessly probing spirit—with that tone, at once so frank and so tender—I felt that I'd found another way of approaching Christ. Not to work from the Gospels, but from a novel that attempted to pinpoint the key conflict of his short life: Where did his humanity end and his divinity begin? Kazantzakis understood something that few have ever understood as keenly in a work of art, be it a novel or a film. He understood that Jesus must have felt as much of an obligation toward his own humanity—an obligation to fulfill his life as a man, in the way we all feel it—as he did toward his divinity.

Jesus is often pictured as serene, somewhat like Siddhartha. In the Pasolini film, he is often angry; the Sermon on the Mount is delivered as a fiery call to arms in that film. But in the Kazantzakis novel, Jesus is no longer just a figure but a uniquely complex character as well—serene at some moments, angry at others. And at all times, conflicted. Perhaps even confused, in the same way that any of us is confused at times about who we are and where we're going. About our intuitions of what we want to do with our lives, which light a spark within us. We don't know where they will lead, we don't fully understand them, but we know that we must fulfill them and see them through to the end. I'm reminded of Stanley Kubrick's comment that when you're making a film, or any work of art, you have to preserve the original spark. That's what life is like, I believe. And it was that way for Jesus, as Kazantzakis so brilliantly imagined it.

I had always thought that if Jesus had returned to walk among us, he would be living with the hookers, the junkies, the bag ladies. He would be trying to set the world aright, one soul at a time. And it's certain that many among us would be laughing at him. Scorning him. We would be upset that someone was calling attention to the misery around us, insisting that we not look away. And he would be suffering.

I found this longing to make a connection between our present and Jesus' present, to make us one with him and make him one with us, in Kazantzakis's novel.

It took many years and a great deal of effort to get my film *The Last Temptation of Christ* made. It's a long story that doesn't bear repeating; most of the details were exhaustively reported at the time. But in the end, despite the difficulties, not only in getting the film made but also in the uproar that followed its release; despite the fact that we were forced to go into production with a small budget and rush through the editing process—despite all those things, I think our film honored the spirit of Kazantzakis's book. Many people accused me of making a film that attacked belief, that attacked faith—just as Kazantzakis himself was accused. As if belief and faith were that flimsy. As if the image of Christ could not withstand interpretation.

If Christ were to walk the earth today, he would be nothing more or nothing less than one of us. He *is* one of us. Whenever you see someone helping a fellow human being who is weaker than he or she, you're seeing his example. Forgiveness and compassion—that is the best we can expect of ourselves, and the best we can expect of others. It was Kazantzakis who helped me to understand that Christ's teachings are eternally, radically new. That was the gift he gave me with *The Last Temptation of Christ*.

WEBLIOGRAPHY

Compiled by Austin S. Lingerfelt

While the editor has made every effort to provide accurate Internet addresses at the time of publication, neither the publisher nor the compiler assumes any responsibility for errors or for changes that occur after publication. The first date in each citation is the date the article was posted, and the second is the date of access.

The Novel (Reviews about or Responses to the Novel)

Derksen, Lorna. "A Response to *The Last Temptation of Christ*." Rev. of *The Last Temptation of Christ*, by Nikos Kazantzakis. *Watershed Online*. Nov. 24, 2003. <http://www.watershedonline.ca/literature/lasttemptation.html>.

"Last Temptation of Christ, The." *BrothersJudd.com*. May 29, 2000. Nov. 24, 2003. <http://www.brothersjudd.com/index.cfm/fuseaction/reviews.detail/book_id/29 2/Last%20Temptat.htm>.

Passatino, Bob, and Gretchen Passatino. "*The Last Temptation of Christ* Denied." *Answers in Action*. Ed. Bob Passatino and Robert Passatino. Nov. 24, 2003. <http://answers.org/issues/last_temptation.html>.

Sermons about the Novel

Loy, Stephen P. "First Sunday in Lent." Mar. 1, 1998. Nov. 24, 2003. <http://www.zianet.com/peacelutheran/Sermon98/Ser0301.htm>.

Rhodes-Wickett, Sharon. "Lenting the Spirit: In Rejection." Apr. 8, 2001. Nov. 24, 2003. <http://www.westwoodumc.org/sermons/2001sermons/s040801.html>.

Shafer, Dr. Byron E. "Tempted in Every Way." Feb. 17, 2002. Nov. 24, 2003. <http://www.rutgerschurch.com/Sermons/sermon021702.html>.

Truemper, David G. "From the Chapel: How Good, Lord, to Be Here!" *Cresset*. Lent 2002. Dec. 2, 2003. <http://www.valpo.edu/cresset/len02chapel.html>.

Walton, Christopher L. "In the Spirit of Jesus."*Philocrites: Commentary on Liberal Religion and Politics*. Apr. 8, 2001. Nov. 24, 2003. <http://www.philocrites.com/sermons/spiritofjesus.html>.

Unique References to the Novel

Caruana, Laurence. "Back to Toronto." *The Journey Thus Far: The Works and Wanderings of Laurence Caruana*. Nov. 24, 2003. <http://www.lcaruana.com/webtext/jourfar/jourfar3.html>.

Edamaruku, Sanal. "P. M. Antony: A Victim of Censorship." Nov. 24, 2003. <http://www.iheu.org/modules/wfsection/article.php?page=1&articleid=204>.

Censorship

Dow, Orrin B. "*The Last Temptation* and the First Freedom." *NCLA Odds and Bookends* 43 (Fall 1963.D231): 9–11. Nov. 24, 2003. <http://www.lib.siu.edu/cni/letter-d2.html>.

The Film (Controversy concerning the Film)

Anker, Roy M. "Lights, Camera, Jesus: Hollywood Looks at Itself in the Mirror of the Messiah." Film. *Christianity Today*. May 22, 2000. Dec. 2, 2003. <http://www.christianitytoday.com/ct/2000/006/4.58.html>.

Bien, Peter. "Scorcese's Spiritual Jesus."*Nikos Kazantzakis Home Page*. 1988. Dec. 2, 2003. <http://www.historical-museum.gr/kazantzakis/bien.html>.

"Can Religion and the Movies Mix?" Film. *BBC News*. Nov. 8, 2002. Dec. 2, 2003. <http://news.bbc.co.uk/1/hi/entertainment/2420305.stm>.

"Chilean Teacher Fired for Showing *The Last Temptation of Christ*." *Catholic World News*. Dec. 2, 2003. <http://www.cwnews.com/news/viewstory.cfm?recnum=6426>.

Ehrenstein, David. "*The Last Temptation of Christ*." Library. *EhrensteinLand.com*. Nov. 28, 2003. <http://www.ehrensteinland.com/htmls/library/last_temptation.html>.

Kelly, Mary Pat. "Catholic Sensibility, American Culture, and Public Life." Paper Presentation. *American Catholics in the Public Square*. June 2–4, 2000. Dec. 2, 2003. <http://www.catholicsinpublicsquare.org/papers/spring2000joint/jointpanel/jointpanel4.htm>. Page 4.

Iannone, Carol. "*The Last Temptation* Reconsidered." *First Things* 60 (Feb. 1996): 50–54. Nov. 28, 2003. <http://www.firstthings.com/ftissues/ft9602/iannone.html>.

International Centre against Censorship and INTERIGHTS. Legal Document That Concerns International Offenses to Religious Beliefs. *INTERIGHTS.* Sep. 14, 1993. Dec. 2, 2003. <http://www.interights.org/pubs/premingeramicus.htm>.

"Jesus Christ! Superstar?" *Electric Elf Test Kitchen.* Dec. 2, 2003. <http://www.eetk.com/jsus.htm>.

Larson, Scott. "Putting Words in Jesus' Mouth."*Scott's Movie Comments.* June 21, 2001. Dec. 2, 2003. <http://www.scottsmovies.com/comments/c010621.html>.

"*Last Temptation of Christ* Screening Draws Protests."*American Libraries.* Sep. 25, 2000. Dec. 2, 2003. <http://archive.ala.org/alonline/news/2000/000925.html>.

Mahan, Jeffrey H. "Celluloid Savior: Jesus in the Movies." *Journal of Religion and Film* 6, no. 1 (Apr. 2002). Dec. 2, 2003. <http://www.unomaha.edu/~wwwjrf/celluloid.htm>.

"Martin Scorcese's *The Last Temptation of Christ.*" Culture Shock. Theatre, Film, and Video. *PBS.* Nov. 28, 2003. <http://www.pbs.org/wgbh/cultureshock/flash-points/theater/lasttemptation_a.html>.

"Martin Scorcese's *The Last Temptation of Christ.*" *Heart of the Beholder.* Dec. 2, 2003. <http://www.beholder.com/last_temptation.htm>.

McPike, Richard K. "Mel Gibson and *The Last Temptation of Christ.*" *Mind the Gap.* July 21, 2003. Dec. 2, 2003. <http://www.livejournal.com/users/fireball1244/2003/07/21/>.

Meyer, Ronald Bruce. "*The Last Temptation of Christ* Released." Reviews. *Ronald-BruceMeyer.com.* Aug. 12, 2003. Nov. 28, 2003. <http://www.ronaldbrucemeyer.com/rants/0812almanac.htm>.

Sauvage, Pierre. "Jesus as *Goy: The Last Temptation of Christ*—One Jewish View." *Chambon Foundation.* Sept. 24, 1998. Nov. 28, 2003. <http://www.chambon.org/sauvage_temptation_en.htm>.

Sina, Ali. "Islamic Game of Victimization."*OpinionEditorials.com.* Sep. 25, 2002. Dec. 2, 2003. <http://www.opinioneditorials.com/freedomwriters/sani_20020925. html>.

Standford, Peter. "He Doesn't Have a Prayer." Observer. *Guardian Unlimited.* Jan. 26, 2003. Dec. 2, 2003. <http://observer.guardian.co.uk/print/0,3858,4591477-102280,00.html>.

Stringer, Phil. "The Entertainment Media."*Independent American Party.* Dec. 2, 2003. <http://www.usiap.org/Viewpoints/Culture/Media/Entertainment Media.html>.

"Text of the Resolution Presented to North Texas Presbytery (PCA) Condemning the Film *The Last Temptation of Christ.*" *First Presbyterian Church of Rowlett.* 1997. Dec. 2, 2003. <http://www.fpcr.org/blue_banner_articles/images7.htm>.

Wilson, Sarah Hinlicky. "Blasphemy or Veracity?" Spirituality. *Damaris Project.* Dec. 2, 2003. <http://www.damarisproject.org/content/Features.asp?Action=Detail&Id=41>.

Critical Analysis of the Film

Greydanus, Steven D. "*The Last Temptation of Christ*: An Essay in Film Criticism and Faith." *DecentFilms.com.* 2001. Nov. 28, 2003. <http://www.decentfilms.com/commentary/lasttemptation.html>.

Ventura, Michael. "The Gospel according to Hollywood." Columns. *Austin Chronicle* 20, no. 33 (Apr. 13, 2001). Dec. 2, 2003. <http://www.austinchronicle.com/issues/dispatch/2001-04-13/cols_ventura.html>.

Whitlark, James. "Stage 1 in *The Last Temptation of Christ*: Chapter 1, Part 3." *The Big Picture: A Post-Jungian Map of Global Cinema.* Dec. 2, 2003. <http://human-threshold-systems.whitlarks.com/bpchp1p3.html>.

Film Reviews

Chaitram, Sandi. "*The Last Temptation of Christ* (1988)." Film Reviews. *BBCi Films.* Rev. Apr. 11, 2001. Dec. 2, 2003. <http://www.bbc.co.uk/films/2001/04/11/last_temptation_of_christ_1988_review.shtml>.

Howe, Desson. "*The Last Temptation of Christ*." *WashingtonPost.com.* Aug. 12, 1988. Nov. 28, 2003. <http://www.washingtonpost.com/wp-srv/style/longterm/movies/videos/thelasttemptationofchristrhowe_a0b1b7.htm>.

Purdy, Jack. "*The Last Temptation of Christ*." Rewind. *Baltimore City Paper Online* (Mar. 29–Apr. 4, 2000). Nov. 28, 2003. <http://www.citypaper.com/2000-03-29/rewind2.html>.

Variety Staff. "*The Last Temptation of Christ*." *Variety.com.* Jan. 1, 1988. Dec. 2, 2003. <http://www.variety.com/index.asp?layout=upsell_review&reviewID=VE11177 92488&cs=1>.

Weaver, Allen Paul, III. "*The Last Temptation of Christ*." *HollywoodJesus.com.* Nov. 28, 2003. <http://www.hollywoodjesus.com/last_temptation.htm>.

DVD Reviews

Anderson, Jeffrey M. "*The Last Temptation of Christ* (1998): The Mean Streets of Jerusalem." *Combustible Celluloid.* Nov. 28, 2003. <http://www.combustiblecelluloid.com/lasttempt.shtml>.

Cressey, Earl. "*The Last Temptation of Christ*." *DVD Talk.* June 27, 2000. Dec. 2, 2003. <http://www.dvdtalk.com/reviews/read.php?id=781>.

Curulli, Anthony. "*The Last Temptation of Christ* (1988)." *Michael D's Region 4 DVD Info Page.* Jan. 5, 2002. Dec. 2, 2003. <http://www.michaeldvd.com.au/Reviews/Reviews.asp?ReviewID=981>.

Jacobson, Colin. "*The Last Temptation of Christ*: Criterion (1998)." *DVD Movie Guide.* Nov. 28, 2003. <http://dvdmg.com/lasttemptationofchrist.shtml>.

Jacobson, Michael. "*The Last Temptation of Christ*." DVD Reviews. *DVD Movie Central*. Dec. 2, 2003. <http://www.dvdmoviecentral.com/ReviewsText/last_temptation_of_christ.htm>.

Langdon, Matt. "*The Last Temptation of Christ*." *Hollywood Bitchslap*. Feb. 24, 2001. Dec. 2, 2003. <http://hollywoodbitchslap.com/review.php?movie=3416&reviewer=119>.

"*Last Temptation of Christ, The* (1988)." DVD Reviews. *Need Coffee*. Dec. 2, 2003. <http://www.needcoffee.com/html/dvd/ltochrist.htm>.

McGinnis, Sean. "*The Last Temptation of Christ*: The Criterion Collection." *DVD Verdict*. May 19, 2000. Nov. 28, 2003. <http://www.dvdverdict.com/reviews/lasttemptation.shtml> or <http://www.dvdverdict.com/reviews/lasttemptation.php>.

O'Hehir, Andrew. "*The Last Temptation of Christ*." Arts and Entertainment. *Salon.com*. Mar. 6, 2001. Nov. 28, 2003. <http://archive.salon.com/ent/movies/dvd//review/2001/03/06/last_temptation/>.

Schulte, Erich. "*The Last Temptation of Christ*." Ruthless Viewing. *Ruthless Reviews*. Dec. 2, 2003. <http://www.ruthlessreviews.com/lasttemptationofchrist.html>.

Stephenson, Cliff. "*The Last Temptation of Christ*." Disc Review. *DVDFile.com*. Jan. 20, 2000. Nov. 28, 2003. <http://www.dvdfile.com/software/review/dvd-video_2/lasttemptationofchrist.htm>.

Sermons about the Film

Clendenin, Dan. "The Journey with Jesus: Notes to Myself." *InterVarsity Christian Fellowship*. Mar. 10, 2003. Dec. 2, 2003. <http://www.stanford.edu/group/ivfaculty/Essays/20030310JJ.shtml>.

Dean, Peter Eaton. "'Lazarus, Come Out!'" The Fifth Sunday in Lent. *St. John's Cathedral, Denver, Colorado*. Mar. 17, 2002. Dec. 2, 2003. <http://www.sjc-den.org/worship/3-17-2002.html>.

Hartshorn, Leo. "The Lost Temptation of Christ."*Peace and Justice Support Network of Mennonite Church USA*. Mar. 1, 1998. Dec. 2, 2003. <http://peace.mennolink.org/articles/leoslost.html>.

Loy, Steven P. "First Sunday in Lent."*Peace Lutheran Church*. Mar. 1, 1998. Dec. 2, 2003. <http://www.zianet.com/peacelutheran/Sermon98/Ser0301.htm>.

Truemper, David G. "From the Chapel: How Good, Lord, to Be Here!" *Cresset*. Lent. Dec. 2, 2003. <http://www.valpo.edu/cresset/len02chapel.html>.

Young, Alexey. "'Who Do Men Say That I Am?'"*Orthodox America*. Dec. 2, 2003. <http://www.roca.org/OA/82/82n.htm>.

Soundtrack

Scrivner, Matthew. "Passion (Music for *The Last Temptation of Christ*)." 2 *Walls Webzine*. Apr. 5, 2001. Dec. 2, 2003. <http://www.2walls.com/REVIEWS/MUSIC/gabriel_peter.asp>.

Weblog Analysis and Criticism

Hanscom, Michael. "*The Last Temptation of Christ*." Books. *Eclecticism*. May 22, 2002. Dec. 2, 2003. <http://www.michaelhanscom.com/eclecticism/2002/05/the_last_tempta.html>.

Wohali. "Wow." *Wohali*. Feb. 22, 2003. Dec. 2, 2003. <http://www.livejournal.com/users/wohali/2003/02/22/>.

Other

King, Susan. "Author Cites the Best and Worst Films for Historical Accuracy." *Los Angeles Times*. *SouthCoast Today*. Feb. 12, 2000. Dec. 2, 2003. <http://www.s-t.com/daily/02-00/02-12-00/b03li072.htm>.

"*Last Temptation of Christ, The*." *IMDB*. Nov. 28, 2003. <http://www.imdb.com/title/tt0095497/>.

"*Last Temptation of Christ, The*." Video/DVD. *Rotten Tomatoes*. Nov. 28, 2003. <http://www.rottentomatoes.com/m/TheLastTemptationofChrist-1011984/about.php>.

"*Last Temptation of Christ, The*." *Wikipedia*. Oct. 7, 2003. Nov. 28, 2003. <http://en.wikipedia.org/wiki/The_Last_Temptation_of_Christ>.

Aland, Kurt. *Synopsis of the Four Gospels.* United Bible Societies, 1982.

Allison, Dale C. *Jesus of Nazareth: Millenarian Prophet.* Minneapolis: Fortress Press, 1998.

American Society for the Defense of Tradition, Family, and Property (ASDTFP). Advertisement. *New York Times*, August 12, 1988, A7.

Ankerberg, John, and John Weldon. *The Facts on "The Last Temptation of Christ": The True Story Behind the Controversial Film.* Eugene, OR: Harvest House Publishers, 1988.

Ansen, David, and Andrew Nurr. "The Arts: Movies, Wrestling with 'Temptation.'" *Newsweek*, August 15, 1988: 56–57.

Babbington, Bruce, and Peter William Evans. *Biblical Epics: Sacred Narratives in the Hollywood Cinema.* Manchester: Manchester University Press, 1993.

Bak, John S. "Christ's Jungian Shadow in *The Last Temptation.*" In *God's Struggler: Religion in the Writings of Nikos Kazantzakis*, edited by Darren J. N. Middleton and Peter A. Bien, 153–68. Macon, GA: Mercer University Press, 1996.

Barrett, Mary Ellin. "Scorsese's 'Temptation': Not Exactly by the Book." *USA Today*, July 12, 1988, D6.

Bartlett, Anthony W. *Cross Purposes: The Violent Grammar of Christian Atonement.* Harrisburg, PA: Trinity Press International, 2001.

Baugh, Lloyd. *Imaging the Divine: Jesus and Christ-Figures in Film.* Kansas City, MO: Sheed & Ward, 1997.

Beaton, Roderick. "Writing, Identity and Truth in Kazantzakis's Novel *The Last Temptation.*" *Kampos: Cambridge Papers in Modern Greek* 5 (1997): 1–21.

Beutner, Ed. "The 'Lust' Temptation of Christ?" *The Fourth R: An Advocate for Religious Liberty* 2, no. 2 (1989): 1, 7–8.

Bien, Peter A. *Kazantzakis: Politics of the Spirit*. Princeton: Princeton University Press, 1989.

———. "Kazantzakis's Long Apprenticeship to Christian Themes." In *God's Struggler: Religion in the Writings of Nikos Kazantzakis*, edited by Darren J. N. Middleton and Peter A. Bien, 113–31. Macon, GA: Mercer University Press, 1996.

———. "Nikos Kazantzakis's Novels on Film." *Journal of Modern Greek Studies* 18 (2000): 161–69.

———. "Scorsese's Spiritual Jesus." *New York Times*, August 11, 1988, A25.

———. *Tempted by Happiness: Kazantzakis' Post-Christian Christ*. Wallingford, PA: Pendle-Hill Publications, 1984.

Billy Graham Ministries. Press release. July 18, 1988.

Bird, Brian. "Film Protesters Vow Long War on Universal." *Christianity Today*, September 16, 1988, 41–43.

Birney, Alice L. *The Literary Lives of Jesus: An International Bibliography of Poetry, Drama, Fiction, and Criticism*. New York: Garland, 1989.

Blake, R. A. "Redeemed in Blood: The Sacramental Universe of Martin Scorsese." *The Journal of Popular Film and Television* 24 (1996): 2–9.

Blenkinsopp, Joseph. "My Entire Soul Is a Cry: The Religious Passion of Nikos Kazantzakis." *Commonweal*, February 26, 1971, 514–18.

Bliss, Michael. *The Word Made Flesh: Catholicism and Conflict in the Films of Martin Scorsese*. London: Scarecrow Press, 1995.

Bloch, Adèle. "Kazantzakis and the Image of Christ." *Literature and Psychology* 15 (1965): 2–11.

Bockmuehl, Markus, ed. *The Cambridge Companion to Jesus*. Cambridge: Cambridge University Press, 2001.

Boersma, Hans. *Violence, Hospitality, and the Cross: Reappropriating the Atonement Tradition*. Grand Rapids, MI: Baker Academic, 2004.

Borg, Marcus J. *Jesus in Contemporary Scholarship*. Valley Forge, PA: Trinity Press International, 1994.

———. *Meeting Jesus Again for the First Time: The Historical Jesus and the Heart of Contemporary Faith*. San Francisco: HarperSanFrancisco, 1994.

———. *The God We Never Knew: Beyond Dogmatic Religion to a More Authentic Contemporary Faith*. San Francisco: HarperSanFrancisco, 1997.

Braxton, Greg. "'The Last Temptation of Christ': Scorsese Ends Long Quest to Make Kazantzakis Novel." *Los Angeles Times*, August 12, 1988, 6:1.

Bulgakov, Sergius. *The Orthodox Church*. New York: Morehouse, 1935.

Cabasilas, Nicholas. *The Life in Christ*. New York: St. Vladimir's Seminary Press, 1974.

Calian, Carnegie Samuel. "Kazantzakis: Prophet of Non-Hope." *Theology Today* 28 (1971): 37–49.

———. *Theology without Boundaries*. Louisville, KY: Westminster John Knox Press, 1992.

Chilson, Richard. "The Christ of Nikos Kazantzakis." *Thought* 47 (1972): 69–89.

Connelly, Marie Katheryn. *Martin Scorsese: An Analysis of His Feature Films with a Filmography of His Whole Career.* Jefferson, NC: McFarland, 1993.

Crossan, John Dominic. *Jesus: A Revolutionary Biography.* San Francisco: Harper-SanFrancisco, 1994.

———. *Who Killed Jesus? Exposing the Roots of Anti-Semitism in the Gospel Story of the Death of Jesus.* San Francisco: HarperSanFrancisco, 1995.

Dart, John. "Some Clerics See No Evil in Temptation." *Los Angeles Times,* July 14, 1988, 6:9.

Dobson, James. Editorial. *Focus on the Family Citizen,* September 1988, 4.

Dombrowski, Daniel A. *Kazantzakis and God.* Albany, NY: State University of New York Press, 1987.

Doulis, Tom. "Kazantzakis and the Meaning of Suffering." *Northwest Review* 6 (1963): 33–57.

Driver. Tom F. "The Last Temptation of Christ." *Christianity and Crisis* 48 (1988): 338–44.

Ehrenstein, David. *The Scorsese Picture.* New York: Carroll Publishing, 1992.

Ehrman, Bart D. *Jesus: The Apocalyptic Prophet of the New Millenium.* Oxford: Oxford University Press, 1999.

———. *Lost Christianities: The Battles for Scripture and the Faiths We Never Knew.* Oxford: Oxford University Press, 2003.

———. *Lost Scriptures: Books That Did Not Make It into the New Testament.* Oxford: Oxford University Press, 2003.

Flinn, Caryl. *Strains of Utopia: Gender, Nostalgia, and Hollywood Film Music.* Princeton: Princeton University Press, 1992.

Ford, David F., and Mike Higton, eds. *Jesus.* Oxford: Oxford University Press, 2002.

Forward, Martin. *Jesus: A Short Biography.* Oxford: Oneworld, 1998.

Fox, Richard Wightman. *Jesus in America: Personal Savior, Cultural Hero, National Obsession.* San Francisco: HarperSanFrancisco, 2004.

Fredriksen, Paula. *Jesus of Nazareth: King of the Jews.* New York: Random House, 1999.

Friedman, Lawrence S. *The Cinema of Martin Scorsese.* New York: Continuum, 1998.

Funk, Robert W. *A Credible Jesus: Fragments of a Vision.* Santa Rosa, CA: Polebridge Press, 2002.

———. *Honest to Jesus: Jesus for a New Millennium.* San Francisco: HarperSan-Francisco, 1996.

Funk. Robert W., and the Jesus Seminar. *The Acts of Jesus: The Search for the Authentic Deeds of Jesus.* New York: HarperCollins, 1998.

Funk, Robert W., Roy W. Hoover, and the Jesus Seminar. *The Five Gospels: The Search for the Authentic Words of Jesus.* New York: Macmillan, 1993.

Green, Joel B. *Salvation.* St. Louis, MO: Chalice Press, 2003.

Grün, Anselm. *Images of Jesus.* New York: Continuum, 2002.

Hamilton, William. *A Quest for the Post-Historical Jesus.* London: SCM Press, 1993.

Hampson, Daphne. *After Christianity.* London: SCM Press, 1996.

Hayes, John Haralson. *Son of God to Super Star: Twentieth-Century Interpretations of Jesus*. Nashville, TN: Abingdon Press, 1976.

Hoover, Roy W., ed. *Profiles of Jesus*. Santa Rosa, CA: Polebridge Press, 2002.

Iannone, Carol. "*The Last Temptation* Reconsidered." *First Things*, February 1996, 50–54.

Inbody, Tyron L. *The Many Faces of Christology*. Nashville, TN: Abingdon Press, 2002.

Johnson, Luke Timothy. *The Real Jesus: The Misguided Quest for the Historical Jesus and the Truth of the Traditional Gospels*. San Francisco, CA: HarperSanFrancisco, 1996.

Johnston, Robert K. *Reel Spirituality: Theology and Film in Dialogue*. Grand Rapids, MI: Baker Academic, 2000.

Kamperidis, Lambros. "The Orthodox Sources of *The Saviors of God*." In *God's Struggler: Religion in the Writing of Nikos Kazantzakis* edited by Darren J. N. Middleton and Peter A. Bien, 53–70, Macon, GA: Mercer University Press, 1996.

Kärkkäinen, Veli-Matti. *Christology: A Global Introduction: An Ecumenical, International and Contextual Perspective*. Grand Rapids, MI: Baker Academic, 2003.

Kassabian, Anahid. *Hearing Film: Tracking Identifications in Contemporary Hollywood Film Music*. New York and London: Routledge, 2001.

Kazantzakis, Helen. *Nikos Kazantzakis: A Biography based on His Letters*. Translated by Amy Mims. New York: Simon & Schuster, 1968.

Kazantzakis, Nikos. *O teleftaíos periasmós*. Athens: Difros, 1955.

———. *Report to Greco*. Translated by Peter A. Bien. New York: Simon & Schuster, 1965.

———. *Saint Francis*. Translated by Peter A. Bien. New York: Simon & Schuster, 1962.

———. *The Last Temptation of Christ*. Translated by Peter A. Bien. New York: Simon & Schuster, 1960.

———. *The Saviors of God: Spiritual Exercises*. Translated by Kimon Friar. New York: Simon & Schuster, 1960.

Kelly, Mary Pat. *Martin Scorsese: A Journey*. New York: Thunder's Mouth Press, 1989.

Kinnard, Roy, and Tim Davis. *Divine Images: A History of Jesus on the Screen*. New York: Citadel Press, 1992.

Krietzer, Larry J. *Gospel Images in Fiction and Film: On Reversing the Hermeneutical Flow*. New York: Continuum, 2002.

Langenhorst, Georg. "The Rediscovery of Jesus as a Literary Figure." *Literature and Theology* 9, no. 1 (1995): 85–98.

Last Temptation of Christ, The. Directed by Martin Scorsese. VHS. Los Angeles: Universal Studios, 1988.

Last Temptation of Christ, The. Directed by Martin Scorsese. DVD. Los Angeles: Universal Studios, 2000.

Lastra, James. *Sound Technology and the American Cinema*. New York: Columbia University Press, 2001.

Lea, James F. *Kazantzakis: The Politics of Salvation.* Tuscaloosa, AL: University of Alabama Press, 1979.

Lee, Robert E. A. "'The Last Temptation of Christ': Insulting or Instructing?" *Lutheran,* September 7, 1988, 15–17.

Levitt, Morton. *The Cretan Glance: The World and Art of Nikos Kazantzakis.* Columbus, OH: Ohio State University Press, 1980.

Lossky, Vladimir. *The Mystical Theology of the Eastern Church.* London: James Clarke, 1957.

Malone, Peter. *Movie Christs and Antichrists.* New York: Crossroads, 1990.

McDermott, Jim. "Is It Possible to Portray Christ in Film?" *Christianity and the Arts* 1 (1994): 20–22.

McGrath, Alister E. *Theology: The Basics.* Malden, MA: Blackwell Publishing, 2004.

Medved, Michael. *Hollywood vs. America: Popular Culture and the War on Traditional Values.* New York: HarperCollins, 1992.

Meredith, Lawrence. "The Gospel According to Kazantzakis: How Close Did Scorsese Come?" *Christian Century,* September 14, 1988, 799.

Meyendorff, John. *Byzantine Theology.* New York: Fordham University Press, 1983.

Meyer, Marvin. *The Secret Teachings of Jesus: Four Gnostic Gospels.* New York: Random House, 1984.

Middleton, Darren J. N. "A Heretic in the Garden of the Virgin? Nikos Kazantzakis and the Holy Mount, Athos." *Modern Greek Studies (Australia and New Zealand): A Journal for Greek Letters* 8–9 (2000–2001): 81–99. Translated into French as Middleton, "Un hérétique dans le jardin de la Vierge: Nikos Kazantzaki et La Sainte Montagne, Athos," *Le Regard Crétois: Revue de la Société Internationale des Amis de Nikos Kazantzaki* 27 (Juillet 2003): 44–57.

———. "Apophatic Boldness: Kazantzakis's Use of Negation and Silence to Emphasize Theological Mystery." *The Journal of Contemporary Thought* 39, no. 4 (1998): 453–67.

———. "Kazantzakis and Christian Doctrine: Some Bridges of Understanding." *Journal of Modern Greek Studies* 16, no. 2 (1998): 285–312.

———. *Novel Theology: Nikos Kazantzakis's Encounter with Whiteheadian Process Theism.* Macon, GA: Mercer University Press, 2000.

Middleton, Darren J. N., and Peter A. Bien, eds. *God's Struggler: Religion in the Writings of Nikos Kazantzakis.* Macon, GA: Mercer University Press, 1996.

Miles, Margaret R. *Seeing and Believing: Religion and Values in the Movies.* Boston: Beacon Press, 1996.

Moore, E. T. "A City in Torment over Kazantzakis." *Bulletin of the American Library Association* 57 (1963): 305–6.

Moore, Paul. "'Last Temptation' Not Heretical." *Witness,* October 1988, 12–13.

Murphy, Cullen. "Who Do Men Say That I Am?" *Atlantic Monthly,* December 1986.

Oeglaend, Margaret. *Martin Scorsese: God's Lonely Man.* Master's thesis, California State University, 1991. Ann Arbor: UMI, 1991.

Owens, Lewis. *Creative Destruction: Nikos Kazantzakis and the Literature of Responsibility*. Macon, GA: Mercer University Press, 2002.

Pattison, George. *Anxious Angels: A Retrospective View of Religious Existentialism*. Basingstoke, UK: Macmillan, 1999.

Pelikan, Jaroslav. *Jesus through the Centuries: His Place in the History of Culture*. New Haven: Yale University Press, 1985.

Petrolle, Jean Ellen. "Nikos Kazantzakis and *The Last Temptation*: Irony and Dialectic in a Spiritual Ontology of Body." *Journal of Modern Greek Studies* 11, no. 2 (1993): 271–91.

Phipps, William E. *The Sexuality of Jesus: Theological and Literary Perspectives*. New York: Harper & Row, 1973.

Poland, Larry. *The Last Temptation of Hollywood*. Highland, CA: Mastermedia International, 1988.

Pollby, George. "Kazantzakis's Struggle." *Commonweal*, April 23, 1971, 155, 175.

Porter, Elisabeth J. *Women and Moral Identity*. North Sydney, New South Wales, Australia: Allen & Unwin, 1991.

Prothero, Stephen. *American Jesus: How the Son of God Became a National Icon*. New York: Farrar, Straus and Giroux, 2003.

Racheotes, Nicholas. "Theogony and Theocide: Nikos Kazantzakis and the Mortal Struggle for Salvation." *East European Quarterly* 17 (1991): 363–98.

Renan, Ernest. *The Life of Jesus*. Translated by Charles Edwin Wilbour. New York: Carleton, 1864.

Richards, Lewis. "Christianity in the Novels of Kazantzakis." *Western Humanities Review* 21 (1967): 49–55.

Riley, Robin. *Film, Faith, and Cultural Conflict: The Case of Martin Scorsese's* The Last Temptation of Christ. Westport, CT: Praeger, 2003.

Rosenbaum, Jonathan. "Raging Messiah: *The Last Temptation of Christ*." *Sight and Sound*. 57, no. 4 (1988): 281–82.

Ruether, Rosemary Radford. *Sexism and God-Talk: Toward a Feminist Christology*. Boston: Beacon Press, 1983.

Sanders, E. P. *The Historical Figure of Jesus*. London: Penguin, 1993.

Schmidt, Daryl D. "Sane Eschatology: Albert Schweitzer's Profile of Jesus," *Forum* 1, no. 2 (1998): 241–60.

Schrader, Paul. *Schrader on Schrader*. Edited by David Thompson and Ian Christie. Boston: Faber & Faber, 1989.

Schüssler-Fiorenza, Elizabeth. *In Memory of Her: A Feminist Reconstruction of Christian Origins*. New York: Crossroads, 1983.

Schweitzer, Albert. *The Mystery of the Kingdom of God: The Secret of Jesus' Messiahship and Passion*. Translated by Walter Lowrie. New York: Macmillan, 1960.

———. *The Psychiatric Study of Jesus: Exposition and Criticism*. Edited and translated by Charles R. Joy. Boston: Beacon Press, 1990.

———. *The Quest of the Historical Jesus*. Edited John Bowden. Fortress Press: Minneapolis, 2001.

Scorsese, Martin. *Scorsese on Scorsese*. Edited by David Thompson and Ian Christie. Boston: Faber & Faber, 1989.

Scott, Bernard Brandon. *Hollywood Dreams and Biblical Stories*. Minneapolis: Fortress Press, 1994.

Speake, Graham. *Mount Athos: Renewal in Paradise*. New Haven: Yale University Press, 2002.

Steinberg, Leo. *The Sexuality of Christ in Renaissance Art and in Modern Oblivion*. 2nd ed. Chicago: University of Chicago, 1996.

Stern, Richard C., et al. *Savior on the Silver Screen*. New York and Mahwah, NJ: Paulist Press, 1999.

Tatum, W. Barnes. "A Review of Scorsese's 'Last Temptation,'" *The Fourth R: An Advocate for Religious Liberty* 2, no. 3 (1989): 1, 7–8.

———. *In Quest of Jesus*. Revised and enlarged edition. Nashville, TN: Abingdon Press, 1999.

———. *Jesus at the Movies: A Guide to the First Hundred Years*. Santa Rosa, CA: Polebridge Press, 1996; revised and enlarged edition, 2004.

Taylor, Timothy. "Kazantzakis and the Cinema." *Byzantine and Modern Greek Studies* 6 (1980): 157–68.

Telford, William R. "Jesus and Women in Fiction and Film." In *Transformative Encounters: Jesus and Women Re-Viewed*. Edited by Ingrid Rosa Kitzberger, 353–91. Leiden: Brill, 2000.

Von Gunden, Kenneth. *Postmodern Auteurs: Coppola, Lucas, De Palma, Spielberg and Scorsese*. Jefferson, NC: McFarland, 1991.

Ware, Timothy. *The Orthodox Church*. Baltimore, MD: Penguin, 1963.

Weaver, J. Denny. *The Nonviolent Atonement*. Grand Rapids, MI: Eerdmans, 2001.

Wildman, Wesley J. *Fidelity with Plausibility: Modest Christologies in the Twentieth Century*. Albany, NY: State University of New York Press, 1998.

Will, Fredrick. "Kazantzakis' Making of God: A Study in Literature and Philosophy." *Iowa Review* 3, no. 44 (1972): 109–24.

Willis, Clint, ed. *Son of Man: Great Writing about Jesus Christ*. New York: Thunder's Mouth Press, 2002.

Ziolkowski, Theodore. *Fictional Transfigurations of Jesus*. Princeton: Princeton University Press, 1972.

Lloyd Baugh, a Canadian Jesuit priest, is Ordinary Professor of Theology and Film at the Pontificia Universita Gregoriana in Rome, Italy. Author of *Imaging the Divine: Jesus and Christ Figures in Film* (Sheed & Ward, 1997), he has published widely on the interdisciplinary dynamic between film texts and theology, religion, spirituality, and morality. He also teaches regularly in Canada, the United States, and the Philippines. At present he is completing a monograph with the working title *Imaging the Good: Moral Imperatives in the Decalogue Films of Krzysztof Kieslowski*.

Roderick Beaton is Koraes Professor of Modern Greek and Byzantine History, Language, and Literature at King's College London (University of London), England. He has published widely on Greek literature and culture from the twelfth century to the present, including several scholarly articles on Kazantzakis. He is the author of *An Introduction to Modern Greek Literature* (Oxford University Press, 1994; 2nd ed., 1999) and of *George Seferis: Waiting for the Angel. A Biography* (Yale University Press, 2003).

Peter Bien is Professor Emeritus of English and Comparative Literature at Dartmouth College, Hanover, New Hampshire, USA. He has translated Kazantzakis's *The Last Temptation of Christ*, *Saint Francis*, and *Report to Greco*. On *The Last Temptation*, he has published an analysis entitled *Tempted by Happiness: Kazantzakis' Post-Christian Christ* (Pendle Hill, 1984). In 1989 Princeton University Press published volume 1 of his biographical-critical study *Kazantzakis: Politics of the Spirit*, and he has recently completed the second volume. He also hopes to edit a volume of Kazantzakis's selected letters in English translation.

Mini Chandran is Assistant Professor of English in the Department of Humanities and Social Sciences at the Indian Institute of Technology, Kanpur, Uttar Pradesh, India. She is currently working on issues of literary censorship in India.

She was a journalist for four years before coming to academics and has also translated numerous short stories and essays from English to Malayalam (a regional Indian language).

Peter T. Chattaway is a Film Critic and Freelance Writer based in Vancouver, British Columbia, Canada. A graduate of the History and Religious Studies program at the University of British Columbia, he has taught journalism at Trinity Western University and written on the treatment of biblical and religious subjects in film for such publications as *Books & Culture, Bible Review, Christianity Today, The Vancouver Sun, Christian Week,* and *BC Christian News.*

Charitini Christodoulou is a Doctoral Candidate at the University of Birmingham, England. Her thesis deals with aspects of meaning and interpretation in *The Last Temptation,* using contemporary theories on narrativity and closure. She currently teaches modern Greek at Cyprus College, Nicosia, Cyprus.

Don Cupitt is a Fellow and former Dean of Emmanuel College, Cambridge University, England. He is the founder of the Sea of Faith movement and author of more than thirty books including *Taking Leave of God* (SCM, 1980), *Emptiness and Brightness* (Polebridge, 2001), *Is Nothing Sacred? The Non-Realist Philosophy of Religion: Selected Essays* (Fordham University Press, 2002), and *Life, Life* (Polebridge, 2003).

Daniel A. Dombrowski is Professor of Philosophy at Seattle University, Seattle, Washington, USA. He is the author of fourteen books, the latest of which is *Divine Beauty: The Aesthetics of Charles Hartshorne* (Vanderbilt University Press, 2004). He is also the author of the book *Kazantzakis and God* (SUNY Press, 1997).

Elizabeth H. Flowers is a Doctoral Candidate in American Religious History at Duke University, Durham, North Carolina, USA. Her first publication, "Southern Baptist Evangelicals or Social Gospel Liberals? The Woman's Missionary Union and Social Reform, 1888 to 1928," was the 1999 winner of the Robert G. Torbet Prize Essay, sponsored by the American Baptist Historical Society.

Pamela J. Francis is an Instructor in the Department of Language and Communication at Northwestern State University in Natchitoches, Louisiana, USA. She holds advanced degrees in Religious Studies and English and has published on Lawrence Durrell. Her current research includes work on Palestinian women writers.

C. D. Gounelas is Associate Professor of Modern Greek Literature at Aristotle University, Thessaloniki, Greece. His recent work includes *The Philosophy of Language and Modern Greek Poetry* (Athens: Delphini, 1995) and *Tsirkas' Trilogy: An Essay on Western Marxism* (Athens: Gutenberg-Typotheto, 2002).

Jen Harrison is a Researcher with the Department of Modern Greek at the University of Sydney, Australia. She has recently returned to Australia from the University of Edinburgh, Scotland, where she completed a doctorate comparing Nikos Kazantzakis and Patrick White. Her main motivation for returning to Australia is to help change Australia's appalling treatment of asylum seekers.

Randolph Jordan Randolph Jordan is a Doctoral Candidate with the Interdisciplinary Humanities program at Concordia University, Montreal, Quebec, Canada, where he is currently pursuing research toward a dissertation on the intersections between film sound theory, acoustic ecology, and electroacoustic music. For more information, visit <http://www.soppybagrecords.net/randolph-jordan>.

Vrasidas Karalis is Associate Professor of Modern Greek with the Department of Modern Greek at the University of Sydney, Australia. The editor of *Modern Greek Studies (Australia and New Zealand)*, he has published a number of articles on modern Greek literature and has translated medieval chronicles into modern Greek. His publications in book form include *N. Kazantzakis and the Palimpsest of History* (Athens: Kanakis, 1995), *Reading D. Solomos* (Athens: Ideogramma, 2002), and *On the Poetry of Andreas Aggelakis* (Athens: Hodos Panos, 2003). He is currently working on a critical edition of *The Confession of Faith*, published by the patriarch of Constantinople, Cyril Loukaris (1629).

Melody D. Knowles is Associate Professor of Hebrew Scripture at McCormick Theological Seminary in Chicago, USA. She is the author of *Centrality Practiced: Jerusalem in the Religious Practice of Yehud and the Diaspora in the Persian Period* (Scholars Press, 2005) and is preparing a monograph on the use of historical motifs in the Psalms.

Austin S. Lingerfelt is a graduate student at Texas Christian University, Fort Worth, Texas, USA. He is currently pursuing an advanced degree in literature with a focus on sacred themes.

Darren J. N. Middleton is Associate Professor of Religion at Texas Christian University, Fort Worth, Texas, USA. The author of *Novel Theology: Nikos Kazantzakis's Encounter with Whiteheadian Process Theism* (Mercer University Press, 2000), he is completing a monograph on the relationship between Christian theology and contemporary literature, focusing on Graham Greene, Toni Morrison, John Irving, and others.

Lewis Owens currently teaches Philosophy of Religion and Ethics at Sidney Sussex College, Cambridge University, England. He was the inaugural president of the UK branch of the International Society of Friends of Nikos Kazantzakis and is the author of *Creative Destruction: Nikos Kazantzakis and the Literature of Responsibility* (Mercer University Press, 2002), as well as various articles on Kazantzakis's religious and philosophical thought. His current research includes work on Kazantzakis and Spain, and the life and work of Dmitri Shostakovich.

Eftychia Papanikolaou is Assistant Professor of Musicology at Miami University, Oxford, Ohio, USA. Although her principal research focuses on music of the nineteenth century, she has lectured and published several essays on topics ranging from the music of ancient Greece and music aesthetics to opera and Mahler's fin de siècle Vienna. She is currently writing a monograph on the genre of the romantic symphonic mass, with emphasis on masses by Beethoven, Schubert, Liszt, and other composers of the Austro-German tradition.

Martin Scorsese is an award-winning film director. He has released over twenty-five movies, including *Mean Streets* (1973), *Alice Doesn't Live Here Anymore* (1974), *Taxi Driver* (1976), *Raging Bull* (1980), *Color of Money* (1986), *The Last Temptation of Christ* (1988), *Goodfellas* (1990), *Cape Fear* (1991), and *The Age of Innocence* (1993). His recent work includes *Gangs of New York* (2002) and *The Aviator* (2004).

W. Barnes Tatum is the Jefferson-Pilot Professor of Religion and Philosophy at Greensboro College, Greensboro, North Carolina, USA. He has published numerous articles and reviews related to Jesus and Christian origins. His monographs include *In Quest of Jesus* (rev. ed.; Abingdon, 1999) and *Jesus at the Movies: A Guide to the First Hundred Years* (rev. ed.; Polebridge, 2004).

Allison Whitney holds a PhD in Cinema and Media Studies from the University of Chicago. She is currently the Social Sciences and Humanities Research Council of Canada Postdoctoral Fellow in the Department of Film and Video, Faculty of Fine Arts, at York University, Toronto, Canada. She has also taught on film adaptations of the Bible at McCormick Theological Seminary, Chicago.

INDEX

Abraham, 65
abyss, 53, 99, 101
Acts of Paul and Thecla, 5
Adam, 17n. 33, 62, 67, 68, 149, 151, 161, 165
Alexis Zorbas (Kazantzakis), 8
Allendy, René, 12
Altman, Rick, 207, 208
Ananias, 54
Andrew, Saint, 65, 105, 165
Androutsos, Christos, 61
animism, 49
anthropology
    Gregory of Nyssa's, 63, 64, 68
    Kazantzakis's, xix, 49, 55, 63, 68, 75, 76, 188
    Scorsese's, xix, 188
Antony, P. M., 136, 137–38
apocalypse, 9–10, 23
Apocrypha, 14, 18n. 57
archetypes, 38, 39, 42, 43, 187
Aristophanes, 55
Aristotle, 48, 51, 56
art/literature
    anxiety and, xvi
    challenge of, xv–xvi, 20, 147
    as collective voice, 42–43
    as confrontation, 114

in evangelical practice, 152
healing and, 43
identity in, 114
Jung on, 45n. 20
productive violence of, 114
symbolic order and, 113
ascent
    as motif, 52–53, 64, 102, 103, 142
    nihilism v., 42
Askitiki (Kazantzakis), 101
atomic bomb, 9–10, 35
Augustine, 67, 159, 160

Bakhtin, Mikhail, 114
Barabbas, 26, 40, 45n. 19, 138
Barabbas (Lagerkvist), 13
Being and Time (Heidegger), 79
Bergson, Henri
    Bien and, 102
    Borges and, 91, 92
    dynamism of, 36, 37
    Jung and, 37, 45n. 6
    Kazantzakis and, 2, 8, 10, 19, 30n. 2, 37, 49, 64, 69, 91, 92, 102, 206
    life force (élan vital) of, 19, 37
    time/space in, 92, 94n. 38
Bien, Peter, 10, 45n. 8, 46n. 30, 53, 55, 64, 102, 104–5, 155n. 10

as devil's tool, 127
as flesh, 129
against God, 128
as housewife, 129
as interchangeable, 129, 166, 178
in Jesus films, 178
in Kazantzakis, 64, 111, 113, 125,
    165, 167–68, 178
as mediator, 111
as mother, 128
as obstacle, 129
as other, 112–13
in Paul, 159
as phallus, 112
powerlessness of, 127
as sacrifice, 115
in Scorsese, 167, 168, 178–79, 188,
    191n. 37
self denigration of, 127
as servant, 125–26, 127
as sin, 128
as speaking subject, 113

as temptress, 184
as whore, 129
Wood, Jess W., 147
Wordsworth, William, 49
world
    events, 35–36, 74, 79
    as illusion, 80
    as performance, 100–101
World Psyche, xix, 101, 104
World War II, 74

Yeats, W. B., 77–78
Young, Roger, 163

Zealots
    crucifixion of, 101, 126, 164, 166
    Judas and, 51
    Kazantzakis's research on, 16n. 31
    Mary Magdalene and, 132n. 53
    in Renan/Kazantzakis, 6–7
Zebedee, 126, 164, 165
Zebedee, sons of, 5, 178, 179